Translator - Seung-Ah Lee
English Adaptation - Jason Deitrich
Retouch and Lettering - Yoohae Yang
Copy Editor - Aaron Sparrow
Cover Layout - Patrick Hook
Graphic Designer - John Lo

Editor - Julie Taylor
Digital Imaging Manager - Chris Buford
Pre-Press Manager - Antonio DePietro
Production Managers - Jennifer Miller, Mutsumi Miyazaki
Art Director - Matt Alford
Managing Editor - Jill Freshney
VP of Production - Ron Klamert
President & C.O.O. - John Parker
Publisher & C.E.O. - Stuart Levy

E-mail: info@TOKYOPOP.com
Come visit us online at www.TOKYOPOP.com

A 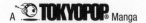 Manga

TOKYOPOP Inc.
5900 Wilshire Blvd. Suite 2000
Los Angeles, CA 90036

Les Bijoux Vol. 3

ISBN: 1-59182-692-6

First TOKYOPOP printing: June 2004

10 9 8 7 6 5 4 3 2 1

Printed in the USA

LAST TIME IN LES BIJOUX...

The world is divided into 12 *Mines*, each ruled by a tyrannical *Habit*. It is a time of war and oppression, when the *Spars*, the working class, live in mortal fear of the Habits. In the midst of this chaos, in the Mine of *Neige*, a strange thing happened. A miraculous child was born from a union between a dwarf and a hunchback...a child who takes on the form of a male and female.

Now the child, *Lapis Lazuli*, has grown up. After his parents were slaughtered by the Habit *Diamond*, Lapis swore revenge against the lord of Neige. But Lapis only managed to cut out Diamond's right eye before the Habit escaped. Homeless and friendless, Lapis travels across the continent to the Mine of *Soleil*, where he makes two new friends, *Carnelian*, brother to the Habit, and "*Butterfly*," a spiritual guide with the ability to transform into a panther.

Lapis gains new allies and new enemies as he faces his role as the one who will overthrow the tyrannical Habits. After steeling his courage, he departs to find the divine sword of Tourmaline. When two of Lapis' friends are slaughtered before his very eyes, Butterfly and Lapis begin a journey to find all of Lapis' guardians.

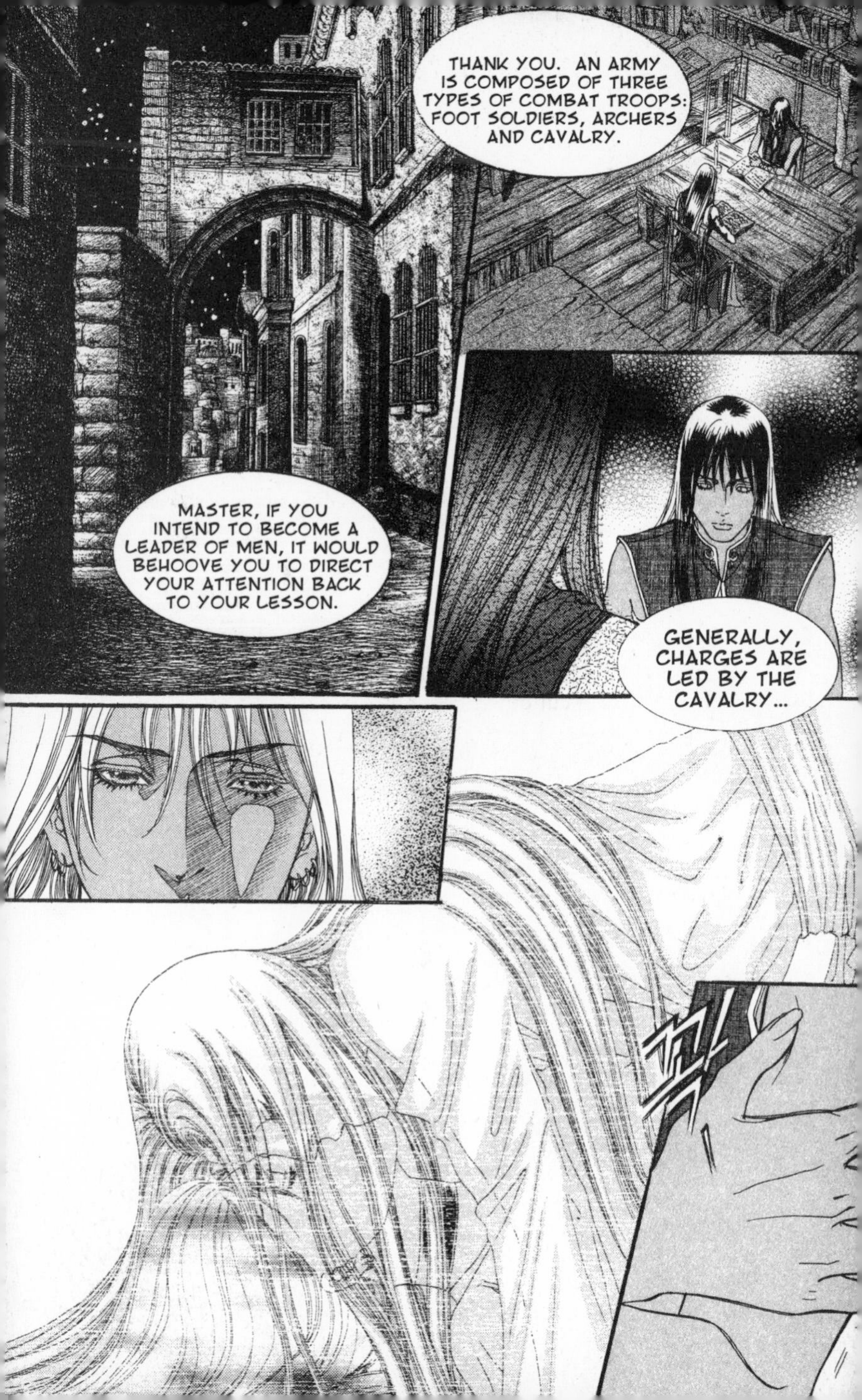
MASTER, IF YOU INTEND TO BECOME A LEADER OF MEN, IT WOULD BEHOOVE YOU TO DIRECT YOUR ATTENTION BACK TO YOUR LESSON.
THANK YOU. AN ARMY IS COMPOSED OF THREE TYPES OF COMBAT TROOPS: FOOT SOLDIERS, ARCHERS AND CAVALRY.
GENERALLY, CHARGES ARE LED BY THE CAVALRY...

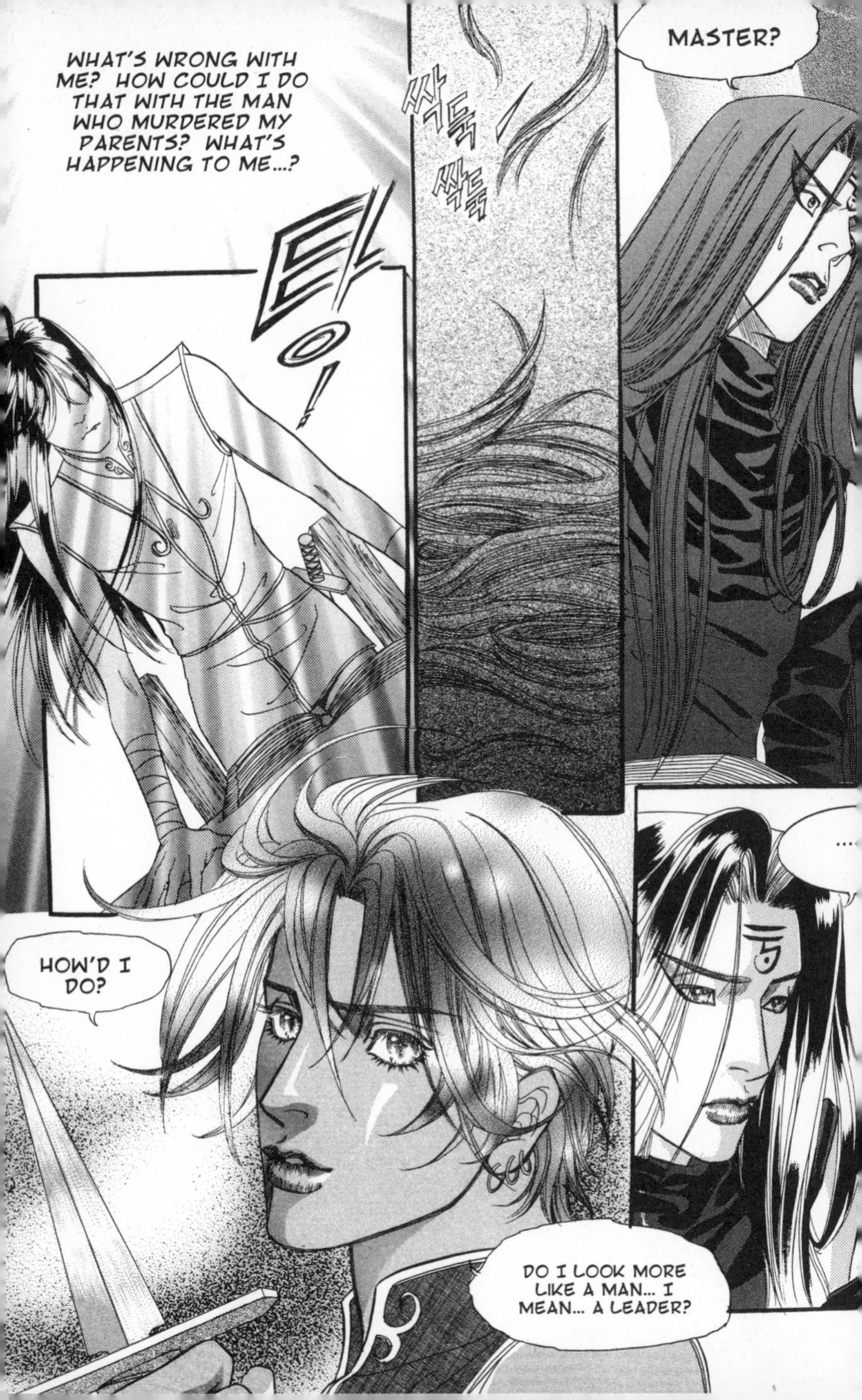
WHAT'S WRONG WITH ME? HOW COULD I DO THAT WITH THE MAN WHO MURDERED MY PARENTS? WHAT'S HAPPENING TO ME...?
싹둑
싹둑
MASTER?
HOW'D I DO?
...
DO I LOOK MORE LIKE A MAN... I MEAN... A LEADER?

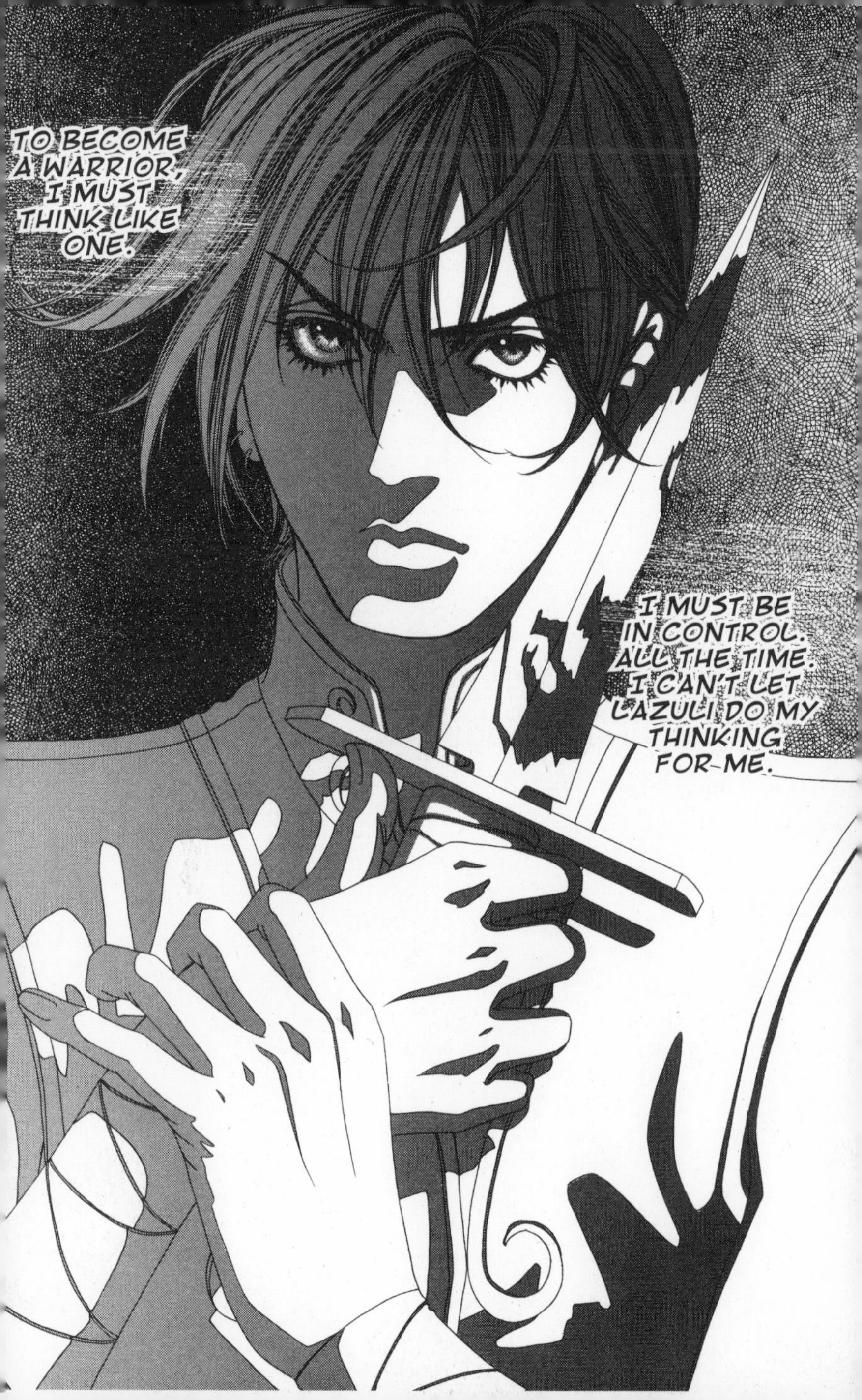
TO BECOME A WARRIOR, I MUST THINK LIKE ONE.
I MUST BE IN CONTROL. ALL THE TIME. I CAN'T LET LAZULI DO MY THINKING FOR ME.

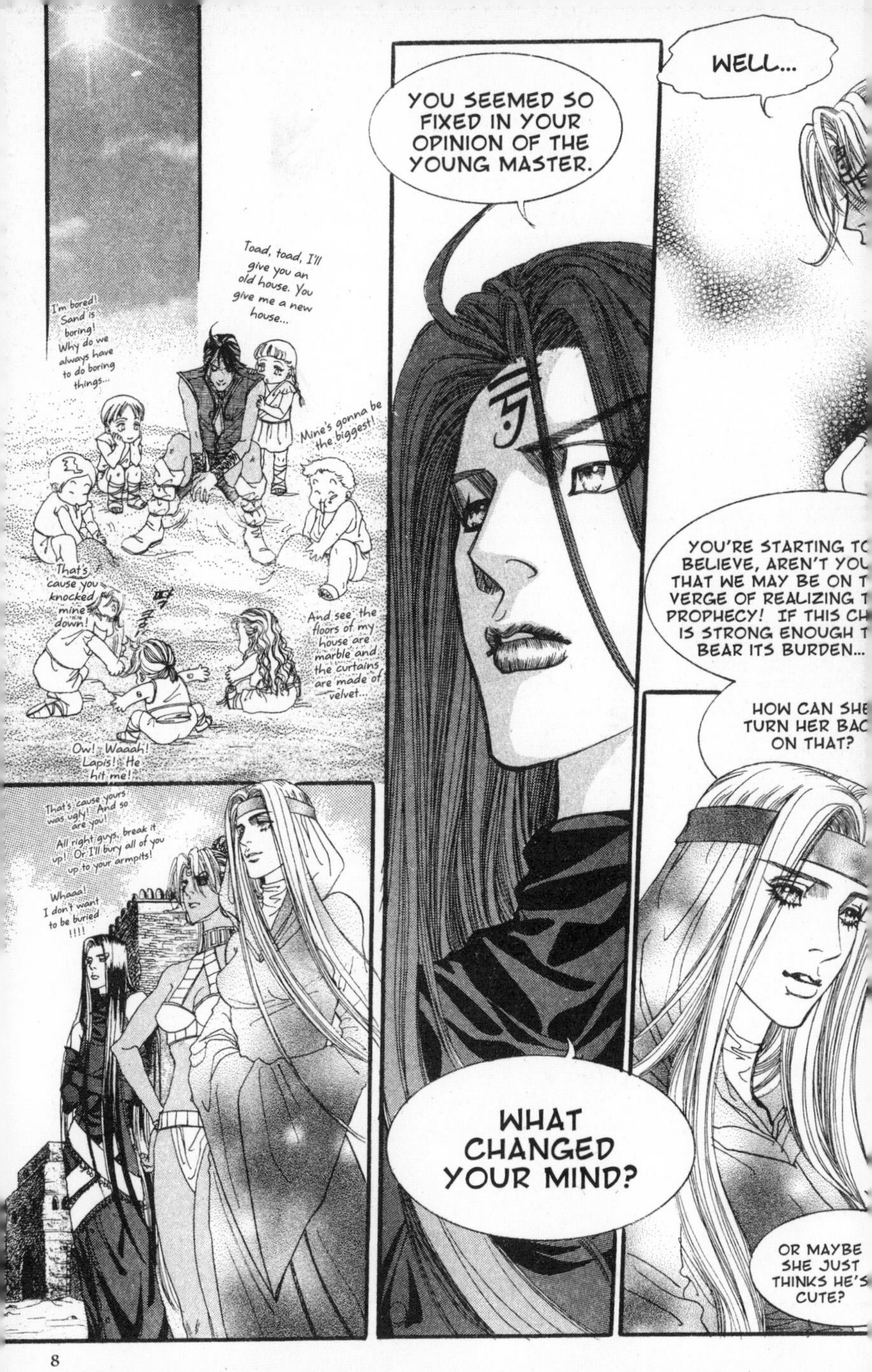
Toad, toad, I'll give you an old house. You give me a new house...
I'm bored! Sand is boring! Why do we always have to do boring things...
Mine's gonna be the biggest!
That's cause you knocked mine down!
And see, the floors of my house are marble and the curtains are made of velvet...
Ow! Waaah! Lapis! He hit me!
That's cause yours was ugly! And so are you!
All right guys, break it up! Or I'll bury all of you up to your armpits!
Whaaa! I don't want to be buried !!!!
YOU SEEMED SO FIXED IN YOUR OPINION OF THE YOUNG MASTER.
WHAT CHANGED YOUR MIND?
WELL...
YOU'RE STARTING T BELIEVE, AREN'T YOU THAT WE MAY BE ON T VERGE OF REALIZING T PROPHECY! IF THIS CH IS STRONG ENOUGH T BEAR ITS BURDEN...
HOW CAN SHE TURN HER BAC ON THAT?
OR MAYBE SHE JUST THINKS HE'S CUTE?

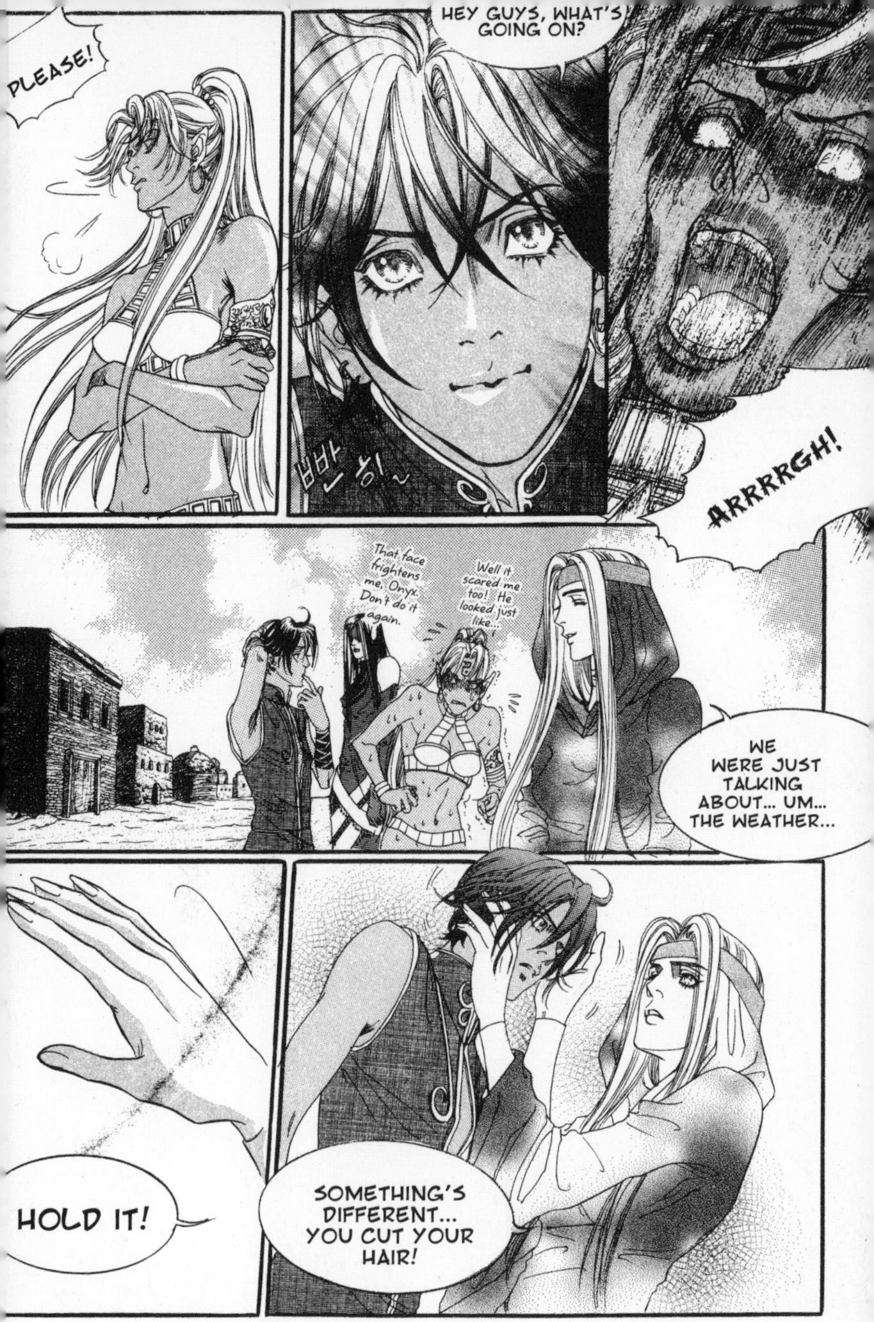
PLEASE!
HEY GUYS, WHAT'S GOING ON?
ARRRRGH!
That face frightens me, Onyx. Don't do it again.
Well it scared me too! He looked just like...
WE WERE JUST TALKING ABOUT... UM... THE WEATHER...
HOLD IT!
SOMETHING'S DIFFERENT... YOU CUT YOUR HAIR!

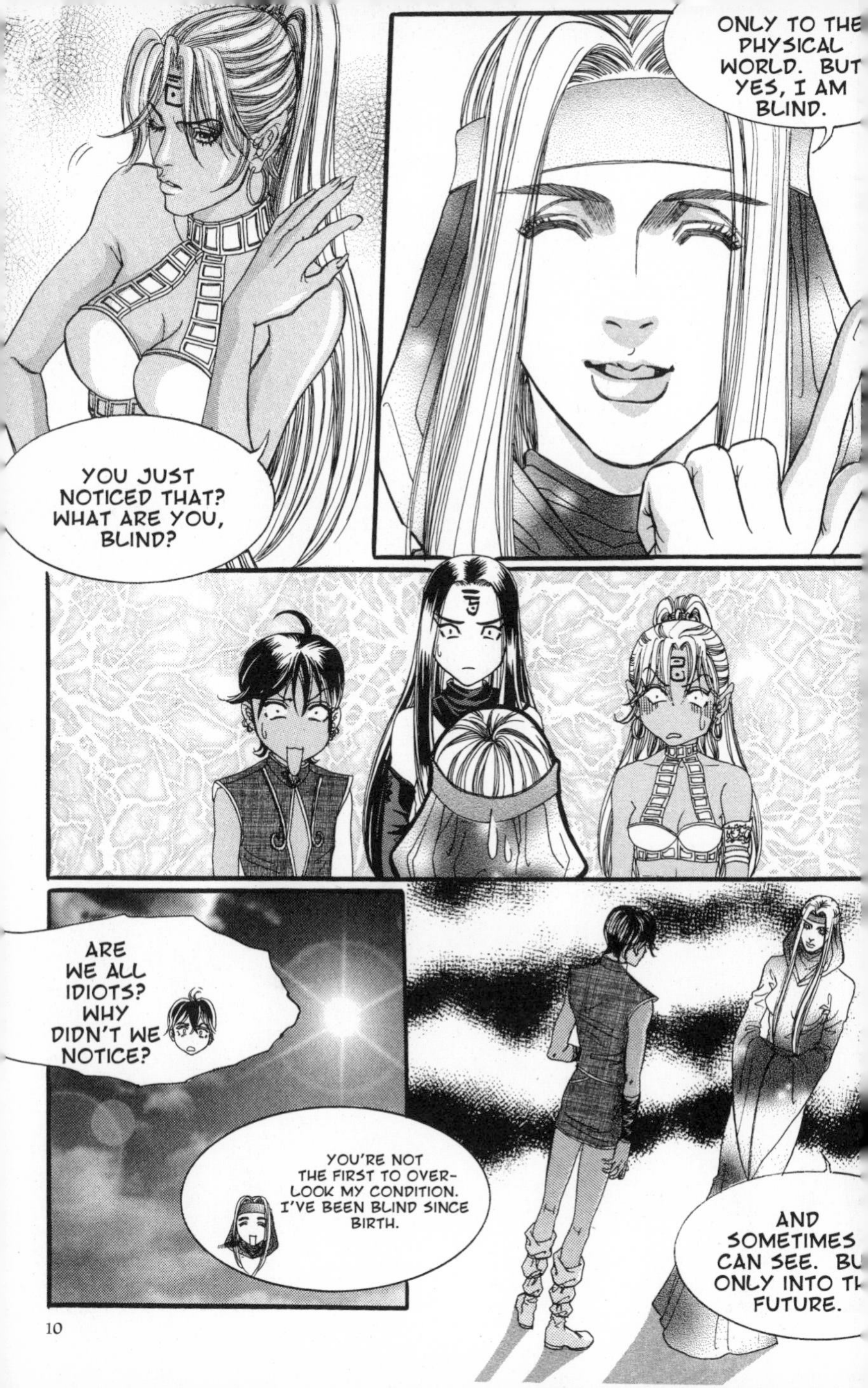
YOU JUST NOTICED THAT? WHAT ARE YOU, BLIND?
ONLY TO THE PHYSICAL WORLD. BUT YES, I AM BLIND.
ARE WE ALL IDIOTS? WHY DIDN'T WE NOTICE?
YOU'RE NOT THE FIRST TO OVER-LOOK MY CONDITION. I'VE BEEN BLIND SINCE BIRTH.
AND SOMETIMES CAN SEE. BU ONLY INTO TH FUTURE.

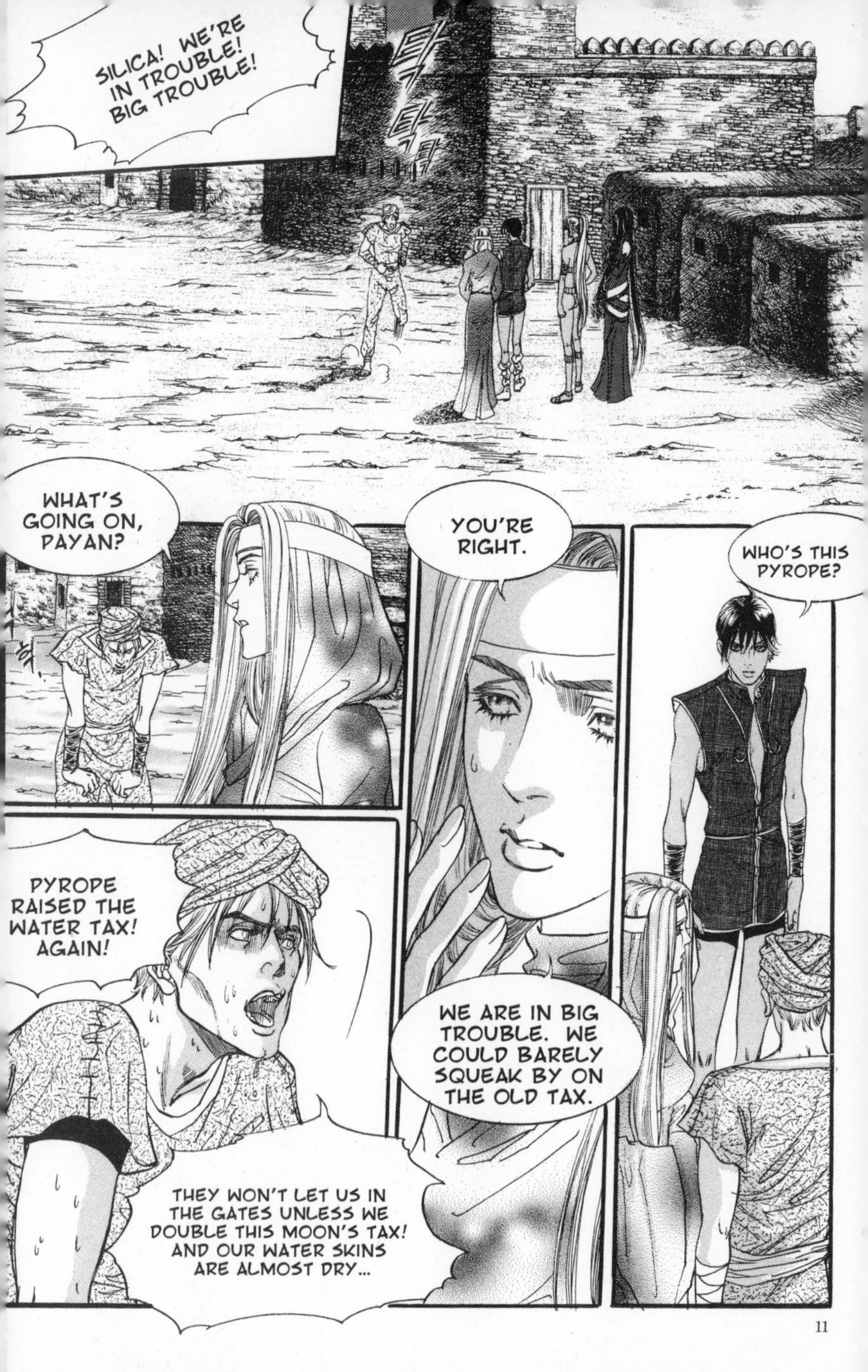
SILICA! WE'RE IN TROUBLE! BIG TROUBLE!
WHAT'S GOING ON, PAYAN?
PYROPE RAISED THE WATER TAX! AGAIN!
THEY WON'T LET US IN THE GATES UNLESS WE DOUBLE THIS MOON'S TAX! AND OUR WATER SKINS ARE ALMOST DRY...
YOU'RE RIGHT.
WE ARE IN BIG TROUBLE. WE COULD BARELY SQUEAK BY ON THE OLD TAX.
WHO'S THIS PYROPE?

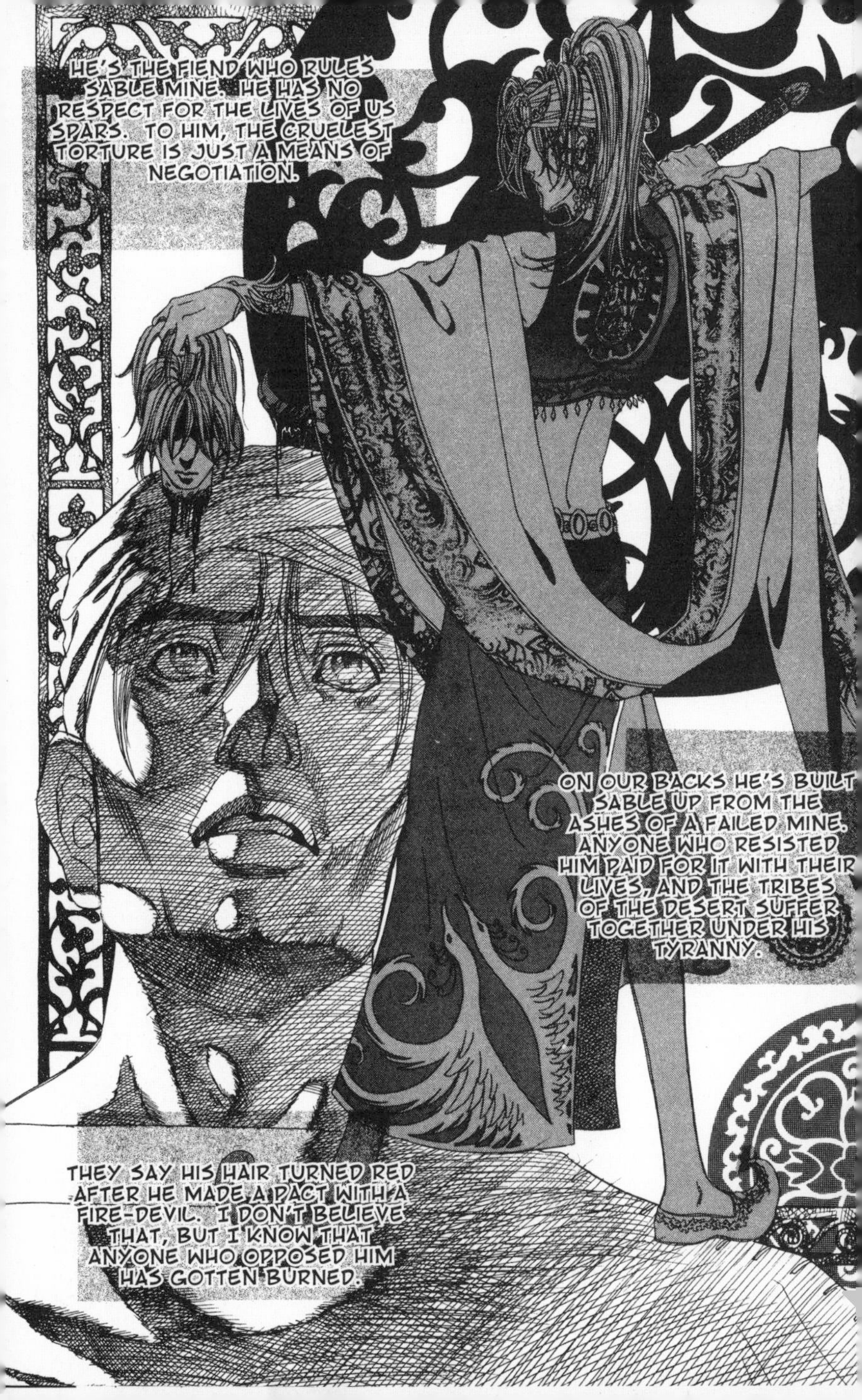
HE'S THE FIEND WHO RULES SABLE MINE. HE HAS NO RESPECT FOR THE LIVES OF US SPARS. TO HIM, THE CRUELEST TORTURE IS JUST A MEANS OF NEGOTIATION.
ON OUR BACKS HE'S BUILT SABLE UP FROM THE ASHES OF A FAILED MINE. ANYONE WHO RESISTED HIM PAID FOR IT WITH THEIR LIVES, AND THE TRIBES OF THE DESERT SUFFER TOGETHER UNDER HIS TYRANNY.
THEY SAY HIS HAIR TURNED RED AFTER HE MADE A PACT WITH A FIRE-DEVIL. I DON'T BELIEVE THAT, BUT I KNOW THAT ANYONE WHO OPPOSED HIM HAS GOTTEN BURNED.

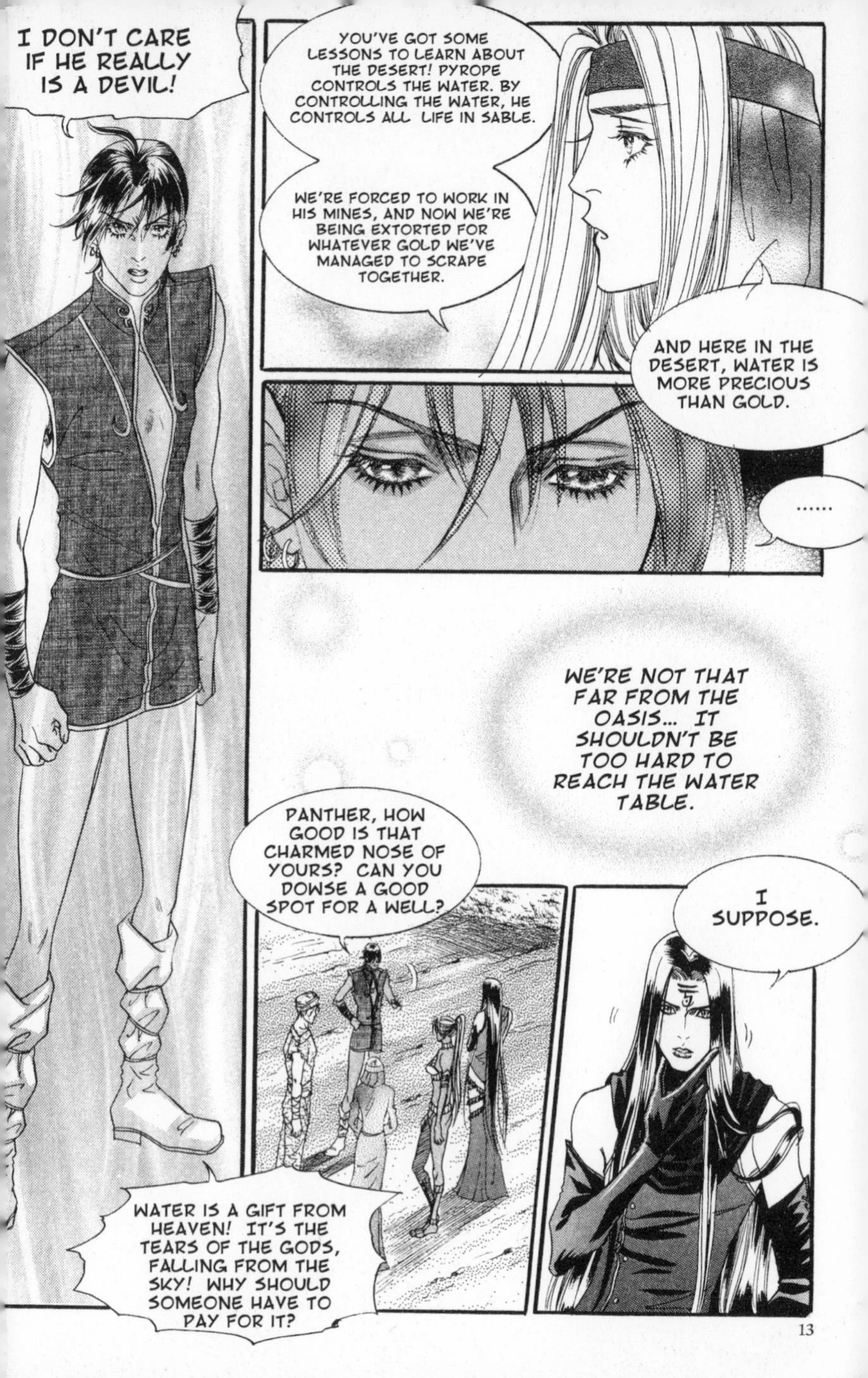
I DON'T CARE IF HE REALLY IS A DEVIL!
WATER IS A GIFT FROM HEAVEN! IT'S THE TEARS OF THE GODS, FALLING FROM THE SKY! WHY SHOULD SOMEONE HAVE TO PAY FOR IT?
YOU'VE GOT SOME LESSONS TO LEARN ABOUT THE DESERT! PYROPE CONTROLS THE WATER. BY CONTROLLING THE WATER, HE CONTROLS ALL LIFE IN SABLE.
WE'RE FORCED TO WORK IN HIS MINES, AND NOW WE'RE BEING EXTORTED FOR WHATEVER GOLD WE'VE MANAGED TO SCRAPE TOGETHER.
AND HERE IN THE DESERT, WATER IS MORE PRECIOUS THAN GOLD.
......
WE'RE NOT THAT FAR FROM THE OASIS... IT SHOULDN'T BE TOO HARD TO REACH THE WATER TABLE.
PANTHER, HOW GOOD IS THAT CHARMED NOSE OF YOURS? CAN YOU DOWSE A GOOD SPOT FOR A WELL?
I SUPPOSE.

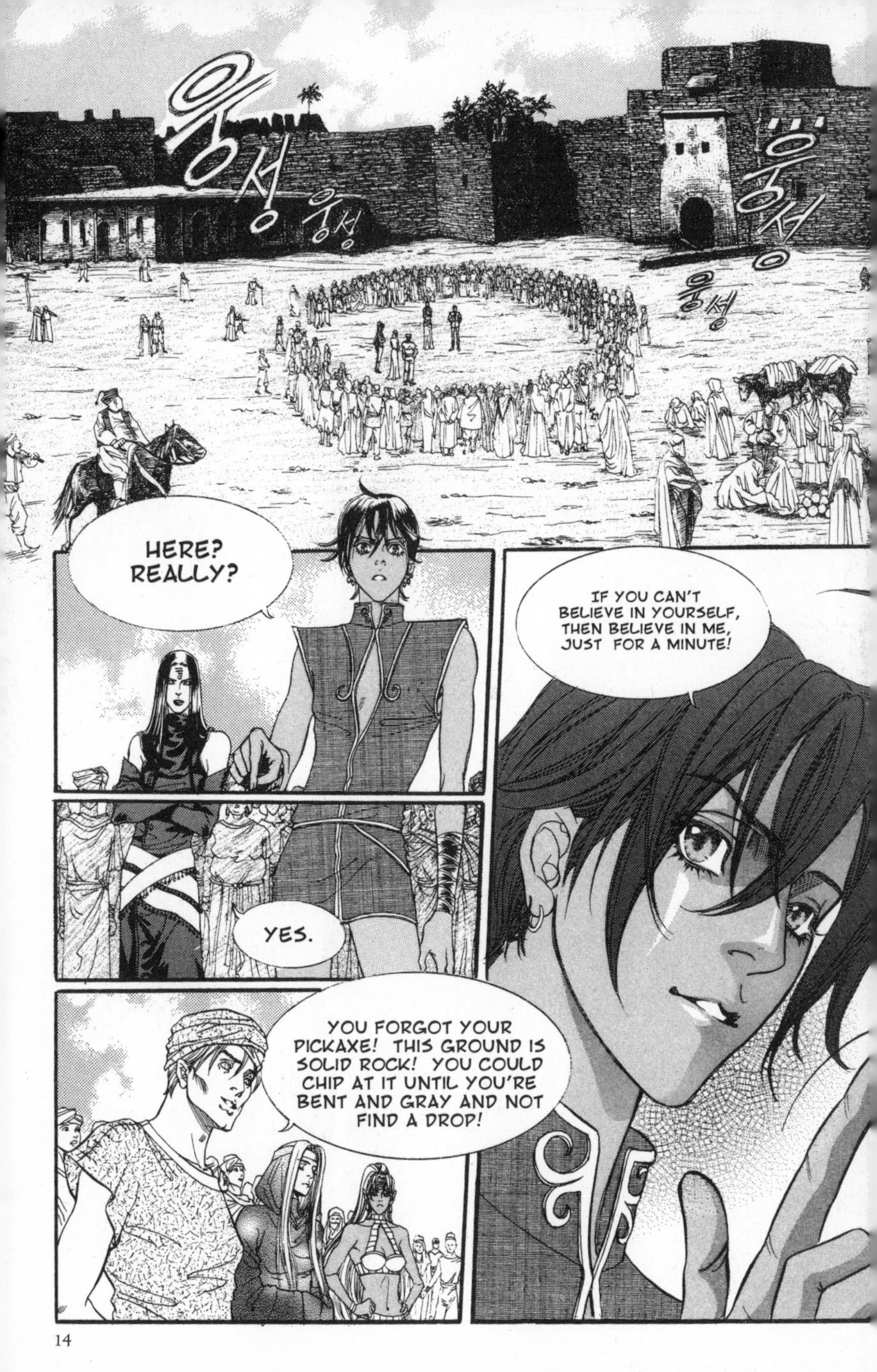
웅성
웅성
웅성
웅성
HERE? REALLY?
YES.
YOU FORGOT YOUR PICKAXE! THIS GROUND IS SOLID ROCK! YOU COULD CHIP AT IT UNTIL YOU'RE BENT AND GRAY AND NOT FIND A DROP!
IF YOU CAN'T BELIEVE IN YOURSELF, THEN BELIEVE IN ME, JUST FOR A MINUTE!

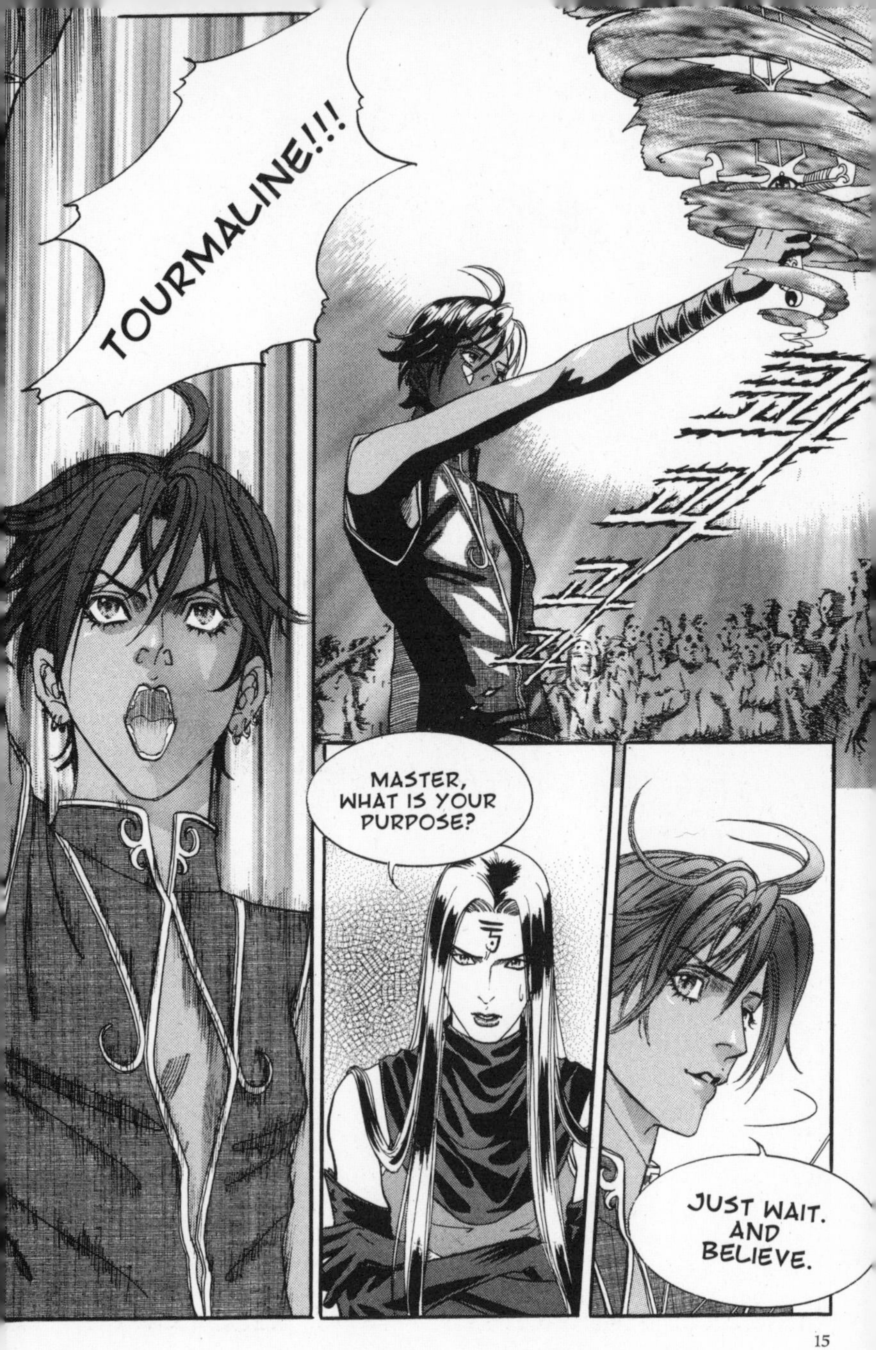
TOURMALINE!!!
MASTER, WHAT IS YOUR PURPOSE?
JUST WAIT. AND BELIEVE.

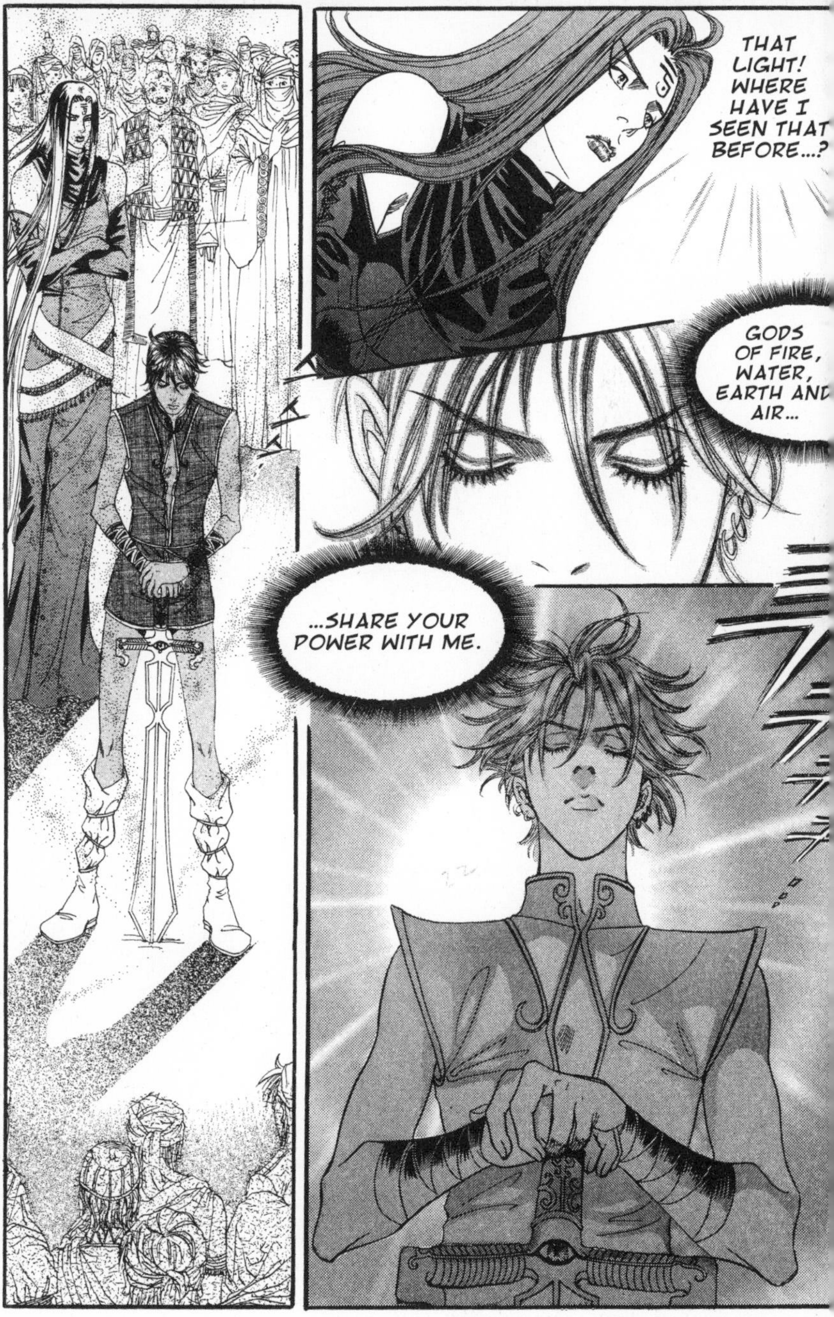
THAT LIGHT! WHERE HAVE I SEEN THAT BEFORE...?
GODS OF FIRE, WATER, EARTH AND AIR...
...SHARE YOUR POWER WITH ME.

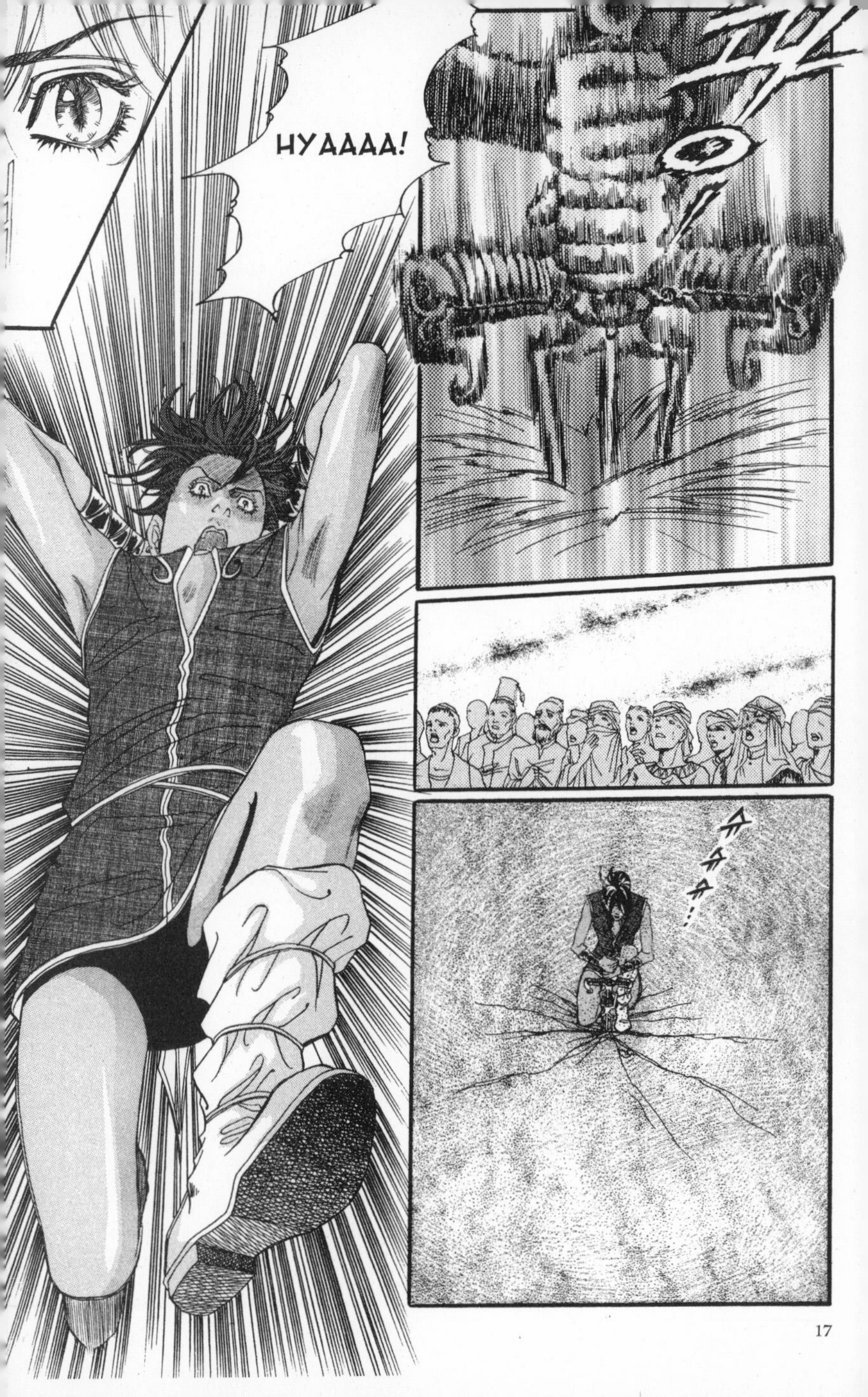
HYAAAA!

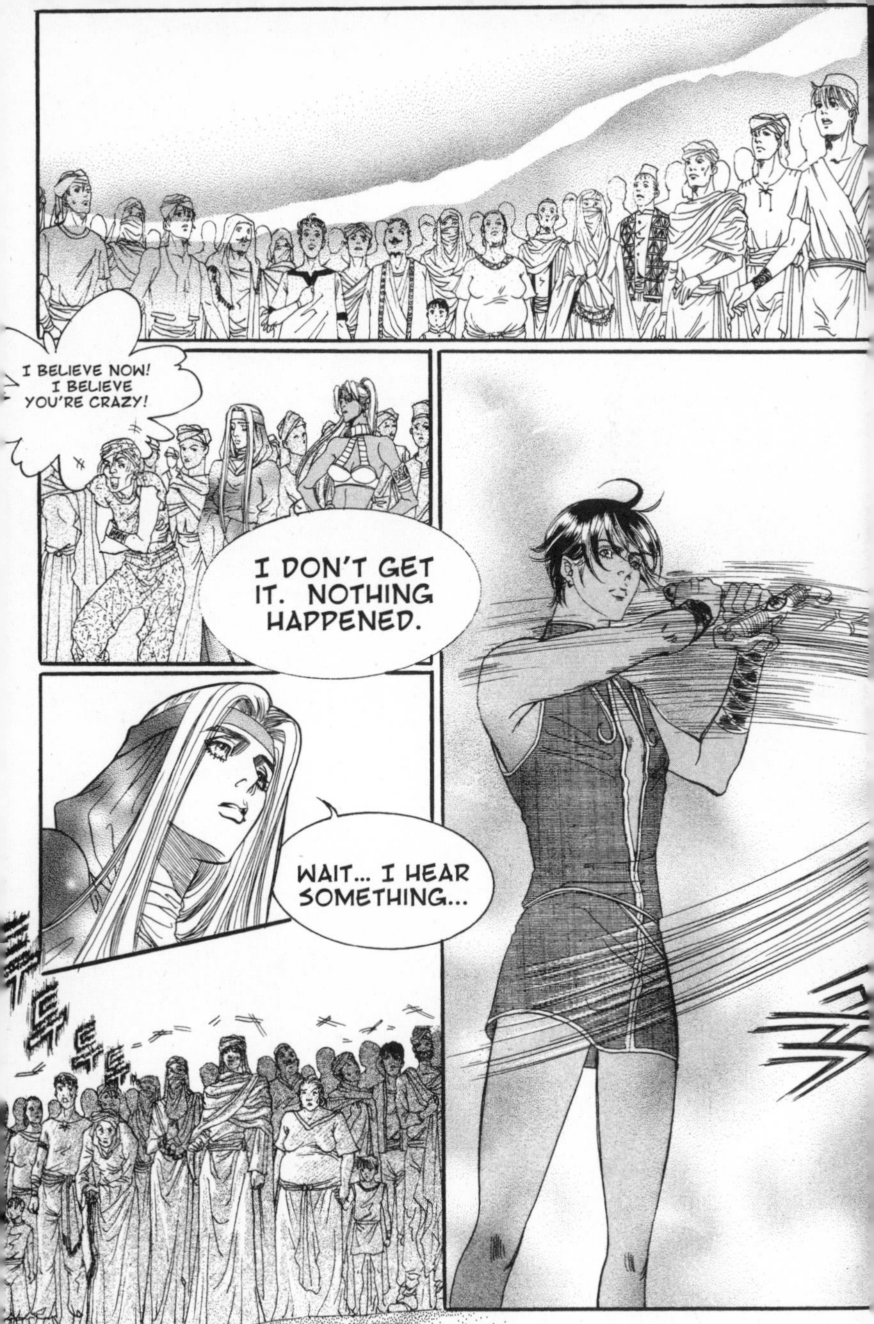
I BELIEVE NOW! I BELIEVE YOU'RE CRAZY!
I DON'T GET IT. NOTHING HAPPENED.
WAIT... I HEAR SOMETHING...

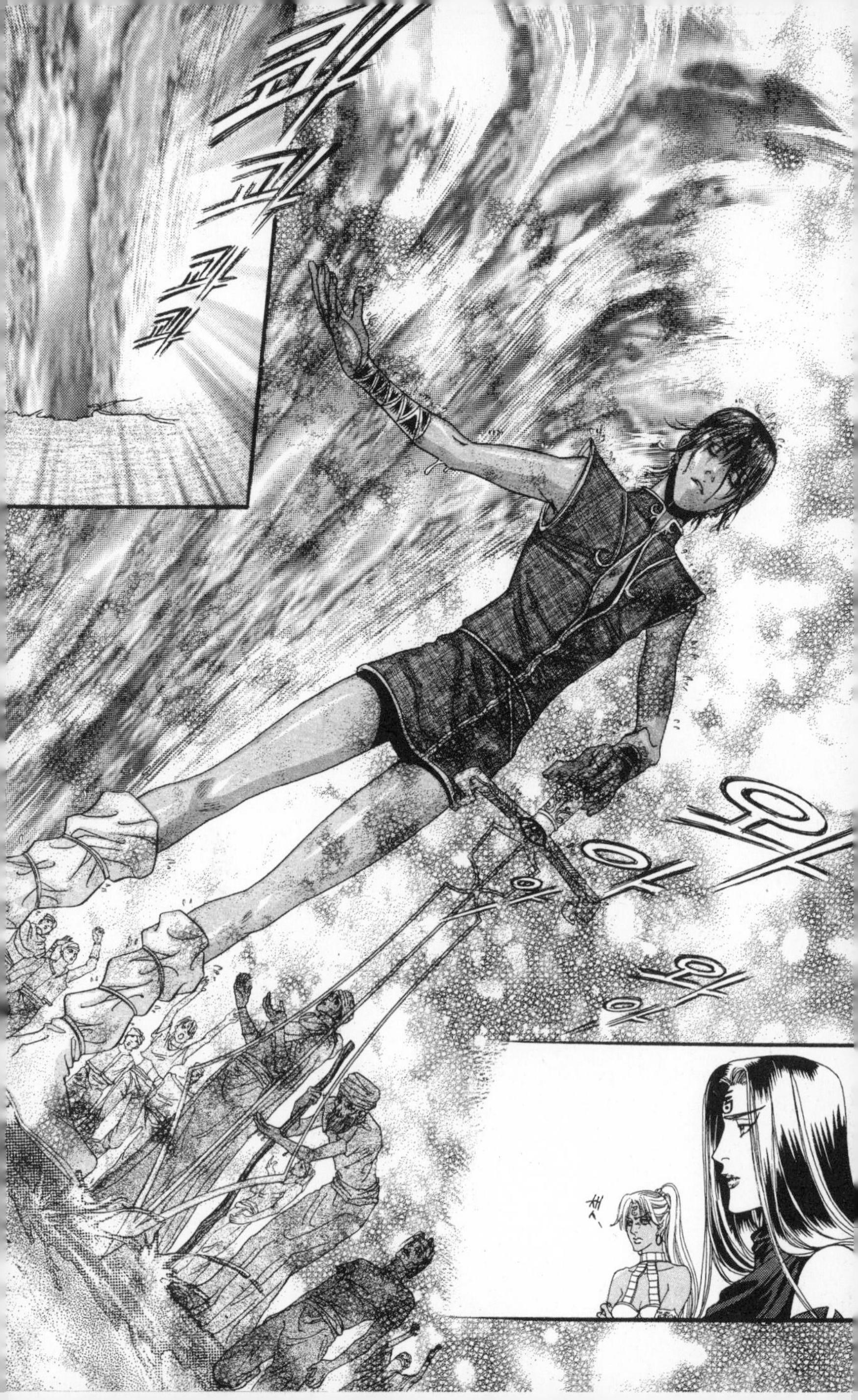
콰콰콰콰
와아아
와아
쳇

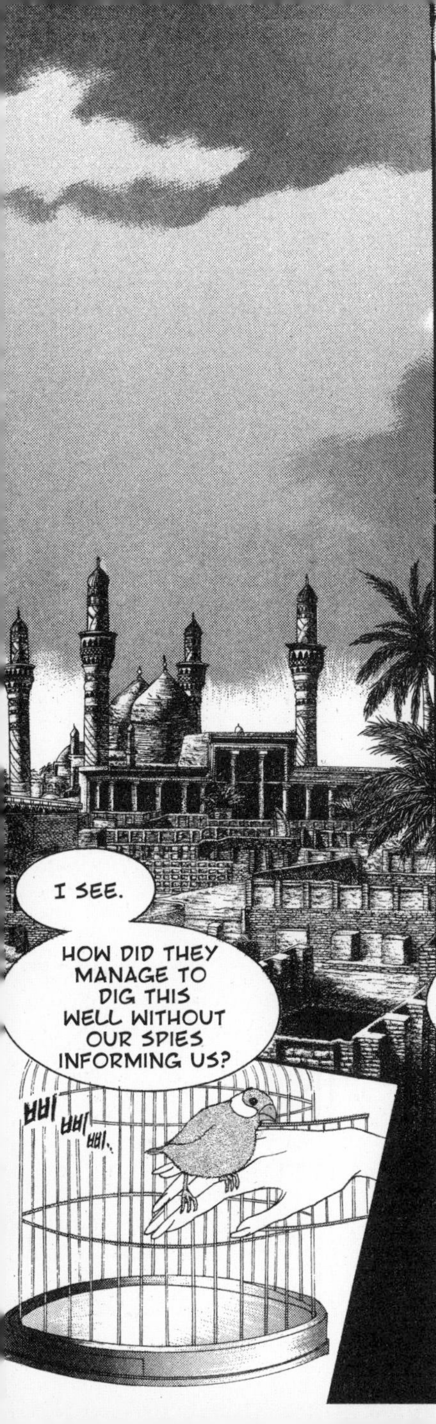
I SEE.
HOW DID THEY MANAGE TO DIG THIS WELL WITHOUT OUR SPIES INFORMING US?
삐
삐
삐..
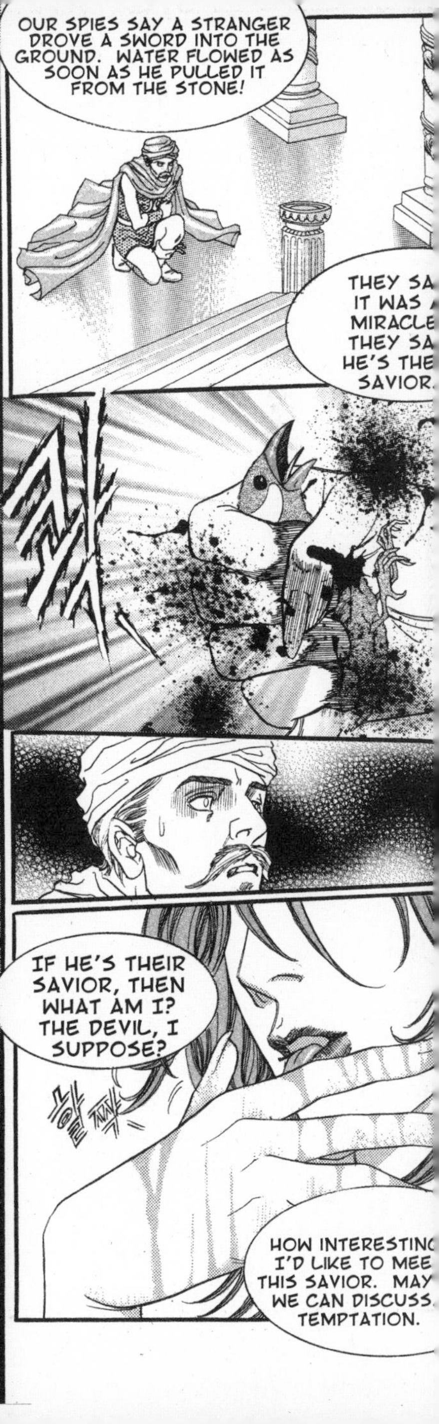
OUR SPIES SAY A STRANGER DROVE A SWORD INTO THE GROUND. WATER FLOWED AS SOON AS HE PULLED IT FROM THE STONE!
THEY SA IT WAS A MIRACLE THEY SA HE'S THE SAVIOR.
IF HE'S THEIR SAVIOR, THEN WHAT AM I? THE DEVIL, I SUPPOSE?
할짝
HOW INTERESTING I'D LIKE TO MEE THIS SAVIOR. MAY WE CAN DISCUSS TEMPTATION.

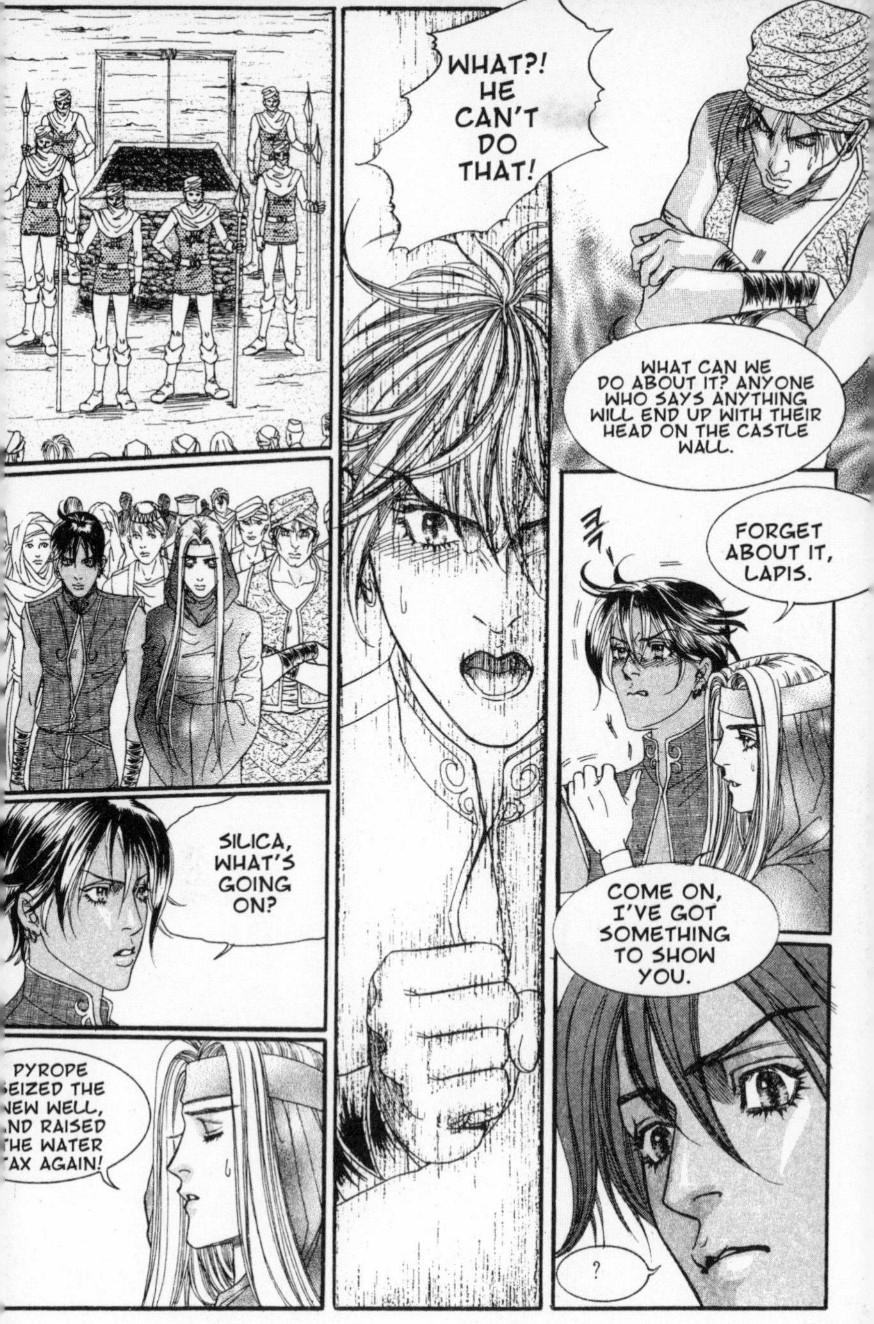
SILICA, WHAT'S GOING ON?
PYROPE SEIZED THE NEW WELL, AND RAISED THE WATER TAX AGAIN!
WHAT?! HE CAN'T DO THAT!
WHAT CAN WE DO ABOUT IT? ANYONE WHO SAYS ANYTHING WILL END UP WITH THEIR HEAD ON THE CASTLE WALL.
FORGET ABOUT IT, LAPIS.
COME ON, I'VE GOT SOMETHING TO SHOW YOU.
?

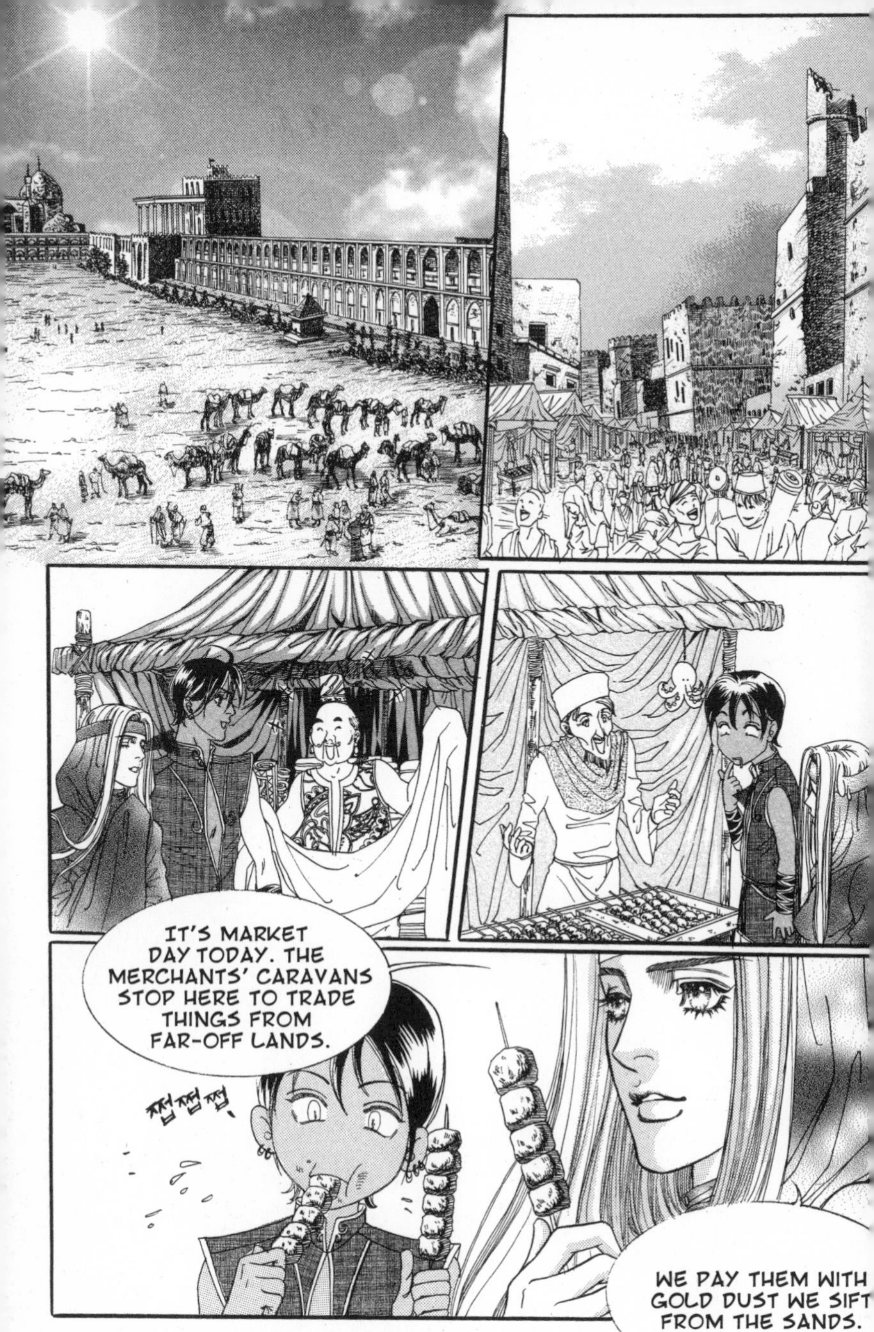
IT'S MARKET DAY TODAY. THE MERCHANTS' CARAVANS STOP HERE TO TRADE THINGS FROM FAR-OFF LANDS.
쩝쩝쩝
WE PAY THEM WITH GOLD DUST WE SIFT FROM THE SANDS.

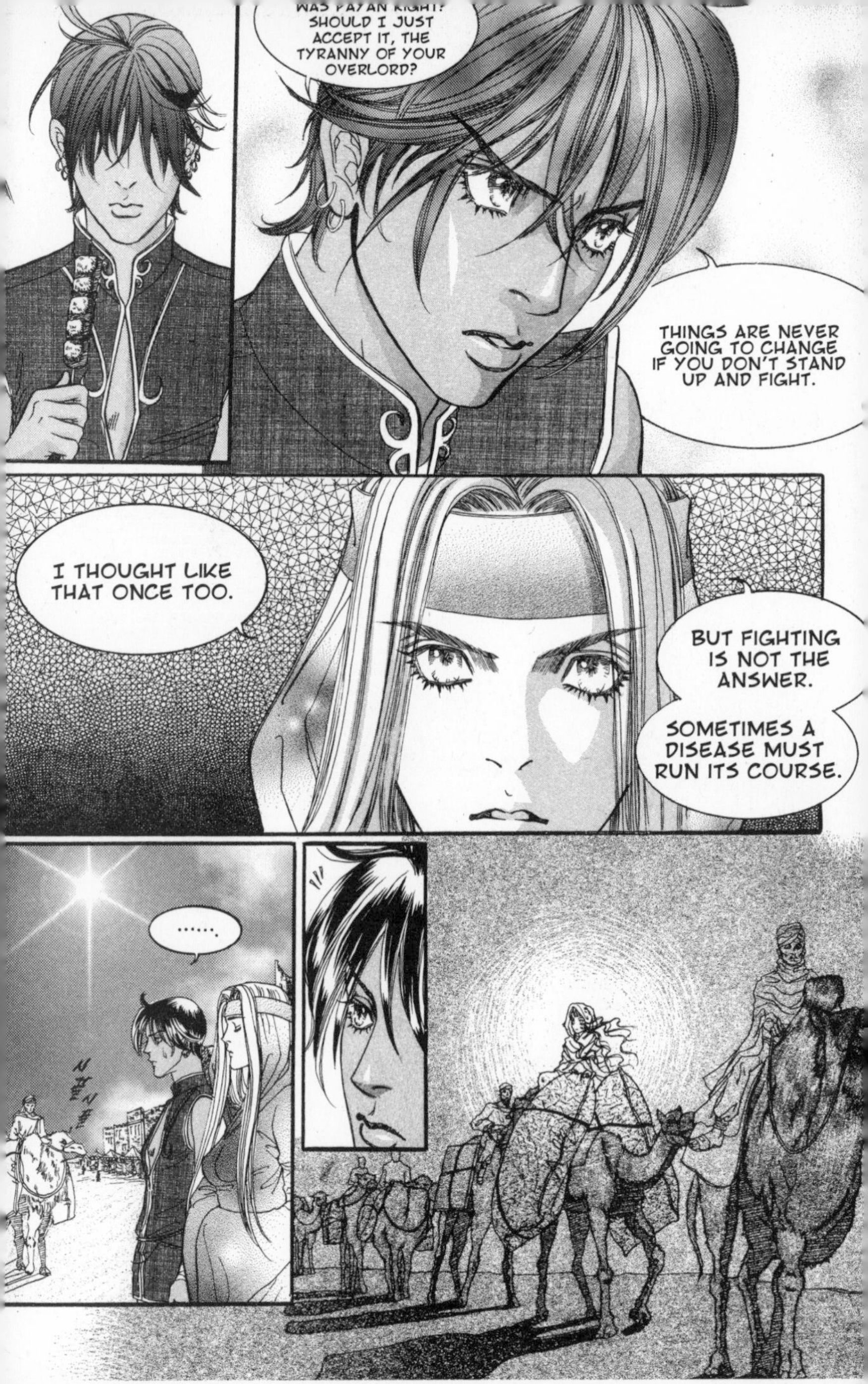
WAS PAYAN RIGHT? SHOULD I JUST ACCEPT IT, THE TYRANNY OF YOUR OVERLORD?
THINGS ARE NEVER GOING TO CHANGE IF YOU DON'T STAND UP AND FIGHT.
I THOUGHT LIKE THAT ONCE TOO.
BUT FIGHTING IS NOT THE ANSWER.
SOMETIMES A DISEASE MUST RUN ITS COURSE.
....

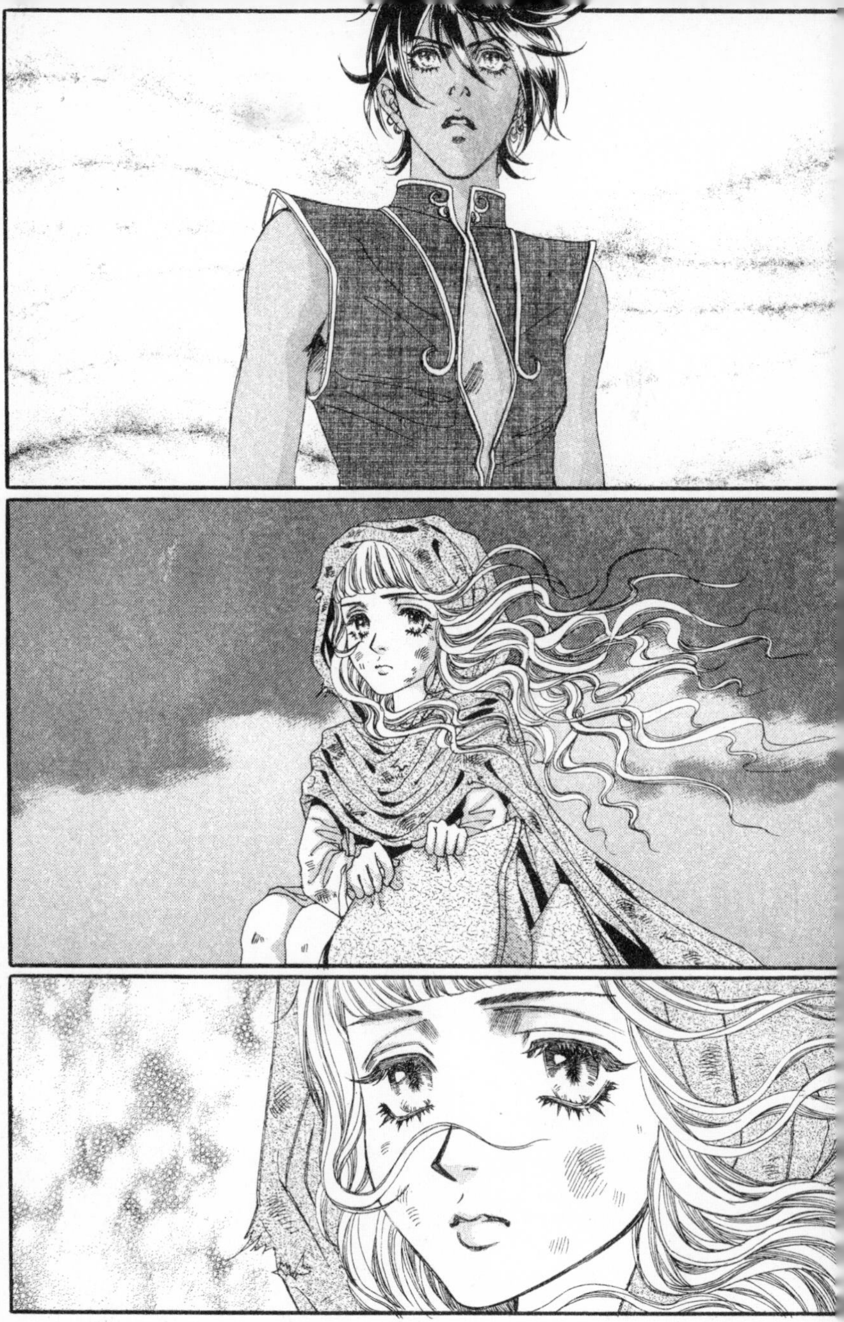

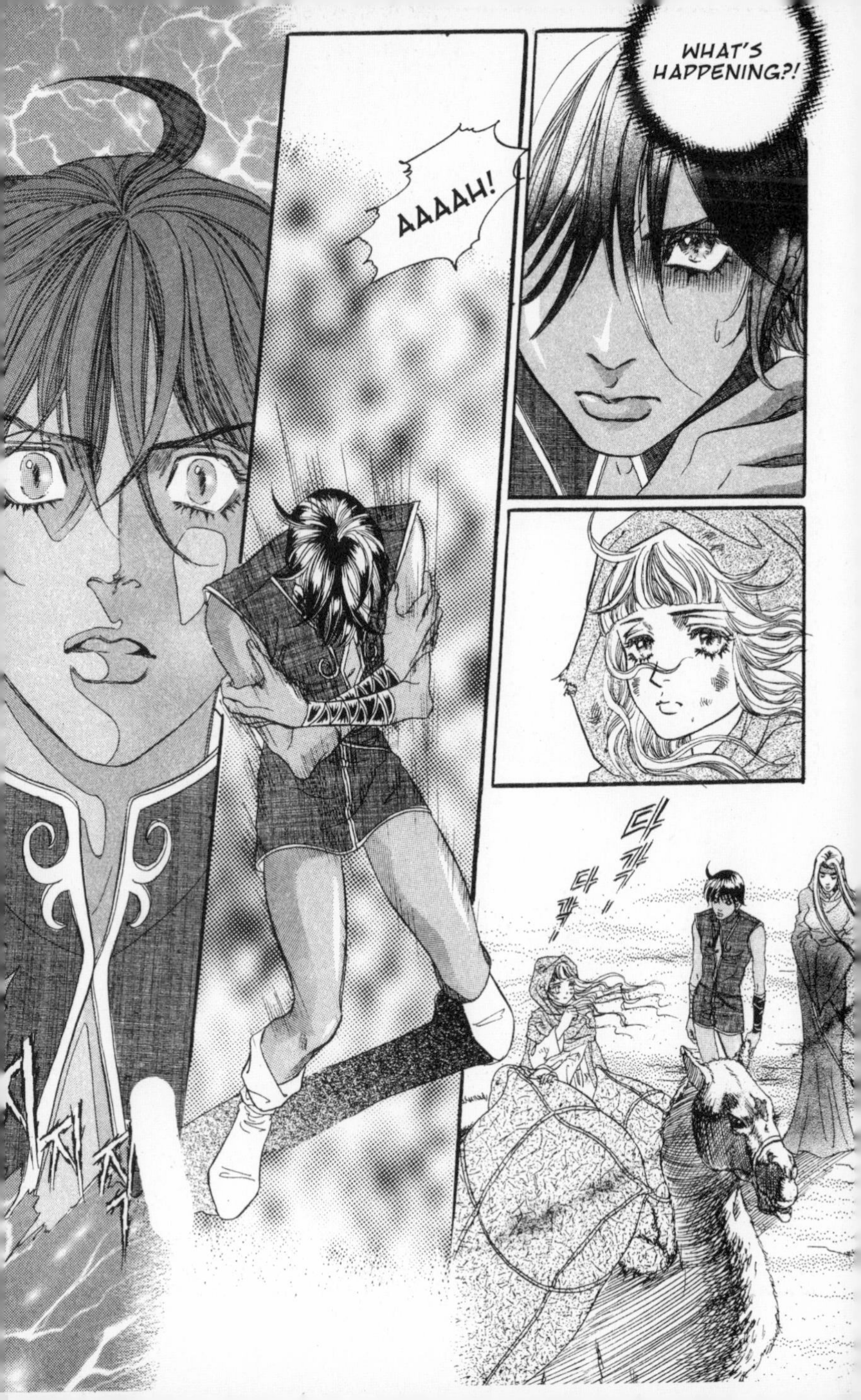
AAAAH!
WHAT'S HAPPENING?!

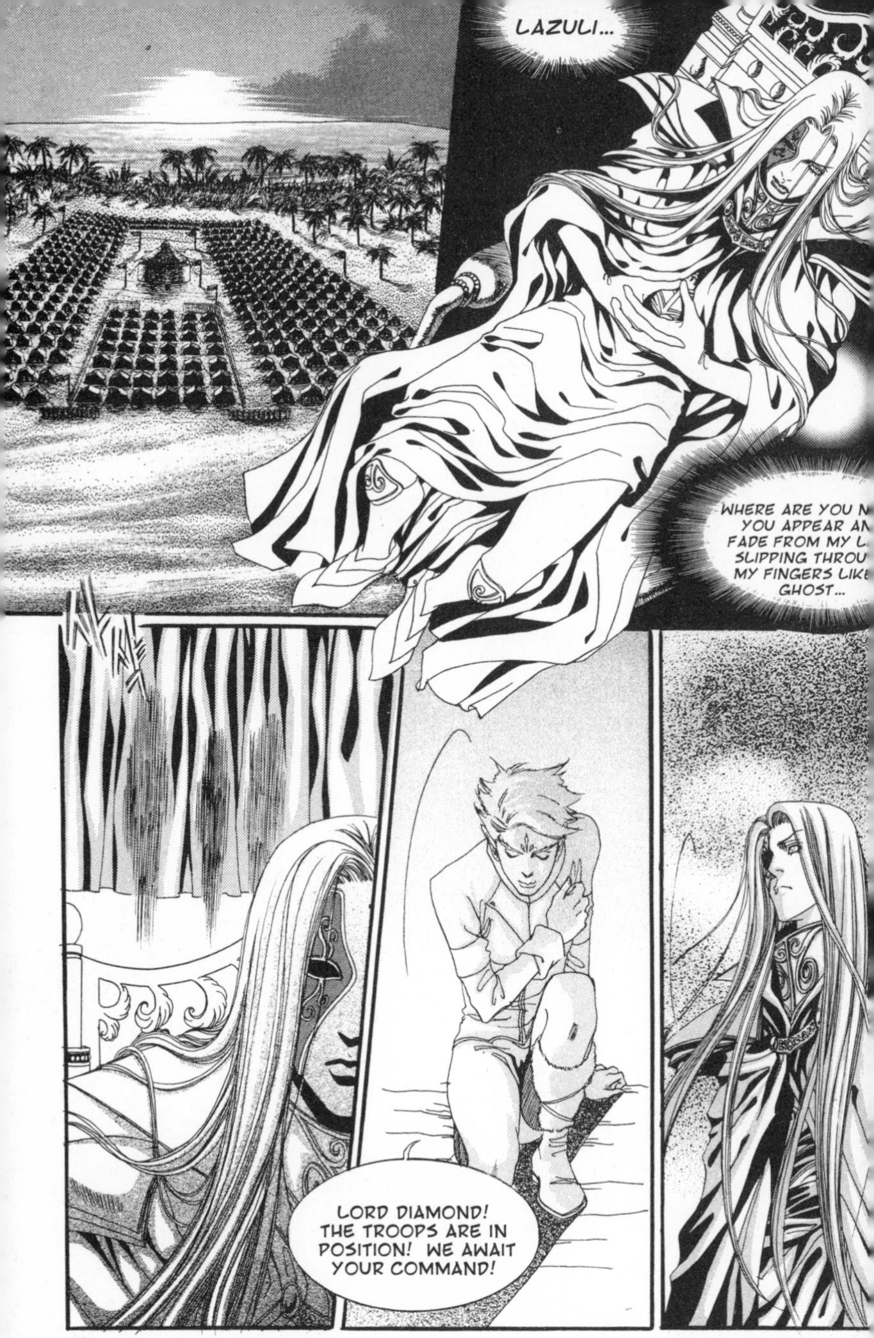
LAZULI...
WHERE ARE YOU N YOU APPEAR AN FADE FROM MY L SLIPPING THROU MY FINGERS LIKE GHOST...
LORD DIAMOND! THE TROOPS ARE IN POSITION! WE AWAIT YOUR COMMAND!

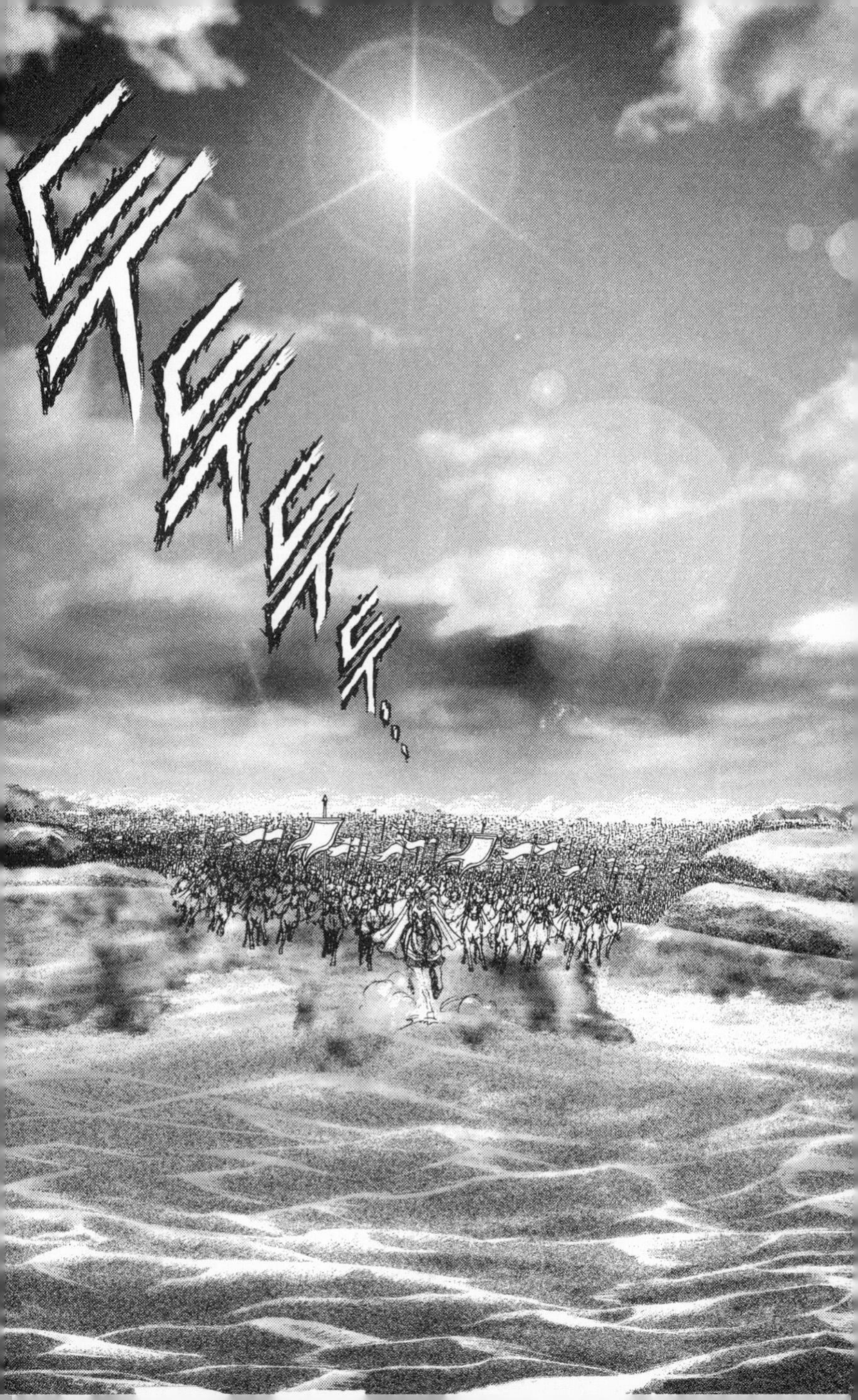
두두두두…

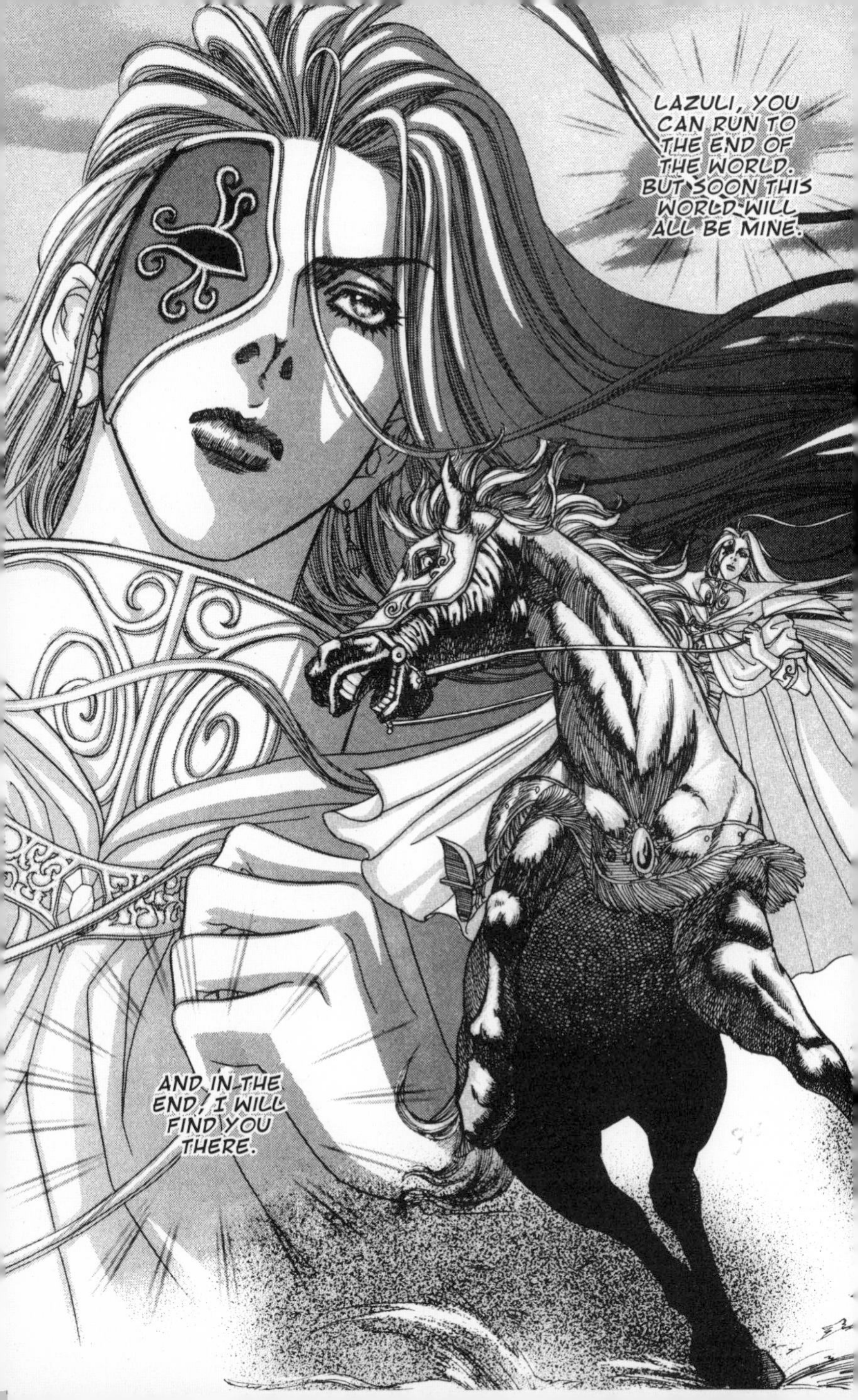
LAZULI, YOU CAN RUN TO THE END OF THE WORLD. BUT SOON THIS WORLD WILL ALL BE MINE.
AND IN THE END, I WILL FIND YOU THERE.

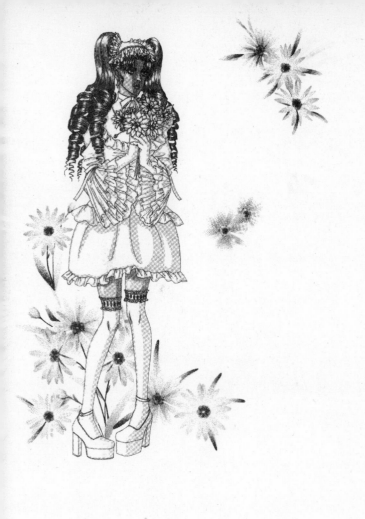

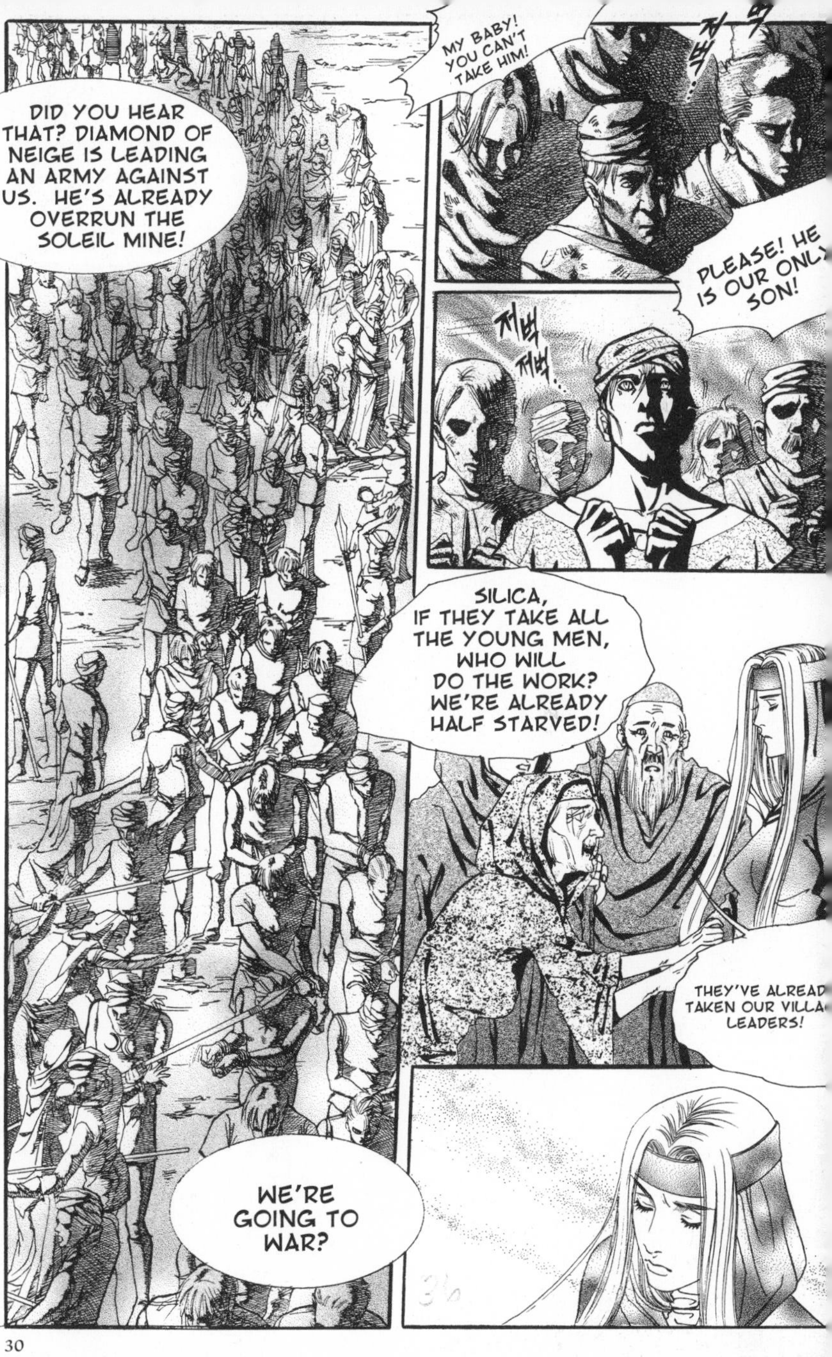
DID YOU HEAR THAT? DIAMOND OF NEIGE IS LEADING AN ARMY AGAINST US. HE'S ALREADY OVERRUN THE SOLEIL MINE!
WE'RE GOING TO WAR?
MY BABY! YOU CAN'T TAKE HIM!
PLEASE! HE IS OUR ONLY SON!
저벅 저벅...
SILICA, IF THEY TAKE ALL THE YOUNG MEN, WHO WILL DO THE WORK? WE'RE ALREADY HALF STARVED!
THEY'VE ALREAD TAKEN OUR VILLA LEADERS!

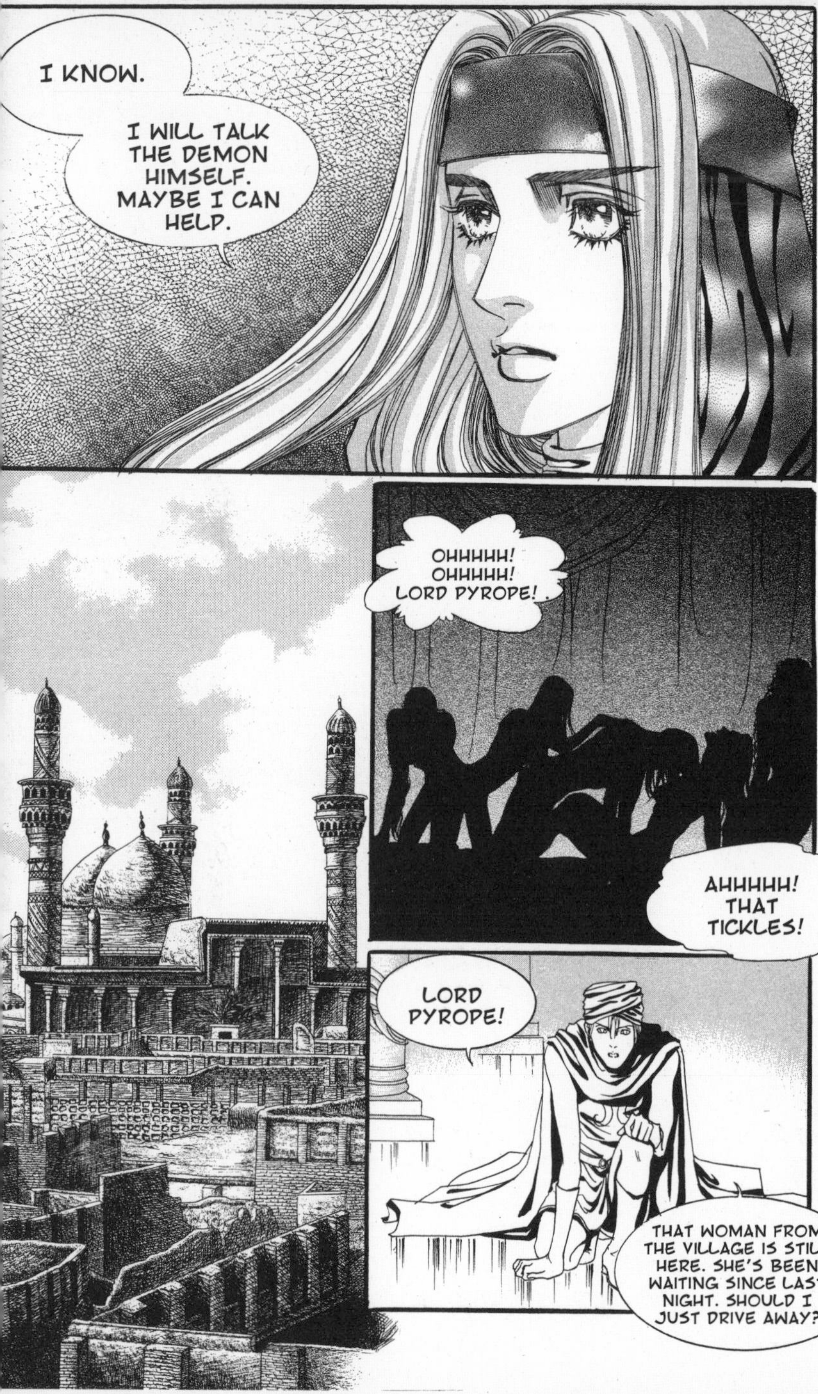
I KNOW.
I WILL TALK THE DEMON HIMSELF. MAYBE I CAN HELP.
OHHHHH! OHHHHH! LORD PYROPE!
AHHHHH! THAT TICKLES!
LORD PYROPE!
THAT WOMAN FROM THE VILLAGE IS STILL HERE. SHE'S BEEN WAITING SINCE LAST NIGHT. SHOULD I JUST DRIVE AWAY?

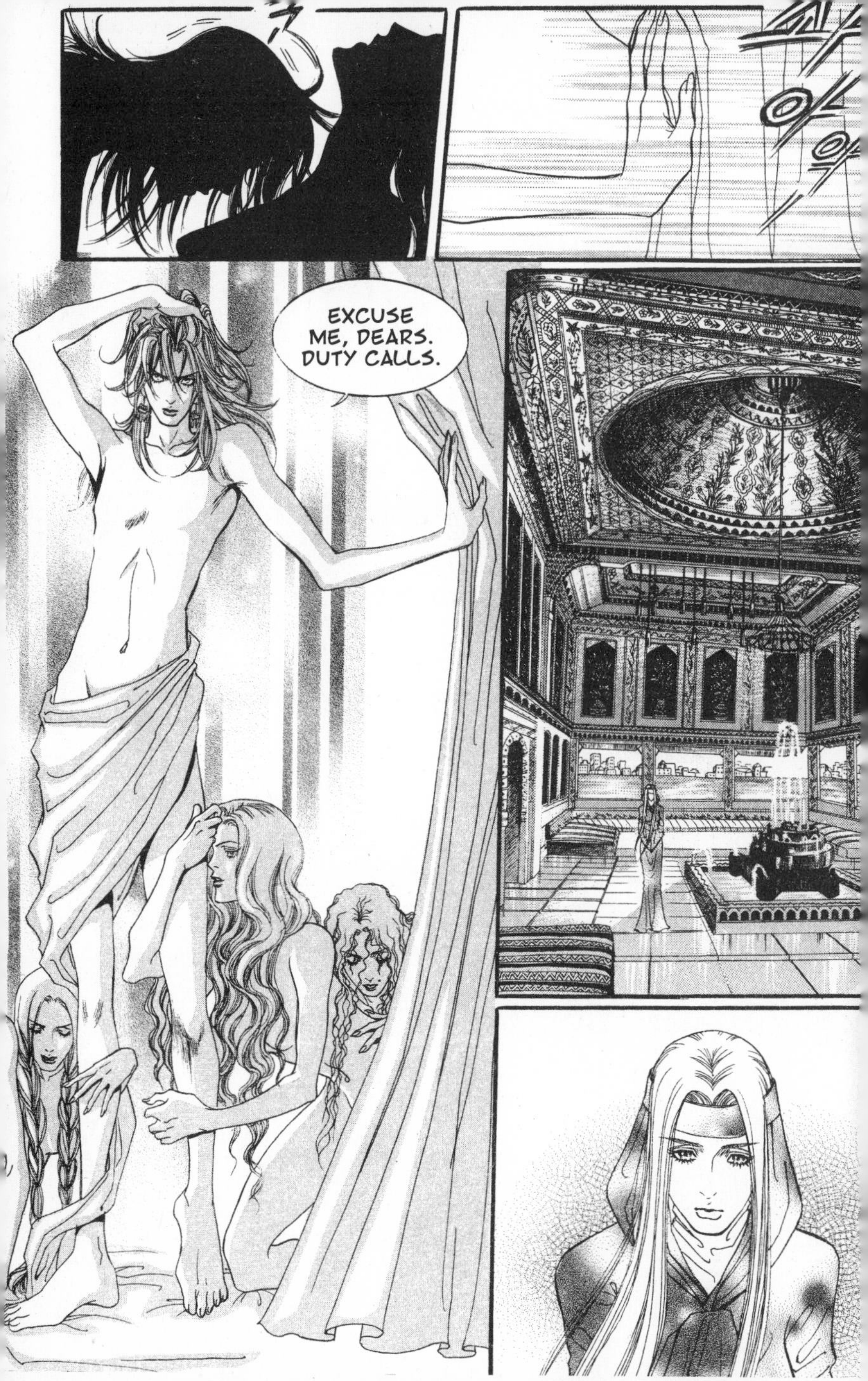
EXCUSE ME, DEARS. DUTY CALLS.

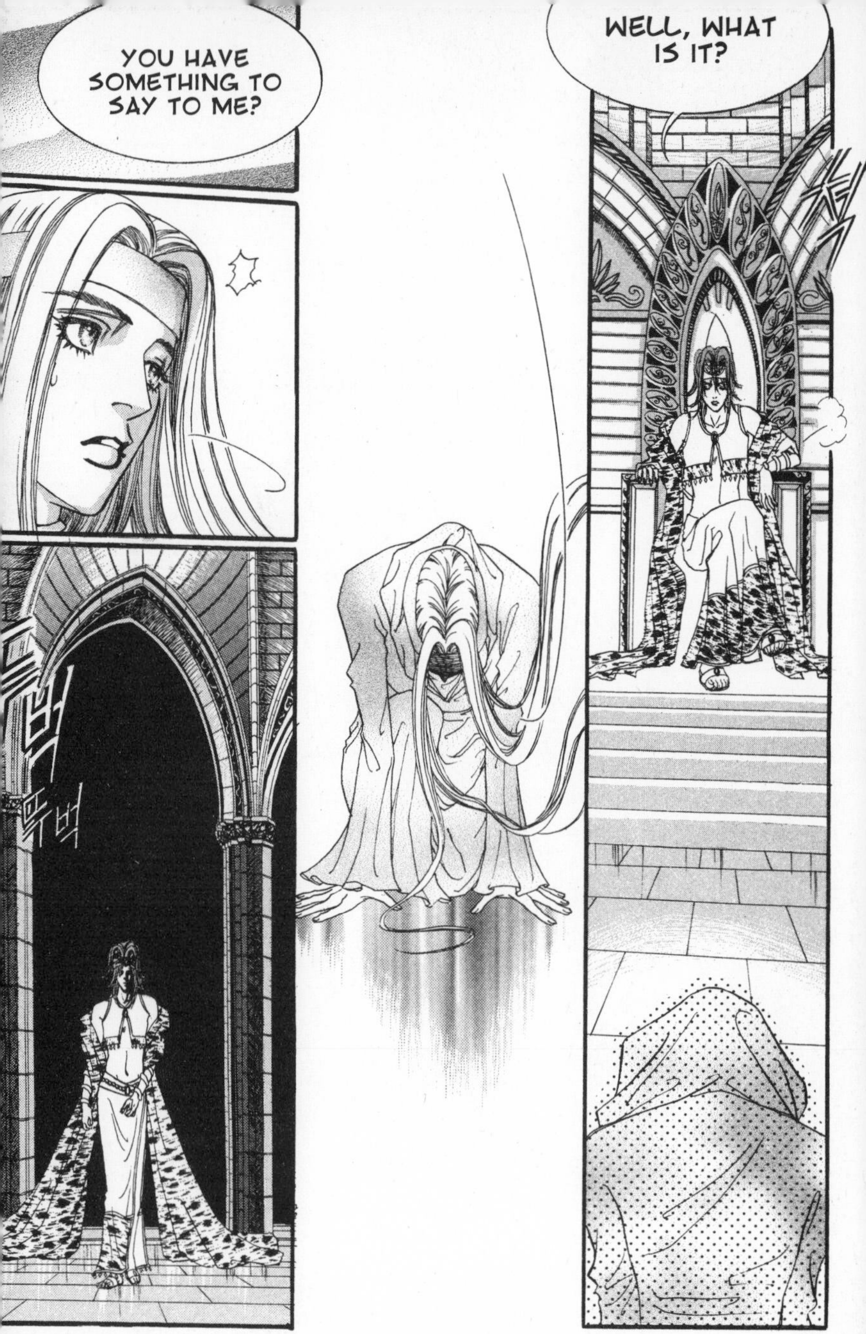
YOU HAVE SOMETHING TO SAY TO ME?
WELL, WHAT IS IT?

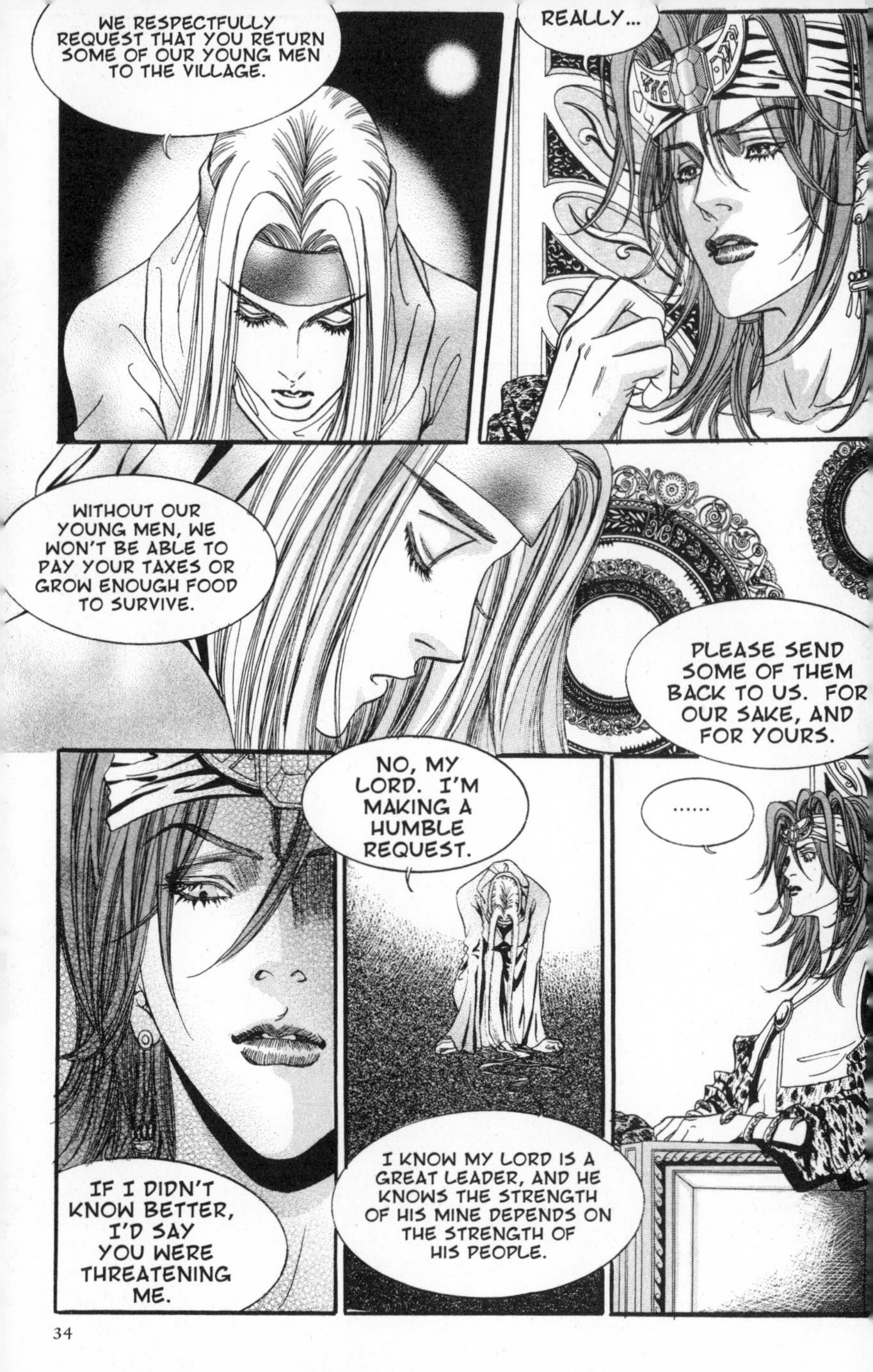
WE RESPECTFULLY REQUEST THAT YOU RETURN SOME OF OUR YOUNG MEN TO THE VILLAGE.
REALLY...
WITHOUT OUR YOUNG MEN, WE WON'T BE ABLE TO PAY YOUR TAXES OR GROW ENOUGH FOOD TO SURVIVE.
PLEASE SEND SOME OF THEM BACK TO US. FOR OUR SAKE, AND FOR YOURS.
IF I DIDN'T KNOW BETTER, I'D SAY YOU WERE THREATENING ME.
NO, MY LORD. I'M MAKING A HUMBLE REQUEST.
I KNOW MY LORD IS A GREAT LEADER, AND HE KNOWS THE STRENGTH OF HIS MINE DEPENDS ON THE STRENGTH OF HIS PEOPLE.
......

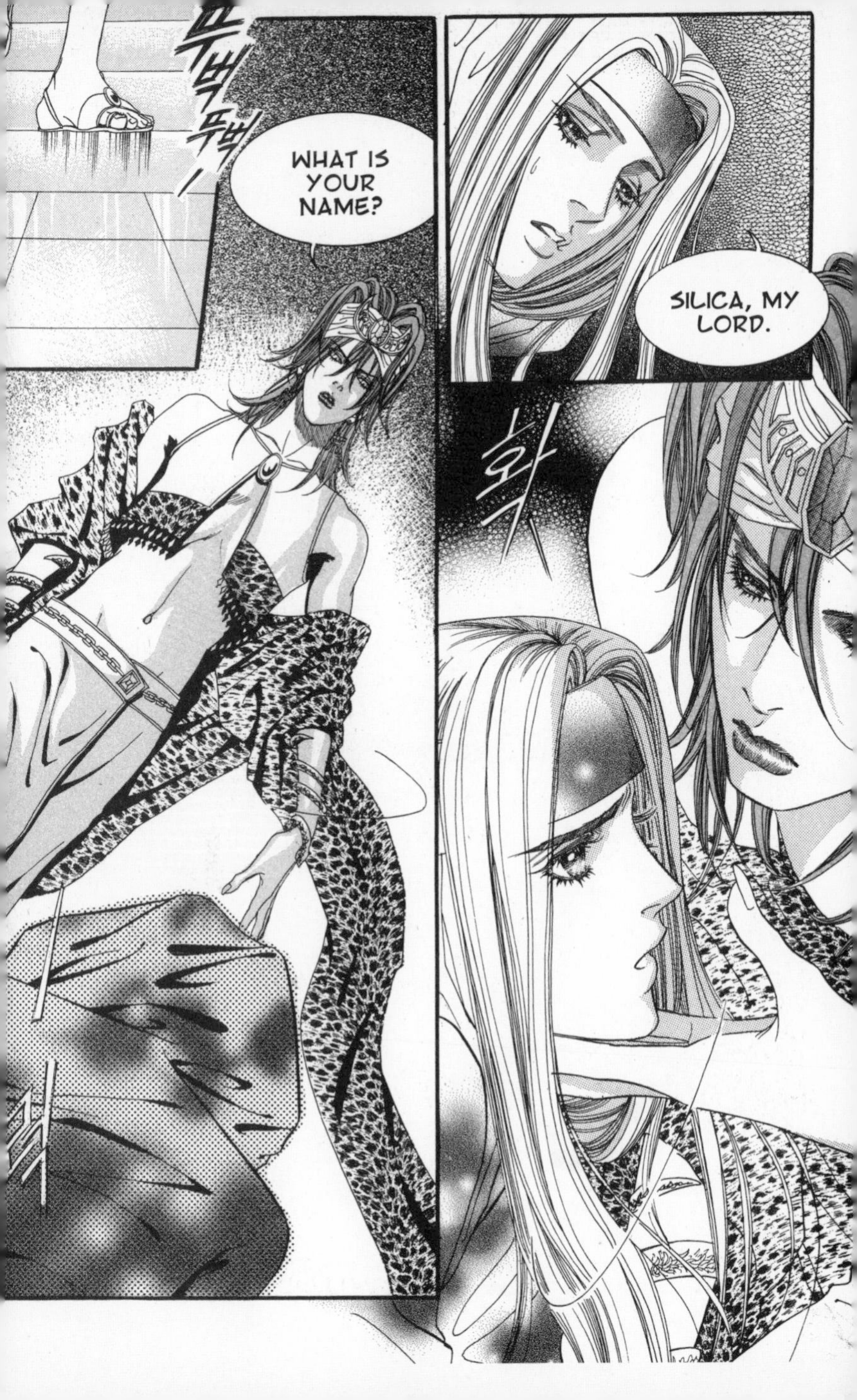
뚜벅뚜벅
WHAT IS YOUR NAME?
SILICA, MY LORD.
확

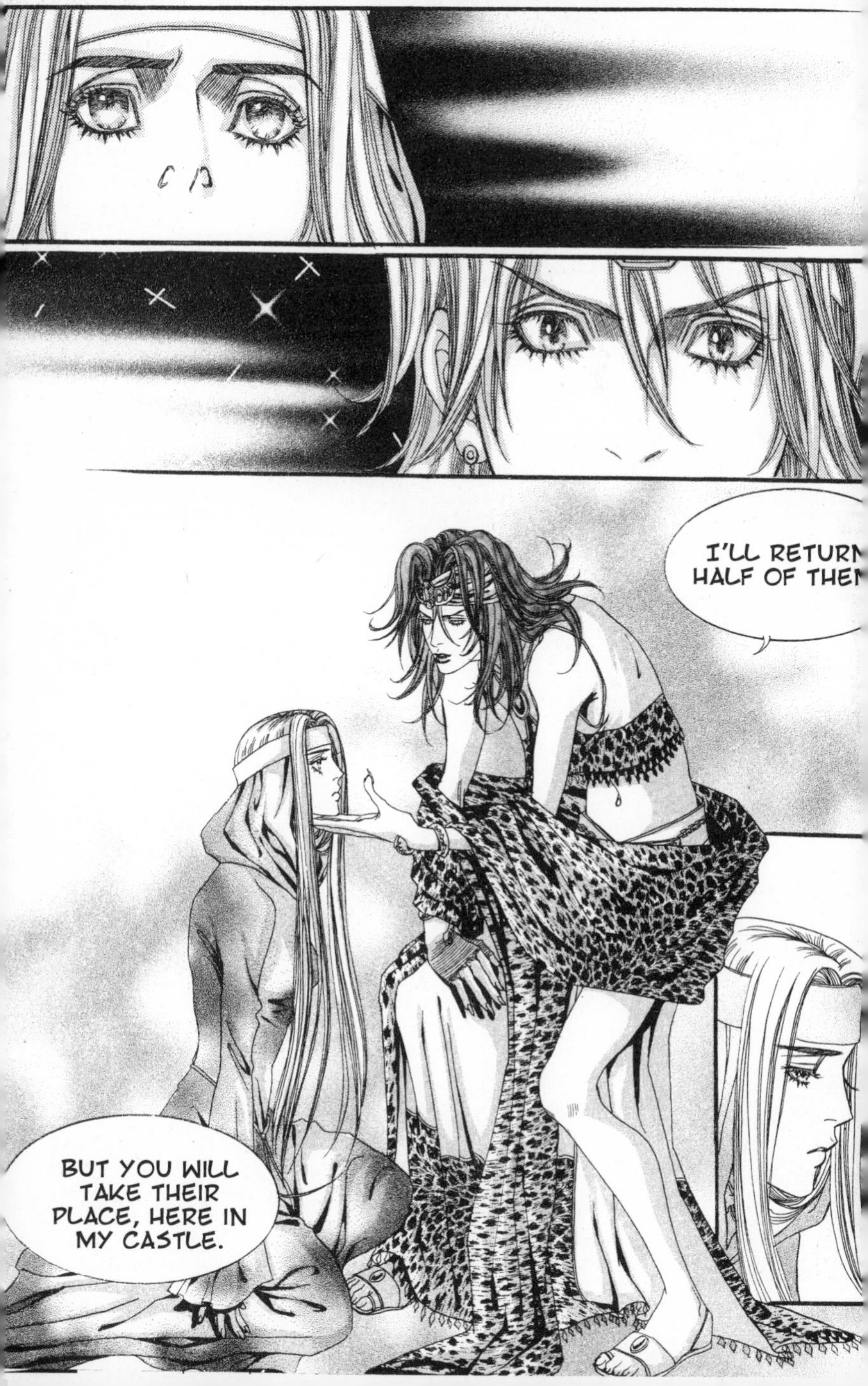
I'LL RETURN HALF OF THEM
BUT YOU WILL TAKE THEIR PLACE, HERE IN MY CASTLE.

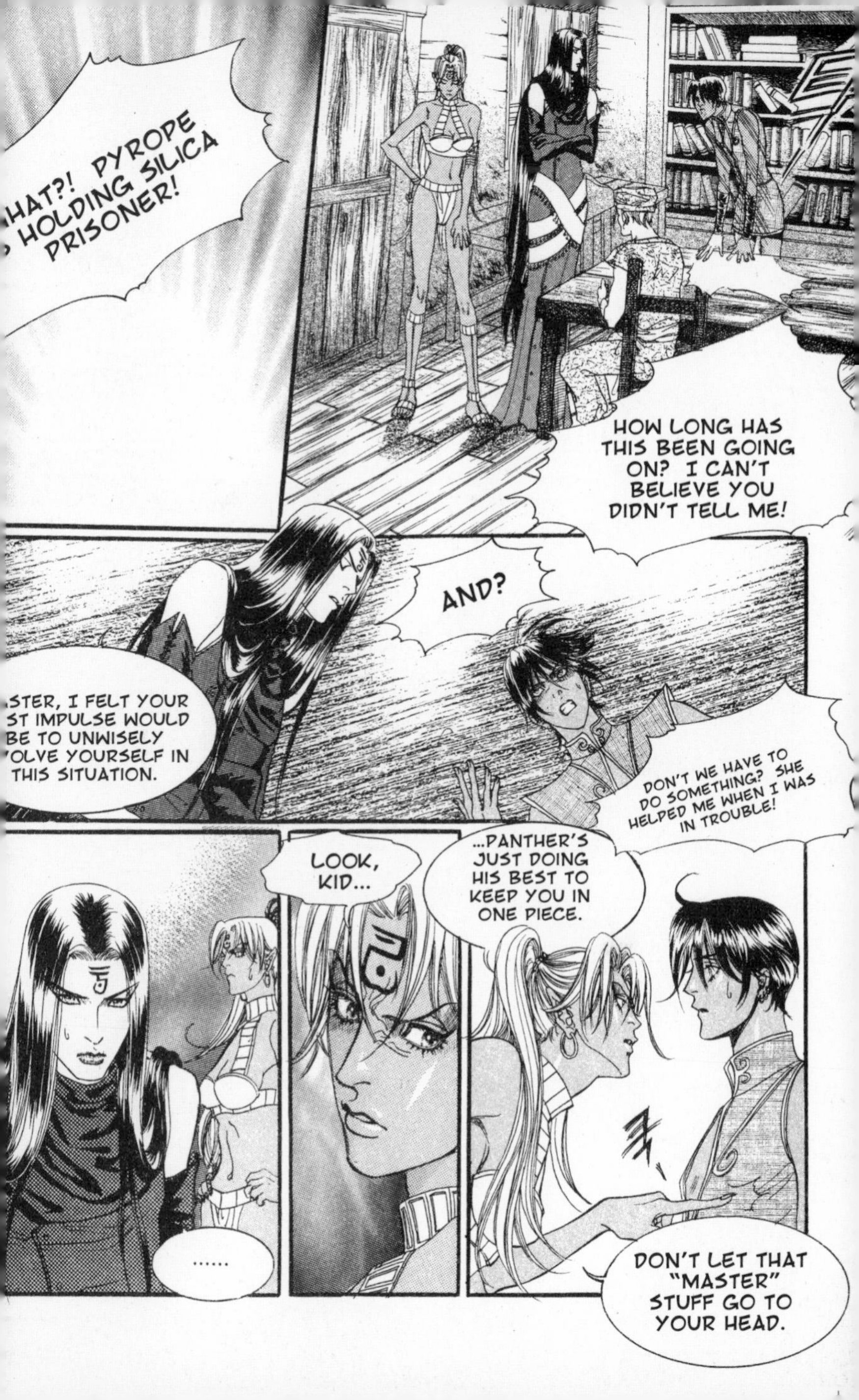
HAT?! PYROPE
HOLDING SILICA
PRISONER!
HOW LONG HAS THIS BEEN GOING ON? I CAN'T BELIEVE YOU DIDN'T TELL ME!
ASTER, I FELT YOUR ST IMPULSE WOULD BE TO UNWISELY VOLVE YOURSELF IN THIS SITUATION.
AND?
DON'T WE HAVE TO DO SOMETHING? SHE HELPED ME WHEN I WAS IN TROUBLE!
......
LOOK, KID...
...PANTHER'S JUST DOING HIS BEST TO KEEP YOU IN ONE PIECE.
DON'T LET THAT "MASTER" STUFF GO TO YOUR HEAD.

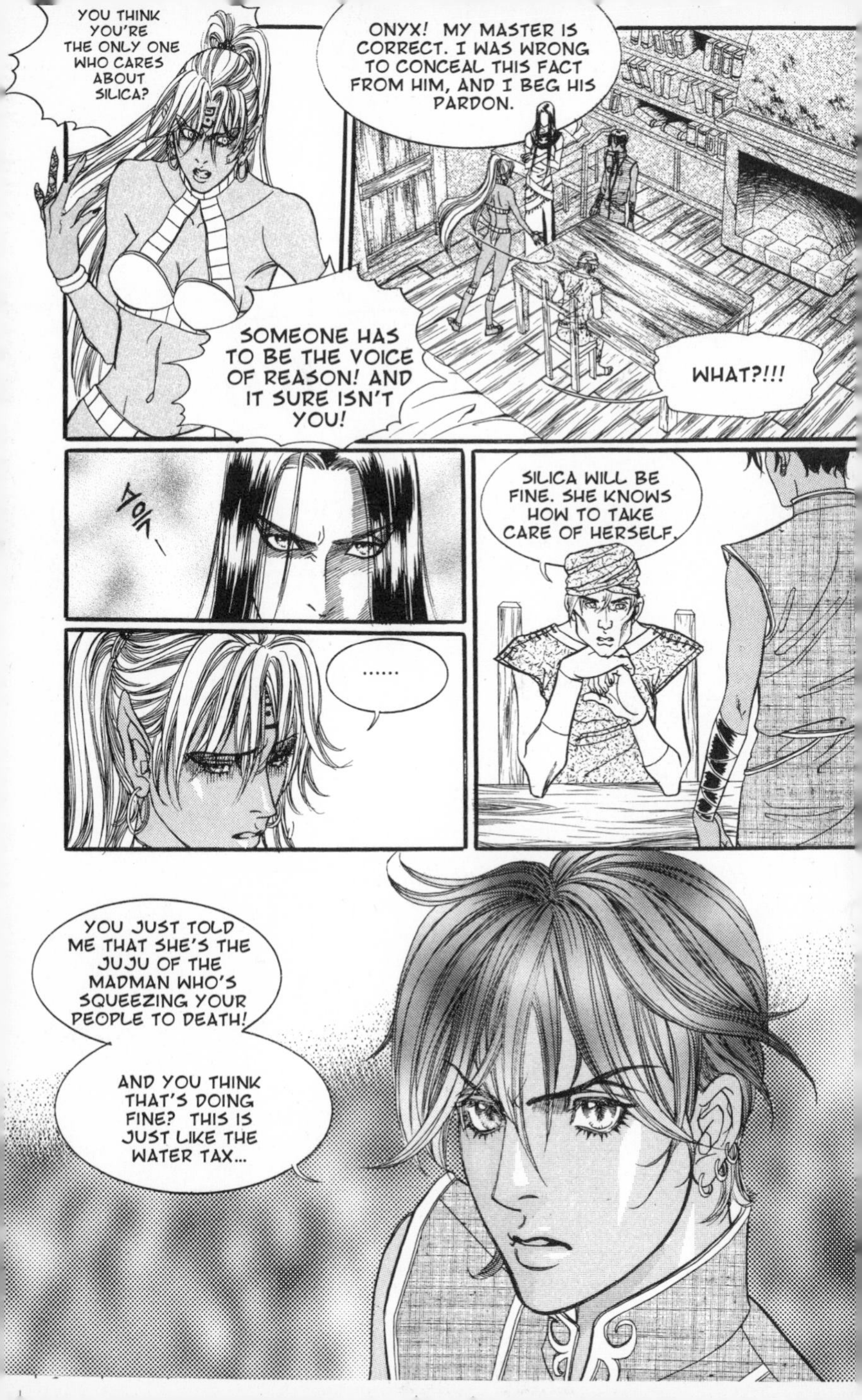
YOU THINK YOU'RE THE ONLY ONE WHO CARES ABOUT SILICA?
SOMEONE HAS TO BE THE VOICE OF REASON! AND IT SURE ISN'T YOU!
ONYX! MY MASTER IS CORRECT. I WAS WRONG TO CONCEAL THIS FACT FROM HIM, AND I BEG HIS PARDON.
WHAT?!!!
......
SILICA WILL BE FINE. SHE KNOWS HOW TO TAKE CARE OF HERSELF.
YOU JUST TOLD ME THAT SHE'S THE JUJU OF THE MADMAN WHO'S SQUEEZING YOUR PEOPLE TO DEATH!
AND YOU THINK THAT'S DOING FINE? THIS IS JUST LIKE THE WATER TAX...

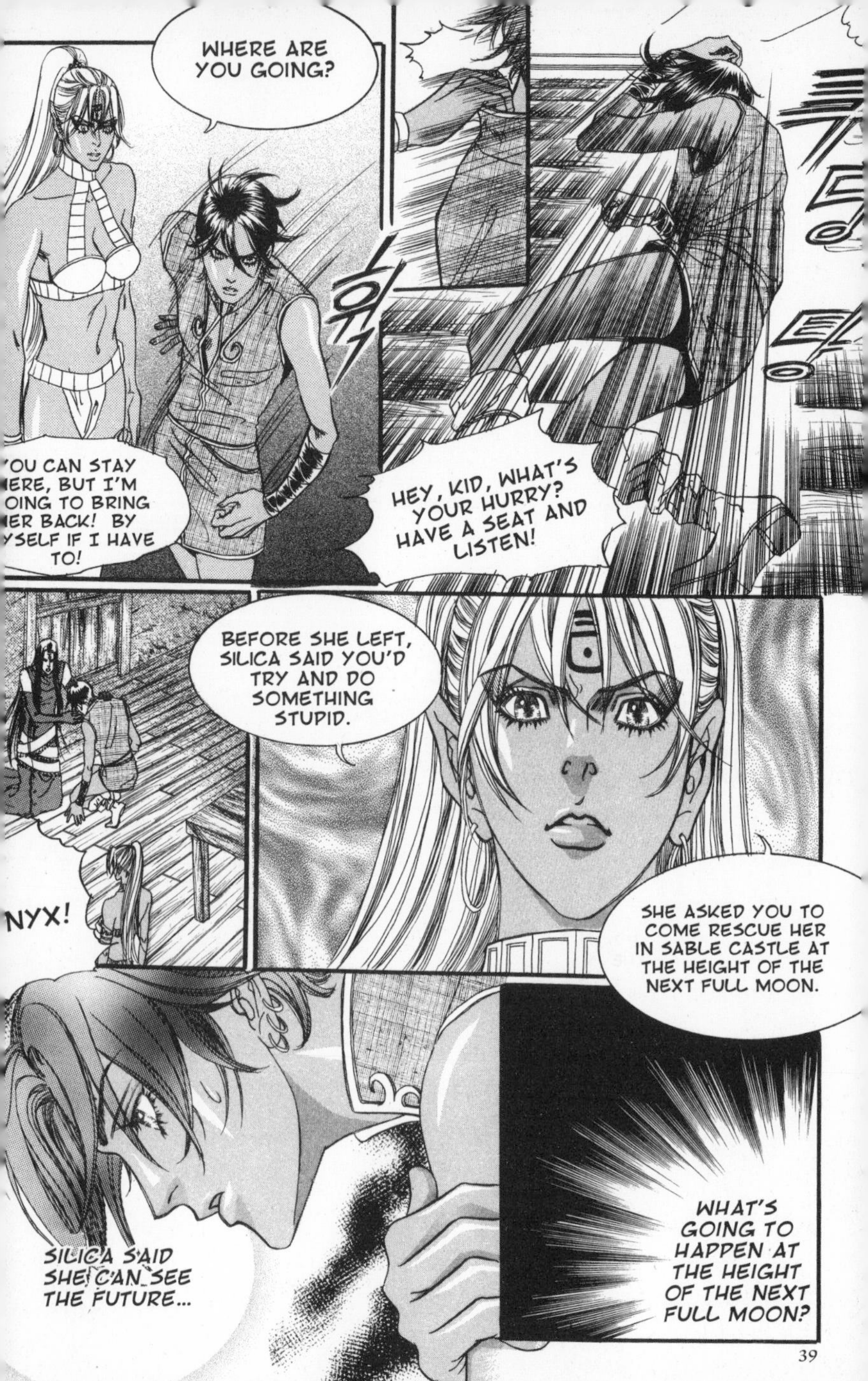
WHERE ARE YOU GOING?
OU CAN STAY ERE, BUT I'M OING TO BRING ER BACK! BY YSELF IF I HAVE TO!
HEY, KID, WHAT'S YOUR HURRY? HAVE A SEAT AND LISTEN!
NYX!
BEFORE SHE LEFT, SILICA SAID YOU'D TRY AND DO SOMETHING STUPID.
SHE ASKED YOU TO COME RESCUE HER IN SABLE CASTLE AT THE HEIGHT OF THE NEXT FULL MOON.
SILICA SAID SHE CAN SEE THE FUTURE...
WHAT'S GOING TO HAPPEN AT THE HEIGHT OF THE NEXT FULL MOON?

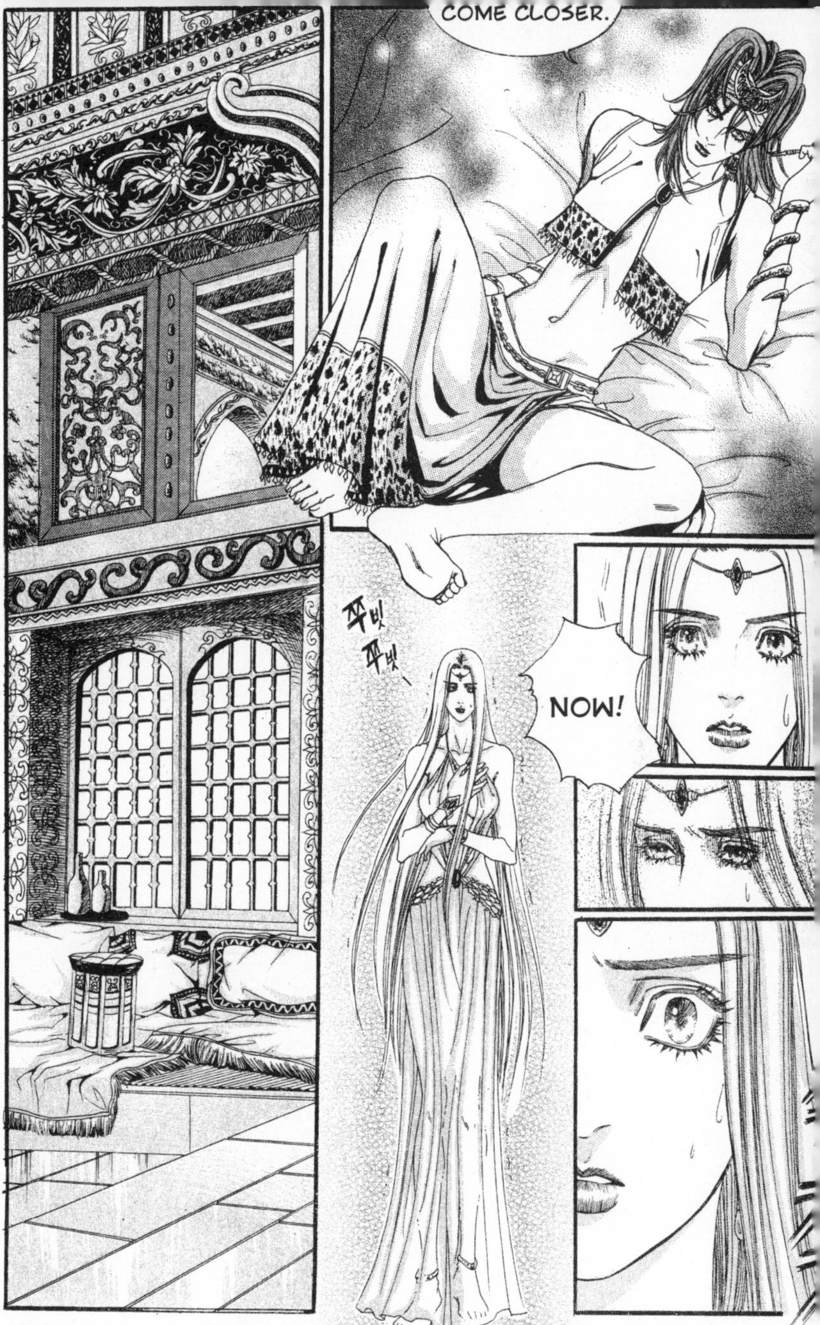
COME CLOSER.
쭈빗
쭈빗
NOW!

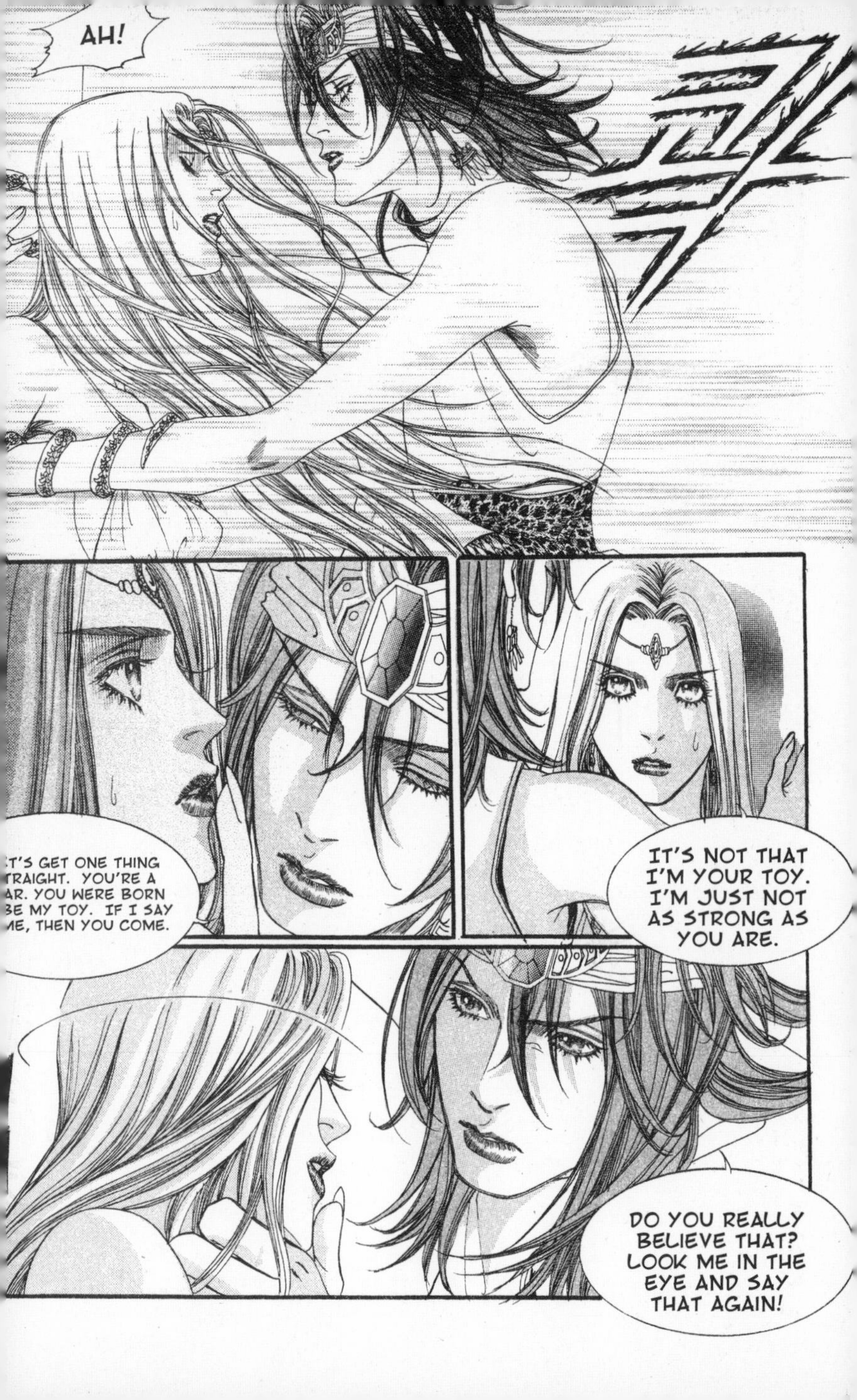
AH!
T'S GET ONE THING TRAIGHT. YOU'RE A AR. YOU WERE BORN BE MY TOY. IF I SAY ME, THEN YOU COME.
IT'S NOT THAT I'M YOUR TOY. I'M JUST NOT AS STRONG AS YOU ARE.
DO YOU REALLY BELIEVE THAT? LOOK ME IN THE EYE AND SAY THAT AGAIN!

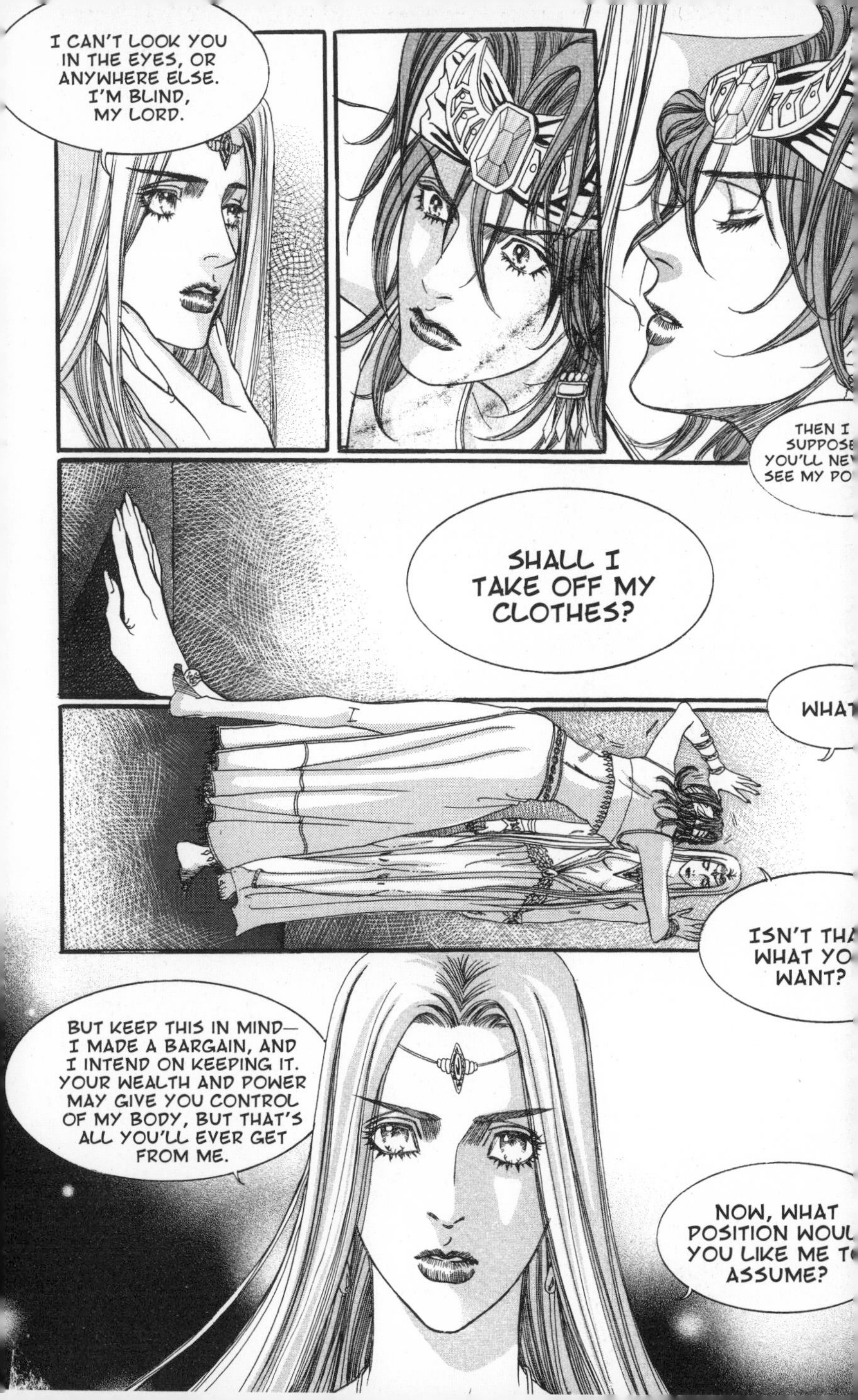
I CAN'T LOOK YOU IN THE EYES, OR ANYWHERE ELSE. I'M BLIND, MY LORD.
THEN I SUPPOSE YOU'LL NE SEE MY PO
SHALL I TAKE OFF MY CLOTHES?
WHA
ISN'T THA WHAT YO WANT?
BUT KEEP THIS IN MIND— I MADE A BARGAIN, AND I INTEND ON KEEPING IT. YOUR WEALTH AND POWER MAY GIVE YOU CONTROL OF MY BODY, BUT THAT'S ALL YOU'LL EVER GET FROM ME.
NOW, WHAT POSITION WOUL YOU LIKE ME T ASSUME?

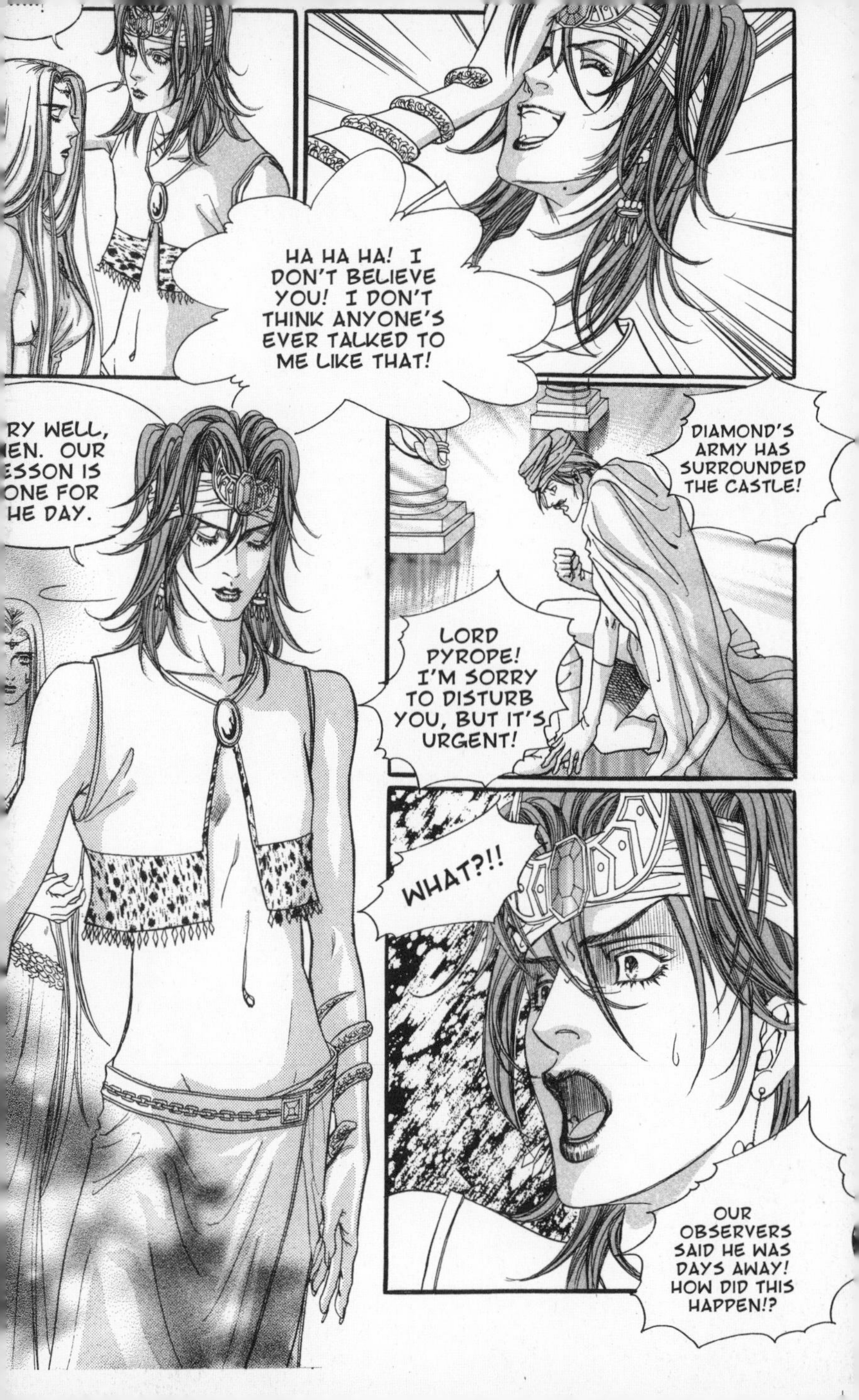
HA HA HA! I DON'T BELIEVE YOU! I DON'T THINK ANYONE'S EVER TALKED TO ME LIKE THAT!
RY WELL, EN. OUR ESSON IS ONE FOR HE DAY.
DIAMOND'S ARMY HAS SURROUNDED THE CASTLE!
LORD PYROPE! I'M SORRY TO DISTURB YOU, BUT IT'S URGENT!
WHAT?!!
OUR OBSERVERS SAID HE WAS DAYS AWAY! HOW DID THIS HAPPEN!?

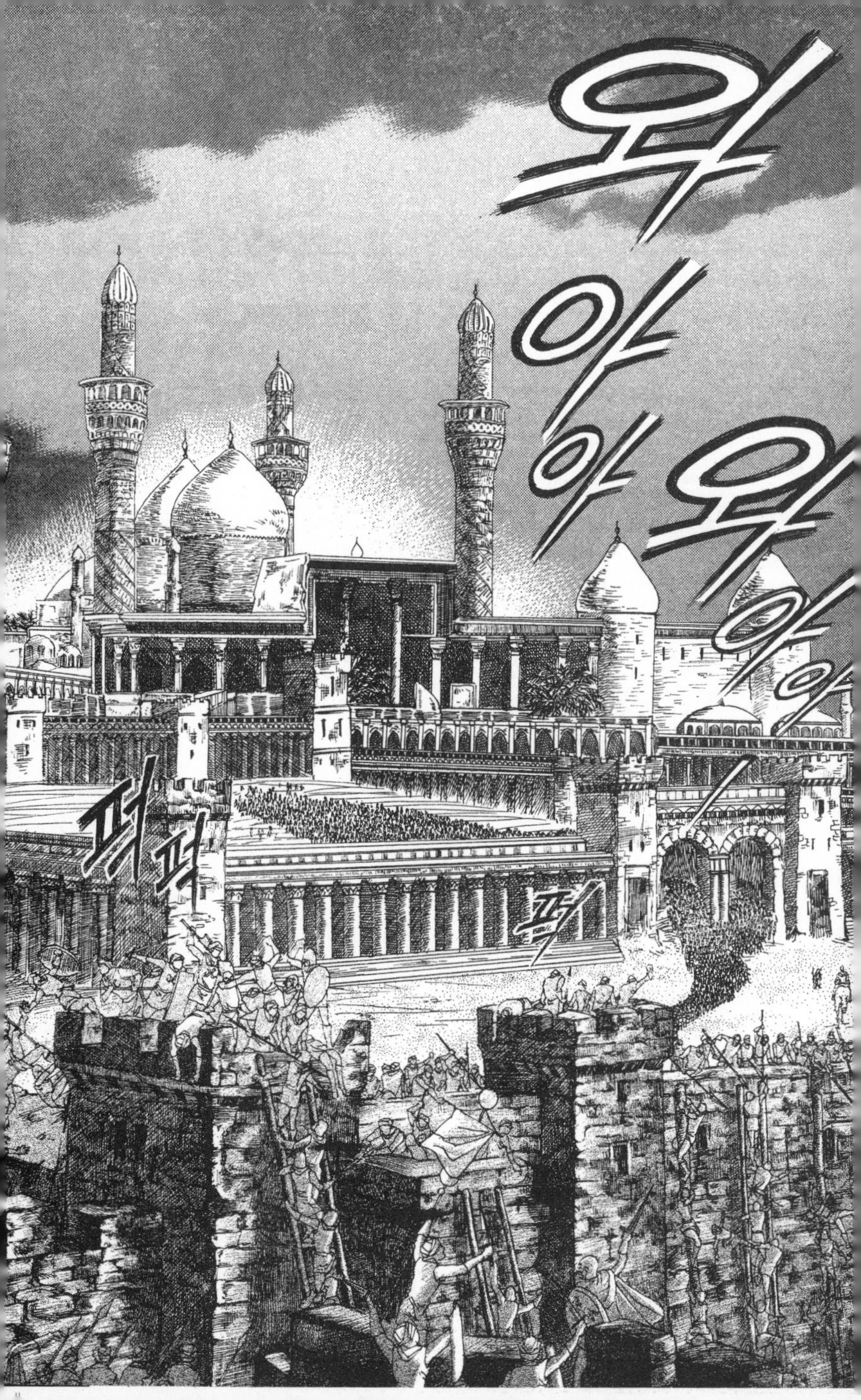
와아아와아아
퍼 퍼
프

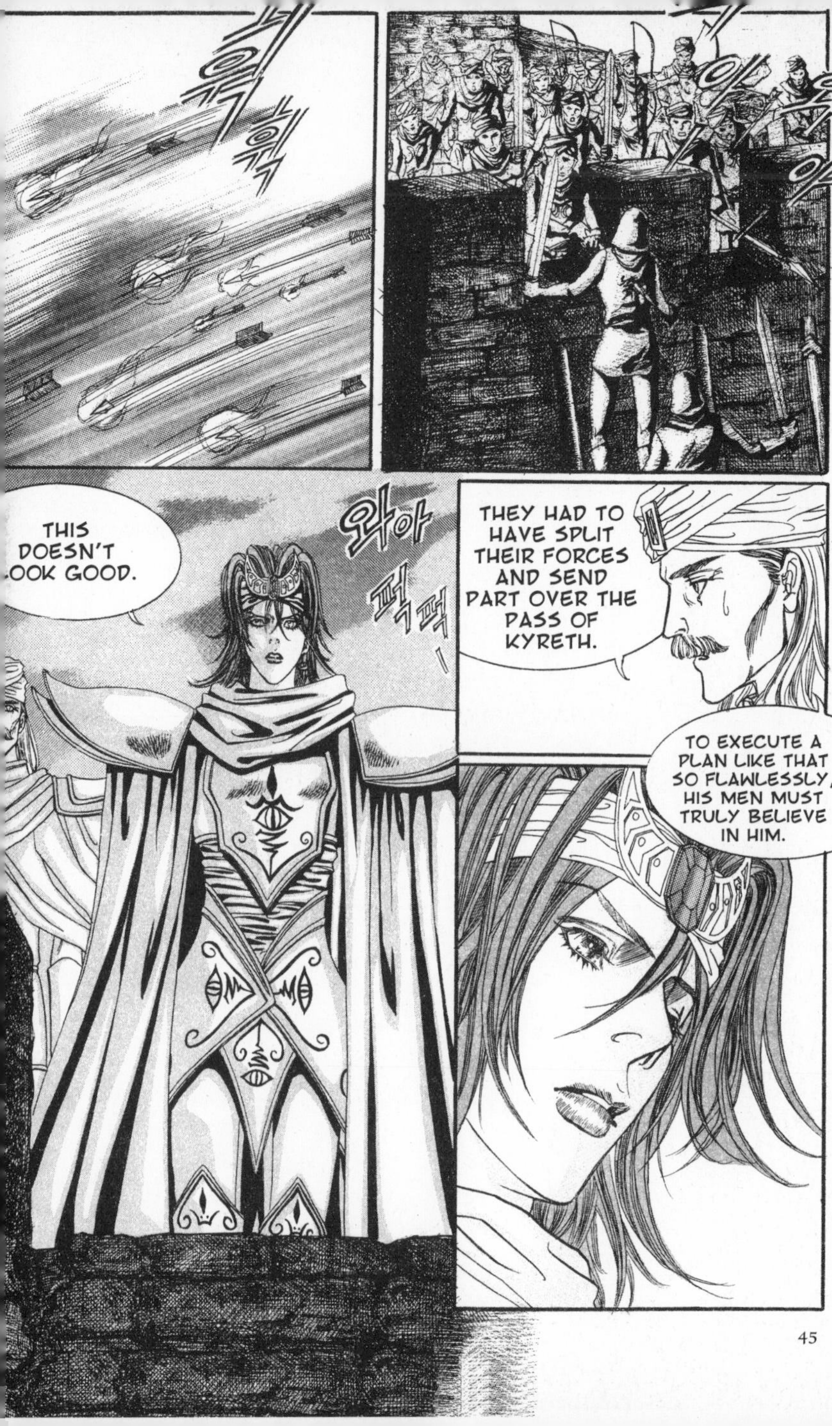
THIS DOESN'T LOOK GOOD.
THEY HAD TO HAVE SPLIT THEIR FORCES AND SEND PART OVER THE PASS OF KYRETH.
TO EXECUTE A PLAN LIKE THAT SO FLAWLESSLY, HIS MEN MUST TRULY BELIEVE IN HIM.

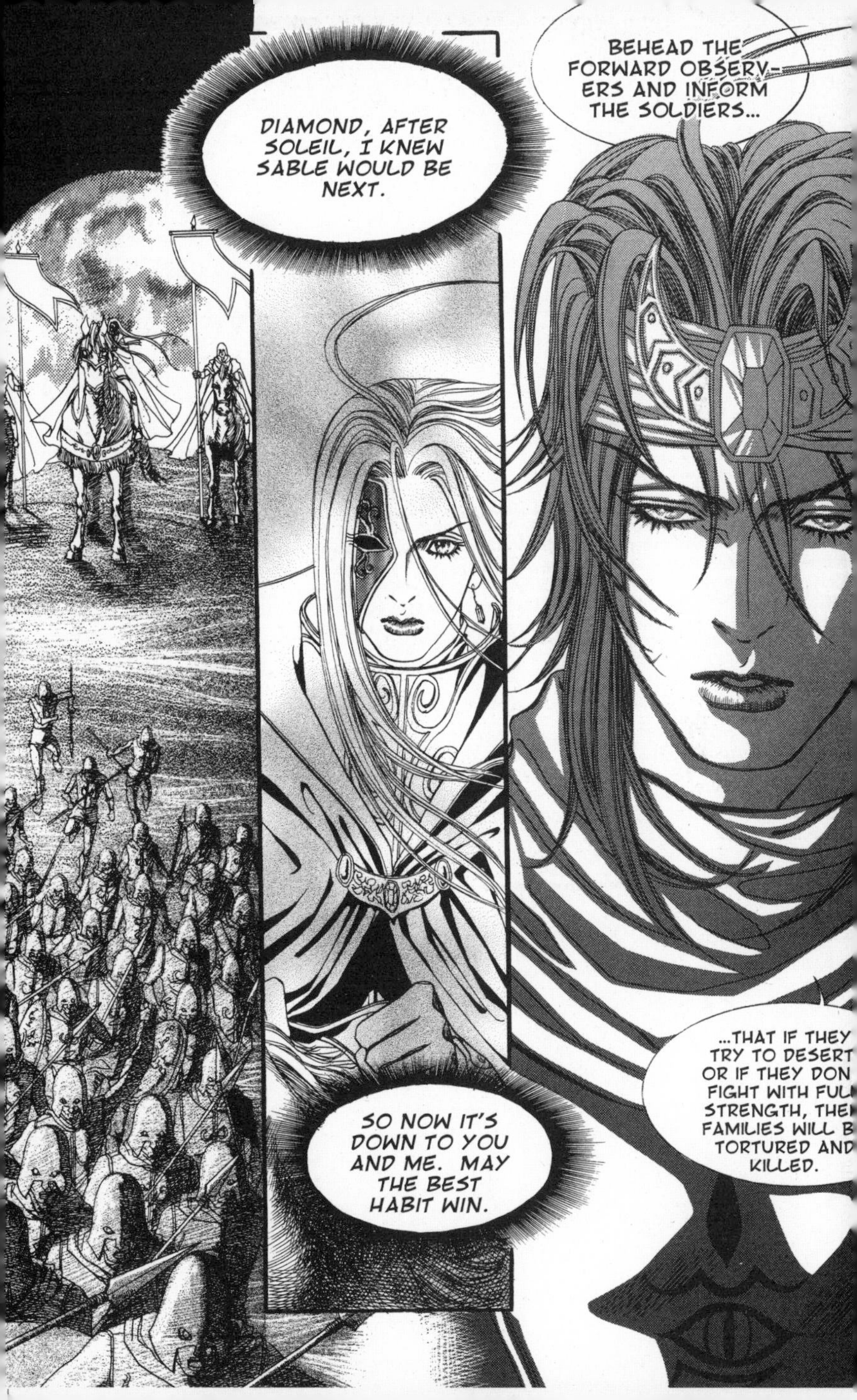
DIAMOND, AFTER SOLEIL, I KNEW SABLE WOULD BE NEXT.
SO NOW IT'S DOWN TO YOU AND ME. MAY THE BEST HABIT WIN.
BEHEAD THE FORWARD OBSERV- ERS AND INFORM THE SOLDIERS...
...THAT IF THEY TRY TO DESERT OR IF THEY DON FIGHT WITH FUL STRENGTH, THE FAMILIES WILL B TORTURED AND KILLED.

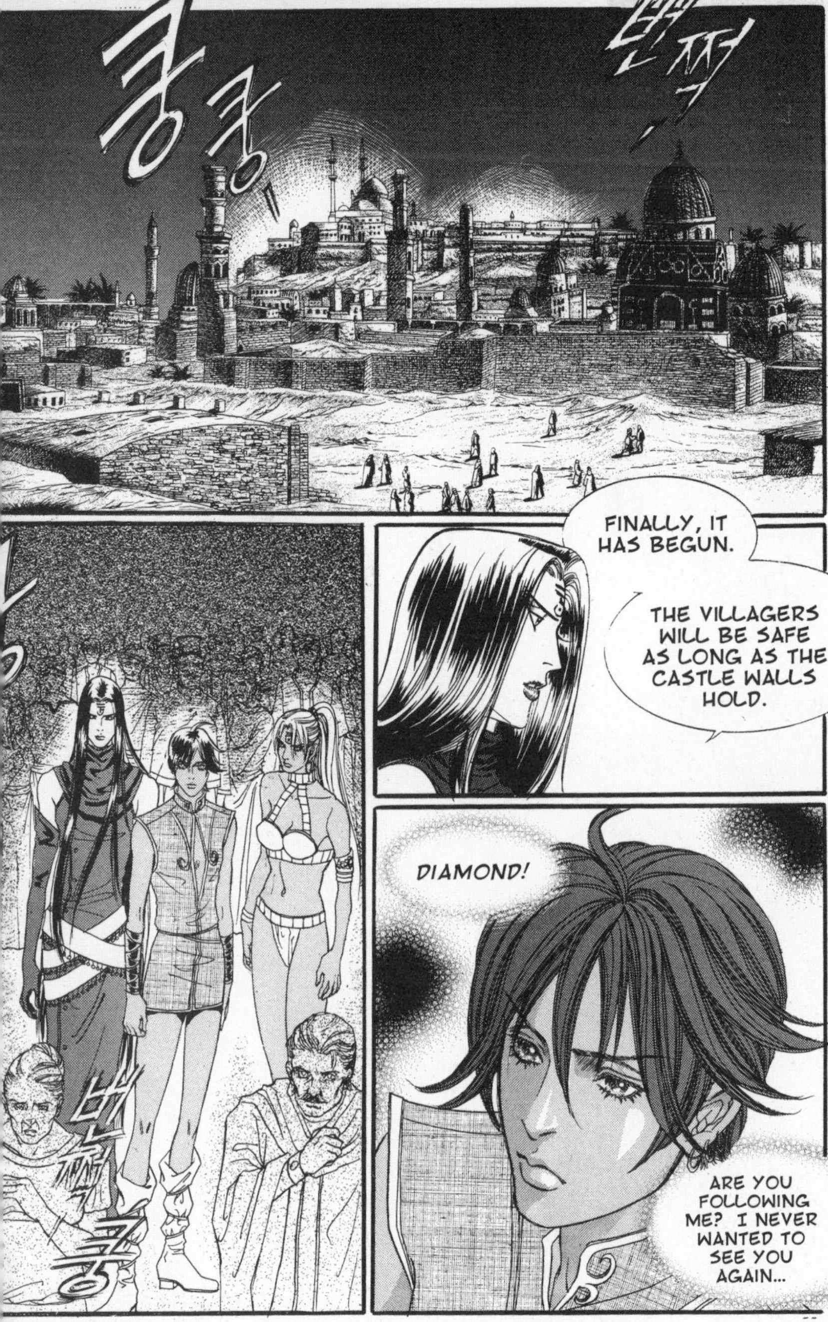
쿵쿵
번쩍
FINALLY, IT HAS BEGUN.
THE VILLAGERS WILL BE SAFE AS LONG AS THE CASTLE WALLS HOLD.
DIAMOND!
ARE YOU FOLLOWING ME? I NEVER WANTED TO SEE YOU AGAIN...

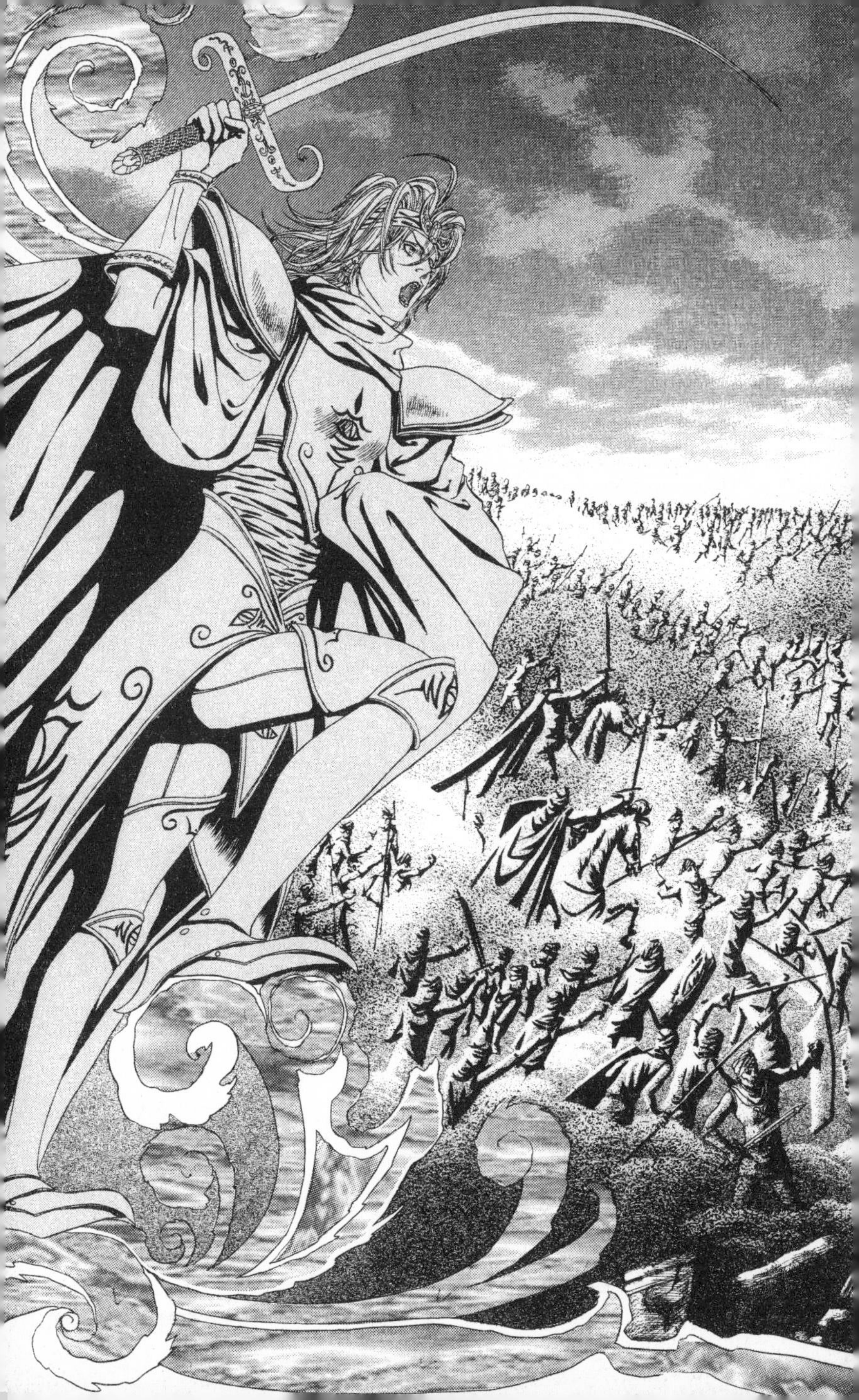

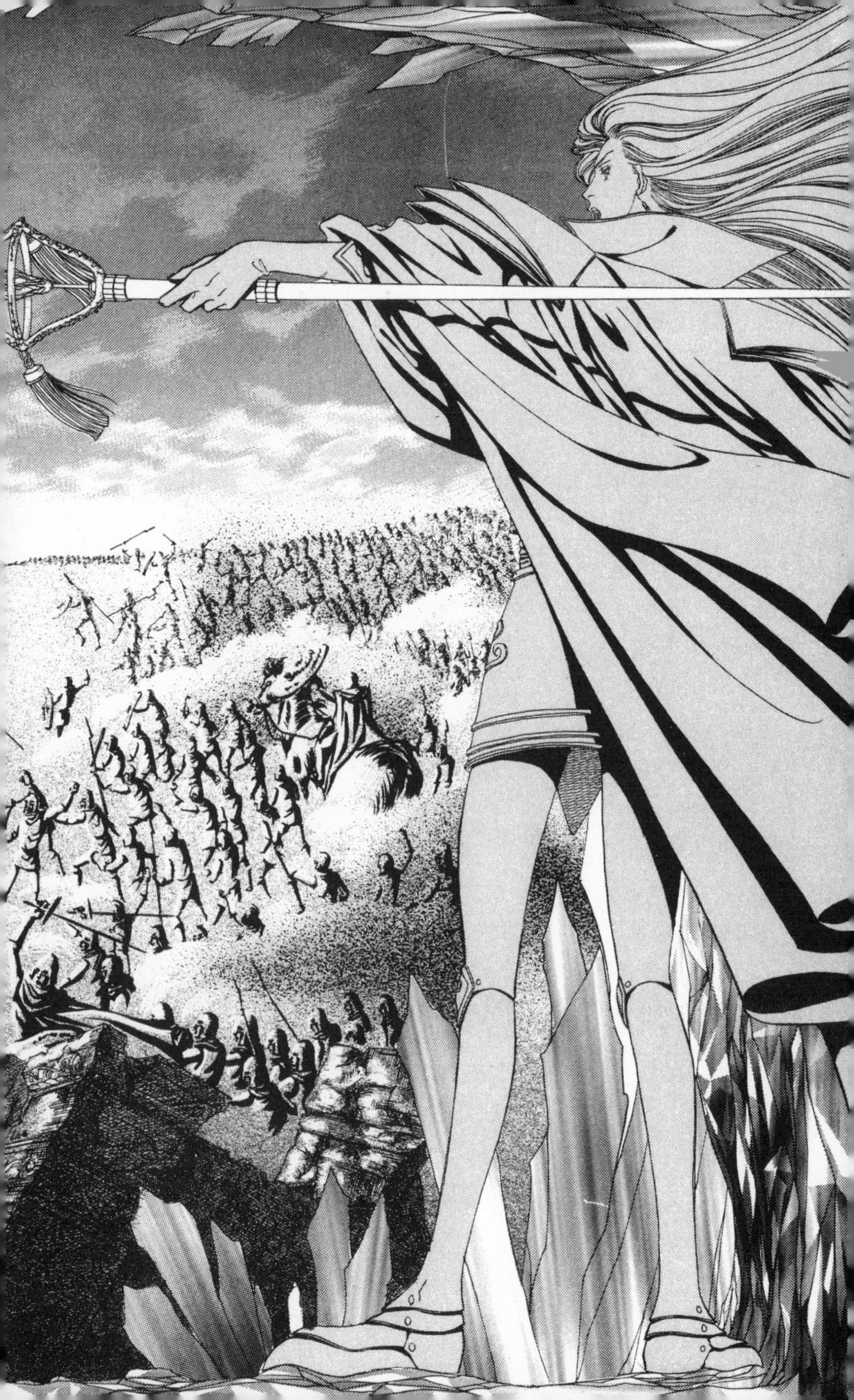

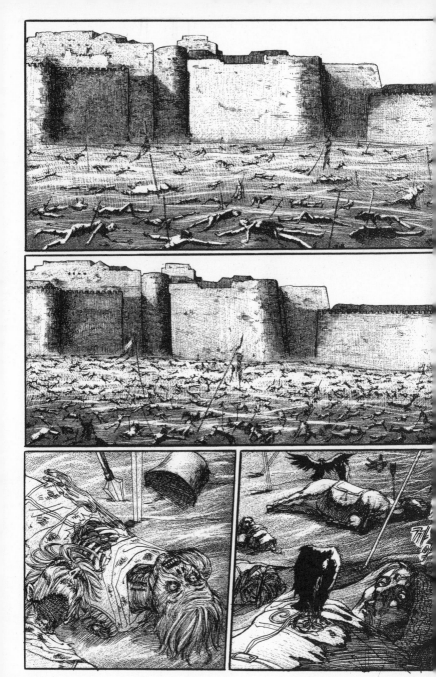

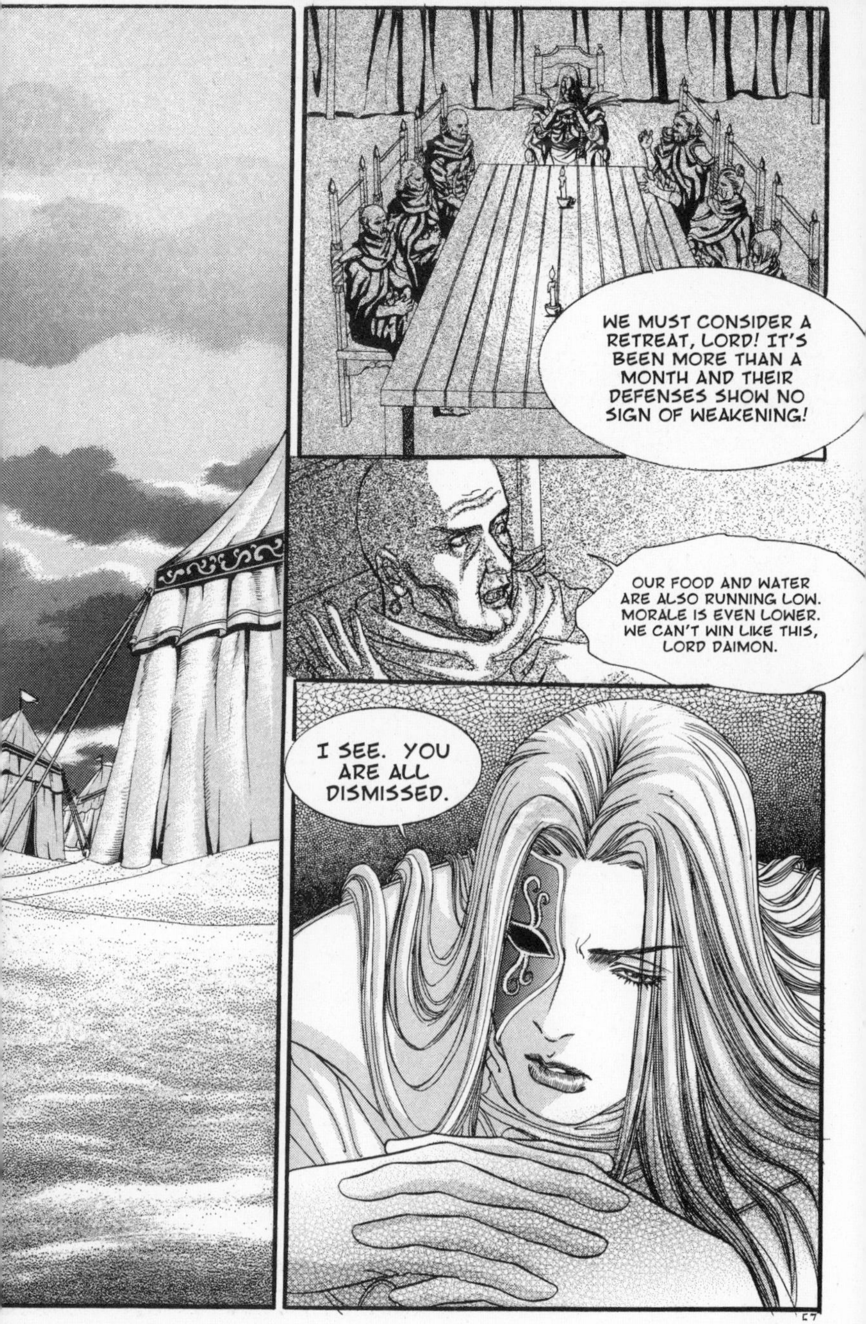
WE MUST CONSIDER A RETREAT, LORD! IT'S BEEN MORE THAN A MONTH AND THEIR DEFENSES SHOW NO SIGN OF WEAKENING!
OUR FOOD AND WATER ARE ALSO RUNNING LOW. MORALE IS EVEN LOWER. WE CAN'T WIN LIKE THIS, LORD DAIMON.
I SEE. YOU ARE ALL DISMISSED.

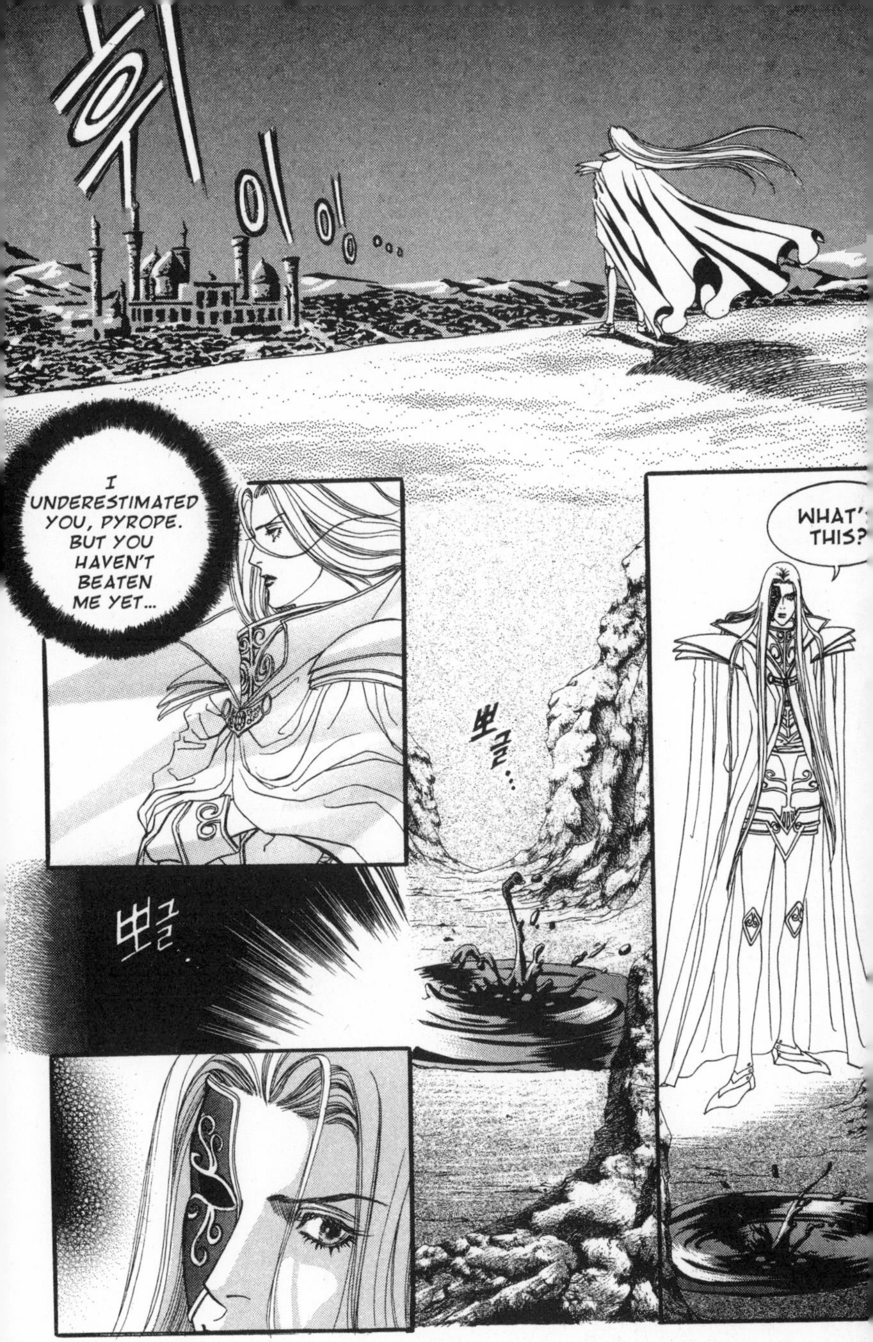
휘이이이...
I UNDERESTIMATED YOU, PYROPE. BUT YOU HAVEN'T BEATEN ME YET...
보글...
WHAT' THIS?
보글.

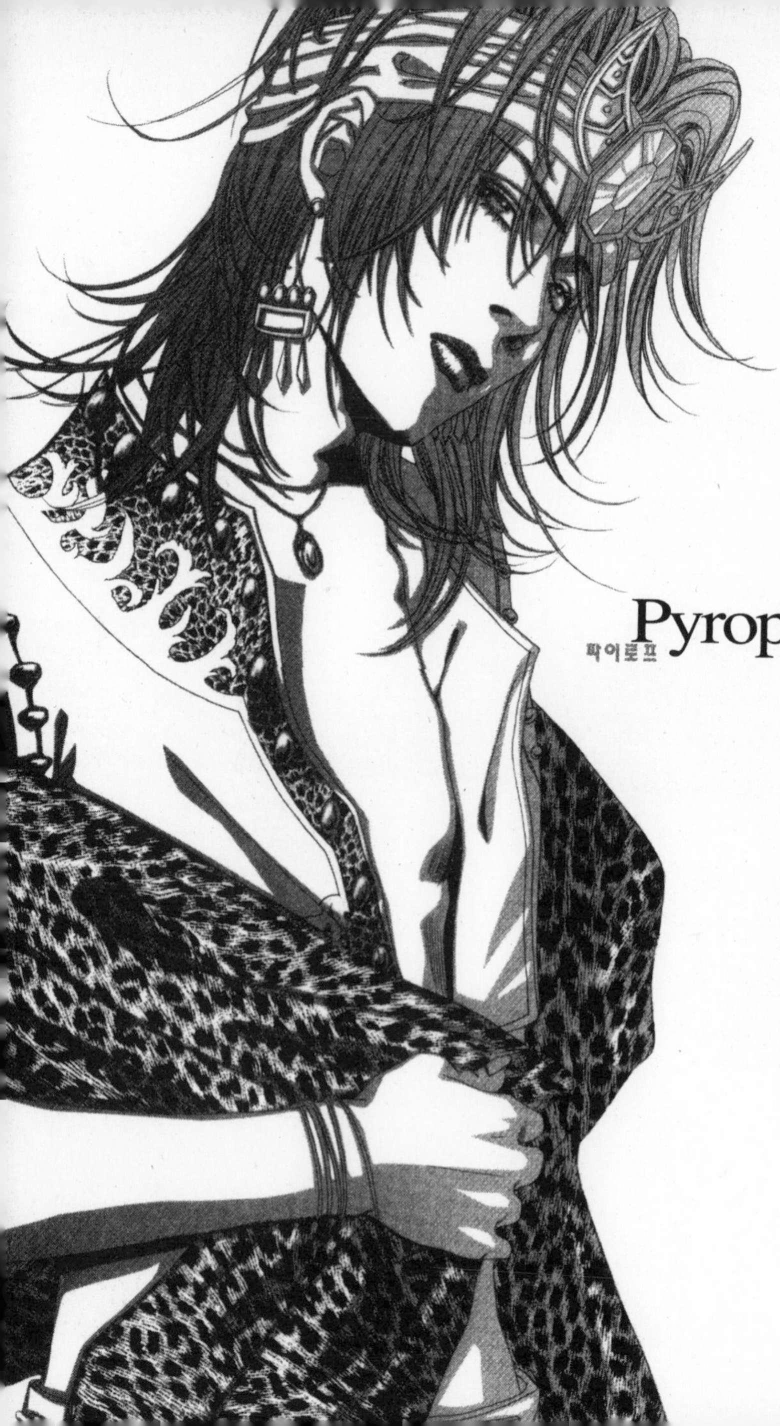

Pyrope

파이로프

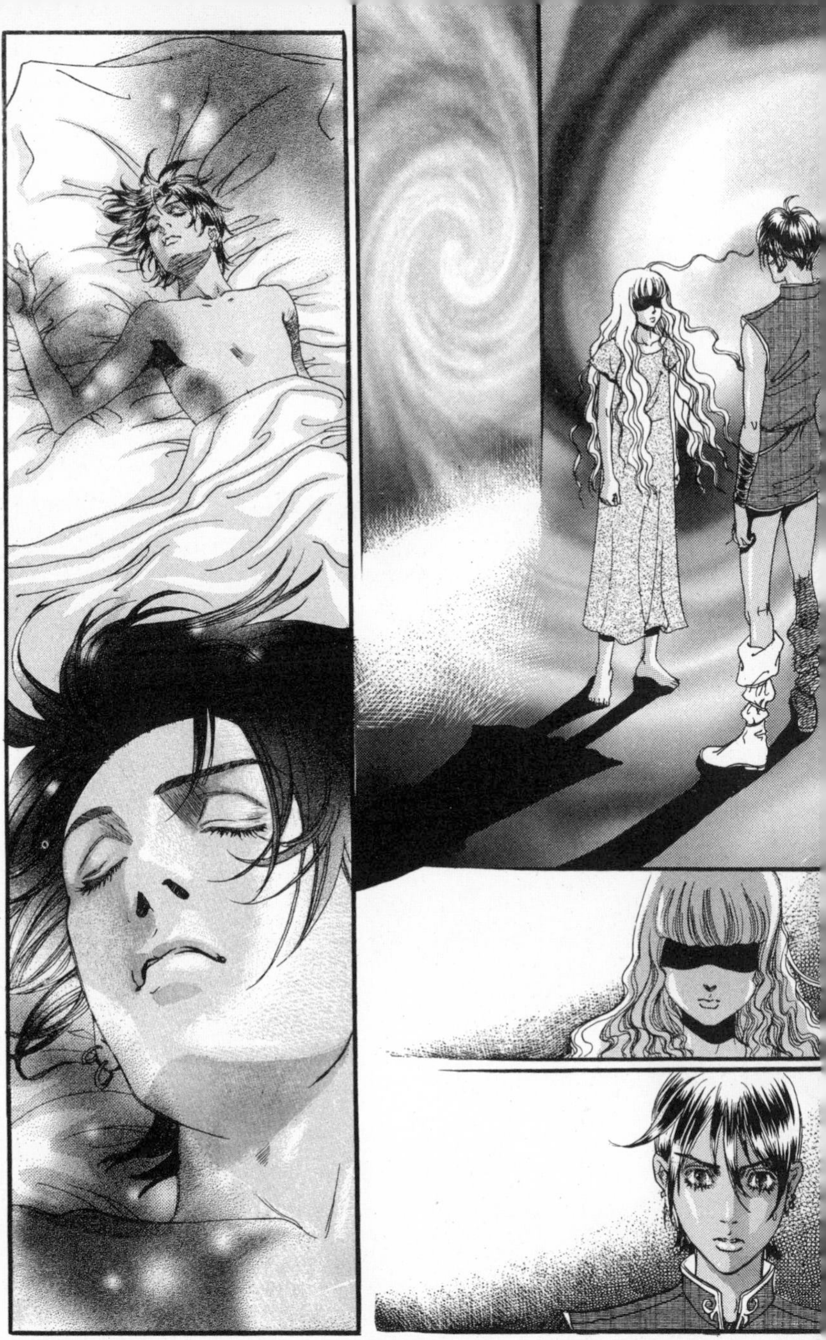

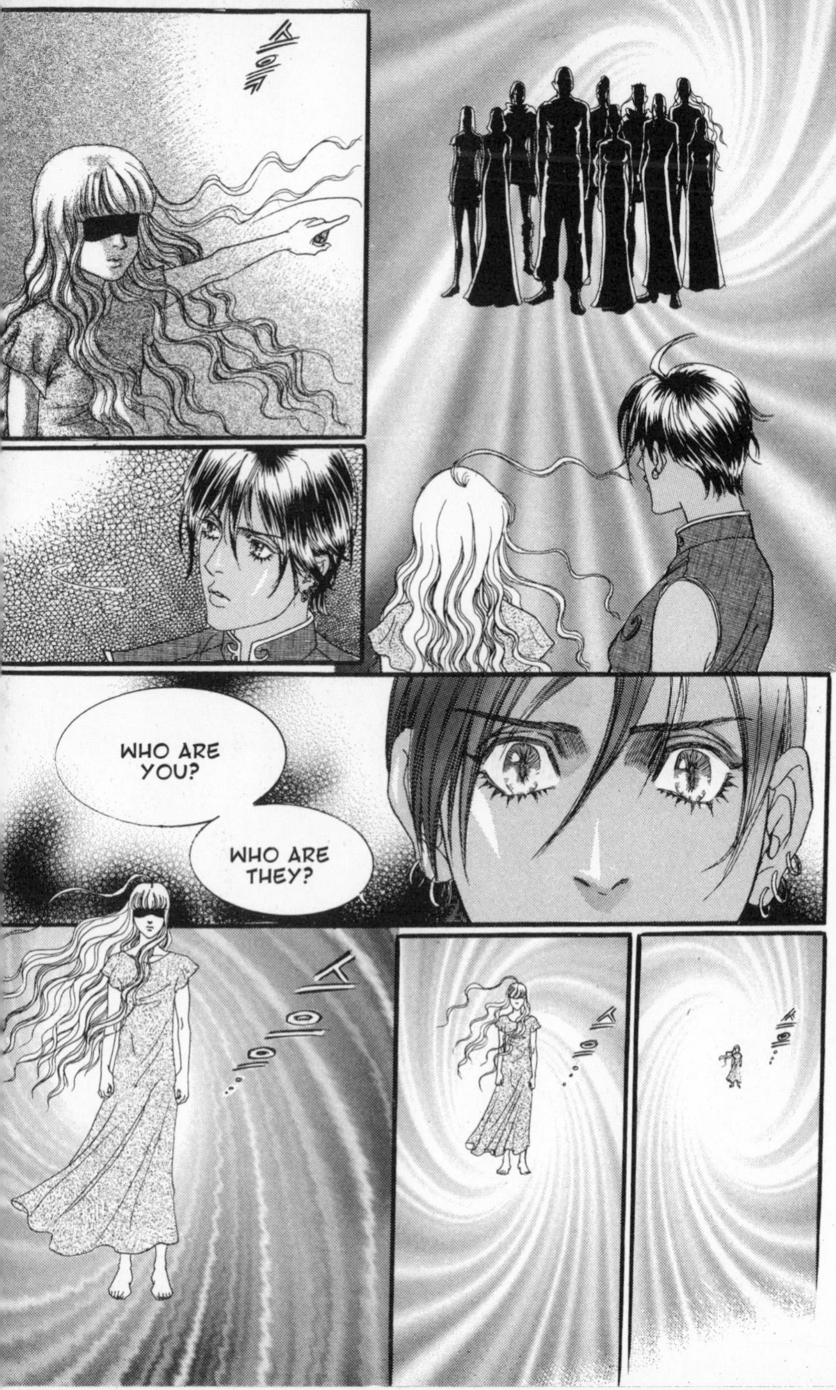
WHO ARE YOU?
WHO ARE THEY?

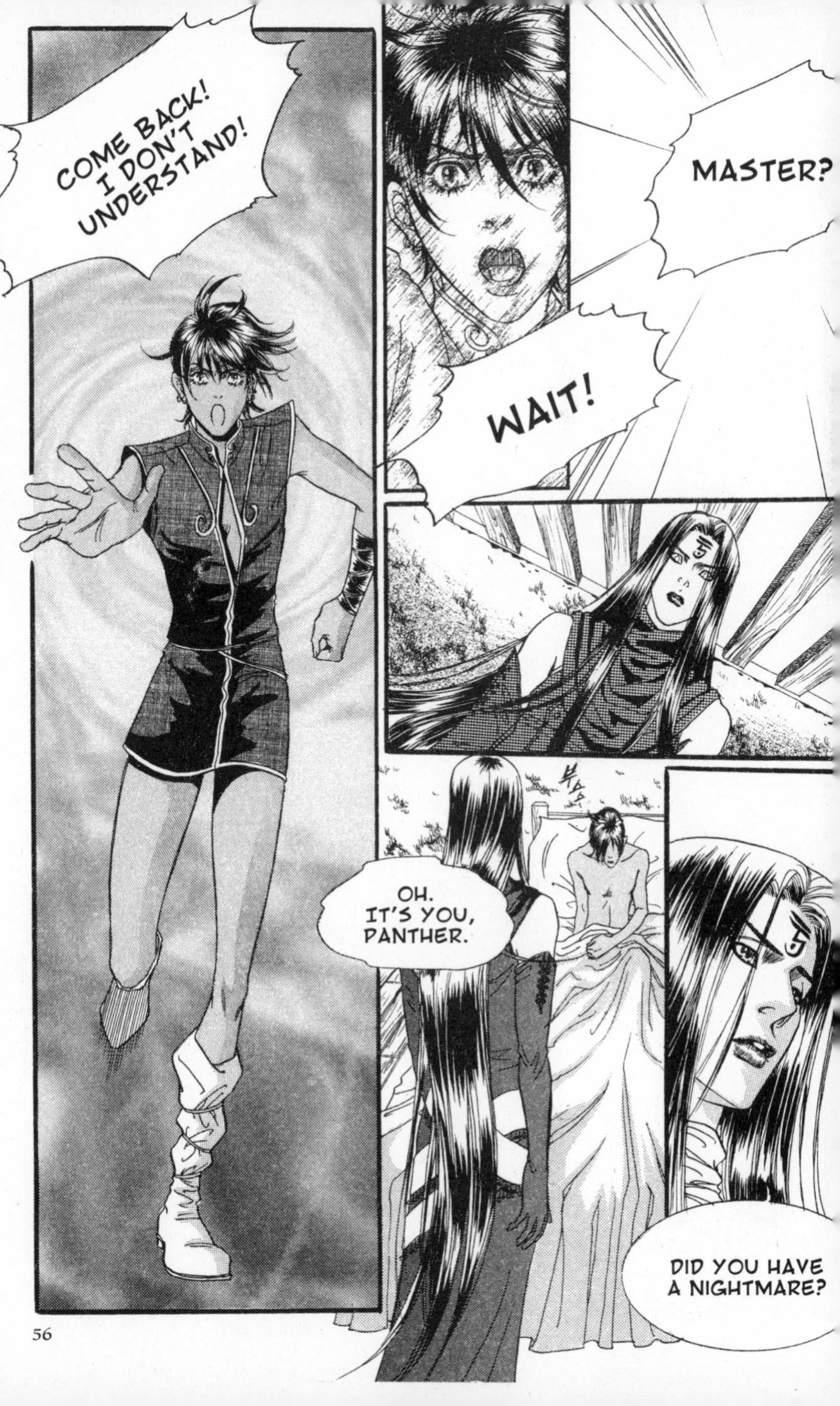
COME BACK! I DON'T UNDERSTAND!
MASTER?
WAIT!
OH. IT'S YOU, PANTHER.
DID YOU HAVE A NIGHTMARE?

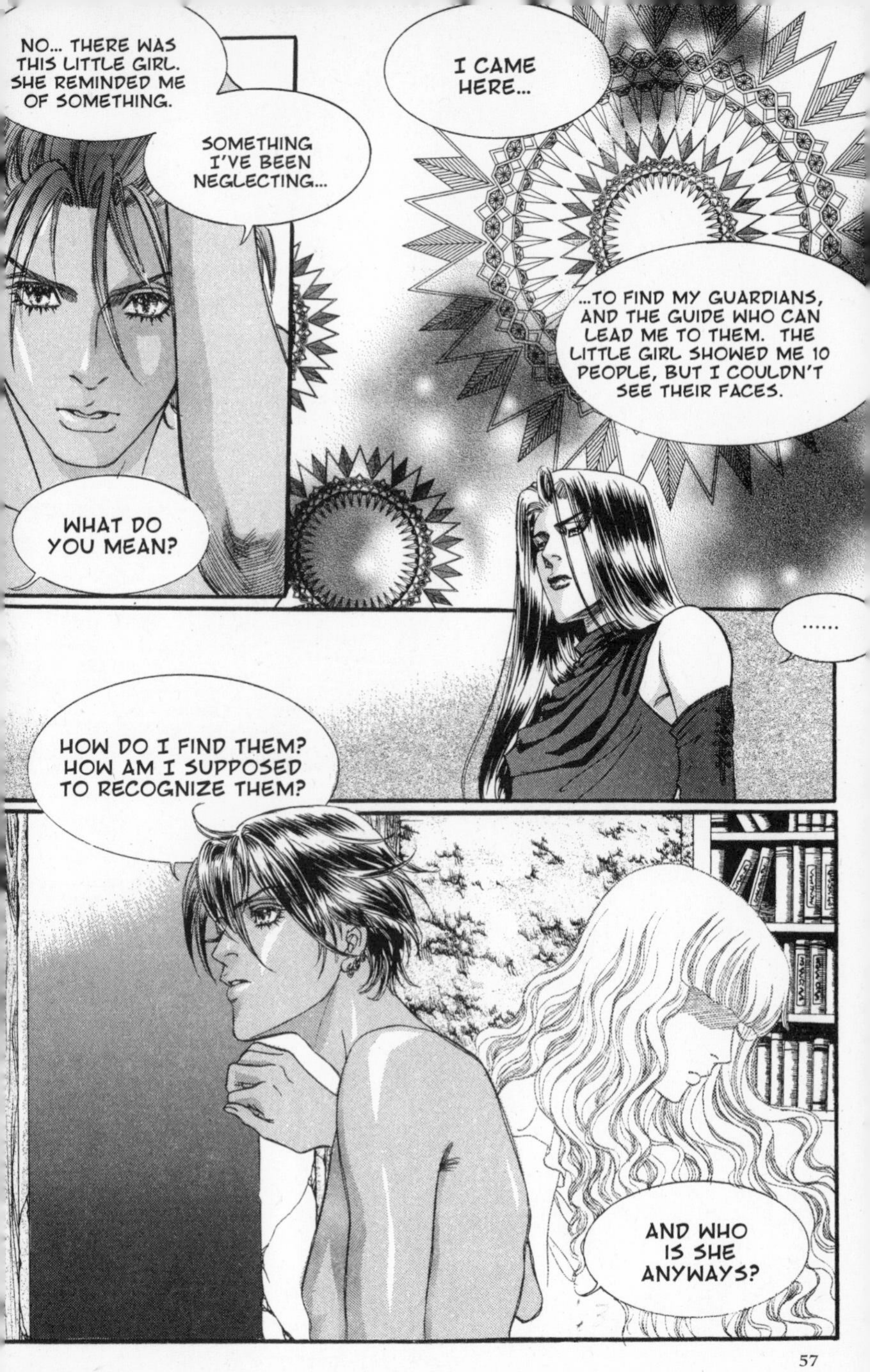
NO... THERE WAS THIS LITTLE GIRL. SHE REMINDED ME OF SOMETHING.
SOMETHING I'VE BEEN NEGLECTING...
WHAT DO YOU MEAN?
I CAME HERE...
...TO FIND MY GUARDIANS, AND THE GUIDE WHO CAN LEAD ME TO THEM. THE LITTLE GIRL SHOWED ME 10 PEOPLE, BUT I COULDN'T SEE THEIR FACES.
......
HOW DO I FIND THEM? HOW AM I SUPPOSED TO RECOGNIZE THEM?
AND WHO IS SHE ANYWAYS?

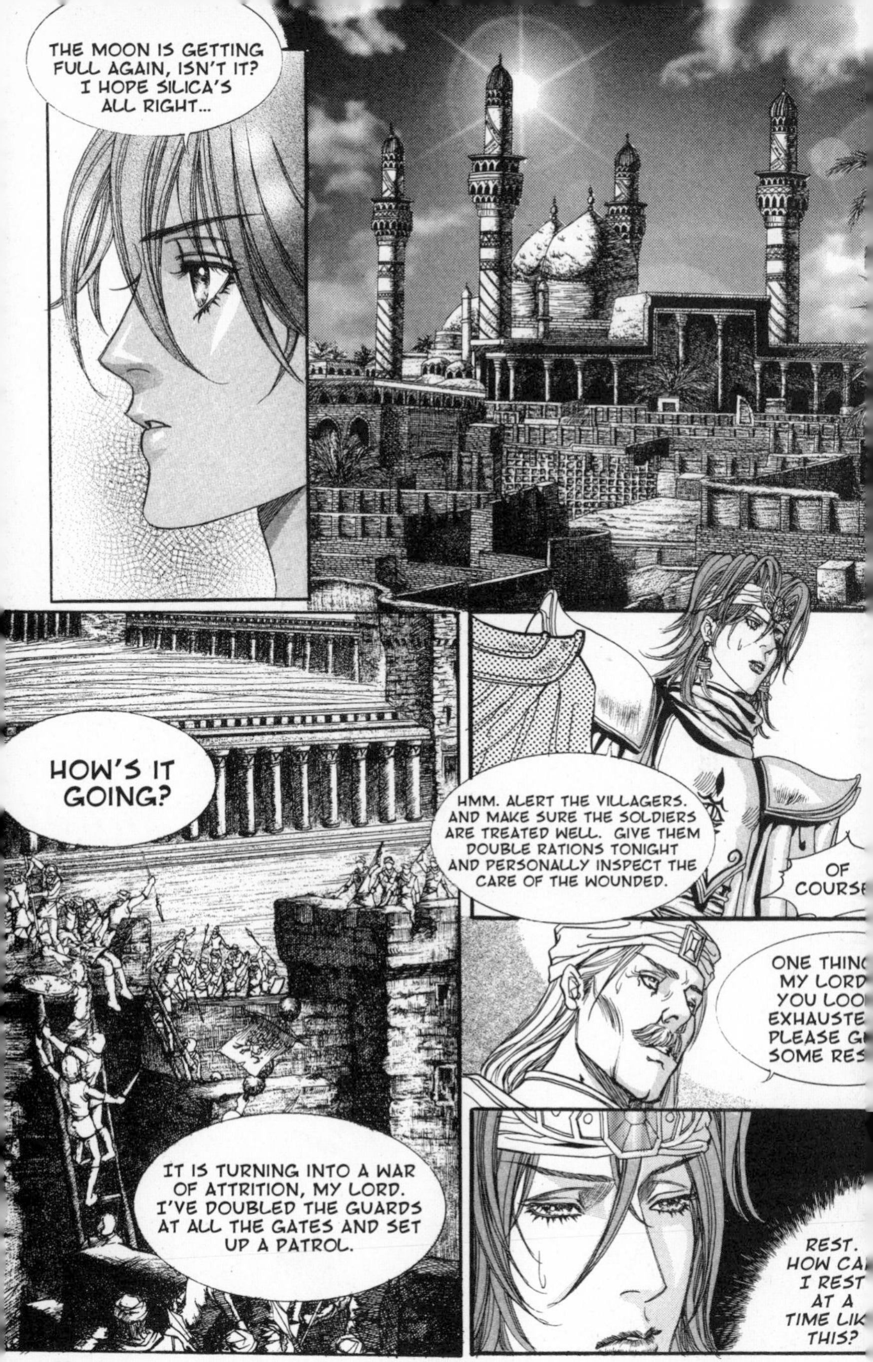
THE MOON IS GETTING FULL AGAIN, ISN'T IT? I HOPE SILICA'S ALL RIGHT...
HOW'S IT GOING?
IT IS TURNING INTO A WAR OF ATTRITION, MY LORD. I'VE DOUBLED THE GUARDS AT ALL THE GATES AND SET UP A PATROL.
HMM. ALERT THE VILLAGERS. AND MAKE SURE THE SOLDIERS ARE TREATED WELL. GIVE THEM DOUBLE RATIONS TONIGHT AND PERSONALLY INSPECT THE CARE OF THE WOUNDED.
OF COURS
ONE THIN MY LORD YOU LOO EXHAUSTE PLEASE G SOME RES
REST. HOW CA I REST AT A TIME LIK THIS?

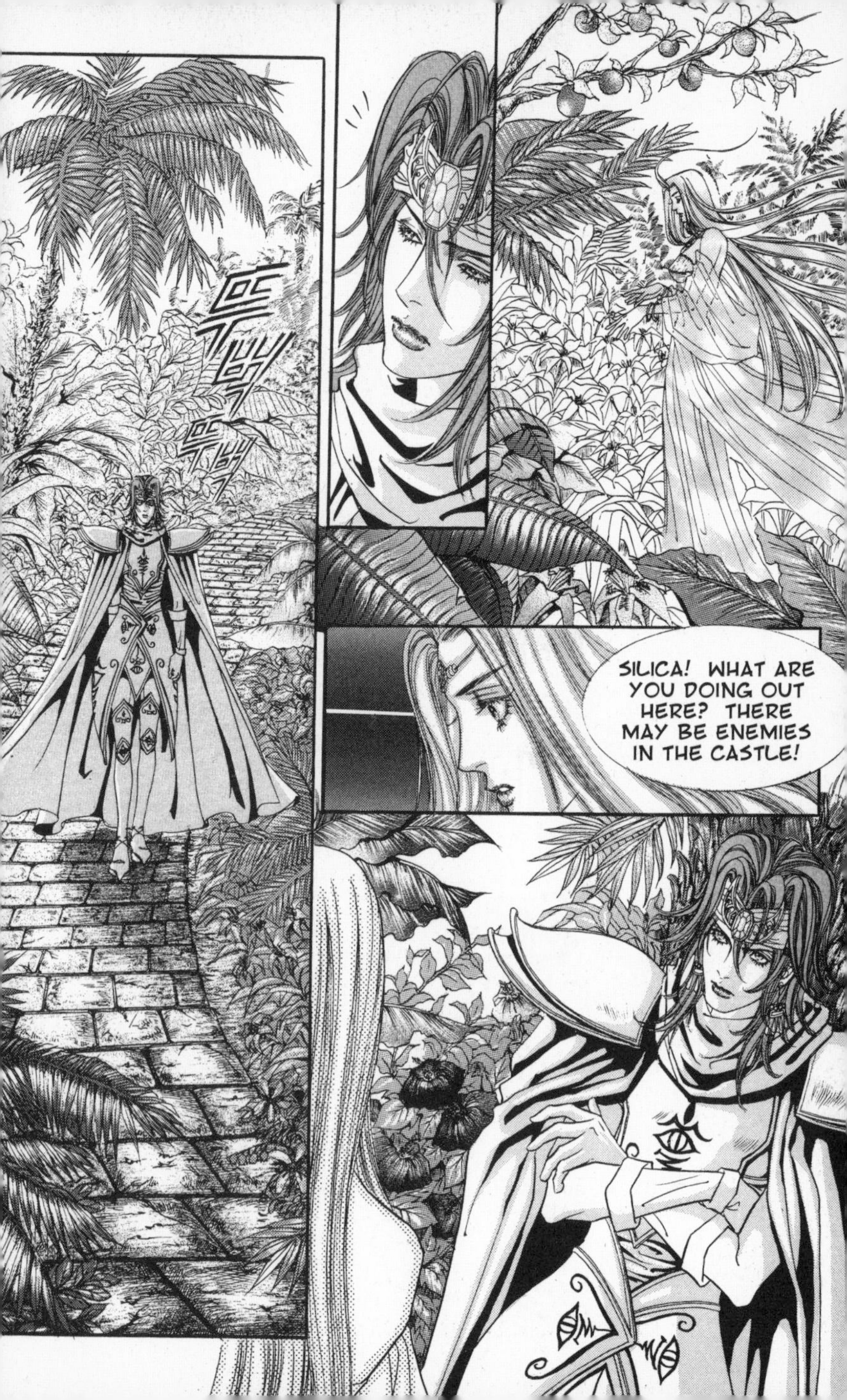
뚜벅 뚜벅
SILICA! WHAT ARE YOU DOING OUT HERE? THERE MAY BE ENEMIES IN THE CASTLE!

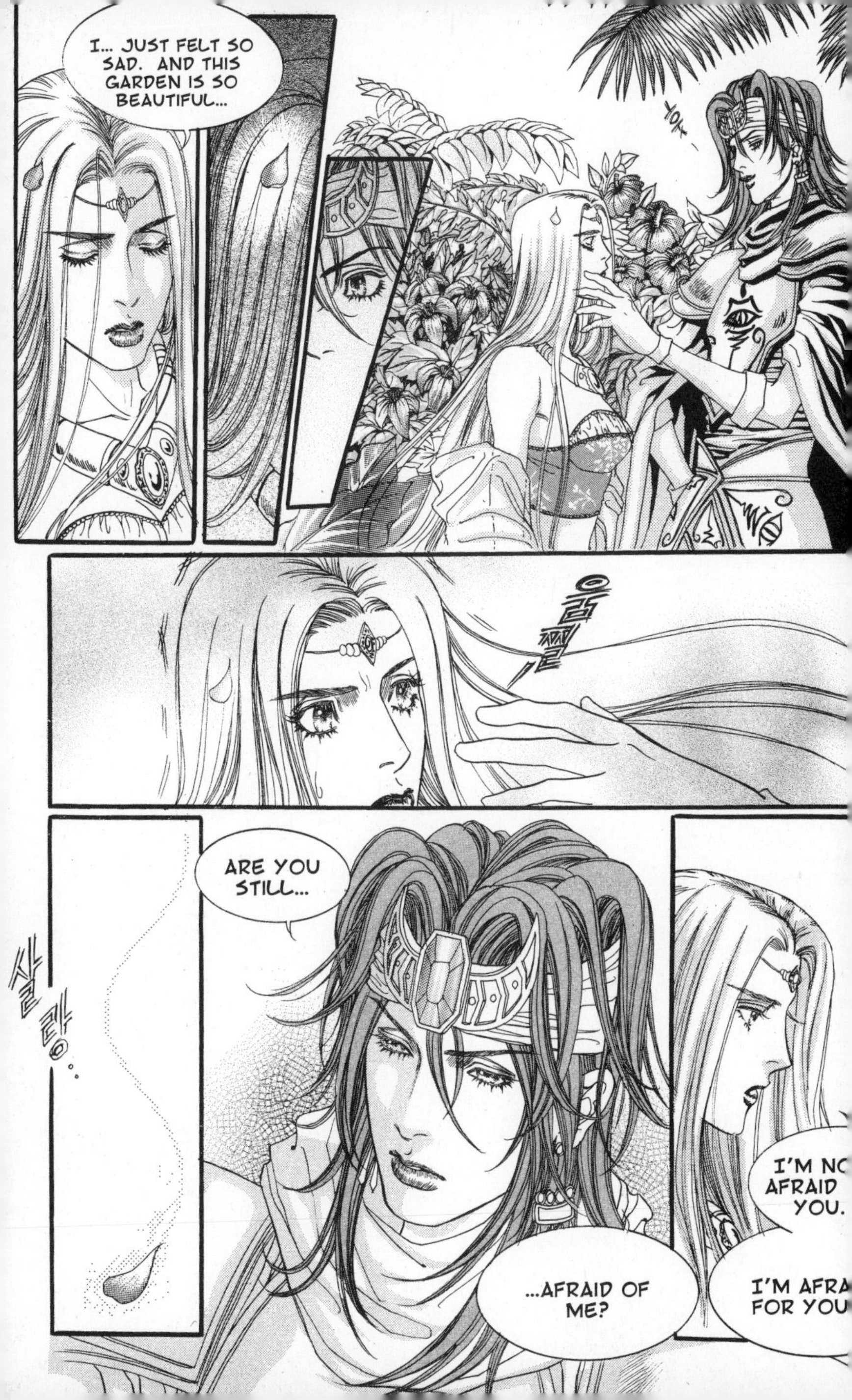

I... JUST FELT SO SAD. AND THIS GARDEN IS SO BEAUTIFUL...
ARE YOU STILL...
살랑..
...AFRAID OF ME?
I'M NO
AFRAID
YOU.
I'M AFRA
FOR YOU

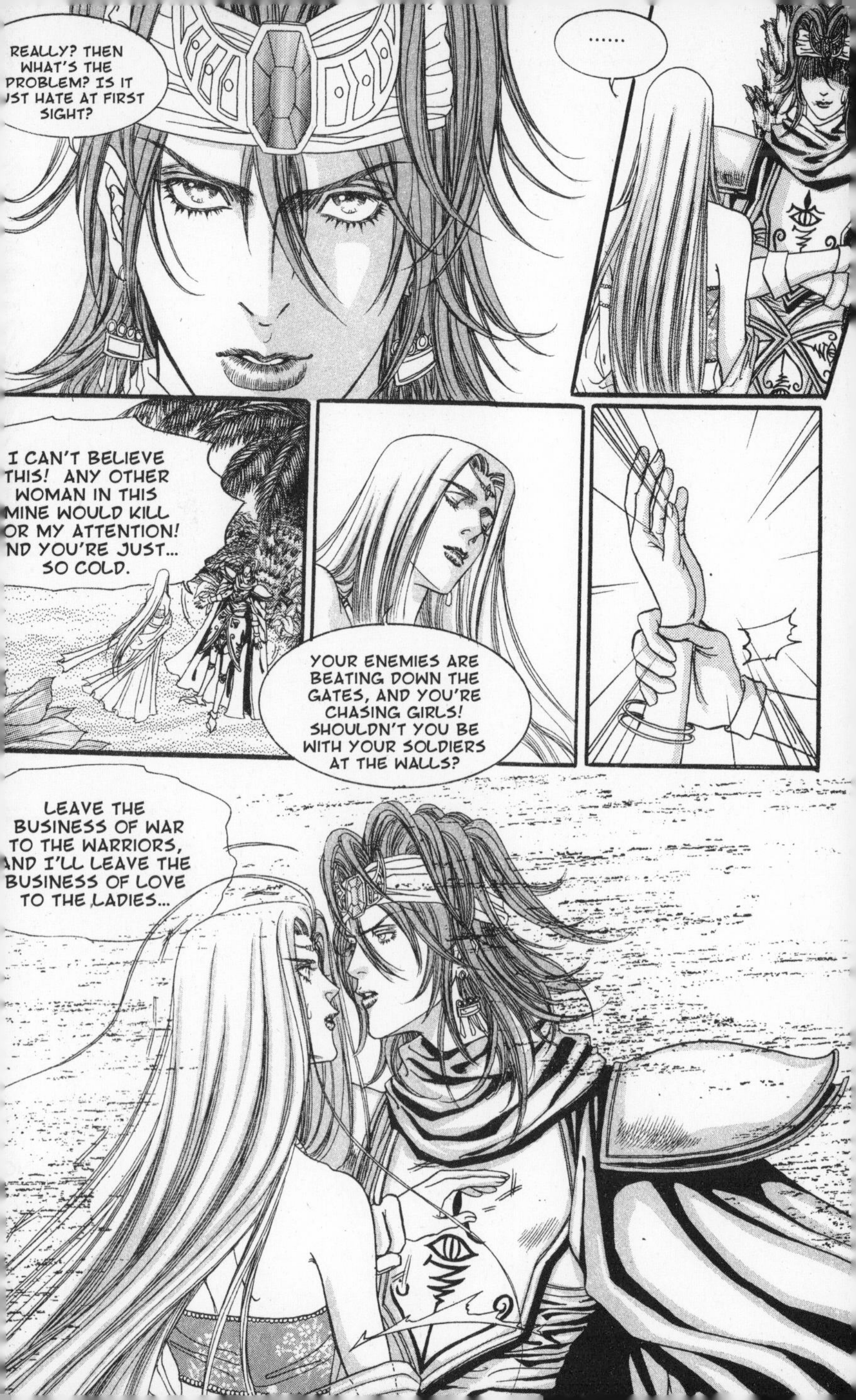
REALLY? THEN WHAT'S THE PROBLEM? IS IT UST HATE AT FIRST SIGHT?
......
I CAN'T BELIEVE THIS! ANY OTHER WOMAN IN THIS MINE WOULD KILL OR MY ATTENTION! ND YOU'RE JUST... SO COLD.
YOUR ENEMIES ARE BEATING DOWN THE GATES, AND YOU'RE CHASING GIRLS! SHOULDN'T YOU BE WITH YOUR SOLDIERS AT THE WALLS?
LEAVE THE BUSINESS OF WAR TO THE WARRIORS, AND I'LL LEAVE THE BUSINESS OF LOVE TO THE LADIES...

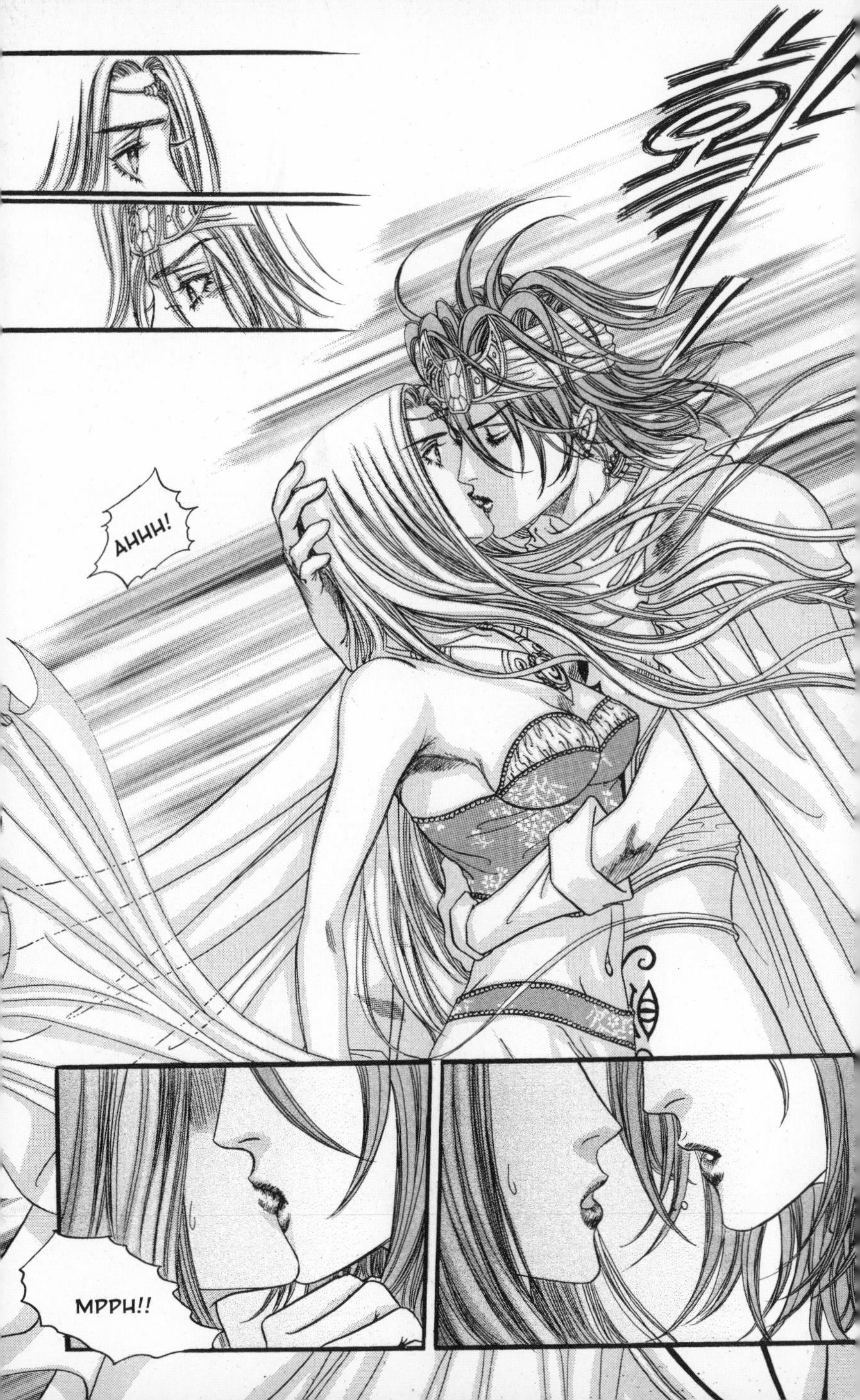
AHHH!
MPPH!!

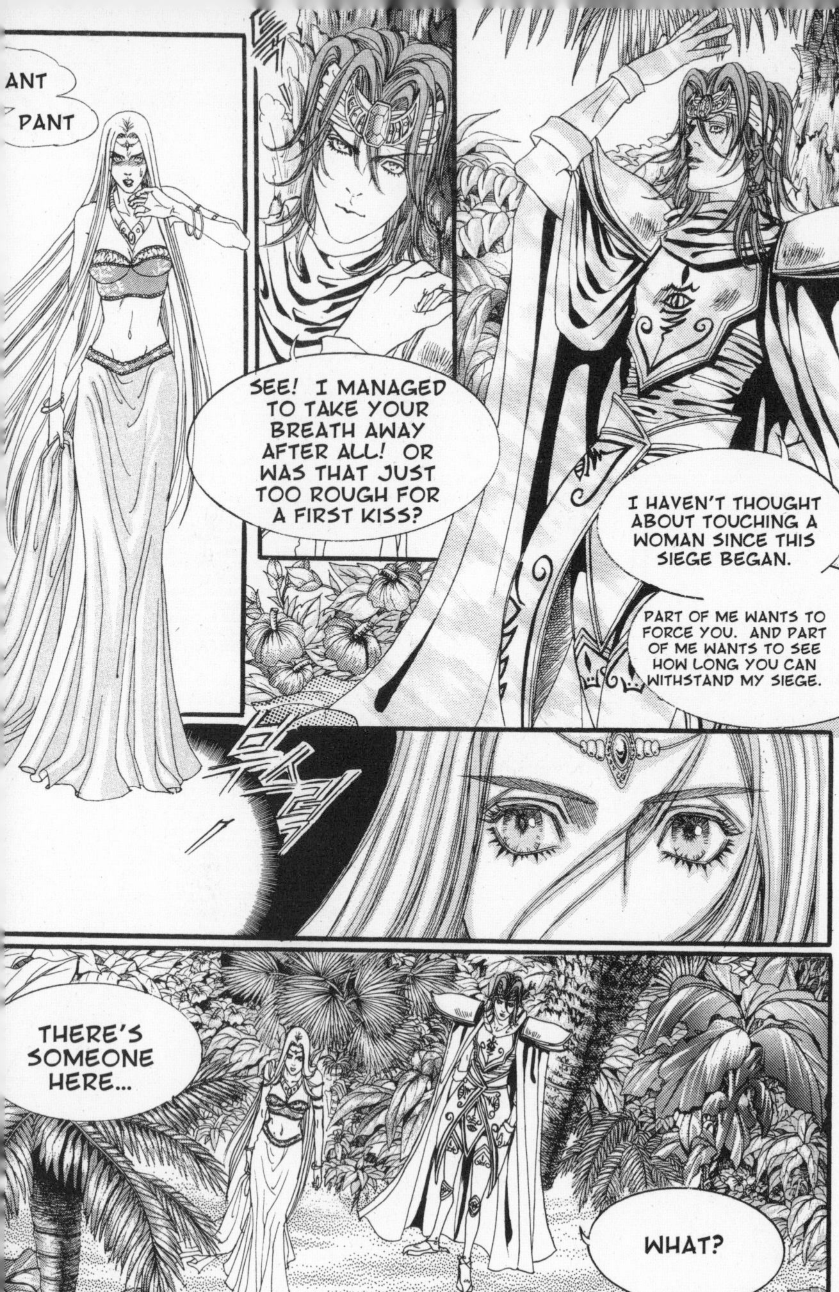
ANT
PANT
SEE! I MANAGED TO TAKE YOUR BREATH AWAY AFTER ALL! OR WAS THAT JUST TOO ROUGH FOR A FIRST KISS?
I HAVEN'T THOUGHT ABOUT TOUCHING A WOMAN SINCE THIS SIEGE BEGAN.
PART OF ME WANTS TO FORCE YOU. AND PART OF ME WANTS TO SEE HOW LONG YOU CAN WITHSTAND MY SIEGE.
THERE'S SOMEONE HERE...
WHAT?

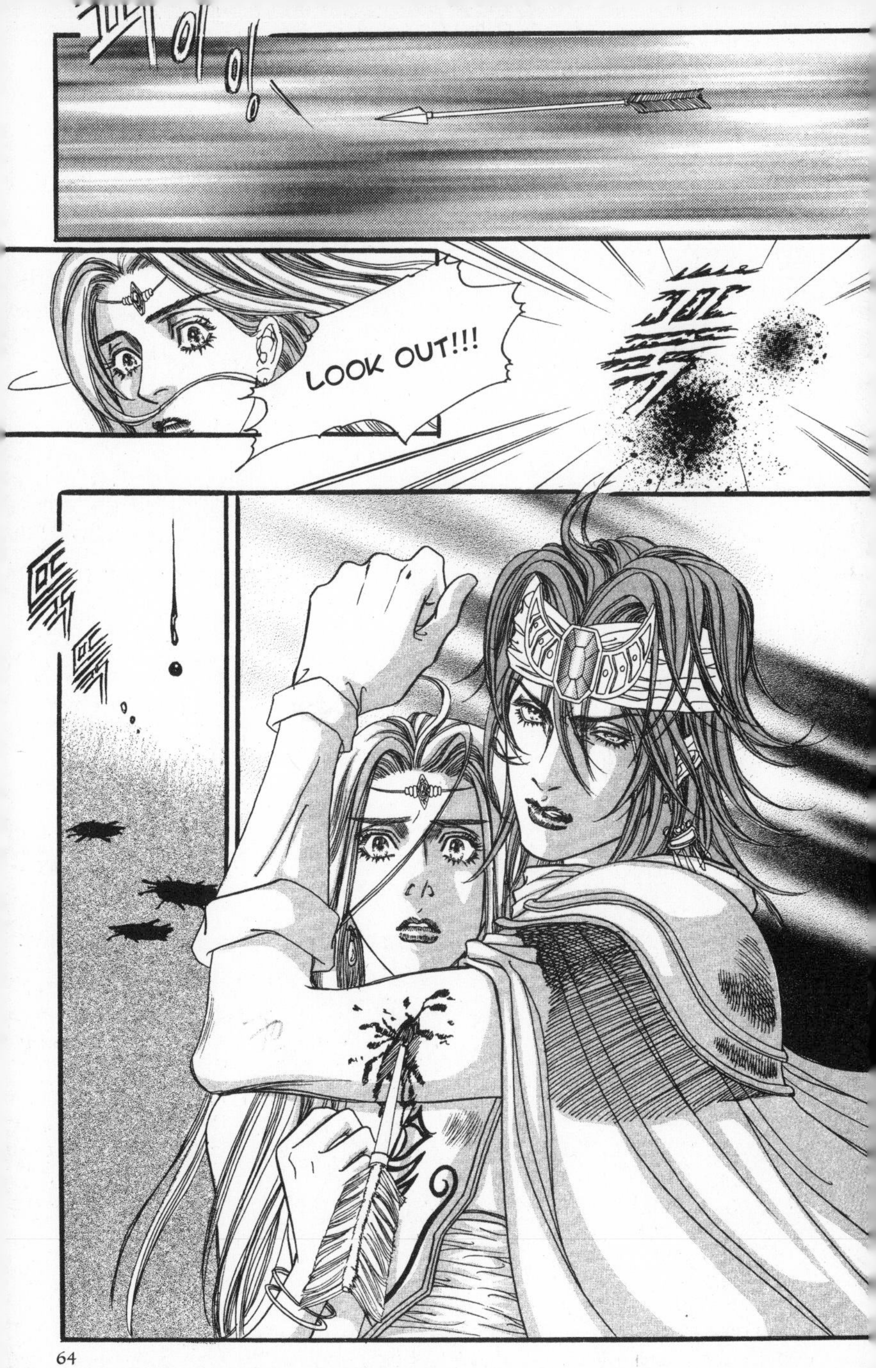
LOOK OUT!!!

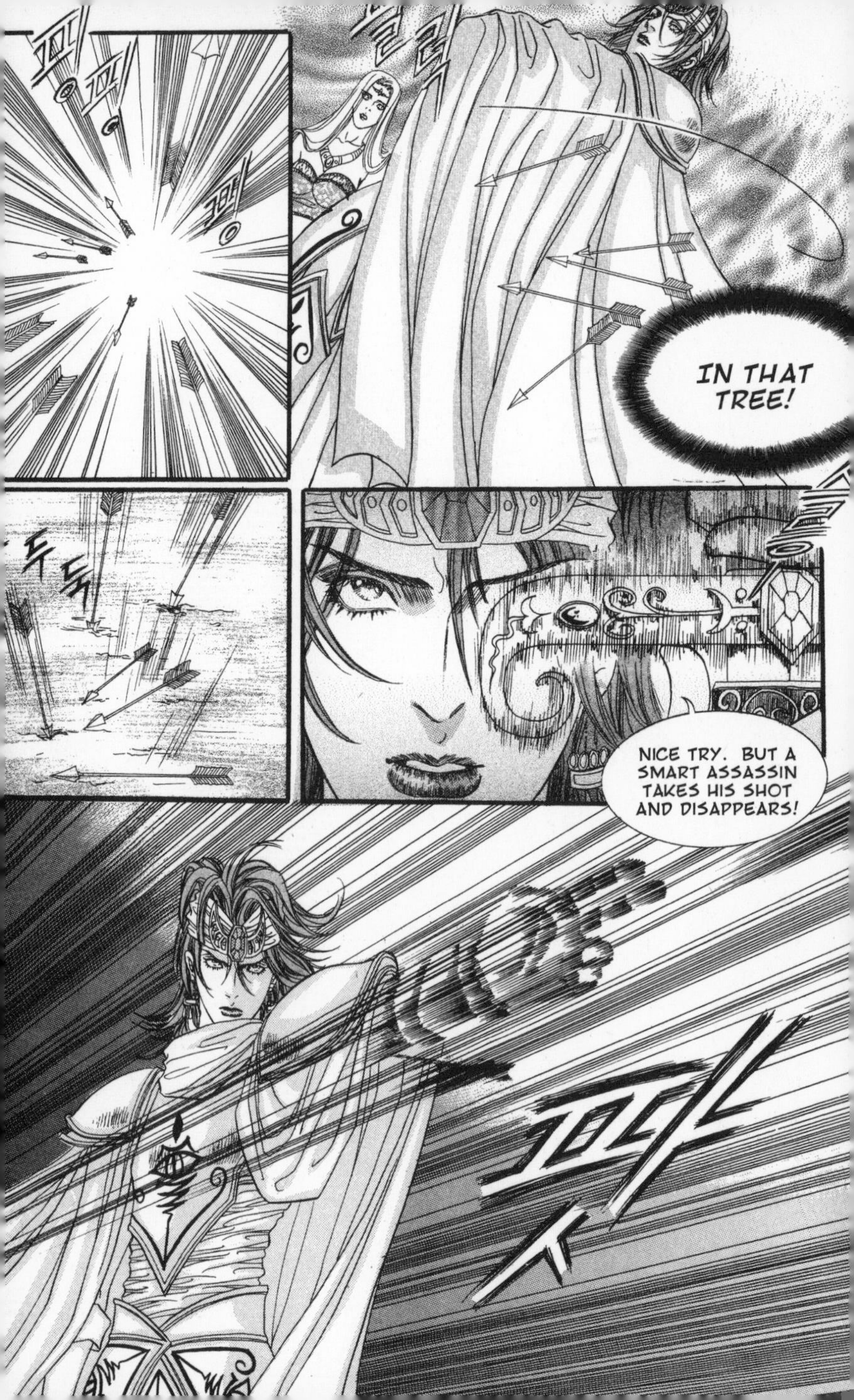
IN THAT TREE!
NICE TRY. BUT A SMART ASSASSIN TAKES HIS SHOT AND DISAPPEARS!

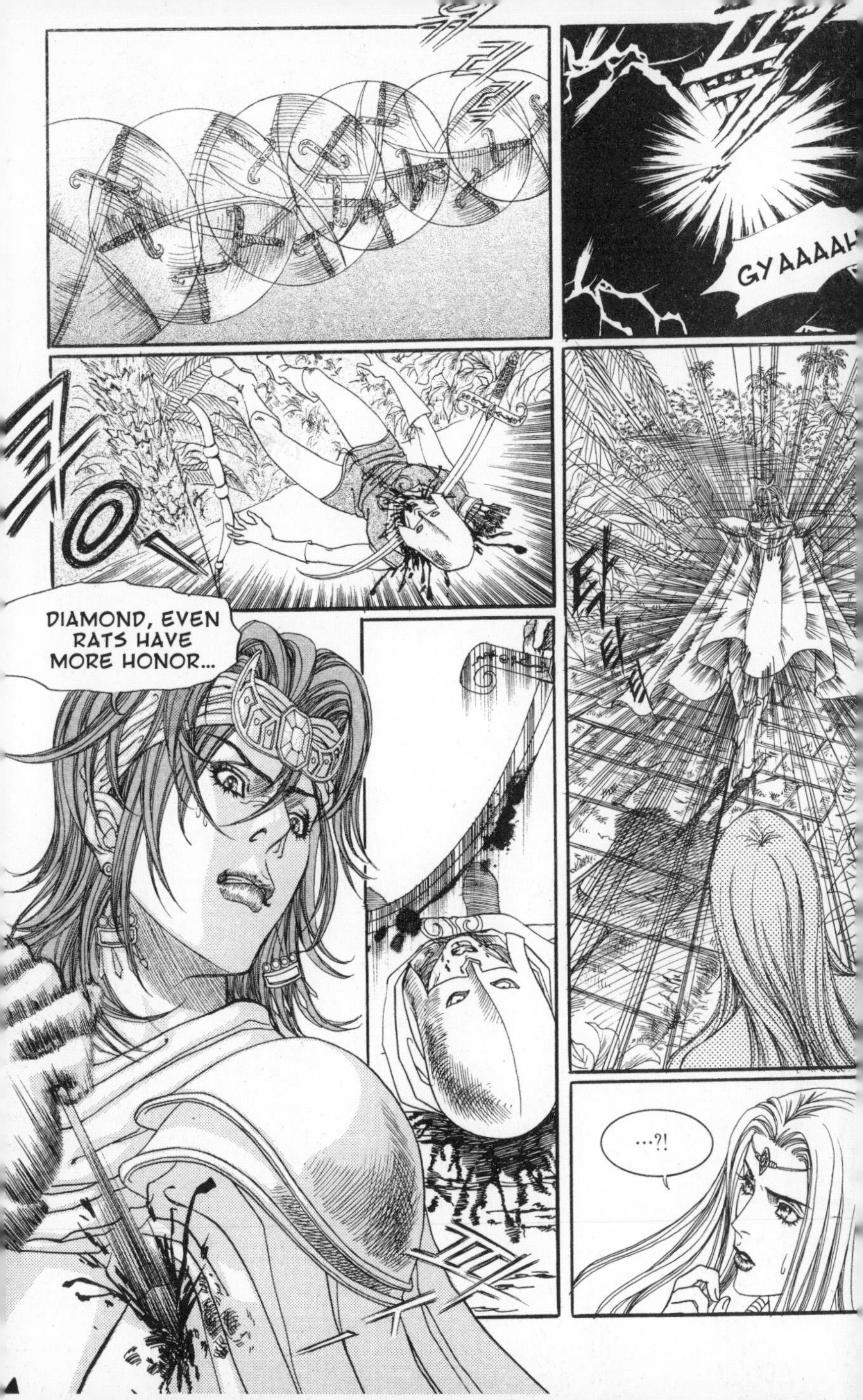
GYAAAAH
DIAMOND, EVEN RATS HAVE MORE HONOR...
...?!

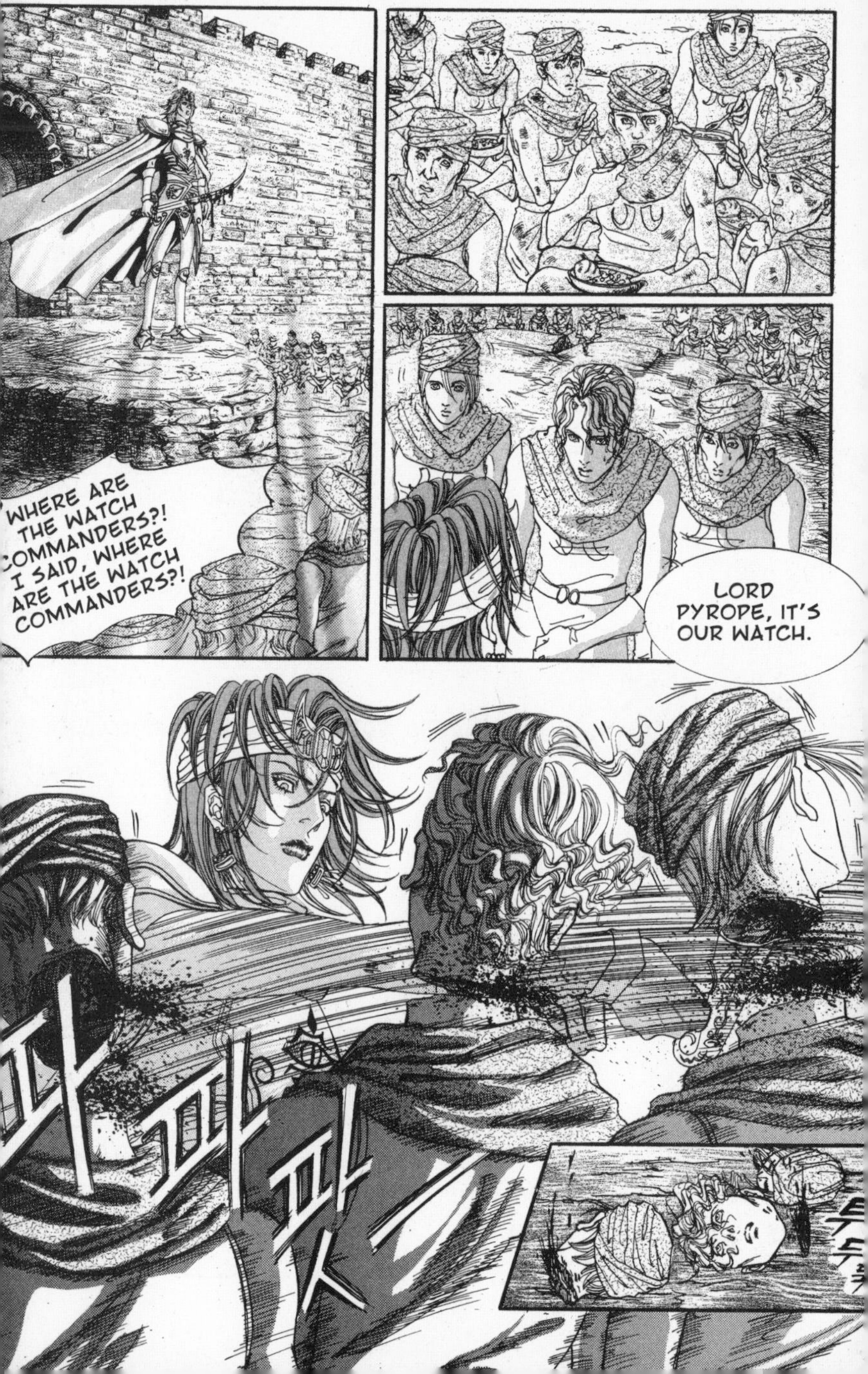
WHERE ARE THE WATCH COMMANDERS?! I SAID, WHERE ARE THE WATCH COMMANDERS?!
LORD PYROPE, IT'S OUR WATCH.

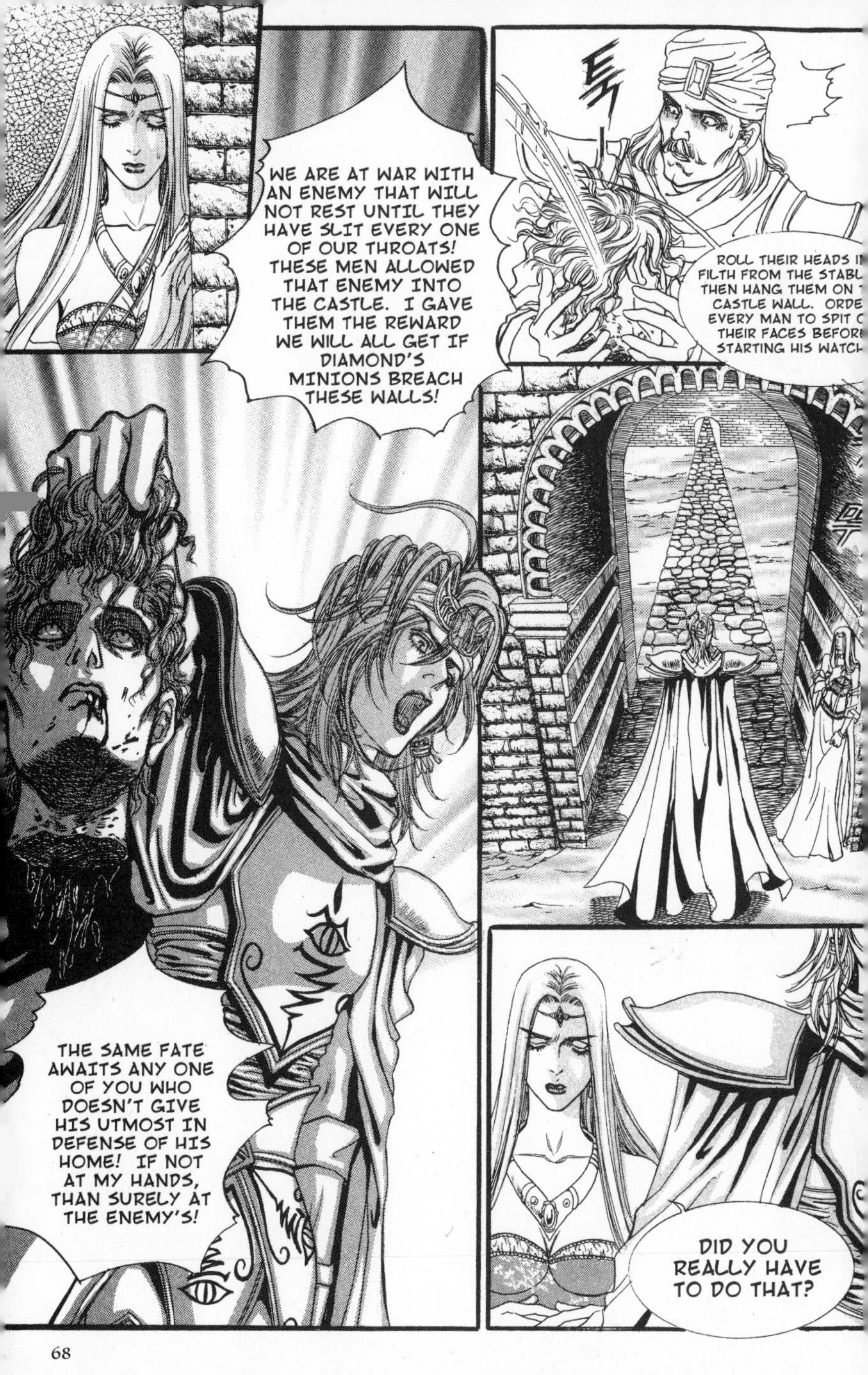
WE ARE AT WAR WITH AN ENEMY THAT WILL NOT REST UNTIL THEY HAVE SLIT EVERY ONE OF OUR THROATS! THESE MEN ALLOWED THAT ENEMY INTO THE CASTLE. I GAVE THEM THE REWARD WE WILL ALL GET IF DIAMOND'S MINIONS BREACH THESE WALLS!
툭
ROLL THEIR HEADS I FILTH FROM THE STABL THEN HANG THEM ON T CASTLE WALL. ORDE EVERY MAN TO SPIT C THEIR FACES BEFOR STARTING HIS WATCH
THE SAME FATE AWAITS ANY ONE OF YOU WHO DOESN'T GIVE HIS UTMOST IN DEFENSE OF HIS HOME! IF NOT AT MY HANDS, THAN SURELY AT THE ENEMY'S!
DID YOU REALLY HAVE TO DO THAT?

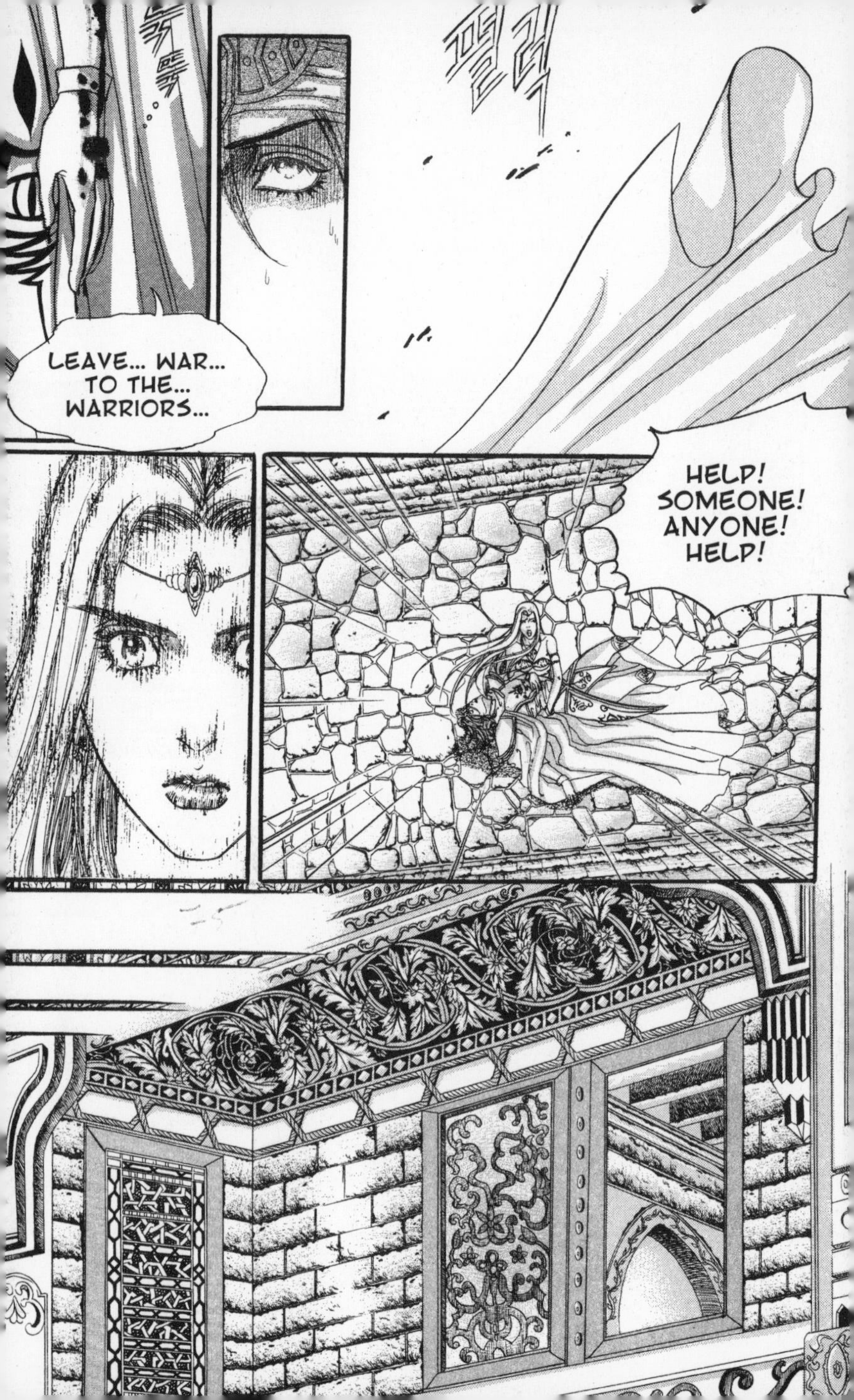
LEAVE... WAR... TO THE... WARRIORS...
펄럭
HELP! SOMEONE! ANYONE! HELP!

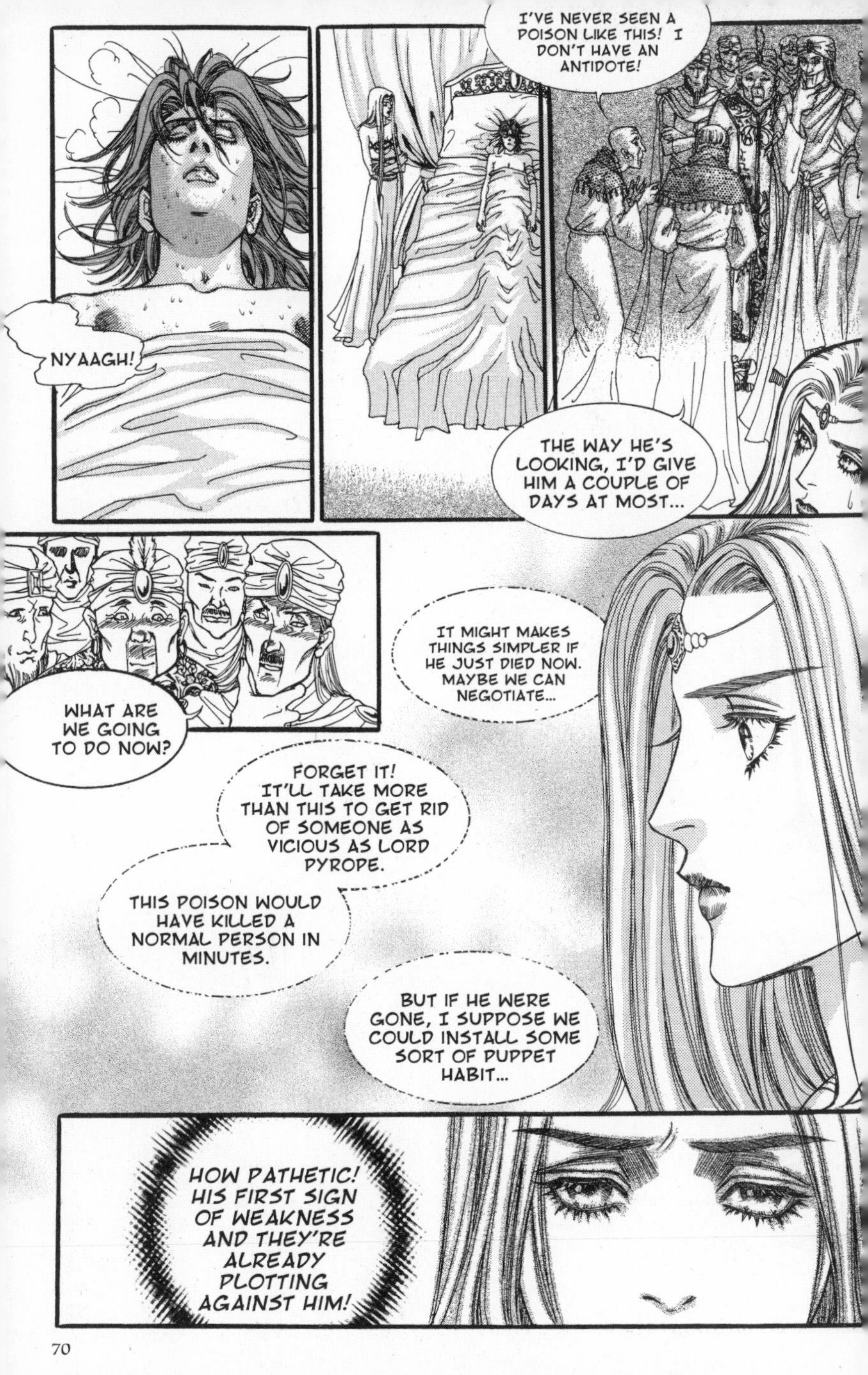
NYAAGH!
I'VE NEVER SEEN A POISON LIKE THIS! I DON'T HAVE AN ANTIDOTE!
THE WAY HE'S LOOKING, I'D GIVE HIM A COUPLE OF DAYS AT MOST...
WHAT ARE WE GOING TO DO NOW?
IT MIGHT MAKES THINGS SIMPLER IF HE JUST DIED NOW. MAYBE WE CAN NEGOTIATE...
FORGET IT! IT'LL TAKE MORE THAN THIS TO GET RID OF SOMEONE AS VICIOUS AS LORD PYROPE.
THIS POISON WOULD HAVE KILLED A NORMAL PERSON IN MINUTES.
BUT IF HE WERE GONE, I SUPPOSE WE COULD INSTALL SOME SORT OF PUPPET HABIT...
HOW PATHETIC! HIS FIRST SIGN OF WEAKNESS AND THEY'RE ALREADY PLOTTING AGAINST HIM!

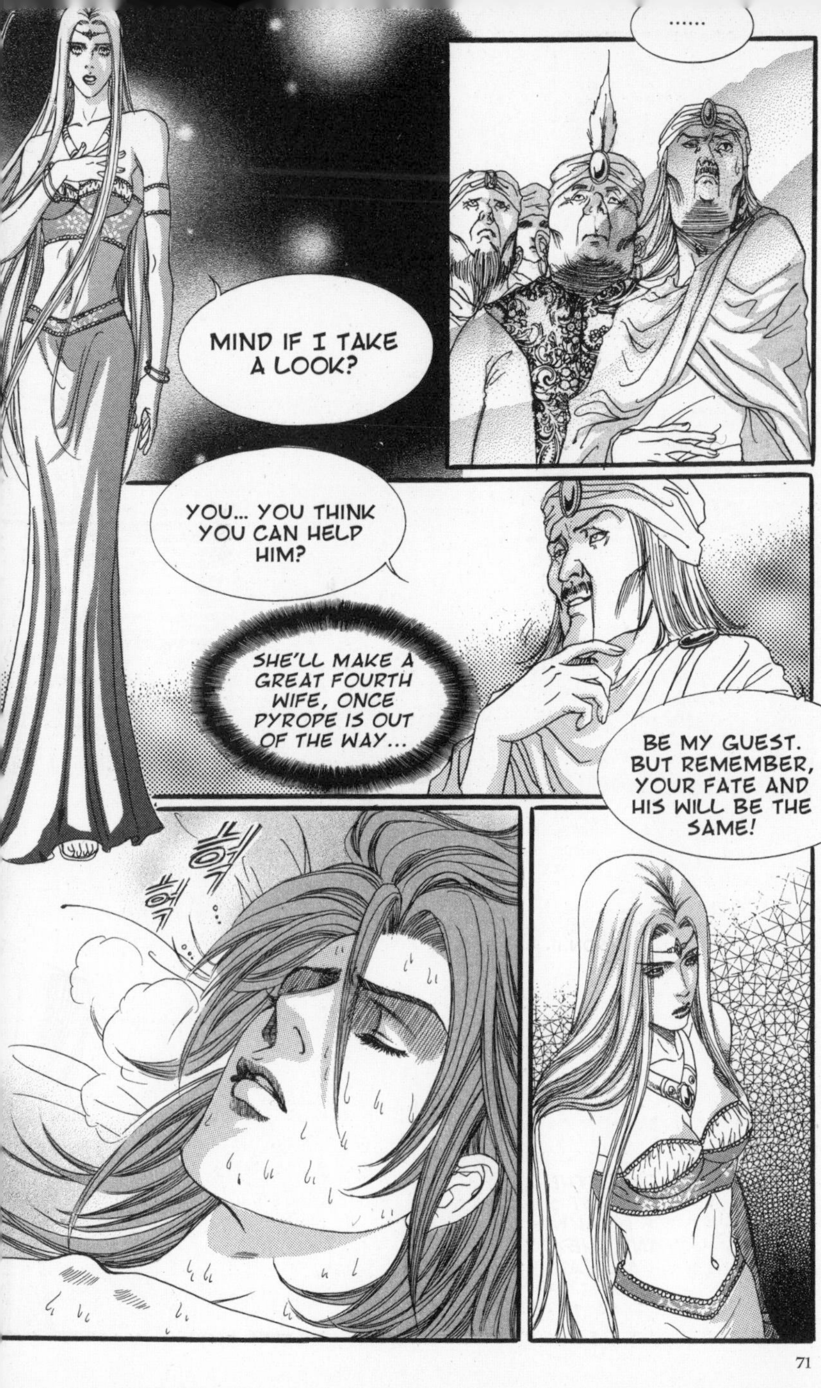
MIND IF I TAKE A LOOK?
......
YOU... YOU THINK YOU CAN HELP HIM?
SHE'LL MAKE A GREAT FOURTH WIFE, ONCE PYROPE IS OUT OF THE WAY...
BE MY GUEST. BUT REMEMBER, YOUR FATE AND HIS WILL BE THE SAME!
헉... 헉...

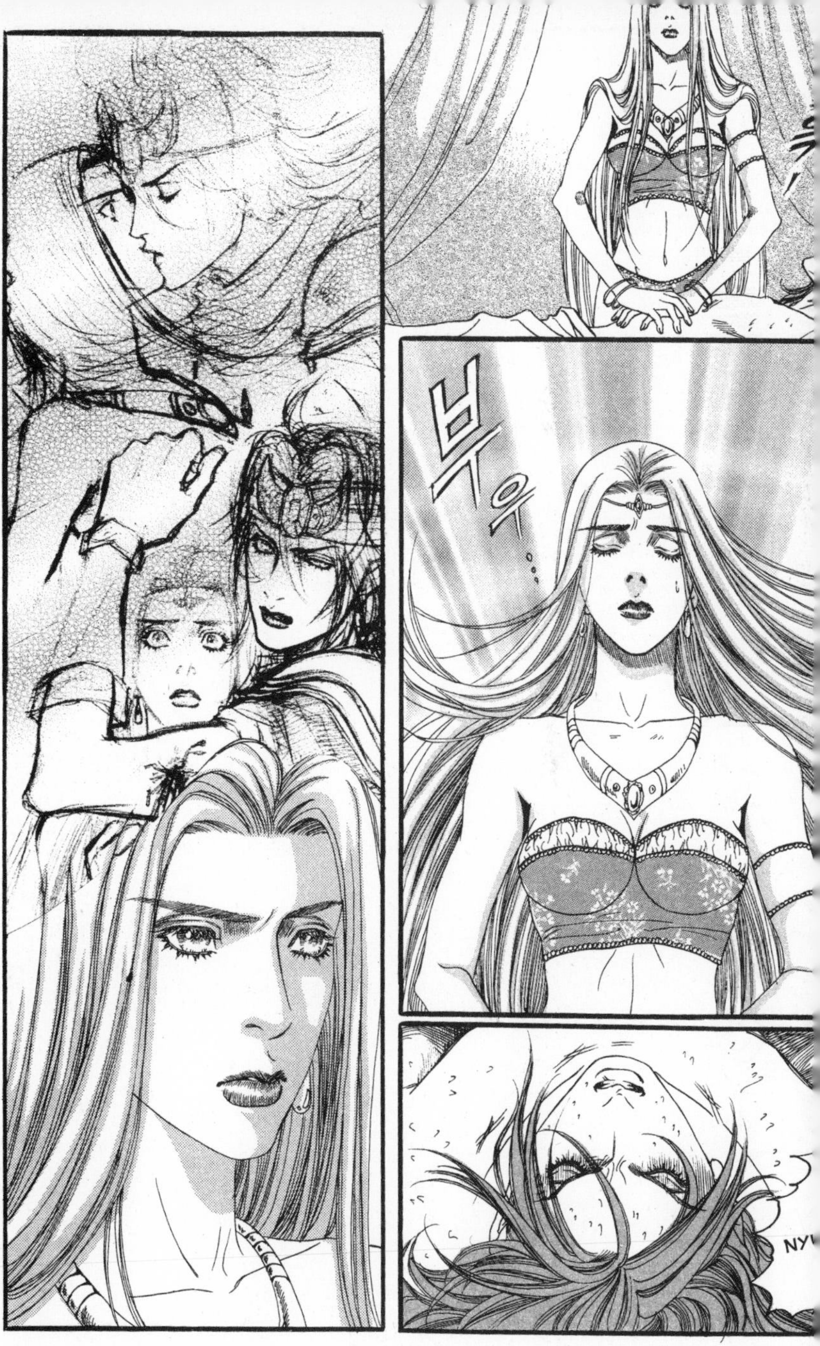
부우...
NYU

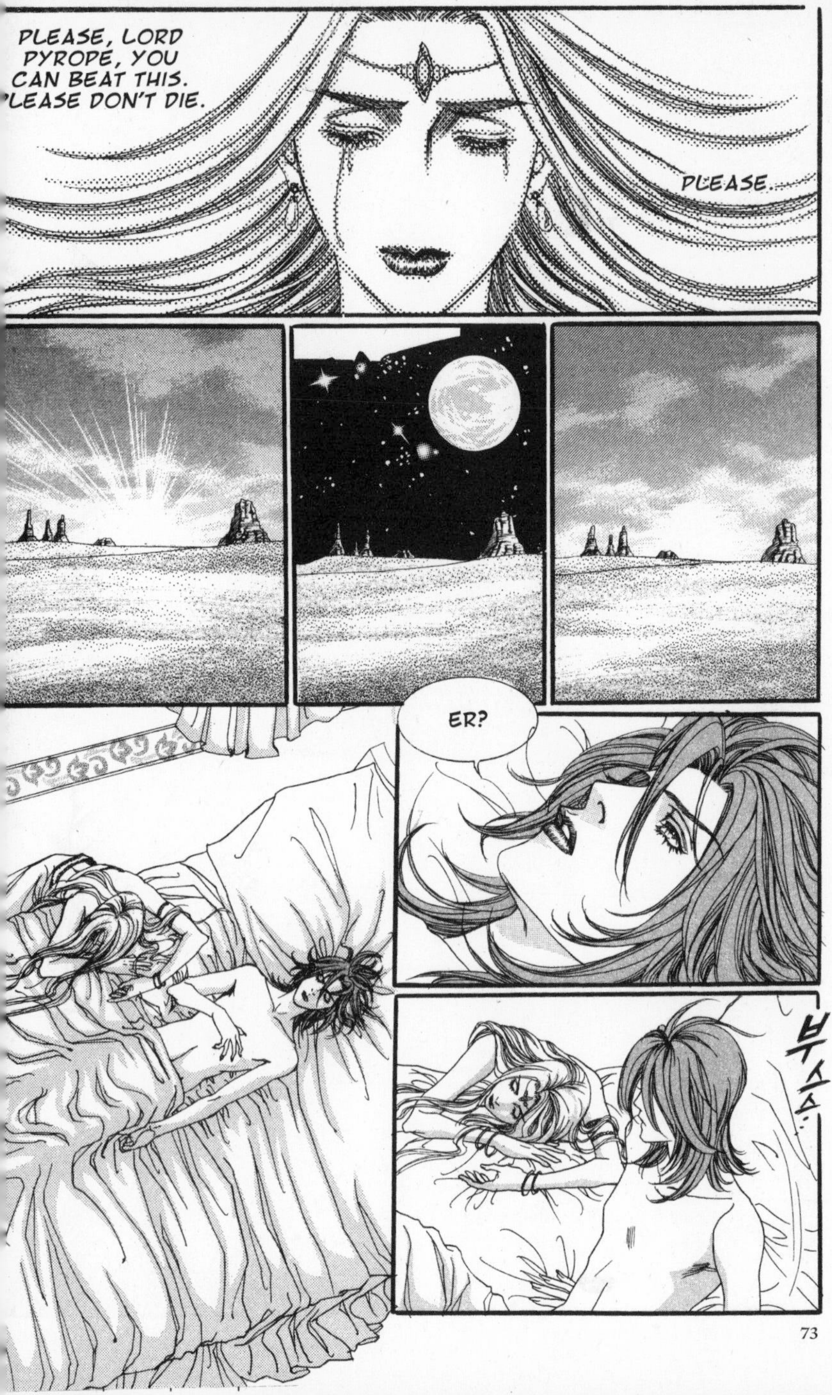
PLEASE, LORD PYROPE, YOU CAN BEAT THIS. PLEASE DON'T DIE.
PLEASE.
ER?
부스스

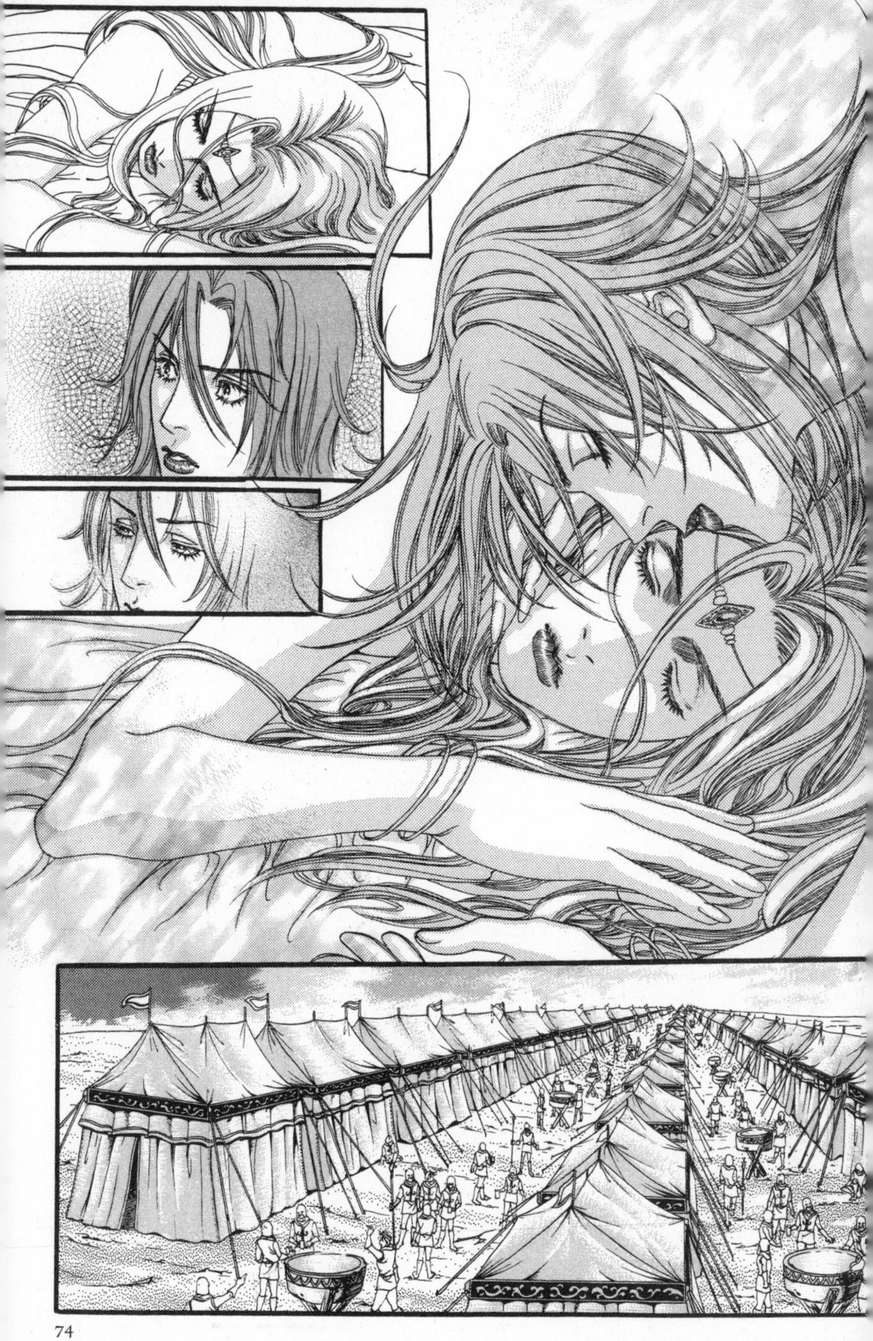

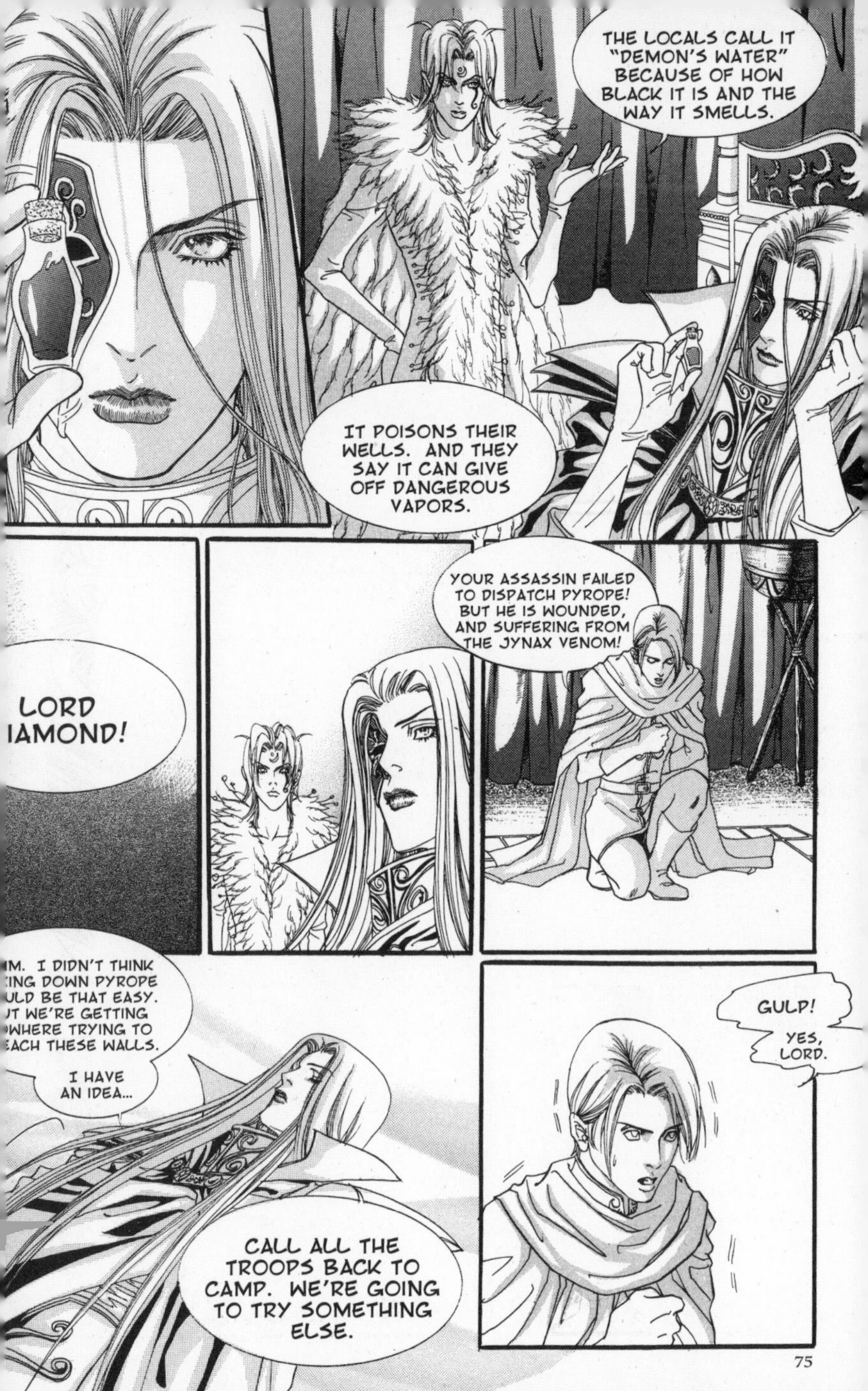
THE LOCALS CALL IT "DEMON'S WATER" BECAUSE OF HOW BLACK IT IS AND THE WAY IT SMELLS.
IT POISONS THEIR WELLS. AND THEY SAY IT CAN GIVE OFF DANGEROUS VAPORS.
LORD IAMOND!
YOUR ASSASSIN FAILED TO DISPATCH PYROPE! BUT HE IS WOUNDED, AND SUFFERING FROM THE JYNAX VENOM!
M. I DIDN'T THINK ING DOWN PYROPE ULD BE THAT EASY. UT WE'RE GETTING WHERE TRYING TO EACH THESE WALLS.
I HAVE AN IDEA...
CALL ALL THE TROOPS BACK TO CAMP. WE'RE GOING TO TRY SOMETHING ELSE.
GULP!
YES, LORD.

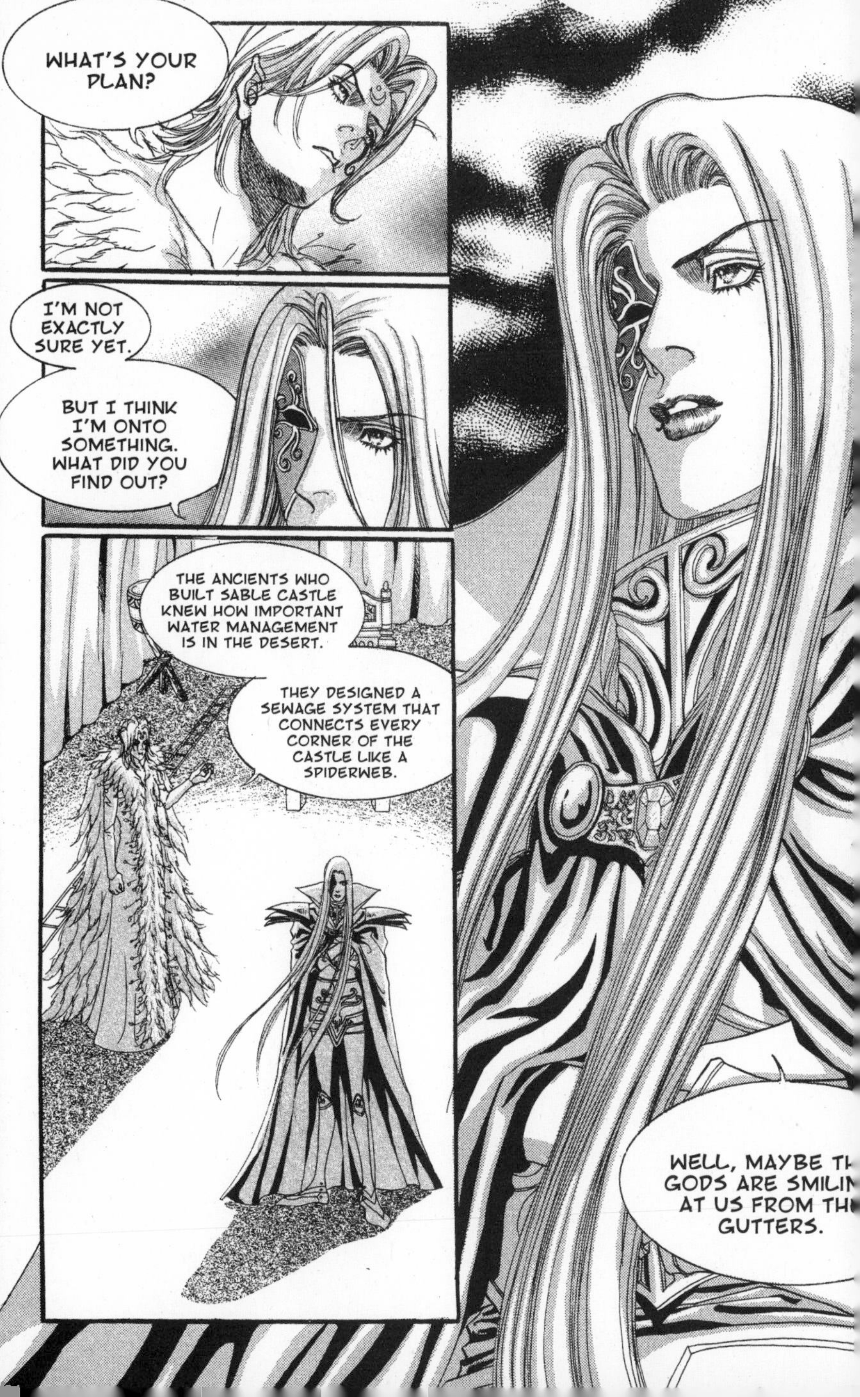
WHAT'S YOUR PLAN?
I'M NOT EXACTLY SURE YET.
BUT I THINK I'M ONTO SOMETHING. WHAT DID YOU FIND OUT?
THE ANCIENTS WHO BUILT SABLE CASTLE KNEW HOW IMPORTANT WATER MANAGEMENT IS IN THE DESERT.
THEY DESIGNED A SEWAGE SYSTEM THAT CONNECTS EVERY CORNER OF THE CASTLE LIKE A SPIDERWEB.
WELL, MAYBE TH GODS ARE SMILIN AT US FROM TH GUTTERS.

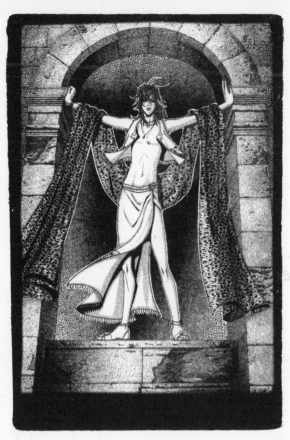

파이로프 Pyrope

Deserted in a
desert mine,
His fiery heart glows
like red stone.
But withered by years of
sun and solitude,
He guards his treasure
by keeping love out.

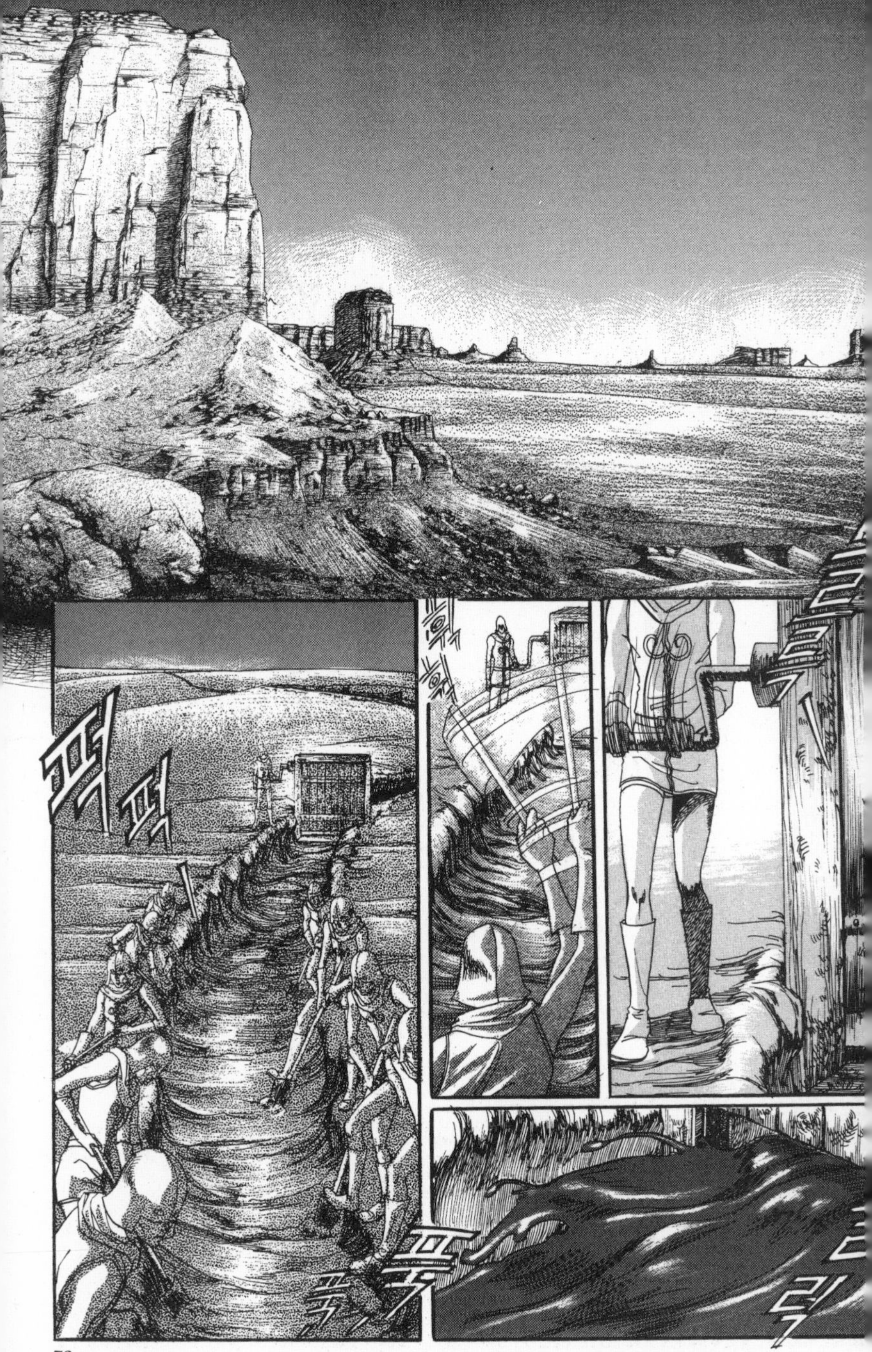
퍽
퍽
휙
휙
드르륵
푹
푹

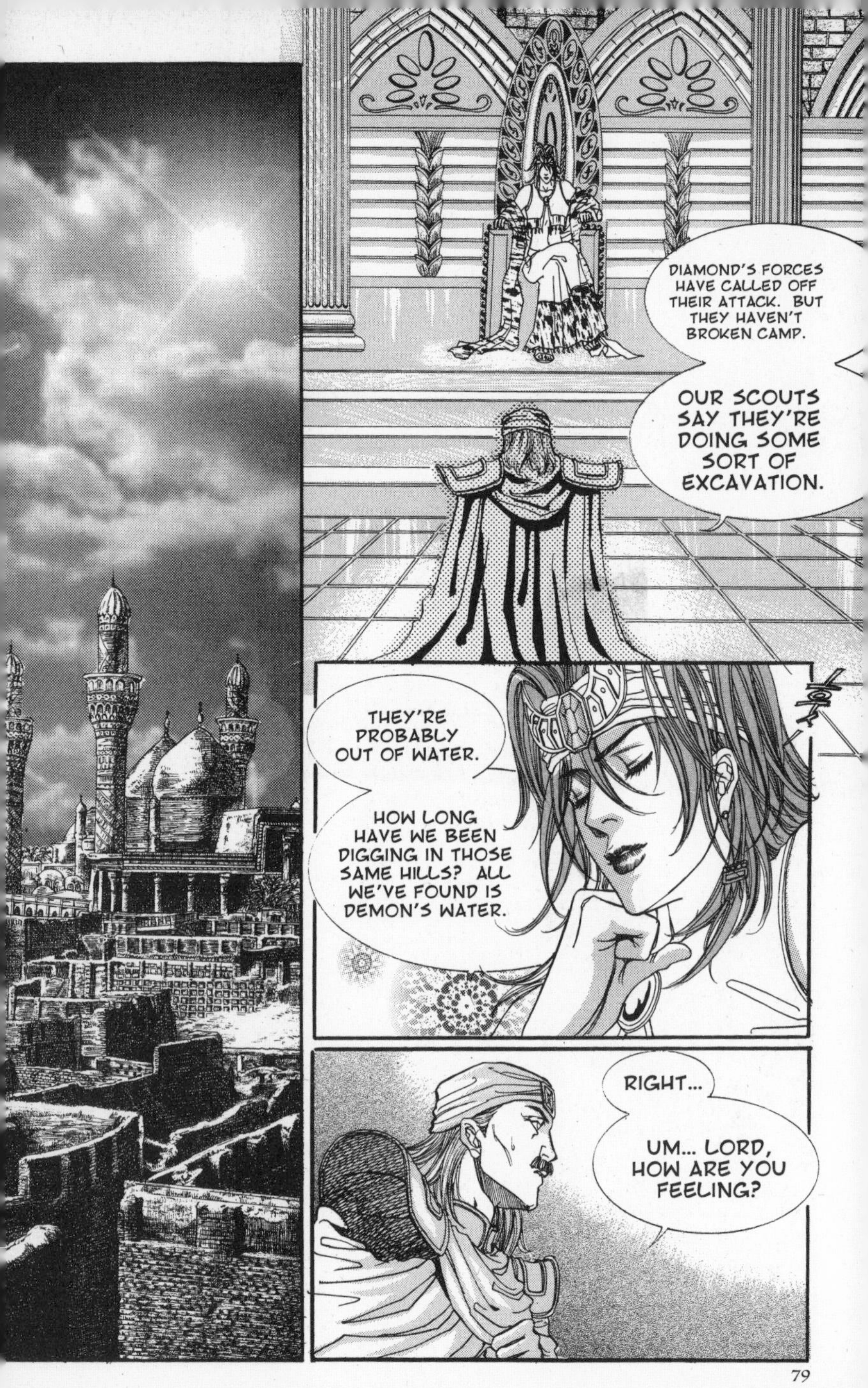
DIAMOND'S FORCES HAVE CALLED OFF THEIR ATTACK. BUT THEY HAVEN'T BROKEN CAMP.
OUR SCOUTS SAY THEY'RE DOING SOME SORT OF EXCAVATION.
THEY'RE PROBABLY OUT OF WATER.
HOW LONG HAVE WE BEEN DIGGING IN THOSE SAME HILLS? ALL WE'VE FOUND IS DEMON'S WATER.
RIGHT...
UM... LORD, HOW ARE YOU FEELING?

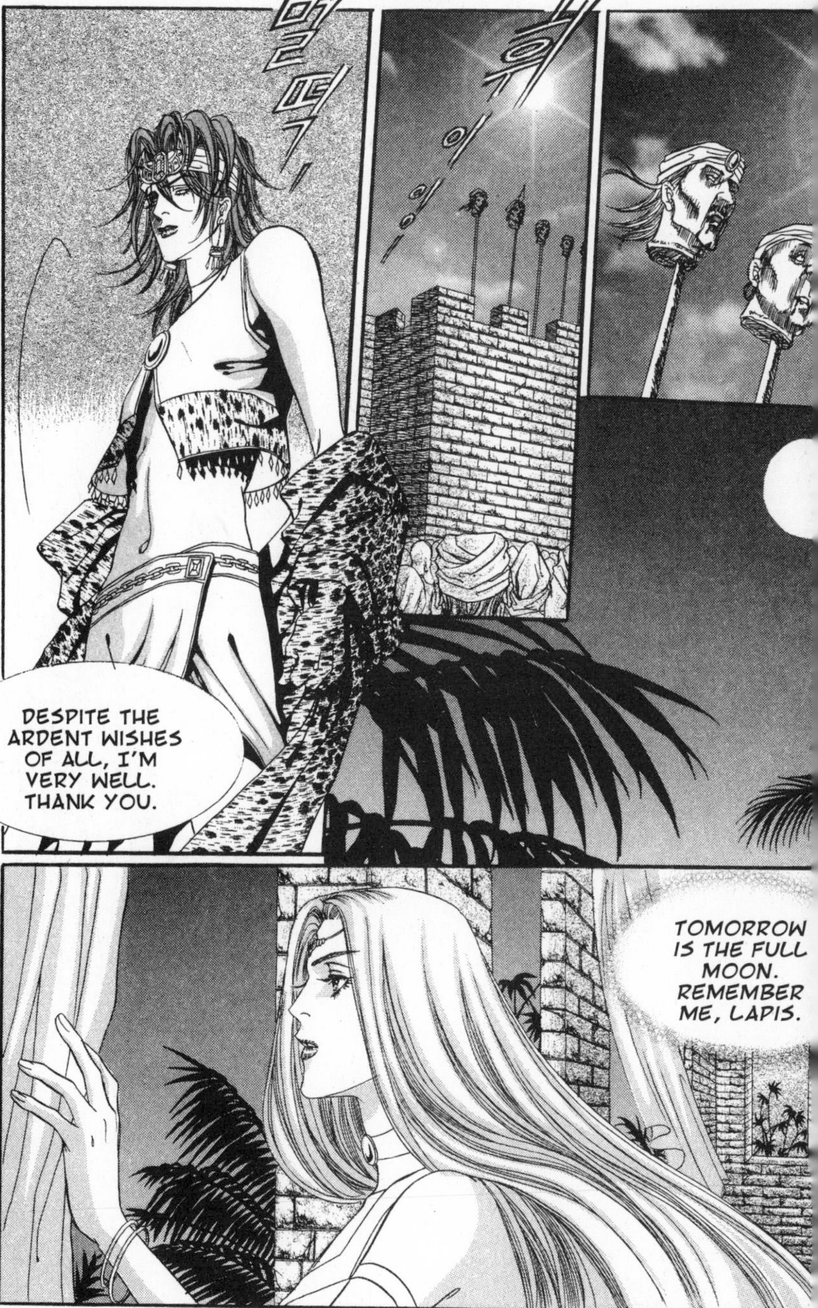
DESPITE THE ARDENT WISHES OF ALL, I'M VERY WELL. THANK YOU.
TOMORROW IS THE FULL MOON. REMEMBER ME, LAPIS.

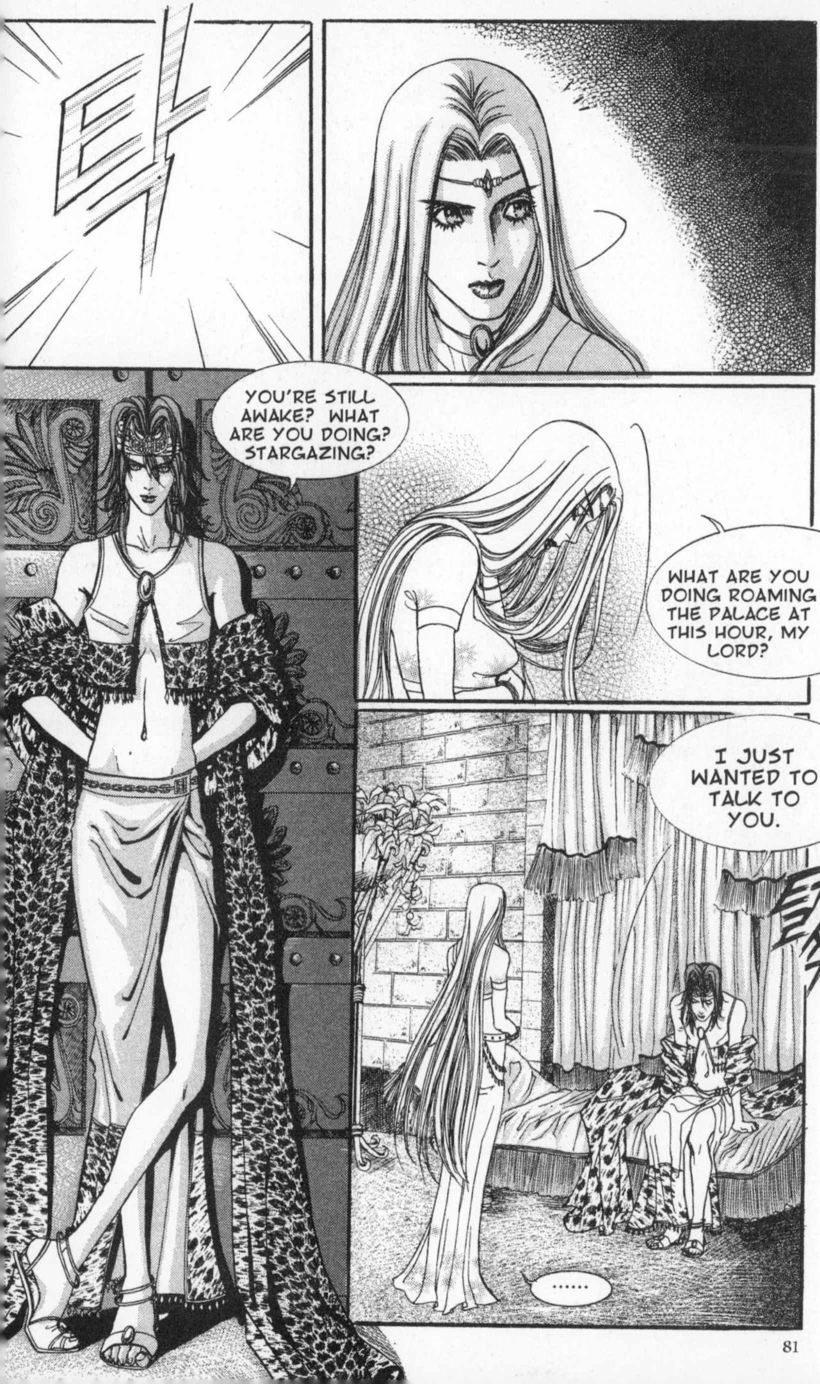

탁
YOU'RE STILL AWAKE? WHAT ARE YOU DOING? STARGAZING?
WHAT ARE YOU DOING ROAMING THE PALACE AT THIS HOUR, MY LORD?
I JUST WANTED TO TALK TO YOU.
털썩
......

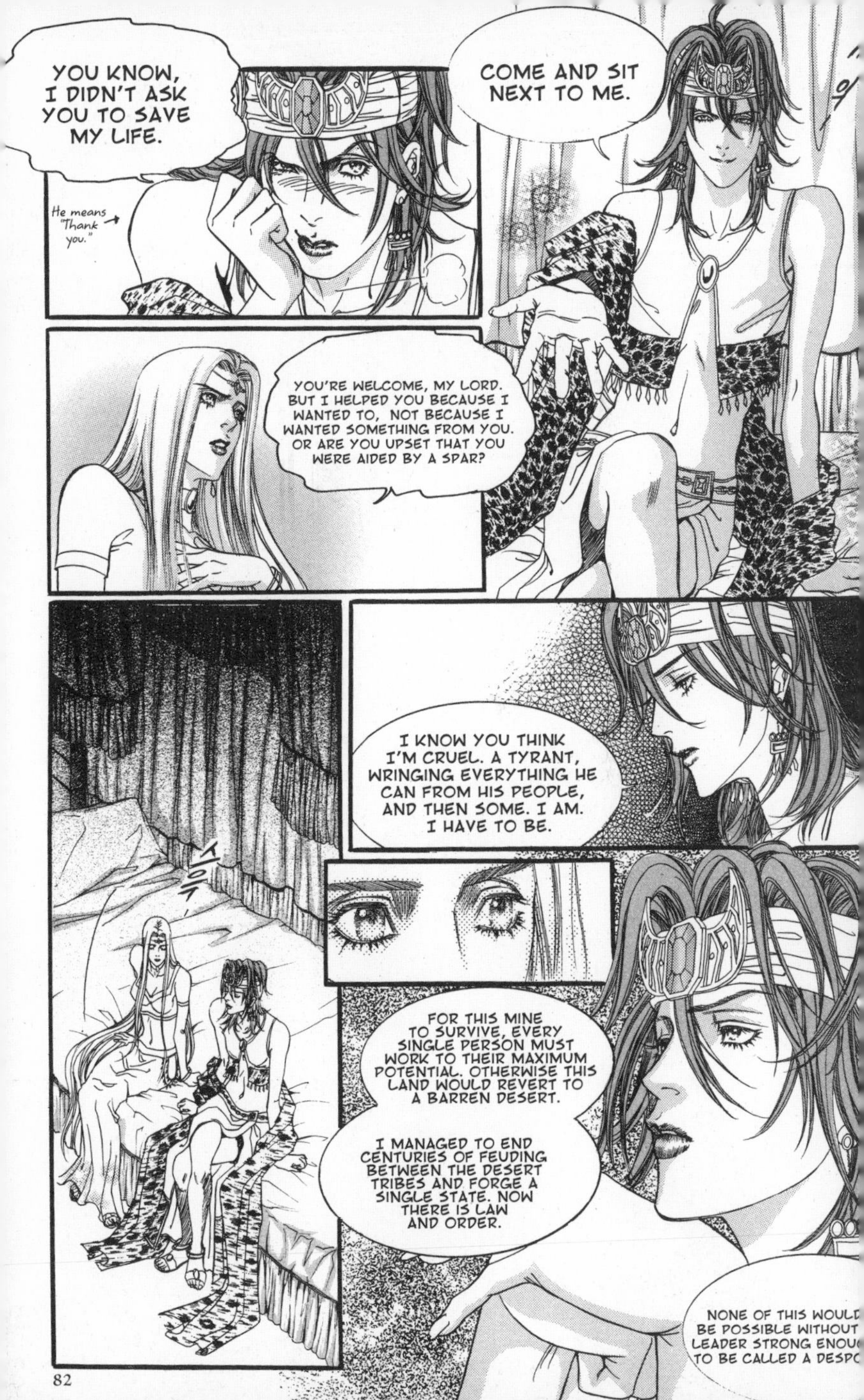
YOU KNOW, I DIDN'T ASK YOU TO SAVE MY LIFE.
He means "Thank you."
COME AND SIT NEXT TO ME.
YOU'RE WELCOME, MY LORD. BUT I HELPED YOU BECAUSE I WANTED TO, NOT BECAUSE I WANTED SOMETHING FROM YOU. OR ARE YOU UPSET THAT YOU WERE AIDED BY A SPAR?
I KNOW YOU THINK I'M CRUEL. A TYRANT, WRINGING EVERYTHING HE CAN FROM HIS PEOPLE, AND THEN SOME. I AM. I HAVE TO BE.
FOR THIS MINE TO SURVIVE, EVERY SINGLE PERSON MUST WORK TO THEIR MAXIMUM POTENTIAL. OTHERWISE THIS LAND WOULD REVERT TO A BARREN DESERT.
I MANAGED TO END CENTURIES OF FEUDING BETWEEN THE DESERT TRIBES AND FORGE A SINGLE STATE. NOW THERE IS LAW AND ORDER.
NONE OF THIS WOULD BE POSSIBLE WITHOUT LEADER STRONG ENOU TO BE CALLED A DESPO

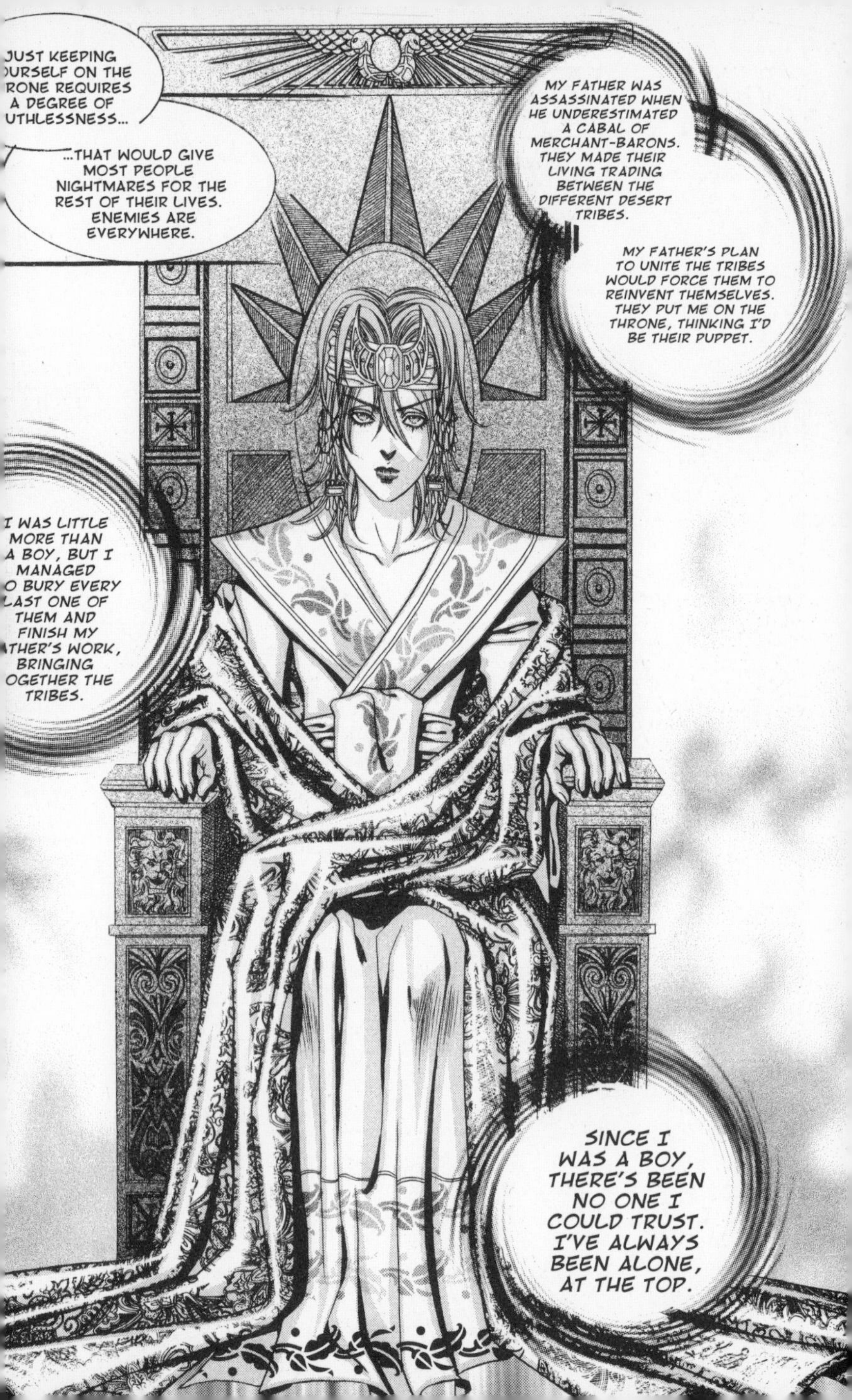
JUST KEEPING URSELF ON THE RONE REQUIRES A DEGREE OF UTHLESSNESS...
...THAT WOULD GIVE MOST PEOPLE NIGHTMARES FOR THE REST OF THEIR LIVES. ENEMIES ARE EVERYWHERE.
MY FATHER WAS ASSASSINATED WHEN HE UNDERESTIMATED A CABAL OF MERCHANT-BARONS. THEY MADE THEIR LIVING TRADING BETWEEN THE DIFFERENT DESERT TRIBES.
MY FATHER'S PLAN TO UNITE THE TRIBES WOULD FORCE THEM TO REINVENT THEMSELVES. THEY PUT ME ON THE THRONE, THINKING I'D BE THEIR PUPPET.
I WAS LITTLE MORE THAN A BOY, BUT I MANAGED O BURY EVERY LAST ONE OF THEM AND FINISH MY ATHER'S WORK, BRINGING OGETHER THE TRIBES.
SINCE I WAS A BOY, THERE'S BEEN NO ONE I COULD TRUST. I'VE ALWAYS BEEN ALONE, AT THE TOP.

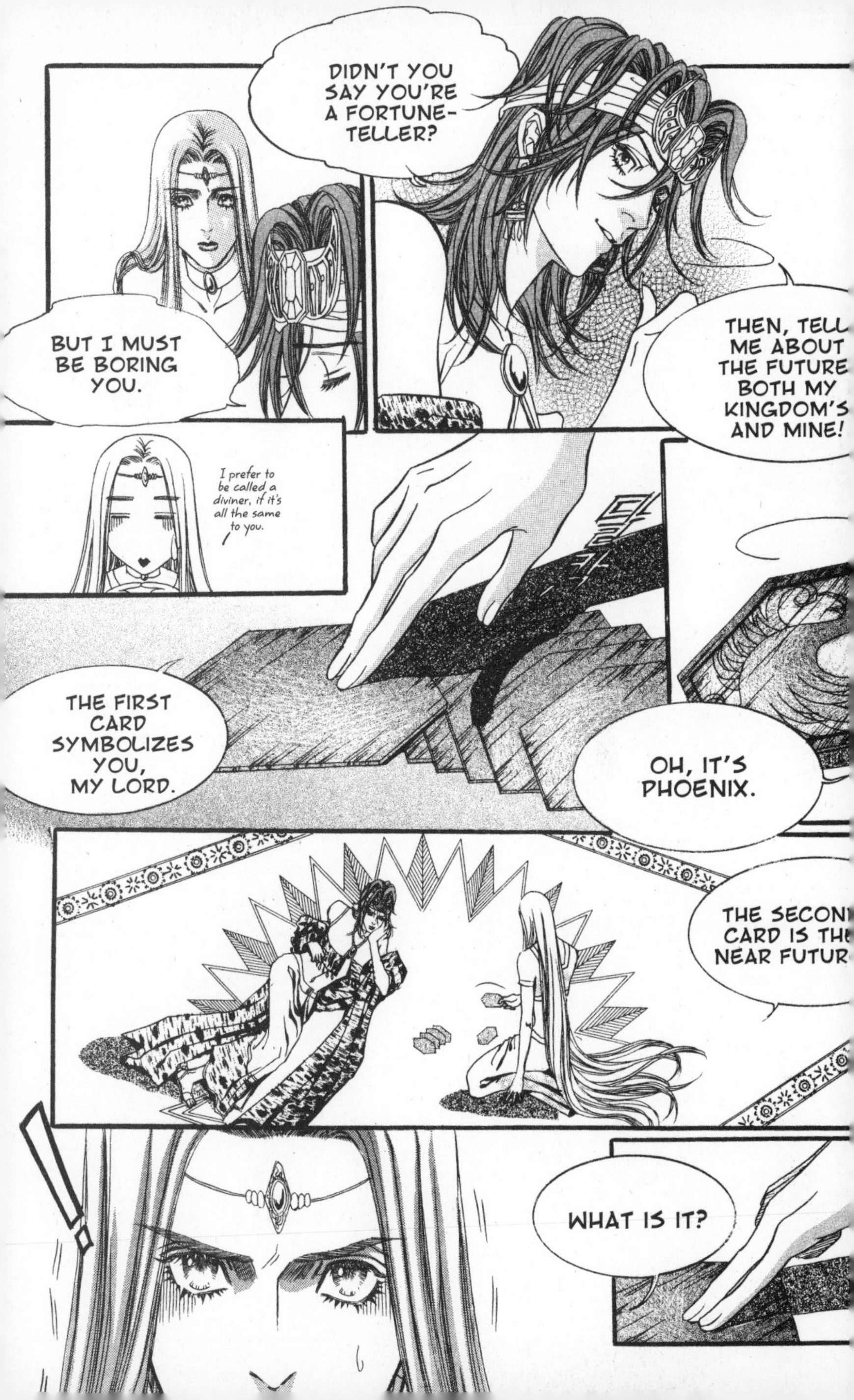

BUT I MUST BE BORING YOU.
DIDN'T YOU SAY YOU'RE A FORTUNE-TELLER?
THEN, TELL ME ABOUT THE FUTURE BOTH MY KINGDOM'S AND MINE!
I prefer to be called a diviner, if it's all the same to you.
THE FIRST CARD SYMBOLIZES YOU, MY LORD.
OH, IT'S PHOENIX.
THE SECON CARD IS TH NEAR FUTUR
WHAT IS IT?

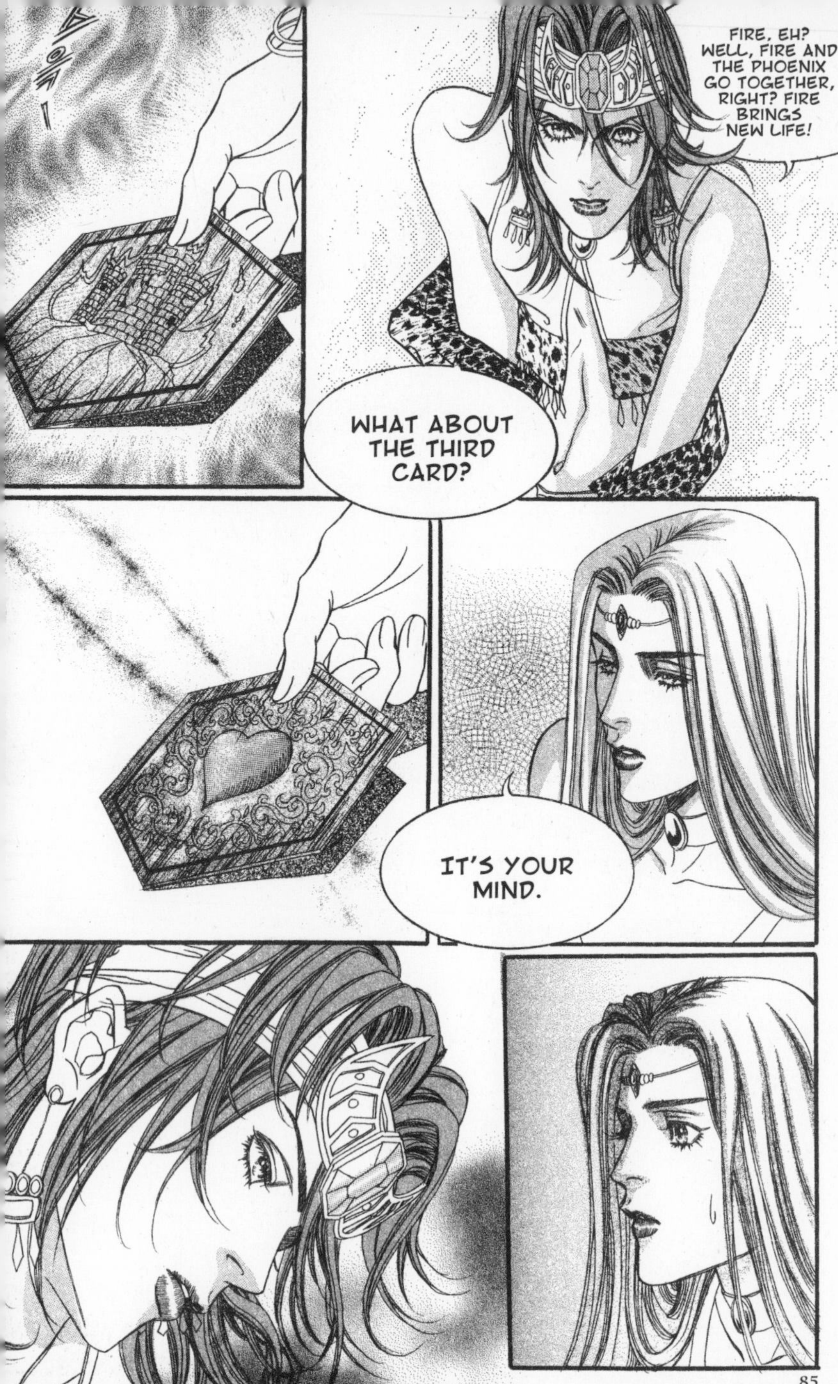
FIRE, EH? WELL, FIRE AND THE PHOENIX GO TOGETHER, RIGHT? FIRE BRINGS NEW LIFE!
WHAT ABOUT THE THIRD CARD?
IT'S YOUR MIND.

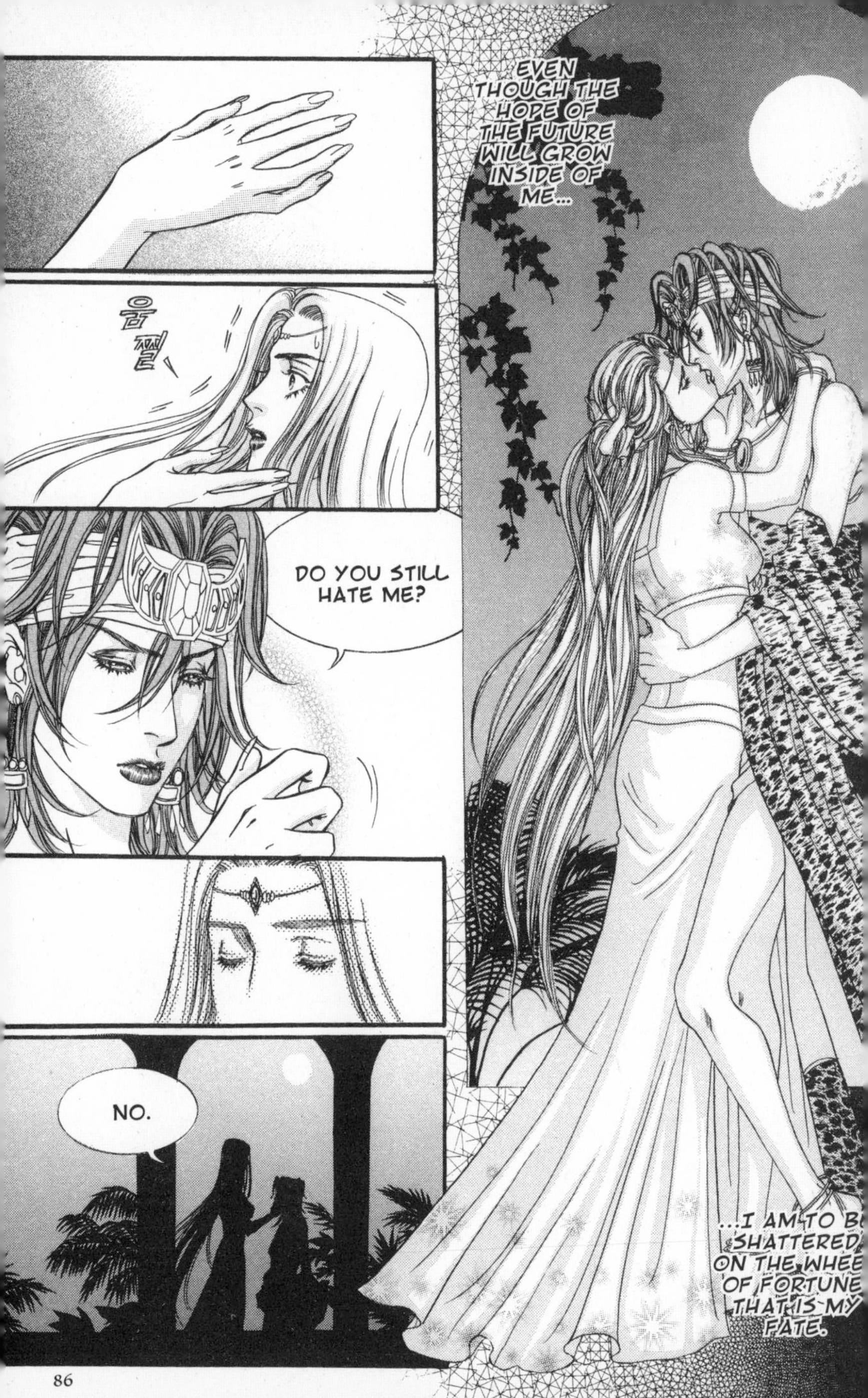
움찔
DO YOU STILL HATE ME?
NO.
EVEN THOUGH THE HOPE OF THE FUTURE WILL GROW INSIDE OF ME...
...I AM TO B SHATTERED ON THE WHEE OF FORTUNE THAT IS MY FATE.

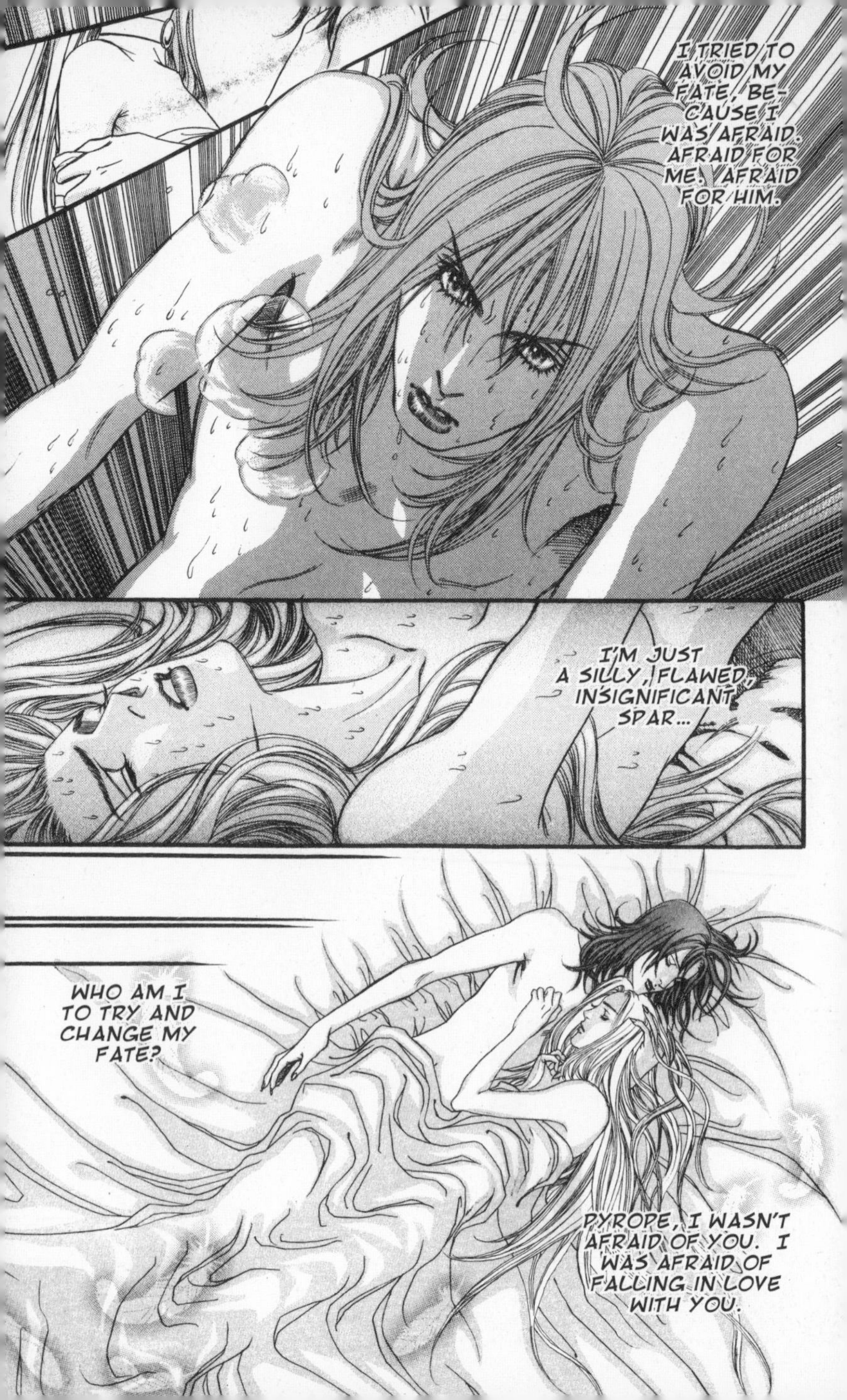
I TRIED TO AVOID MY FATE, BE-CAUSE I WAS AFRAID. AFRAID FOR ME. AFRAID FOR HIM.
I'M JUST A SILLY, FLAWED, INSIGNIFICANT SPAR...
WHO AM I TO TRY AND CHANGE MY FATE?
PYROPE, I WASN'T AFRAID OF YOU. I WAS AFRAID OF FALLING IN LOVE WITH YOU.

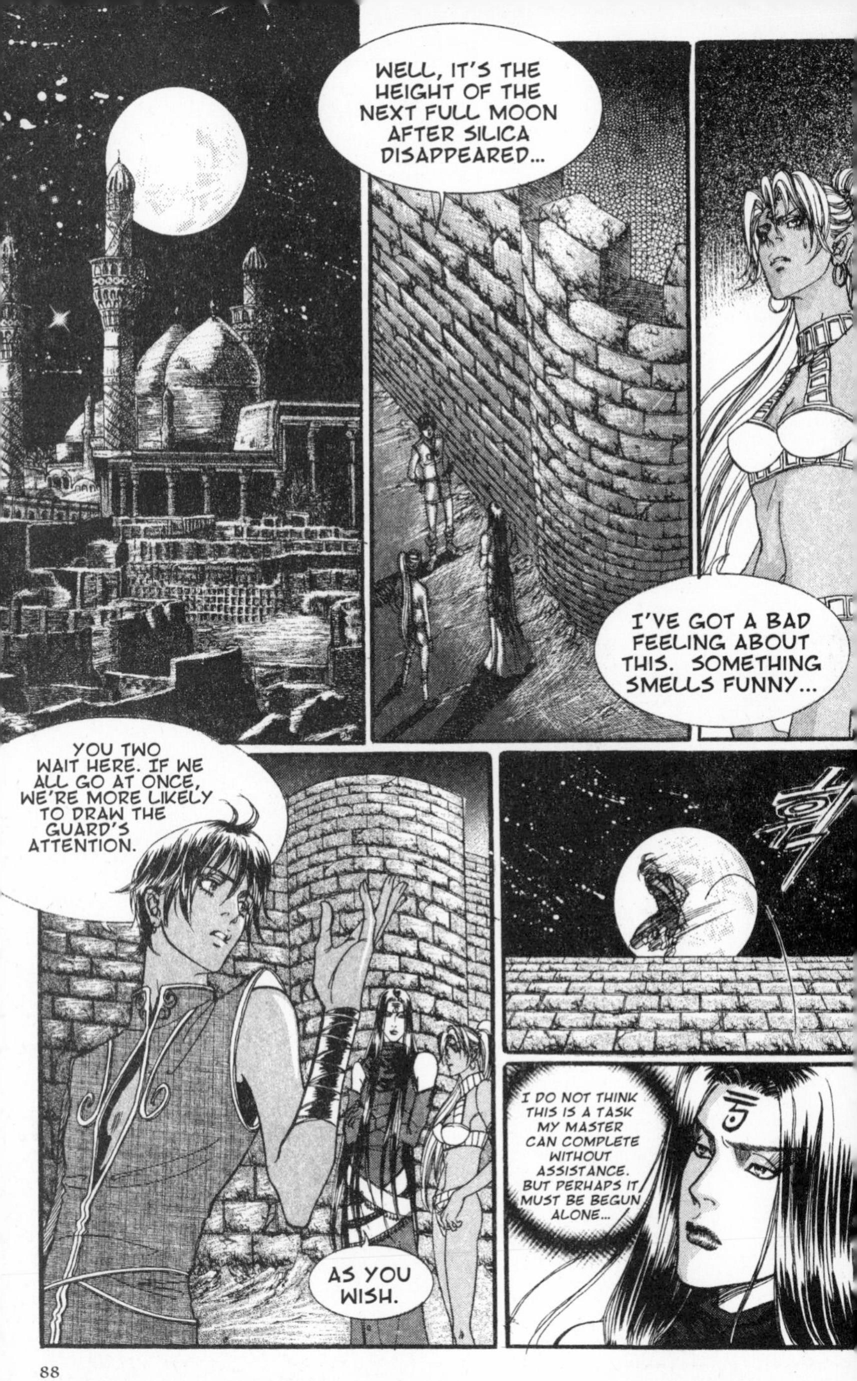
WELL, IT'S THE HEIGHT OF THE NEXT FULL MOON AFTER SILICA DISAPPEARED...
I'VE GOT A BAD FEELING ABOUT THIS. SOMETHING SMELLS FUNNY...
YOU TWO WAIT HERE. IF WE ALL GO AT ONCE, WE'RE MORE LIKELY TO DRAW THE GUARD'S ATTENTION.
AS YOU WISH.
I DO NOT THINK THIS IS A TASK MY MASTER CAN COMPLETE WITHOUT ASSISTANCE. BUT PERHAPS IT MUST BE BEGUN ALONE...

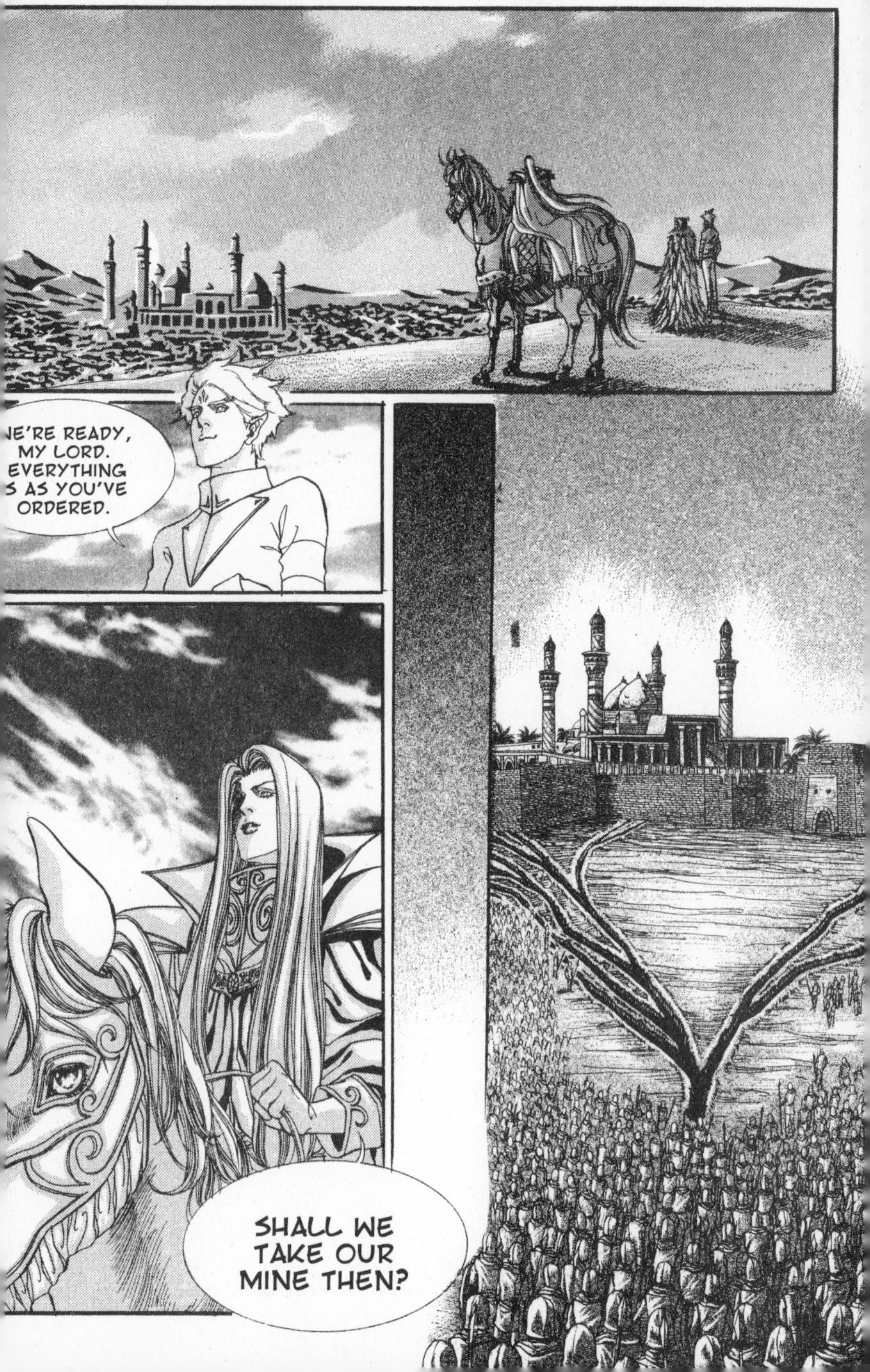

E'RE READY, MY LORD. EVERYTHING S AS YOU'VE ORDERED.
SHALL WE TAKE OUR MINE THEN?

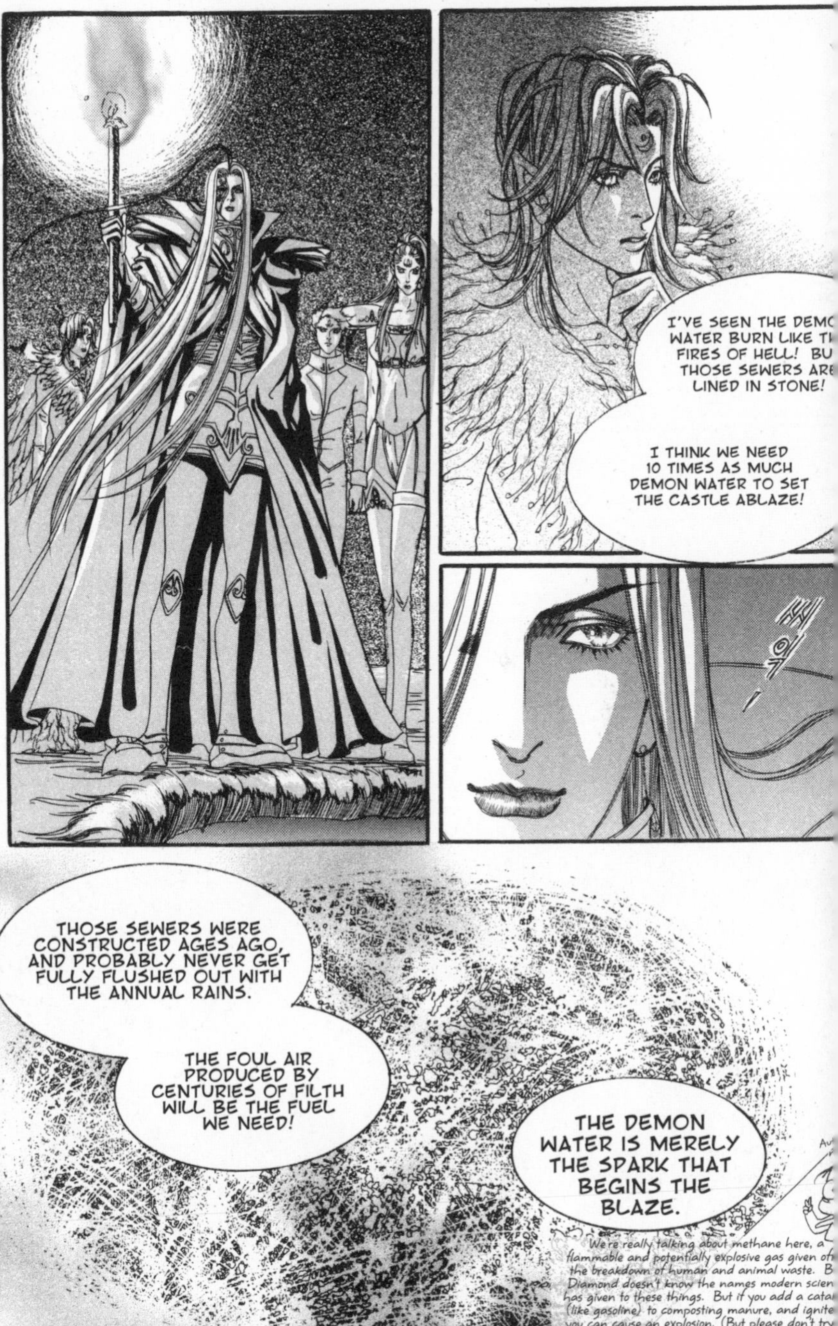
I'VE SEEN THE DEMO
WATER BURN LIKE TH
FIRES OF HELL! BU
THOSE SEWERS ARE
LINED IN STONE!
I THINK WE NEED 10 TIMES AS MUCH DEMON WATER TO SET THE CASTLE ABLAZE!
THOSE SEWERS WERE CONSTRUCTED AGES AGO, AND PROBABLY NEVER GET FULLY FLUSHED OUT WITH THE ANNUAL RAINS.
THE FOUL AIR PRODUCED BY CENTURIES OF FILTH WILL BE THE FUEL WE NEED!
THE DEMON WATER IS MERELY THE SPARK THAT BEGINS THE BLAZE.
We're really talking about methane here, a
flammable and potentially explosive gas given of
the breakdown of human and animal waste. B
Diamond doesn't know the names modern scien
has given to these things. But if you add a catal
(like gasoline) to composting manure, and ignite
you can cause an explosion. (But please don't try
you could end up looking very silly, or dead. Or bo

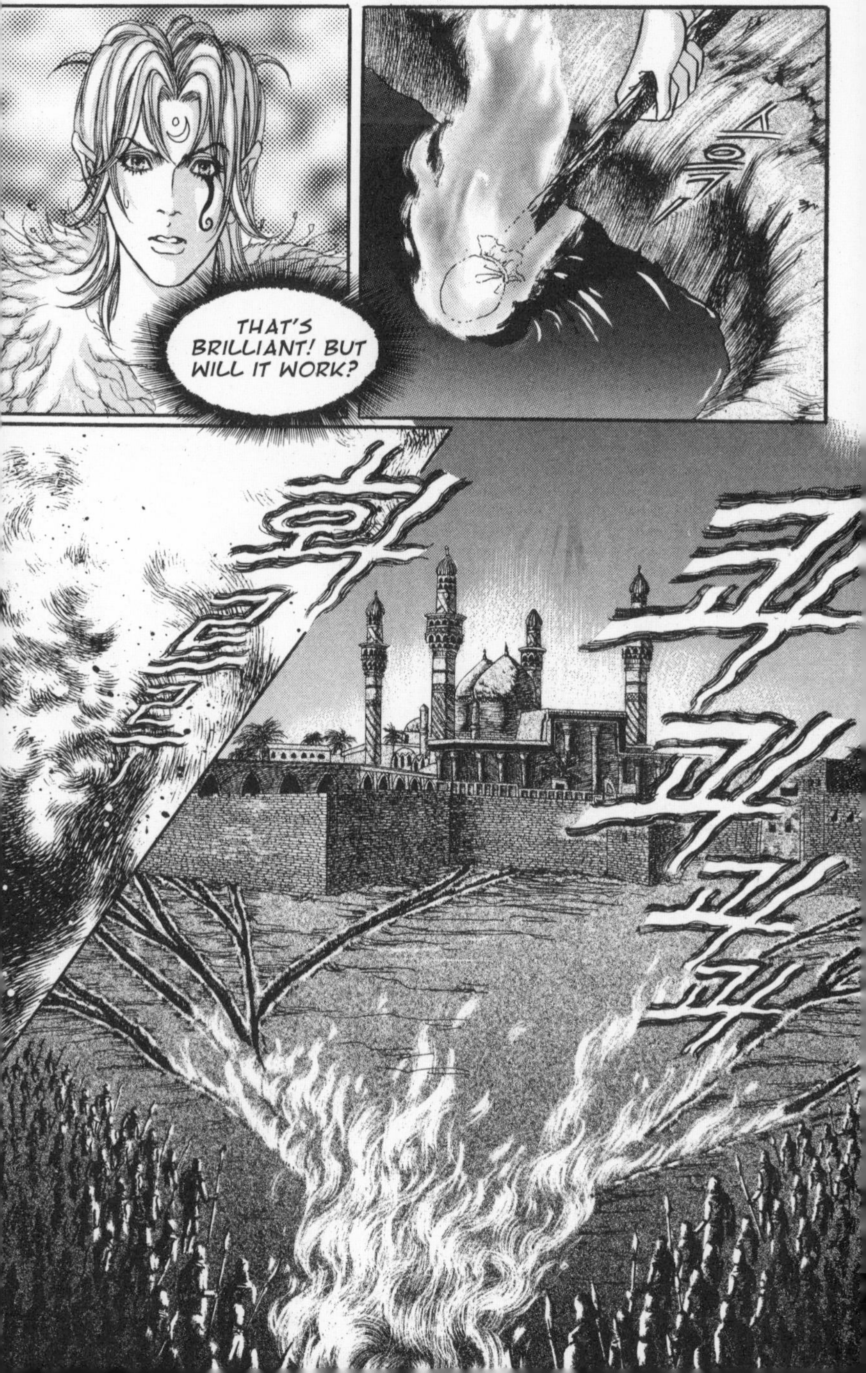
THAT'S BRILLIANT! BUT WILL IT WORK?

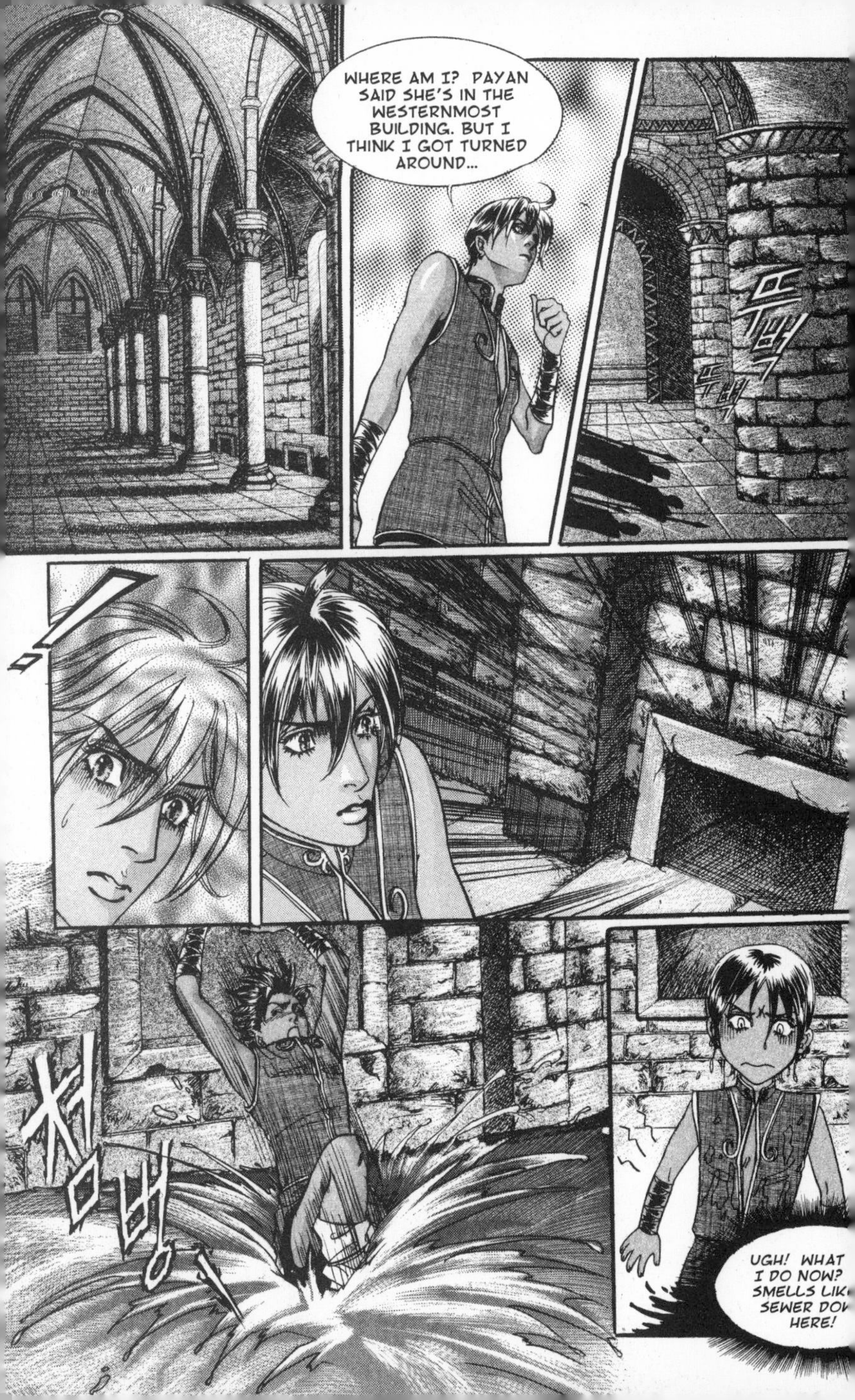
WHERE AM I? PAYAN SAID SHE'S IN THE WESTERNMOST BUILDING. BUT I THINK I GOT TURNED AROUND...
뚜벅
뚜벅
!
첨벙
UGH! WHAT I DO NOW? SMELLS LIK SEWER DOW HERE!

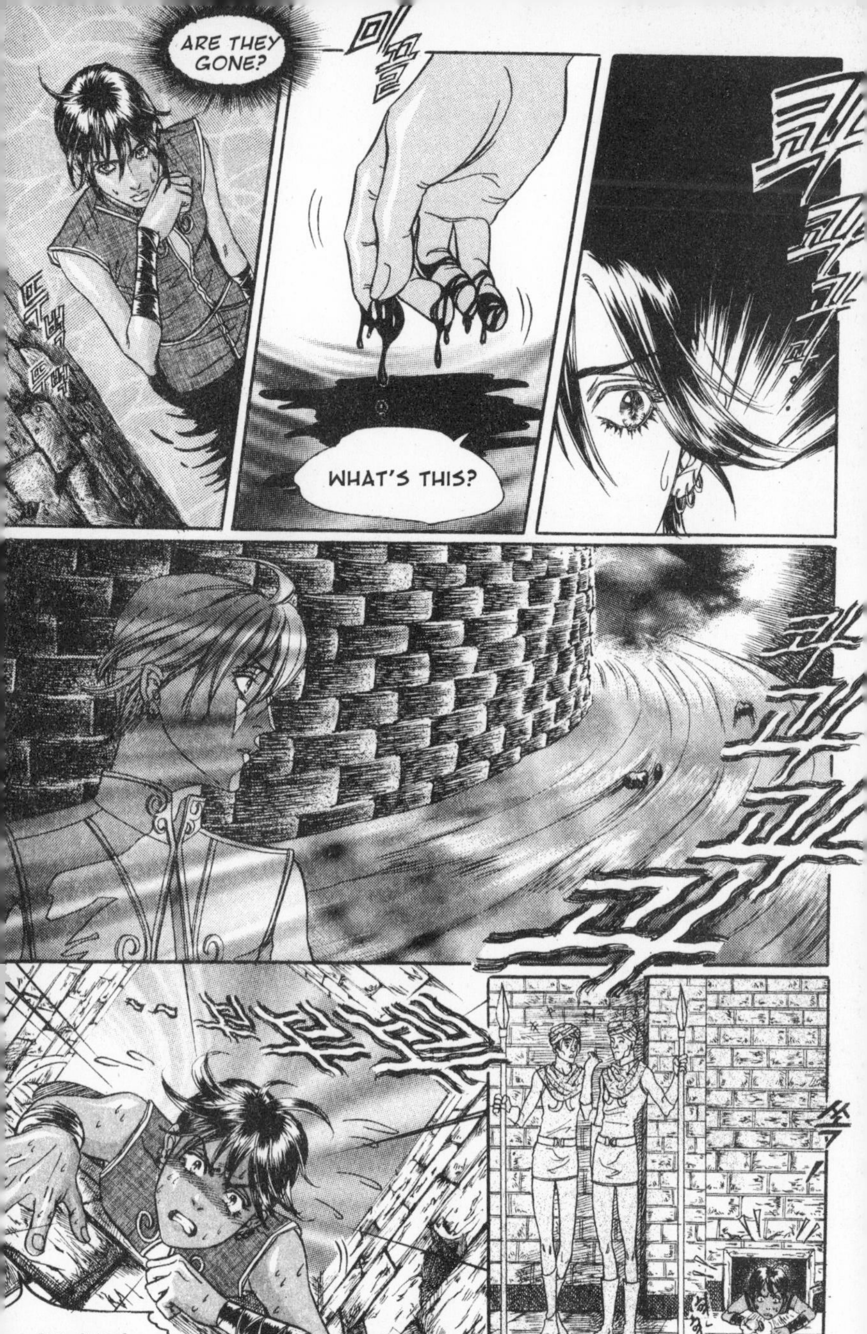
ARE THEY GONE?
WHAT'S THIS?
OH SHIT! WHAT'S THAT?

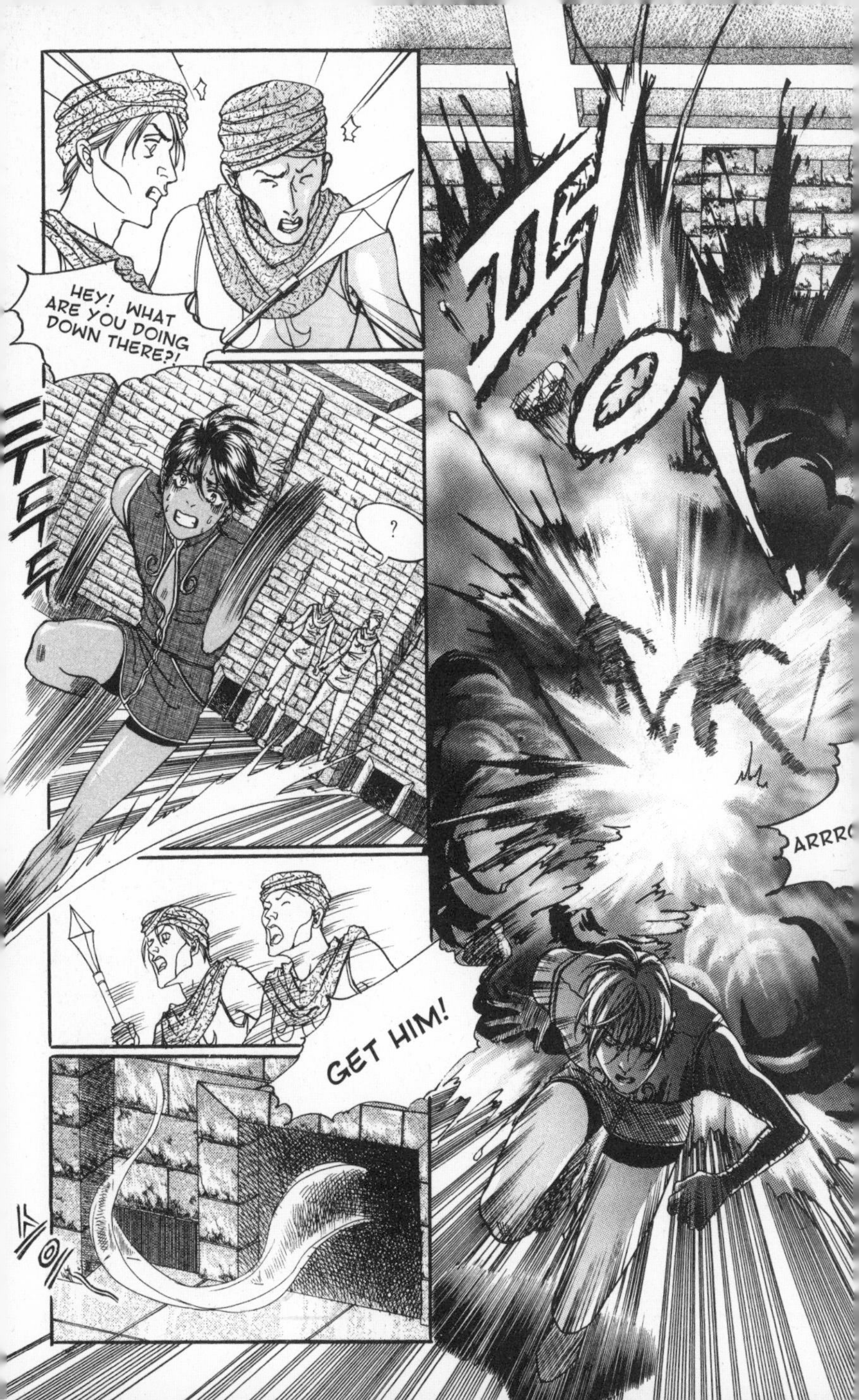
HEY! WHAT ARE YOU DOING DOWN THERE?!
?
GET HIM!
ARRR

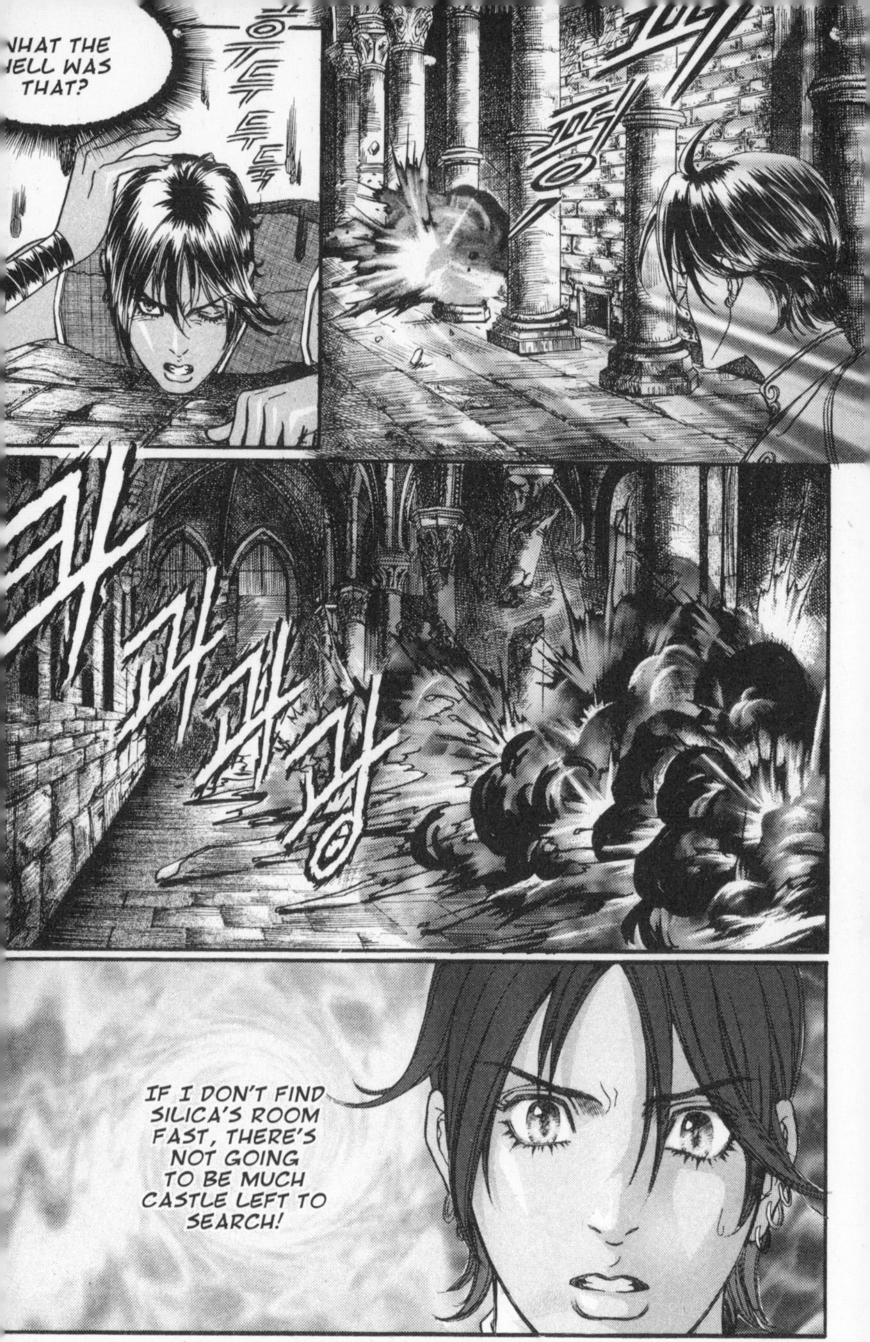
WHAT THE HELL WAS THAT?
IF I DON'T FIND SILICA'S ROOM FAST, THERE'S NOT GOING TO BE MUCH CASTLE LEFT TO SEARCH!

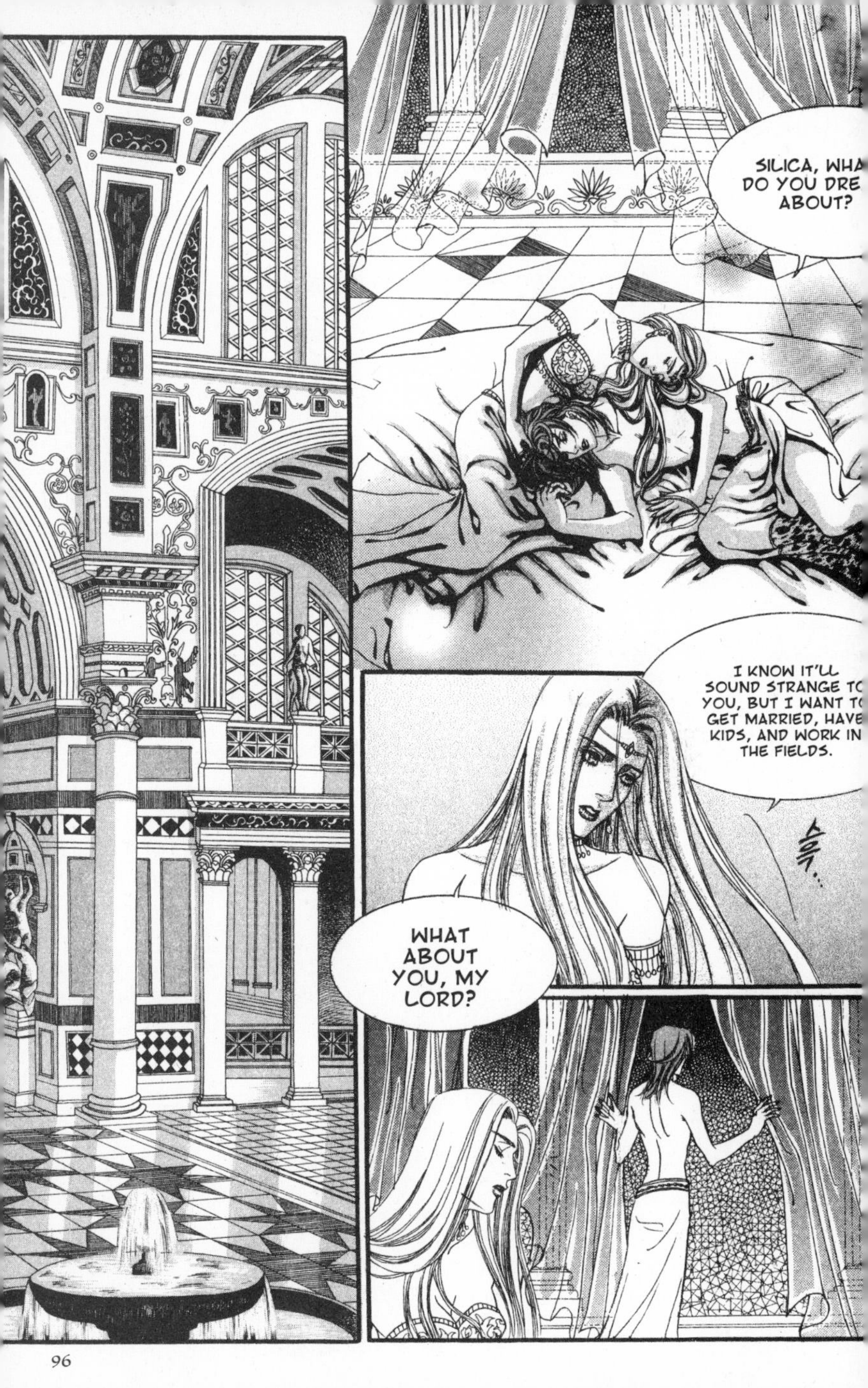
SILICA, WHA DO YOU DRE ABOUT?
I KNOW IT'LL SOUND STRANGE TO YOU, BUT I WANT TO GET MARRIED, HAVE KIDS, AND WORK IN THE FIELDS.
WHAT ABOUT YOU, MY LORD?

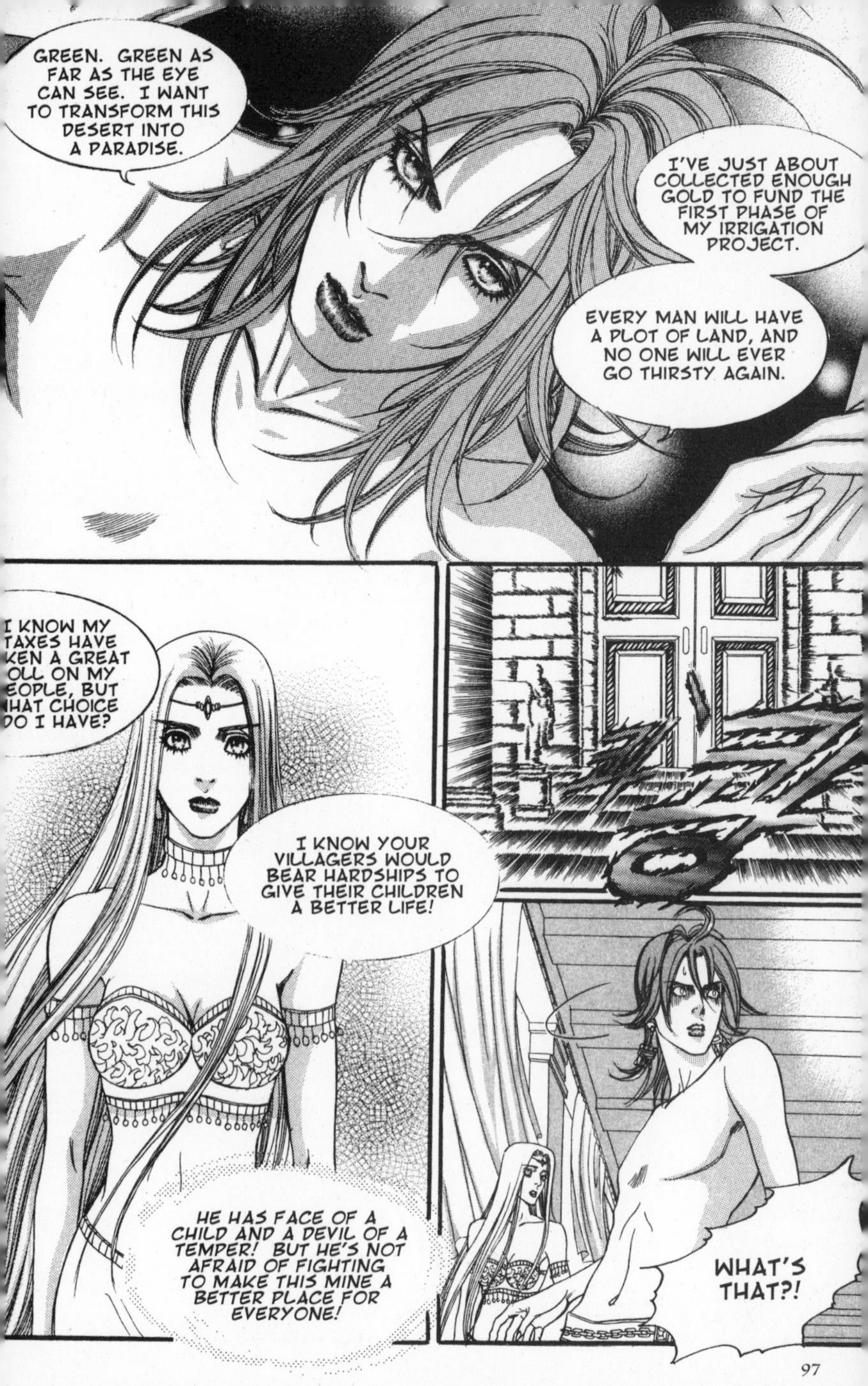
GREEN. GREEN AS FAR AS THE EYE CAN SEE. I WANT TO TRANSFORM THIS DESERT INTO A PARADISE.
I'VE JUST ABOUT COLLECTED ENOUGH GOLD TO FUND THE FIRST PHASE OF MY IRRIGATION PROJECT.
EVERY MAN WILL HAVE A PLOT OF LAND, AND NO ONE WILL EVER GO THIRSTY AGAIN.
I KNOW MY TAXES HAVE KEN A GREAT OLL ON MY EOPLE, BUT HAT CHOICE DO I HAVE?
I KNOW YOUR VILLAGERS WOULD BEAR HARDSHIPS TO GIVE THEIR CHILDREN A BETTER LIFE!
HE HAS FACE OF A CHILD AND A DEVIL OF A TEMPER! BUT HE'S NOT AFRAID OF FIGHTING TO MAKE THIS MINE A BETTER PLACE FOR EVERYONE!
WHAT'S THAT?!

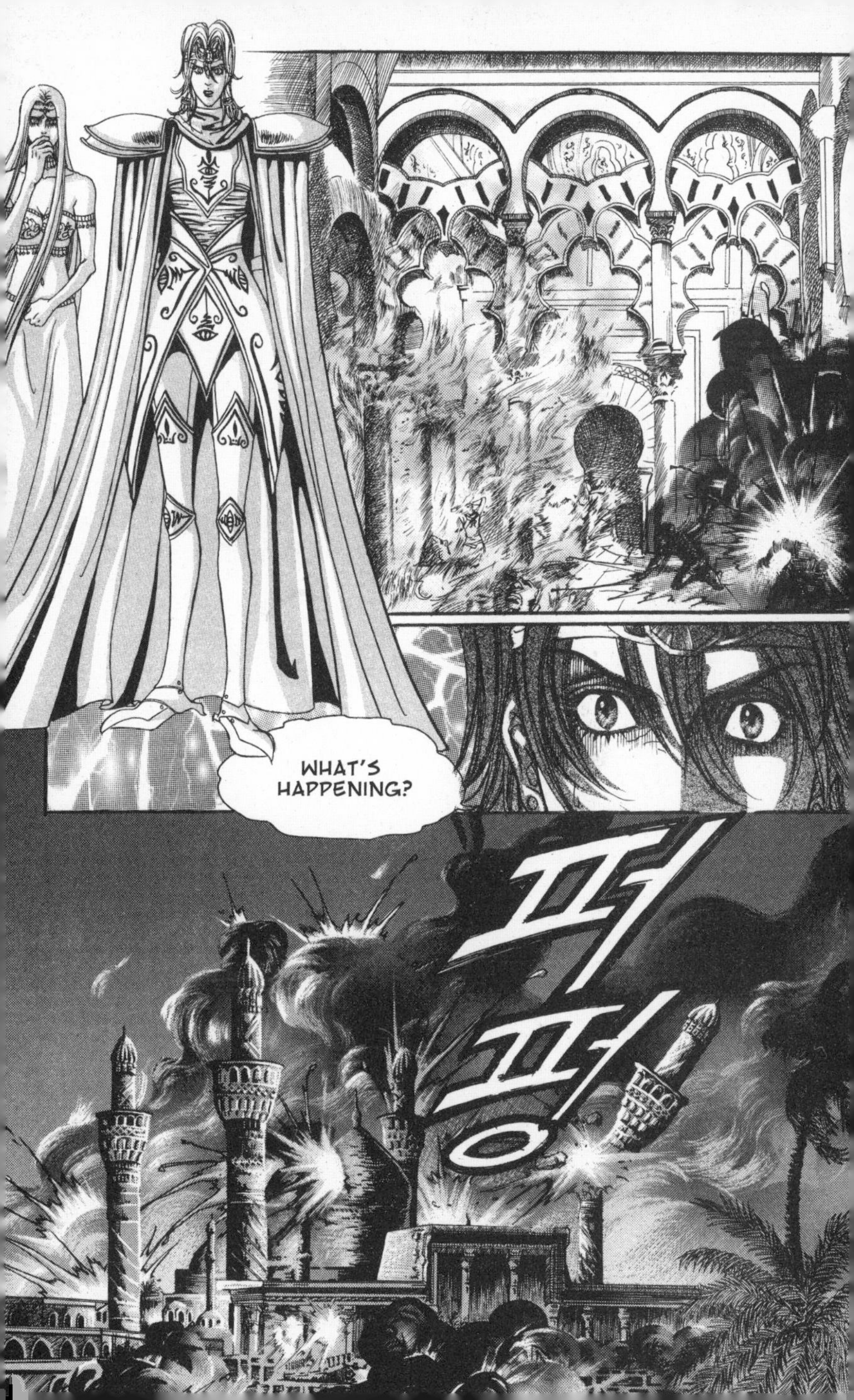
WHAT'S HAPPENING?

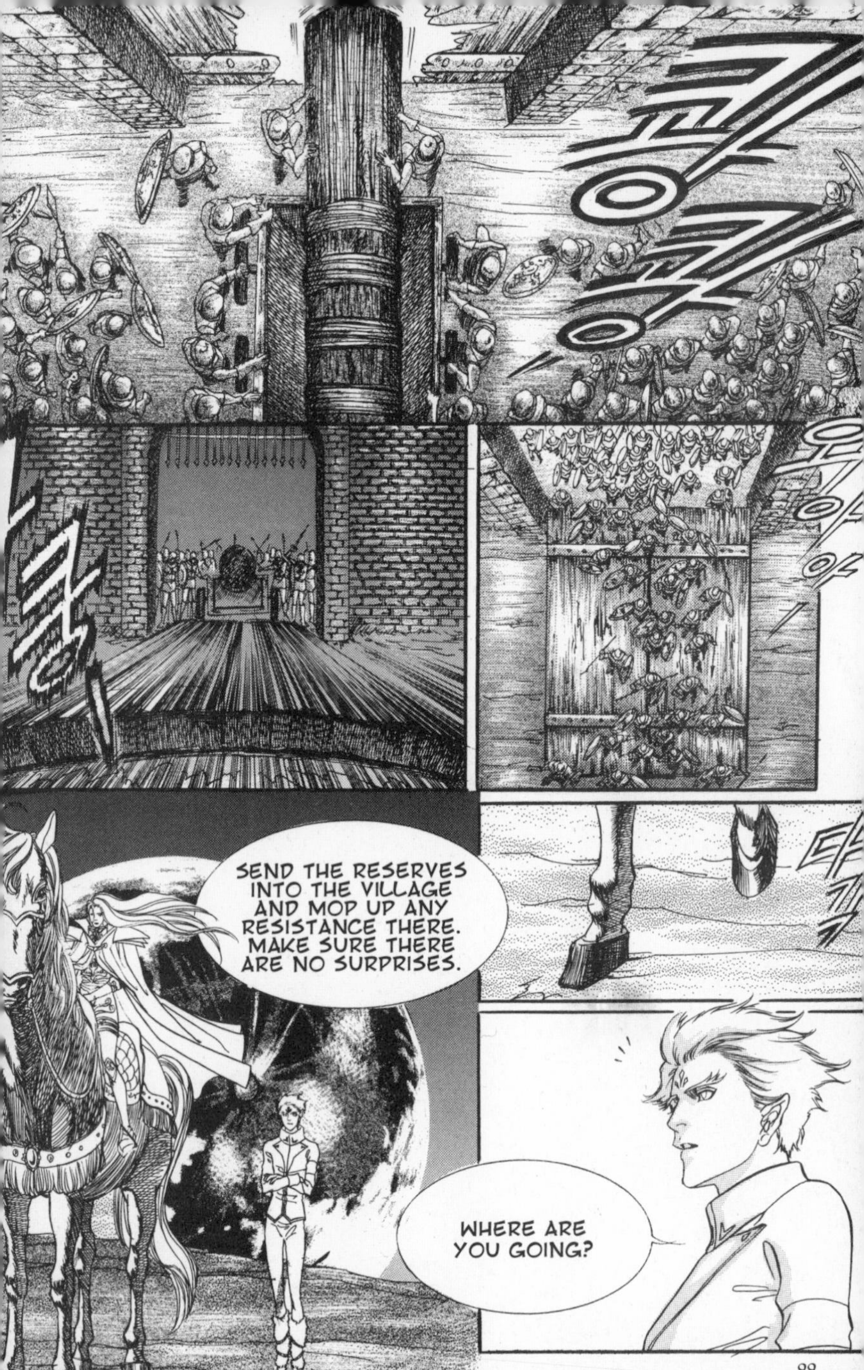
SEND THE RESERVES INTO THE VILLAGE AND MOP UP ANY RESISTANCE THERE. MAKE SURE THERE ARE NO SURPRISES.
WHERE ARE YOU GOING?

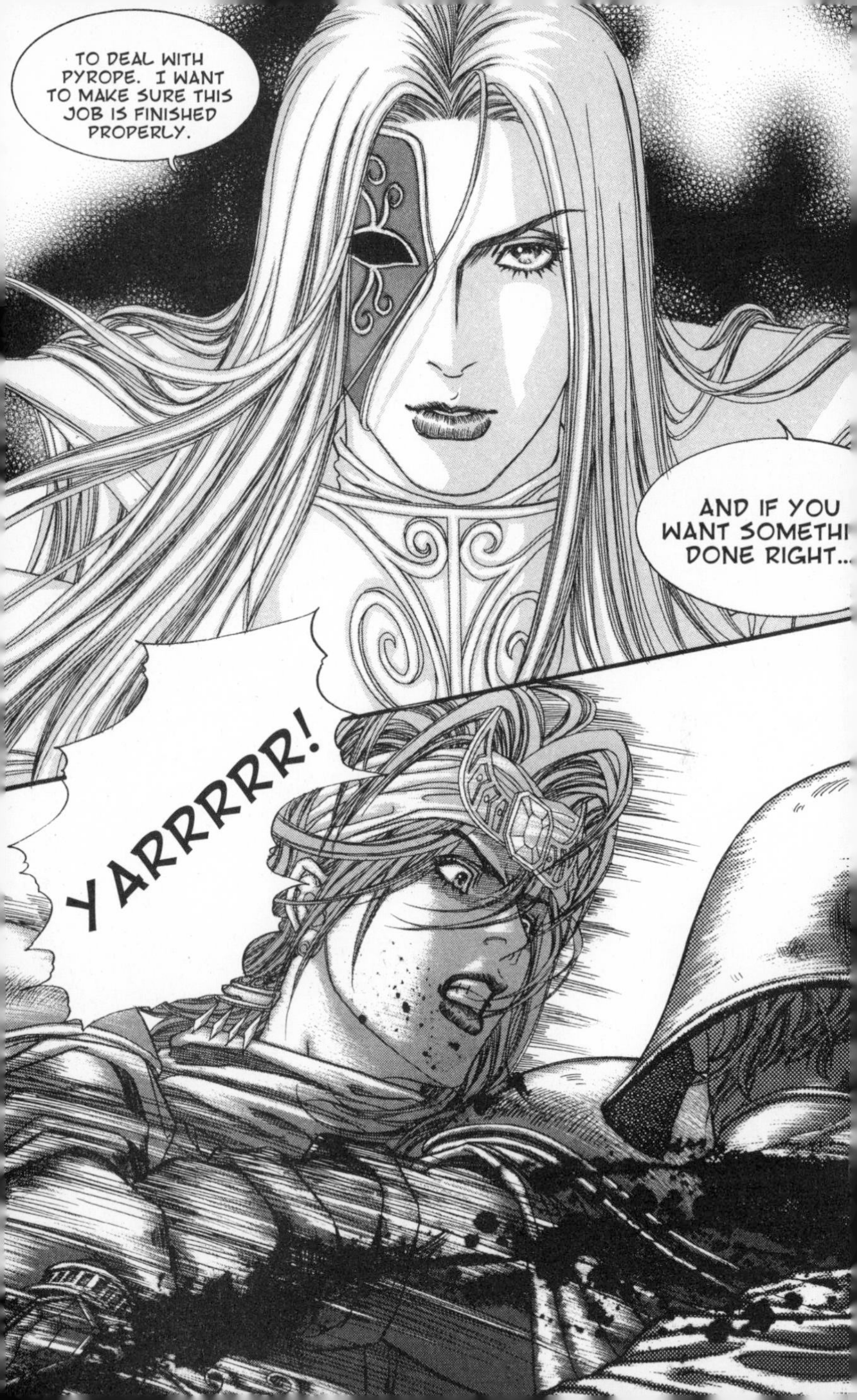

TO DEAL WITH PYROPE. I WANT TO MAKE SURE THIS JOB IS FINISHED PROPERLY.
AND IF YOU WANT SOMETHI DONE RIGHT...
YARRRRR!

Pyrope & Silica

The springs of love bubble and flow,
    In Pyrope's withered heart,
    Bringing life to the desert.

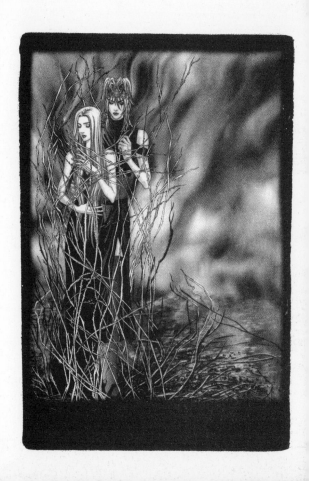

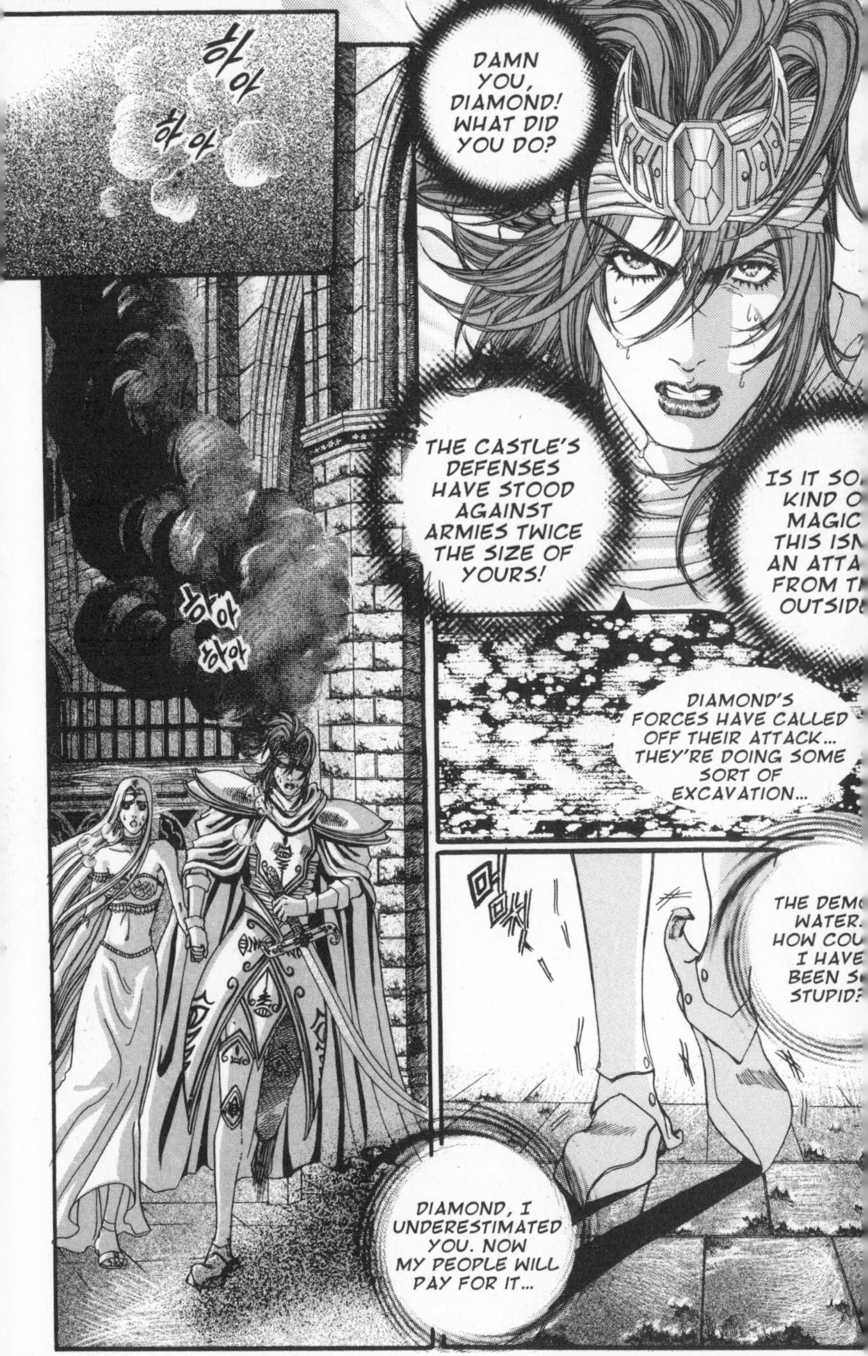
하아
하아
DAMN YOU, DIAMOND! WHAT DID YOU DO?
THE CASTLE'S DEFENSES HAVE STOOD AGAINST ARMIES TWICE THE SIZE OF YOURS!
IS IT SO KIND O MAGIC THIS ISN AN ATTA FROM T OUTSID
하아
하아
DIAMOND'S FORCES HAVE CALLED OFF THEIR ATTACK... THEY'RE DOING SOME SORT OF EXCAVATION...
THE DEM WATER. HOW COU I HAVE BEEN S STUPID?
DIAMOND, I UNDERESTIMATED YOU. NOW MY PEOPLE WILL PAY FOR IT...

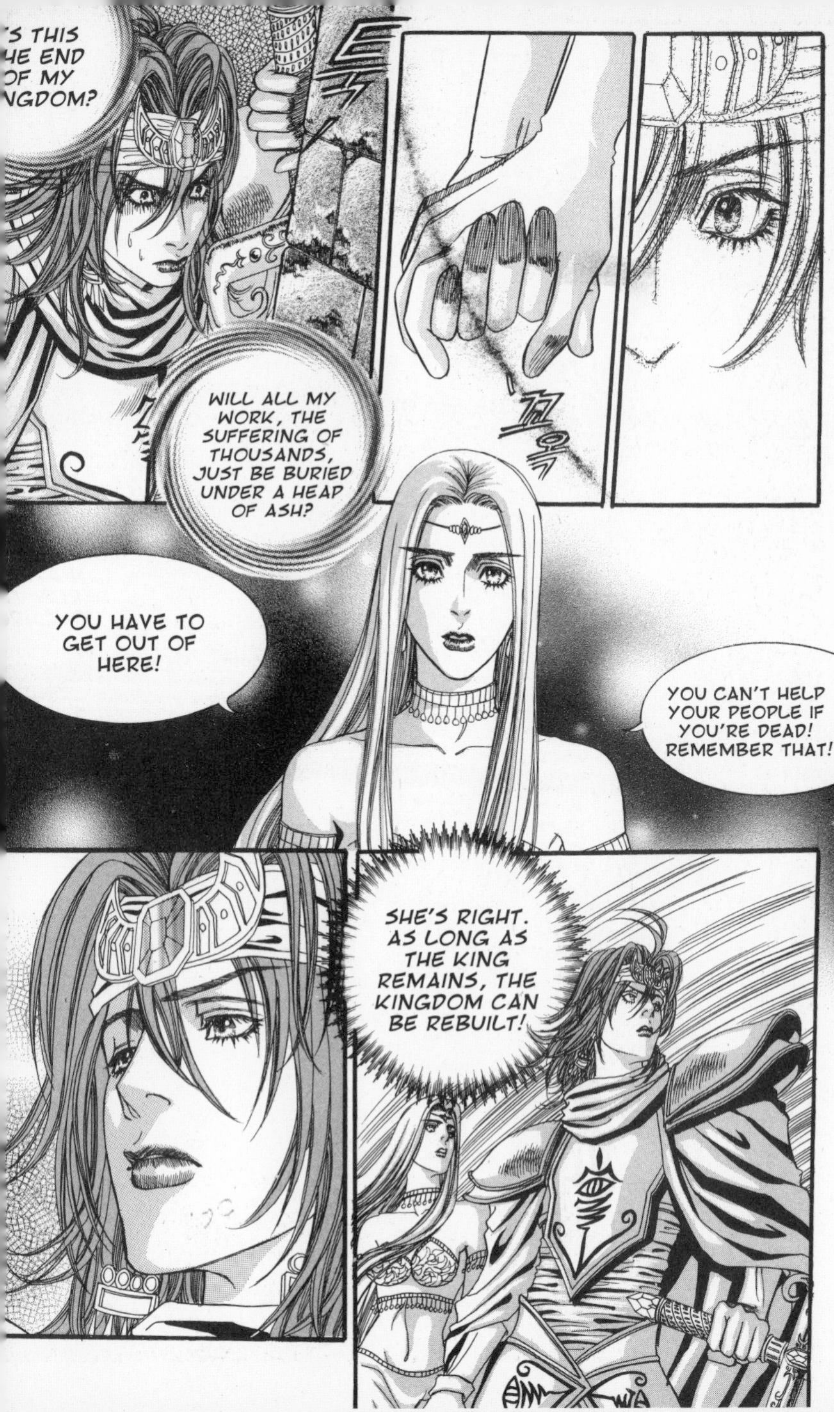
S THIS HE END OF MY NGDOM?
WILL ALL MY WORK, THE SUFFERING OF THOUSANDS, JUST BE BURIED UNDER A HEAP OF ASH?
YOU HAVE TO GET OUT OF HERE!
YOU CAN'T HELP YOUR PEOPLE IF YOU'RE DEAD! REMEMBER THAT!
SHE'S RIGHT. AS LONG AS THE KING REMAINS, THE KINGDOM CAN BE REBUILT!

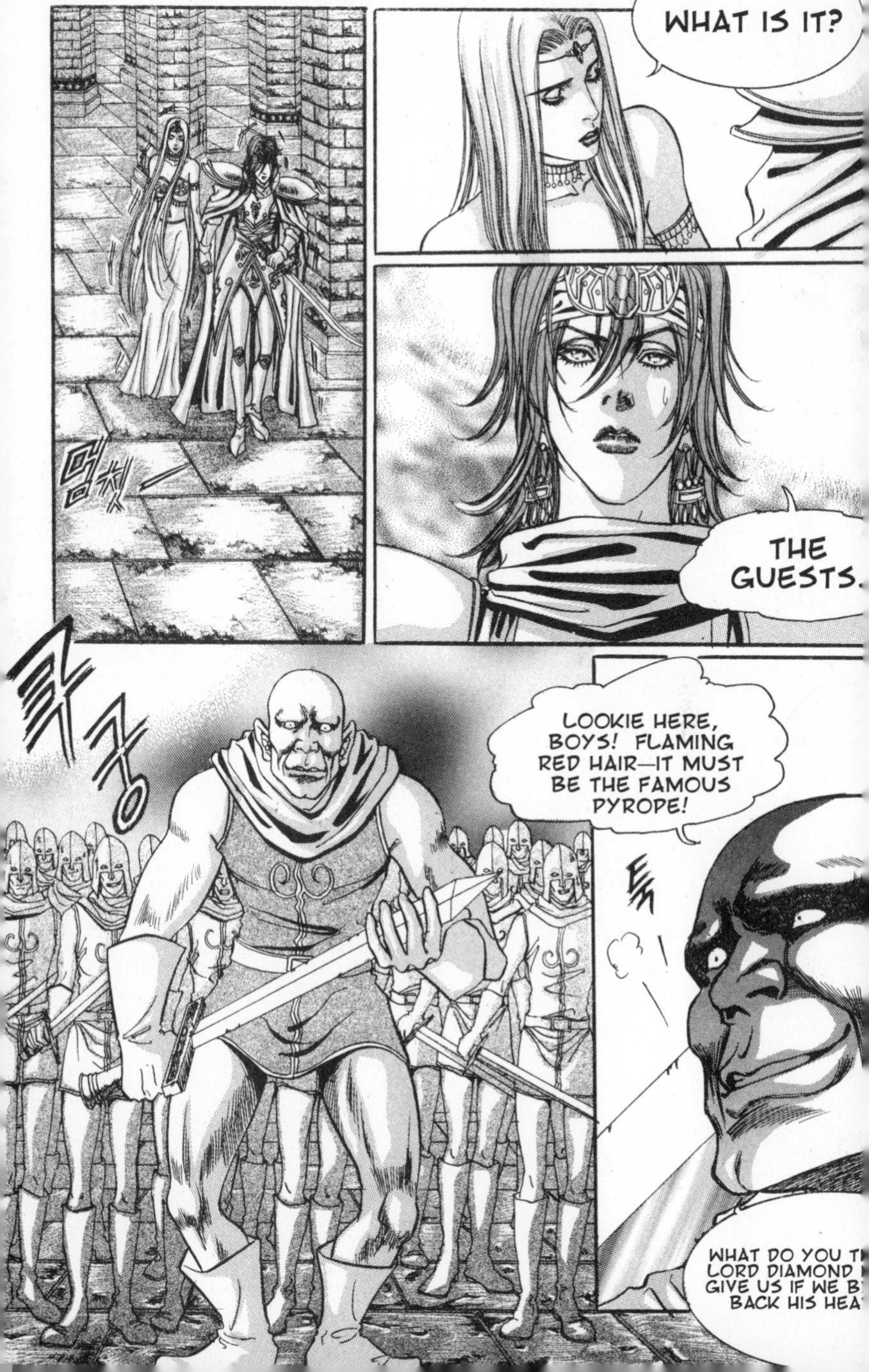

멈칫
WHAT IS IT?
THE GUESTS.
LOOKIE HERE, BOYS! FLAMING RED HAIR—IT MUST BE THE FAMOUS PYROPE!
WHAT DO YOU T LORD DIAMOND GIVE US IF WE B BACK HIS HEA

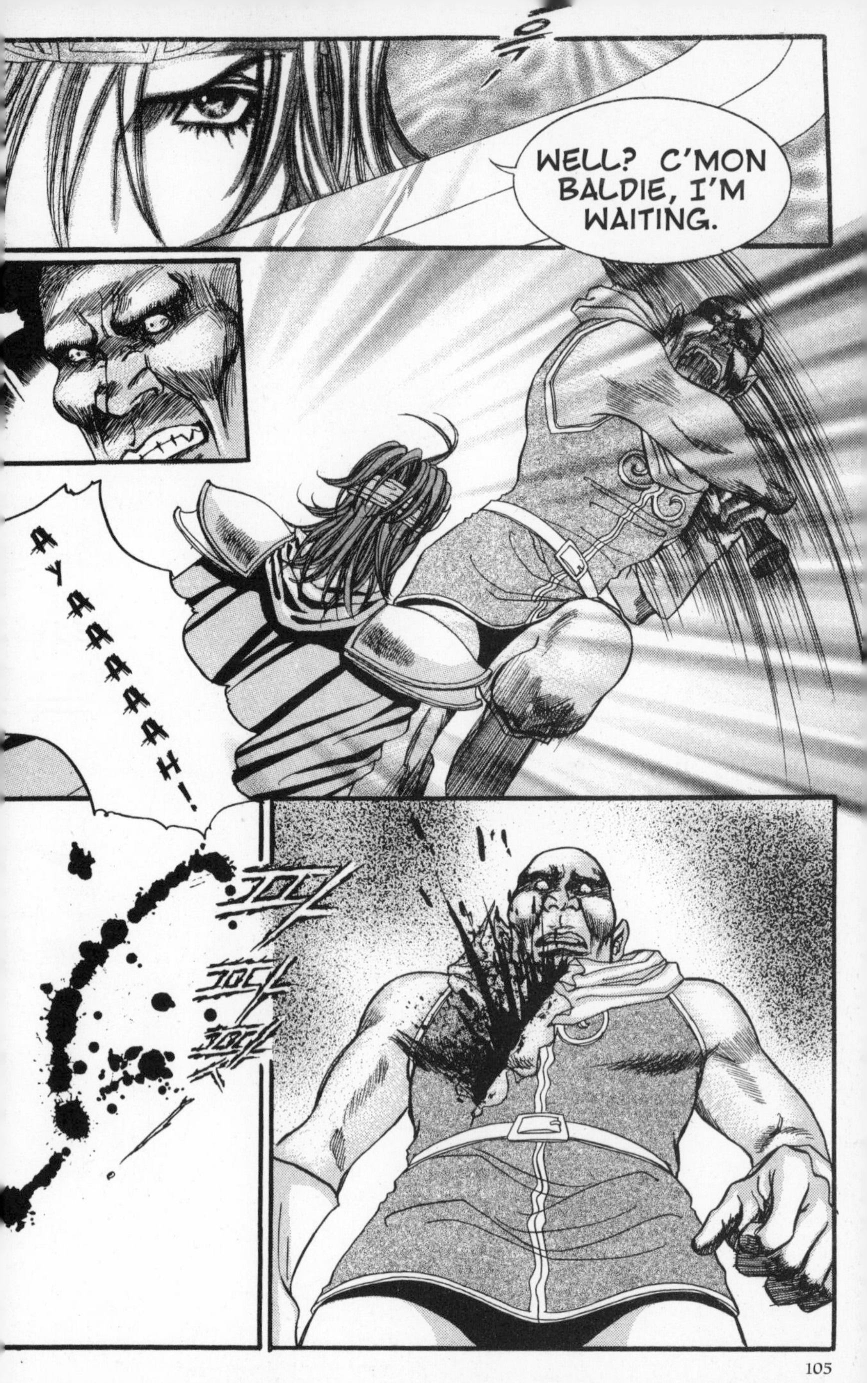
WELL? C'MON BALDIE, I'M WAITING.
AYAAAAAH!

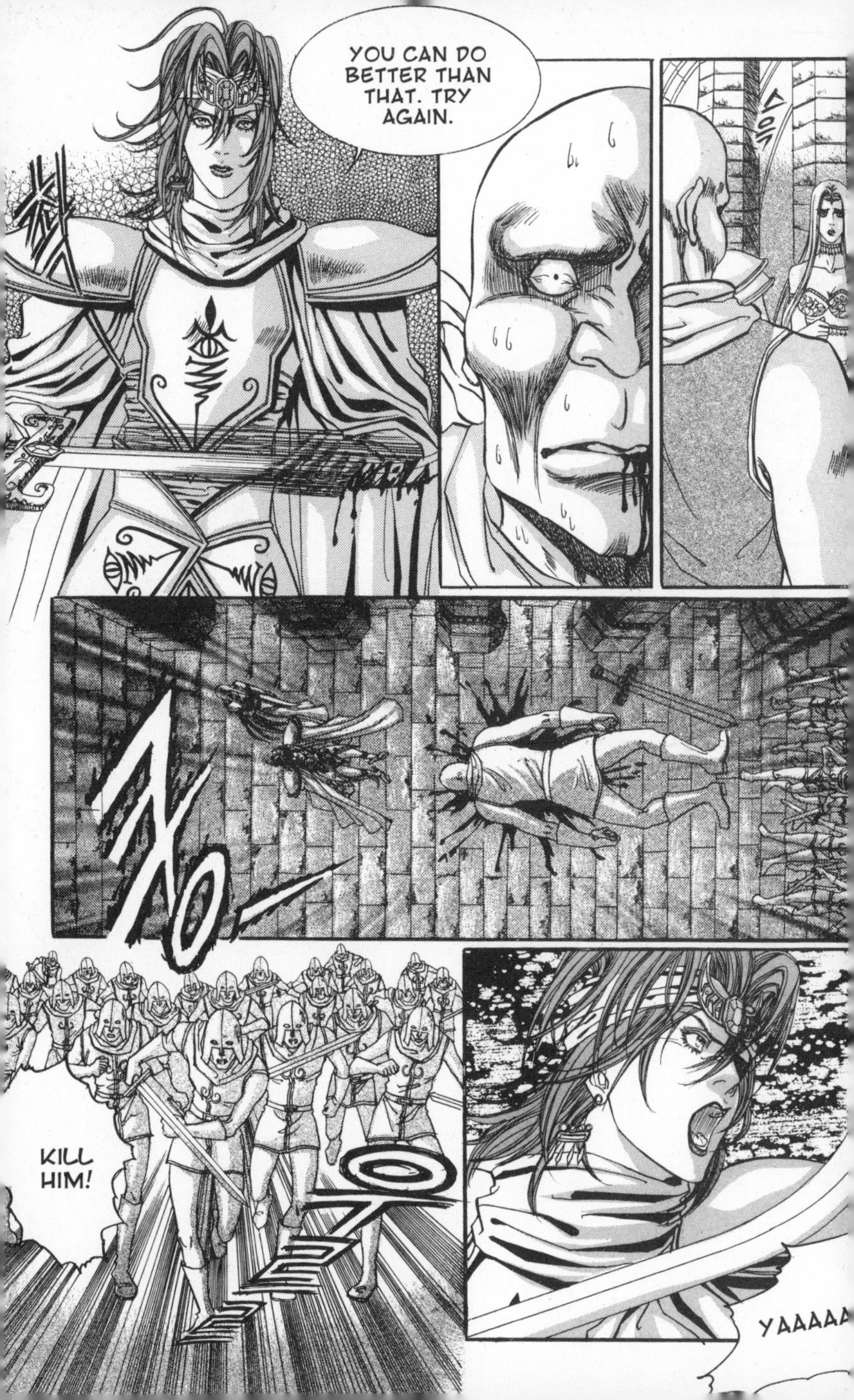
YOU CAN DO BETTER THAN THAT. TRY AGAIN.
KILL HIM!
YAAAAA

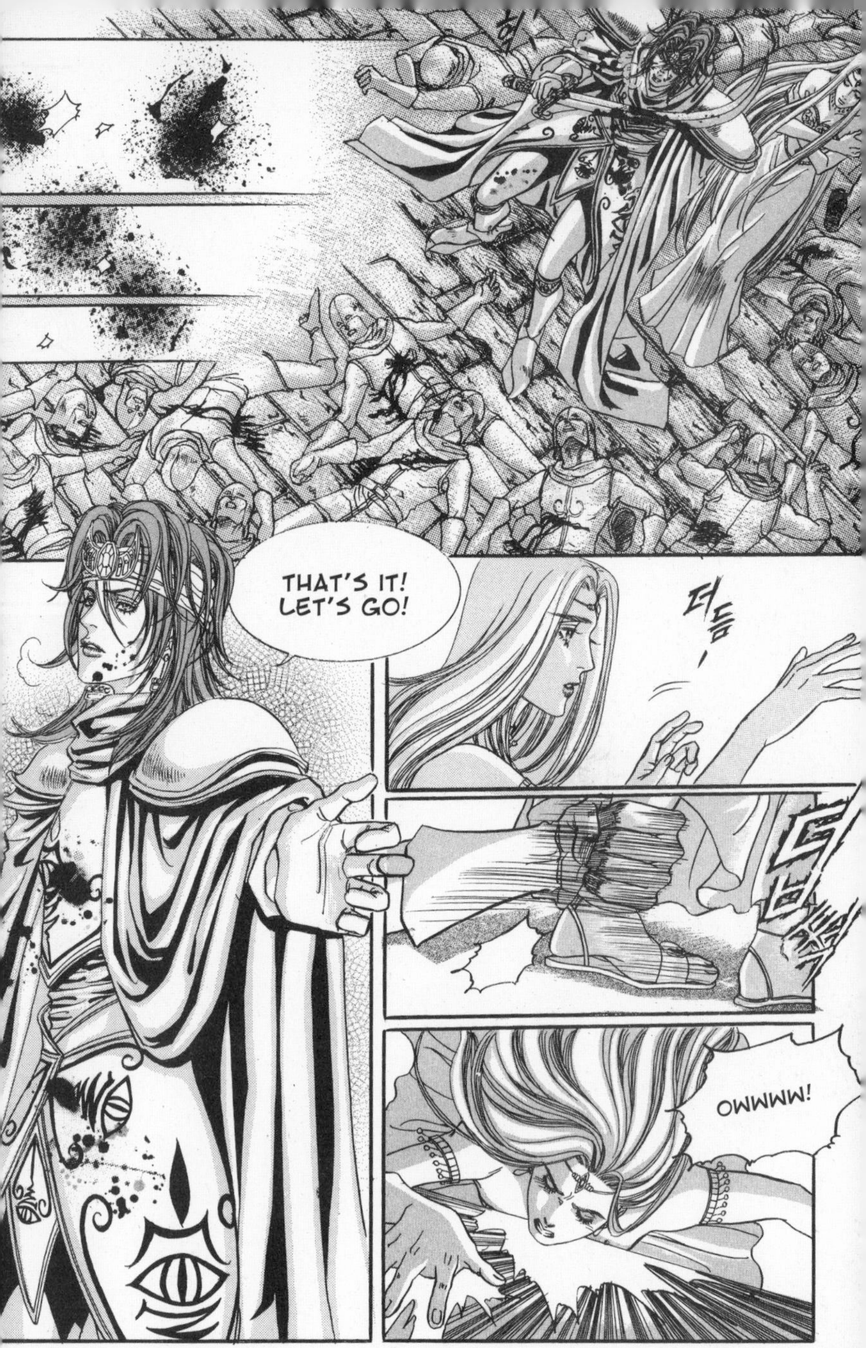
THAT'S IT! LET'S GO!
더듬
OWWWW!

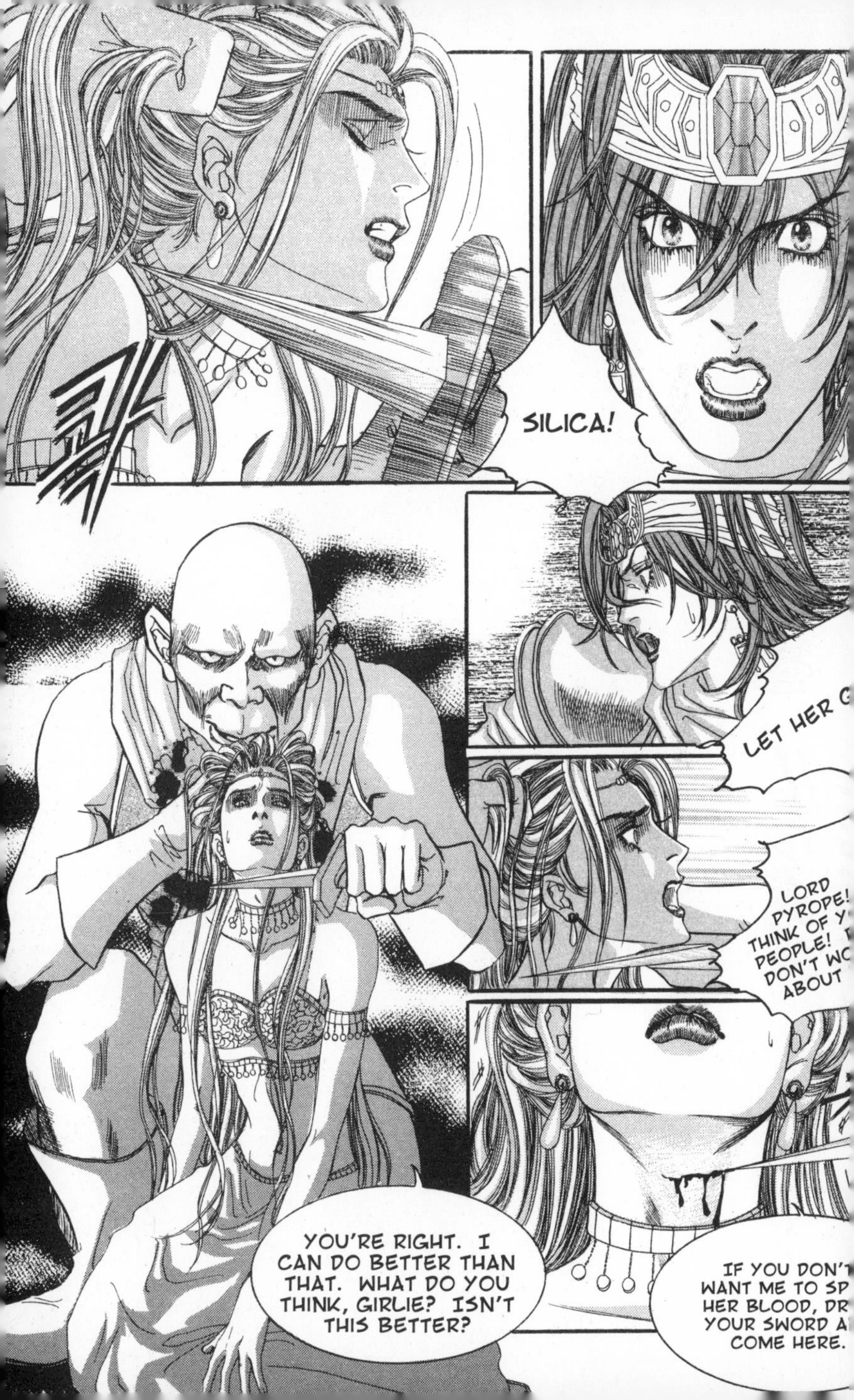
SILICA!
YOU'RE RIGHT. I CAN DO BETTER THAN THAT. WHAT DO YOU THINK, GIRLIE? ISN'T THIS BETTER?
LET HER G
LORD PYROPE! THINK OF Y PEOPLE! DON'T WO ABOUT
IF YOU DON'T WANT ME TO SP HER BLOOD, DR YOUR SWORD A COME HERE.

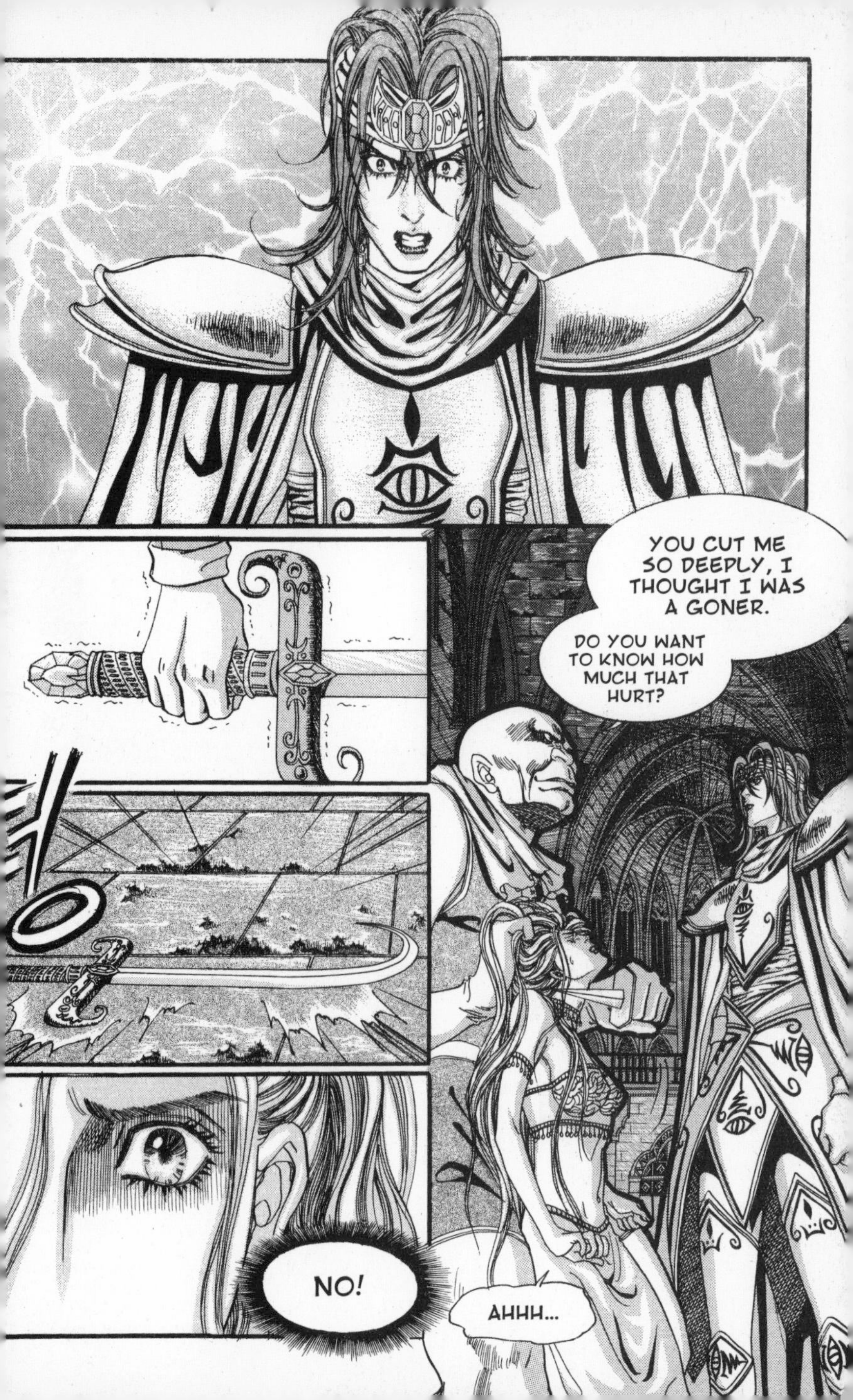
YOU CUT ME SO DEEPLY, I THOUGHT I WAS A GONER.
DO YOU WANT TO KNOW HOW MUCH THAT HURT?
NO!
AHHH...

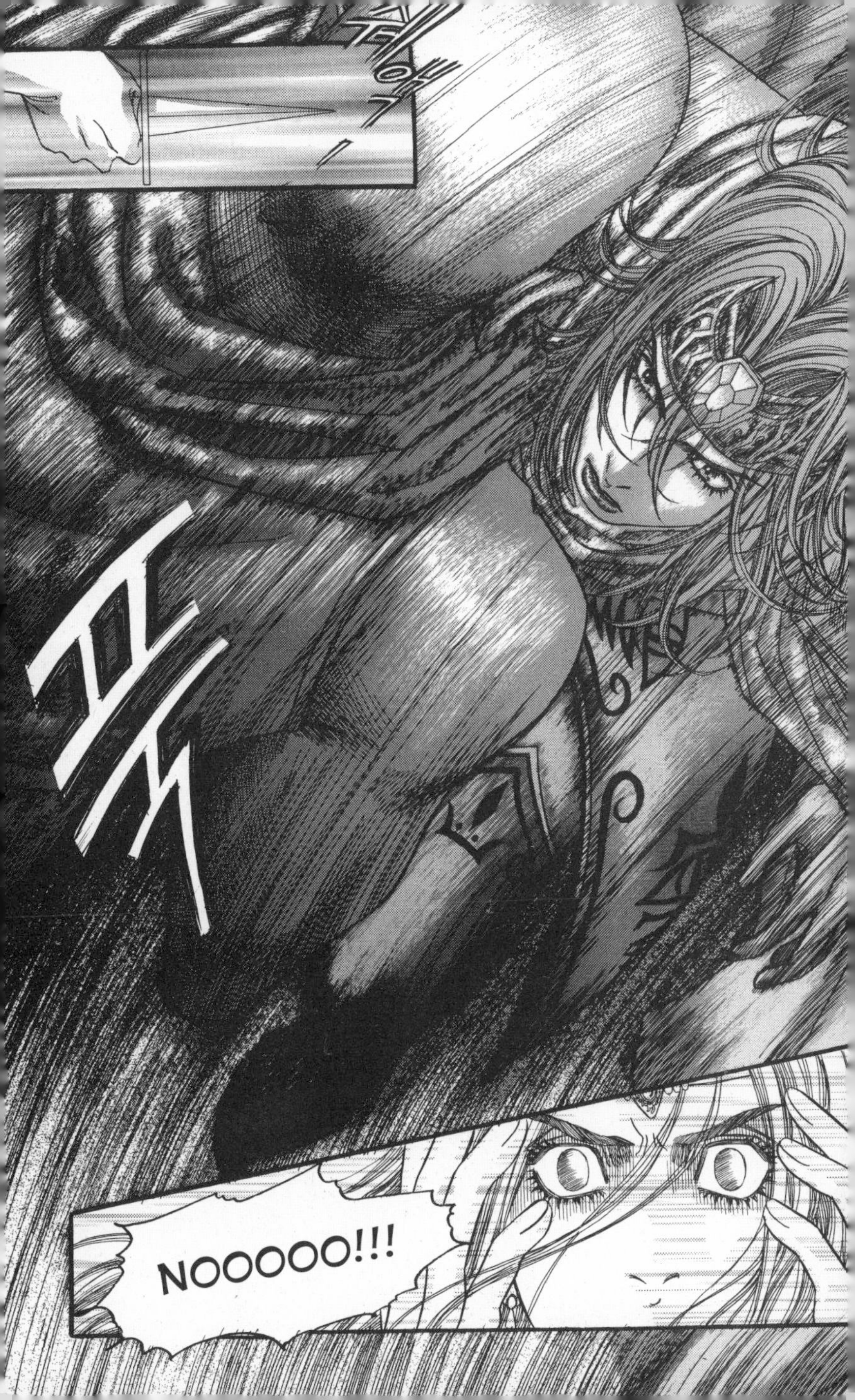
NOOOOO!!!

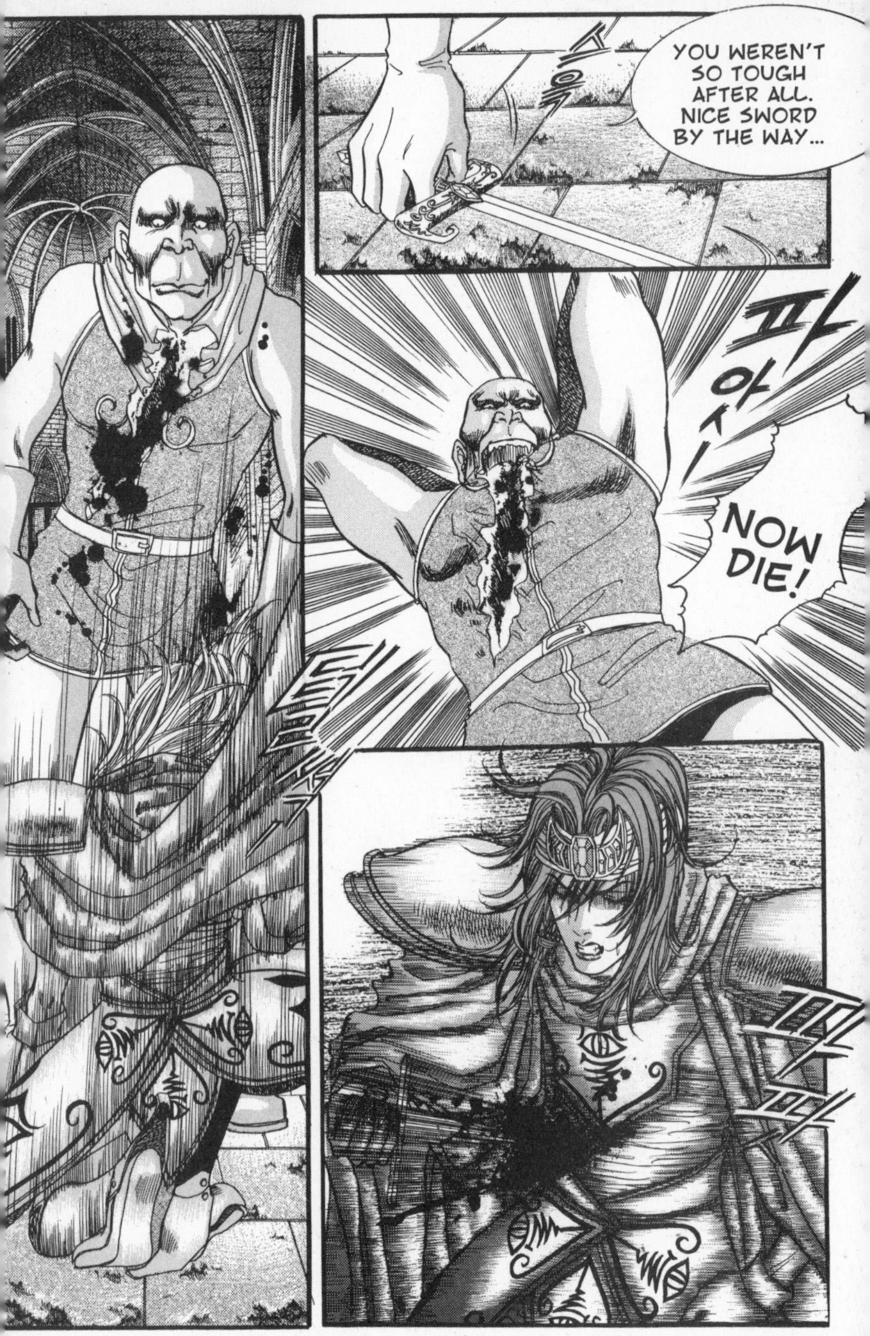
YOU WEREN'T SO TOUGH AFTER ALL. NICE SWORD BY THE WAY...
NOW DIE!

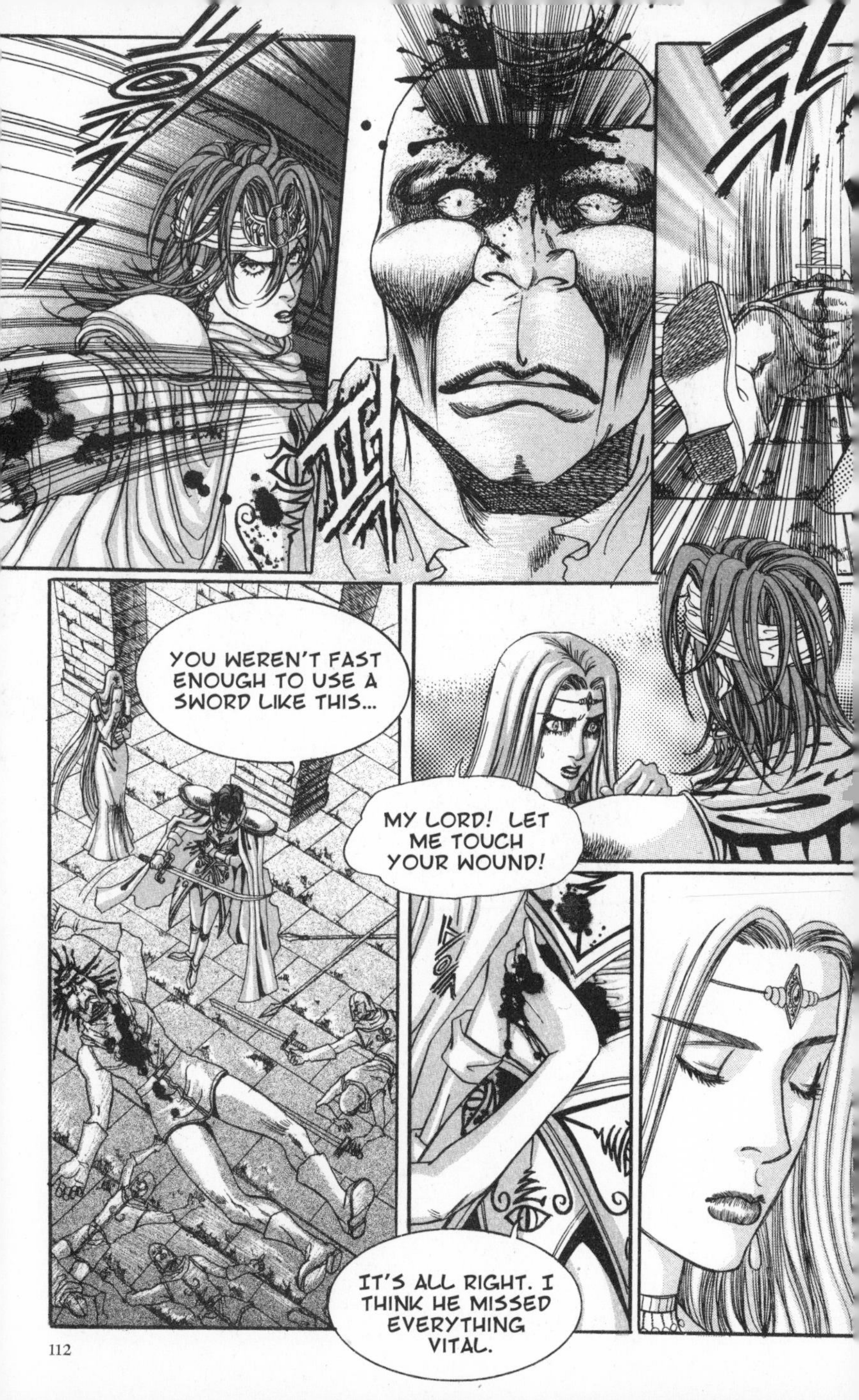
YOU WEREN'T FAST ENOUGH TO USE A SWORD LIKE THIS...
MY LORD! LET ME TOUCH YOUR WOUND!
IT'S ALL RIGHT. I THINK HE MISSED EVERYTHING VITAL.

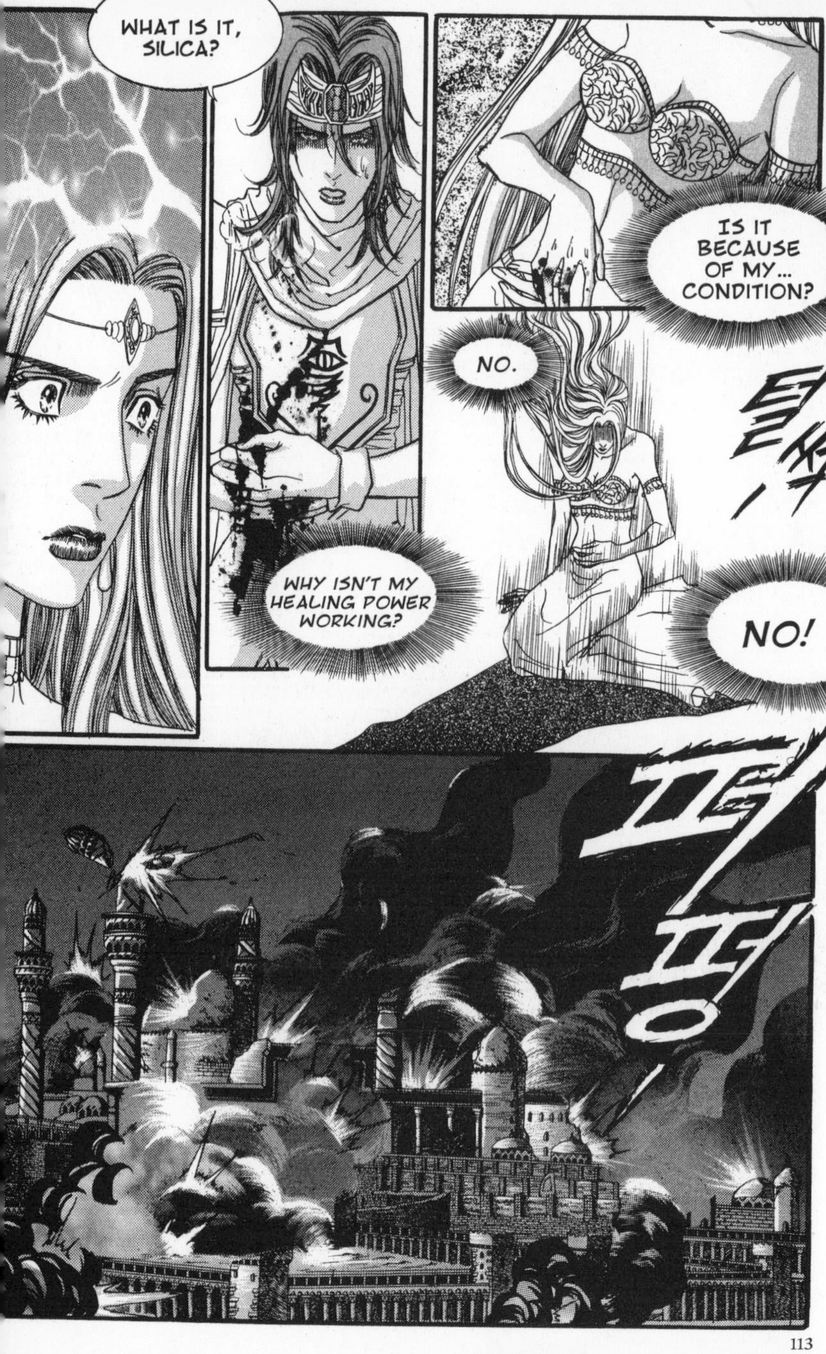
WHAT IS IT, SILICA?
WHY ISN'T MY HEALING POWER WORKING?
IS IT BECAUSE OF MY... CONDITION?
NO.
NO!

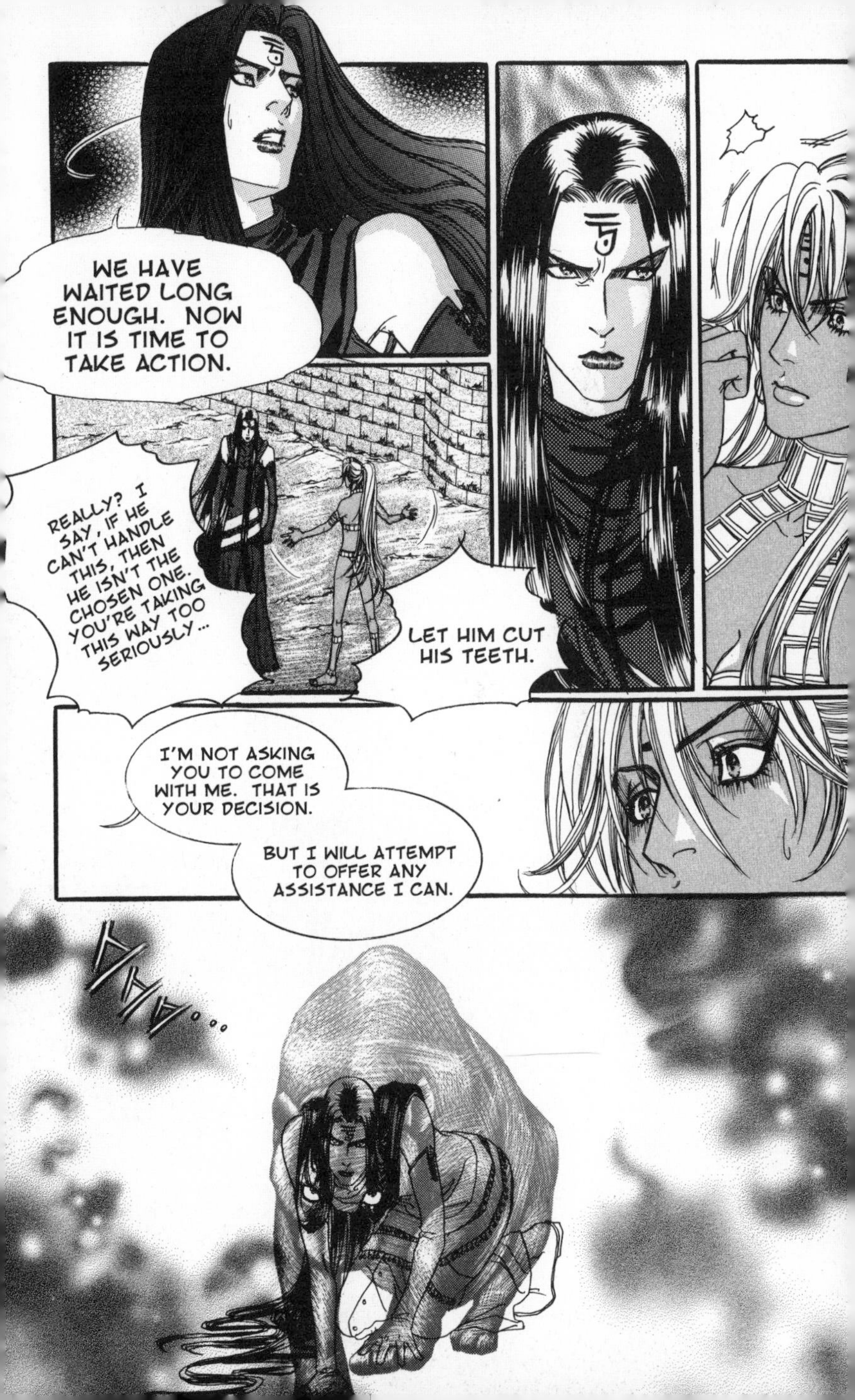
WE HAVE WAITED LONG ENOUGH. NOW IT IS TIME TO TAKE ACTION.
REALLY? I SAY, IF HE CAN'T HANDLE THIS, THEN HE ISN'T THE CHOSEN ONE. YOU'RE TAKING THIS WAY TOO SERIOUSLY...
LET HIM CUT HIS TEETH.
I'M NOT ASKING YOU TO COME WITH ME. THAT IS YOUR DECISION.
BUT I WILL ATTEMPT TO OFFER ANY ASSISTANCE I CAN.

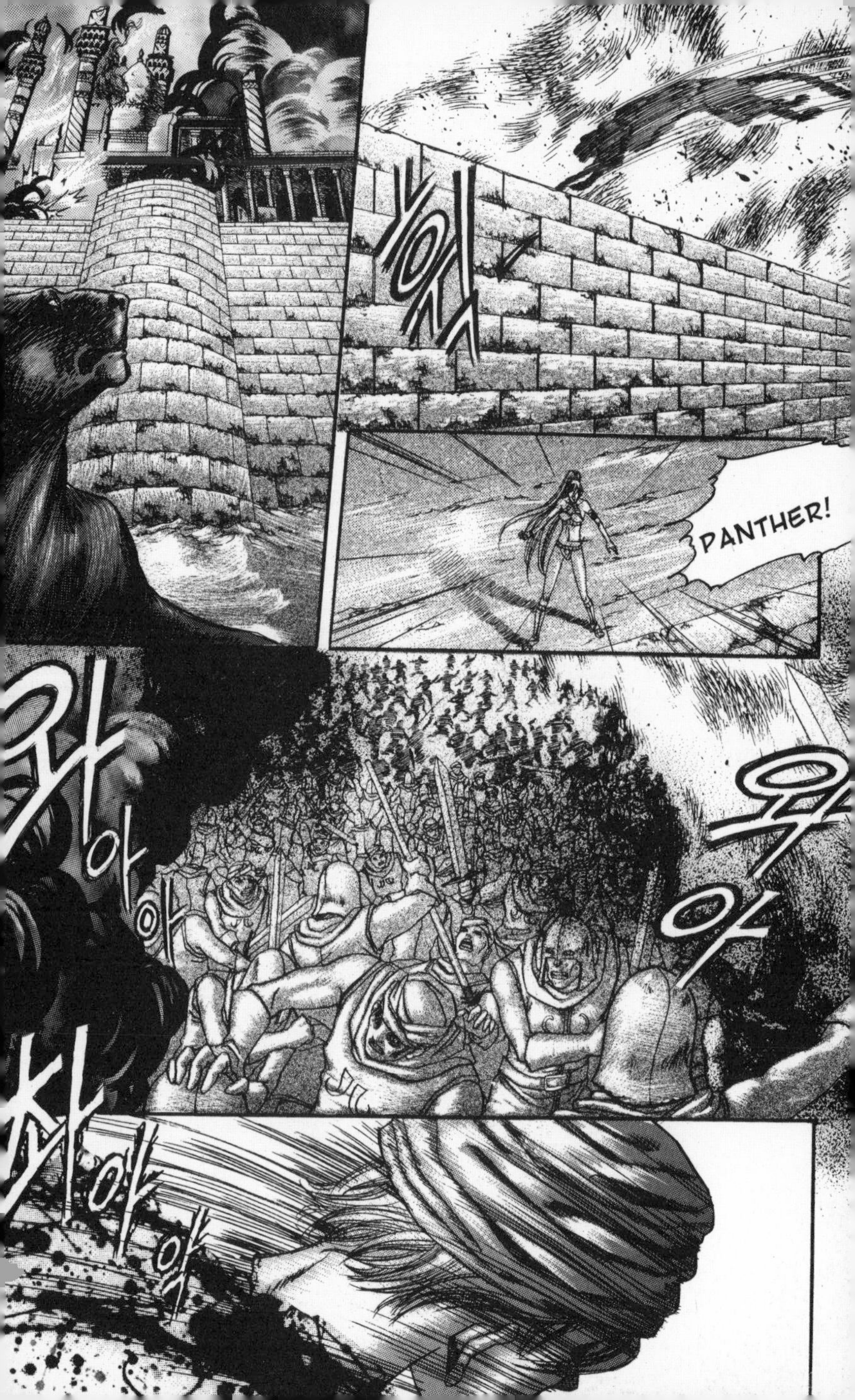
PANTHER!
와아아
와아

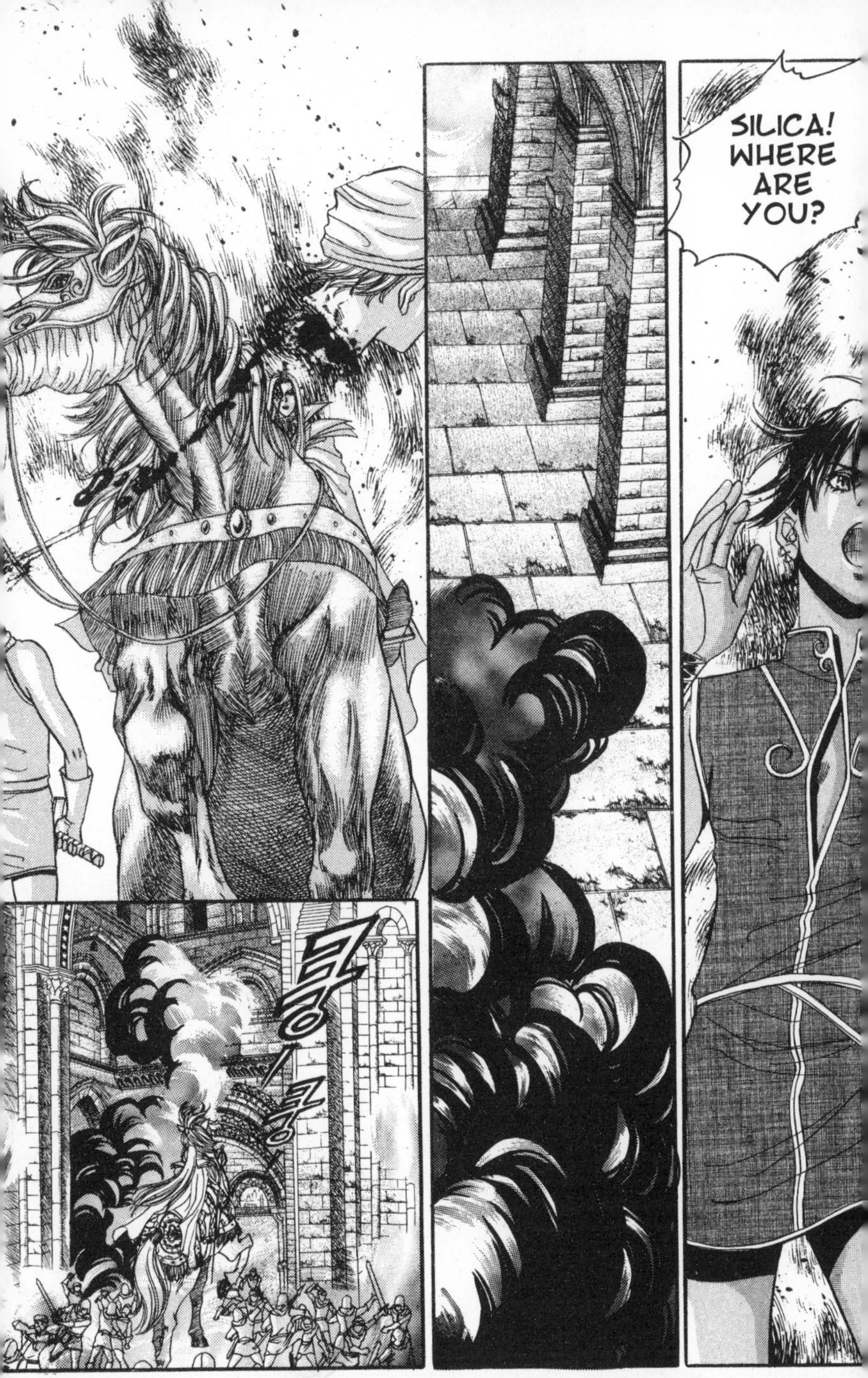
SILICA! WHERE ARE YOU?

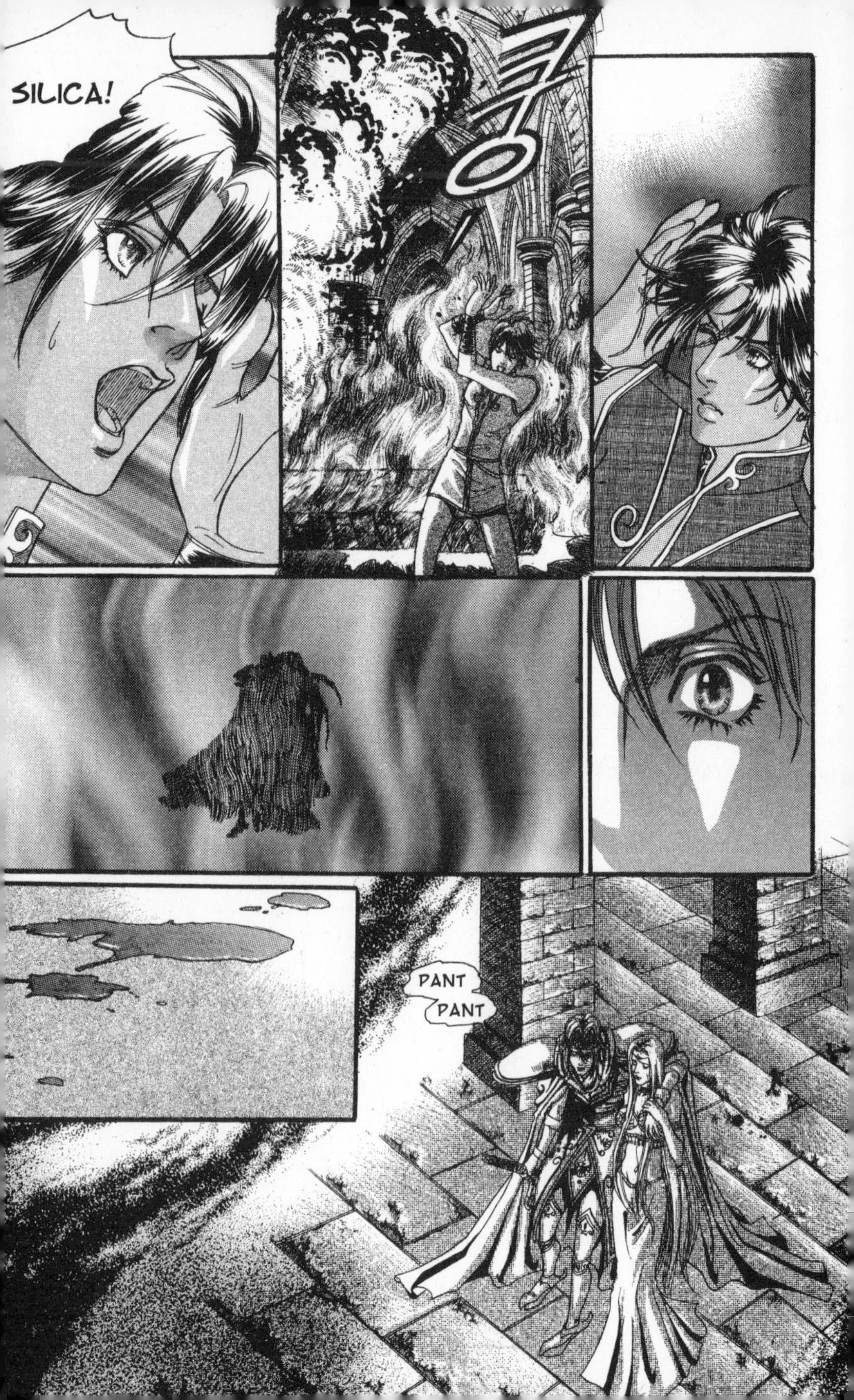
SILICA!
PANT
PANT

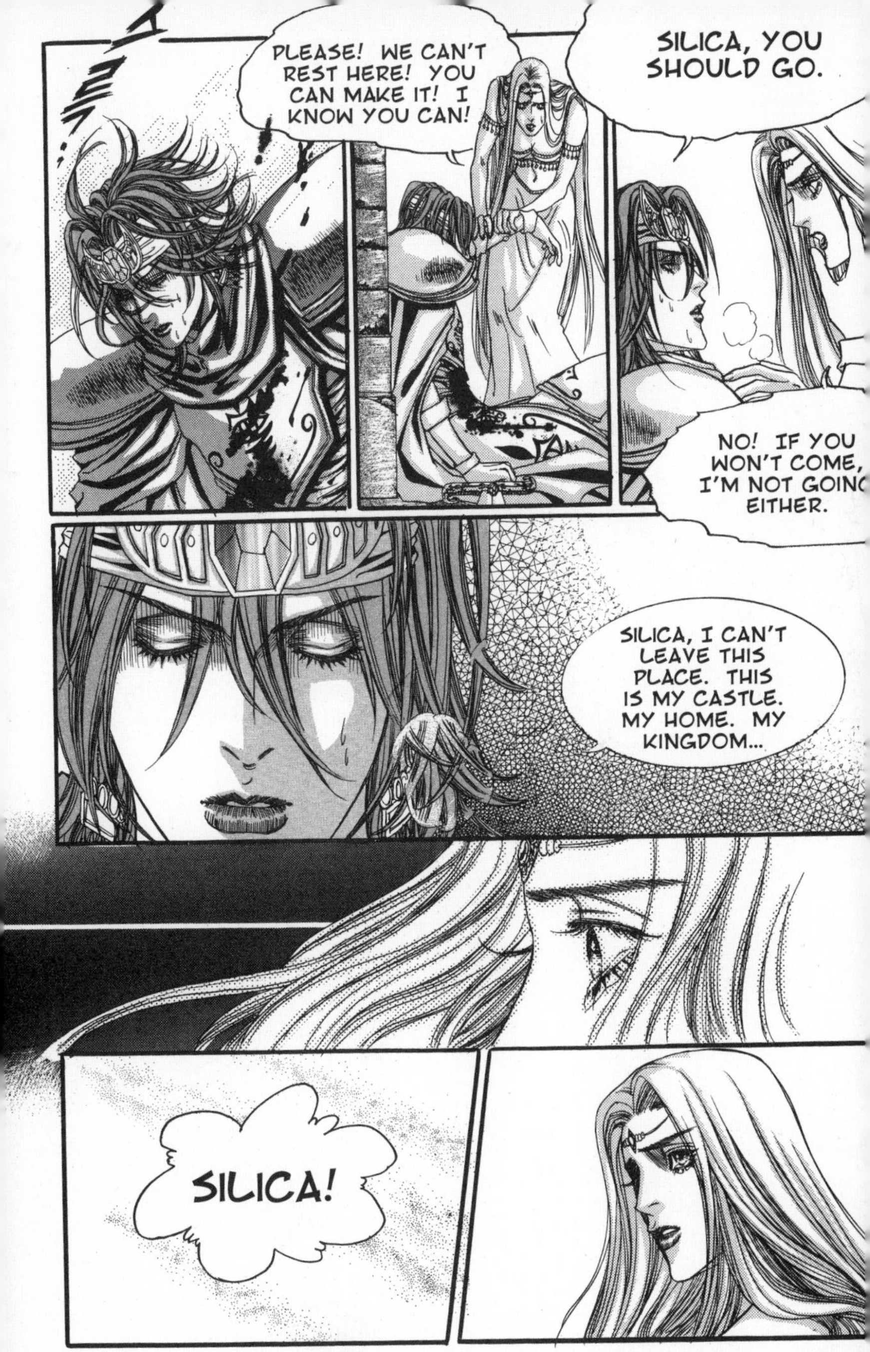
PLEASE! WE CAN'T REST HERE! YOU CAN MAKE IT! I KNOW YOU CAN!
SILICA, YOU SHOULD GO.
NO! IF YOU WON'T COME, I'M NOT GOING EITHER.
SILICA, I CAN'T LEAVE THIS PLACE. THIS IS MY CASTLE. MY HOME. MY KINGDOM...
SILICA!

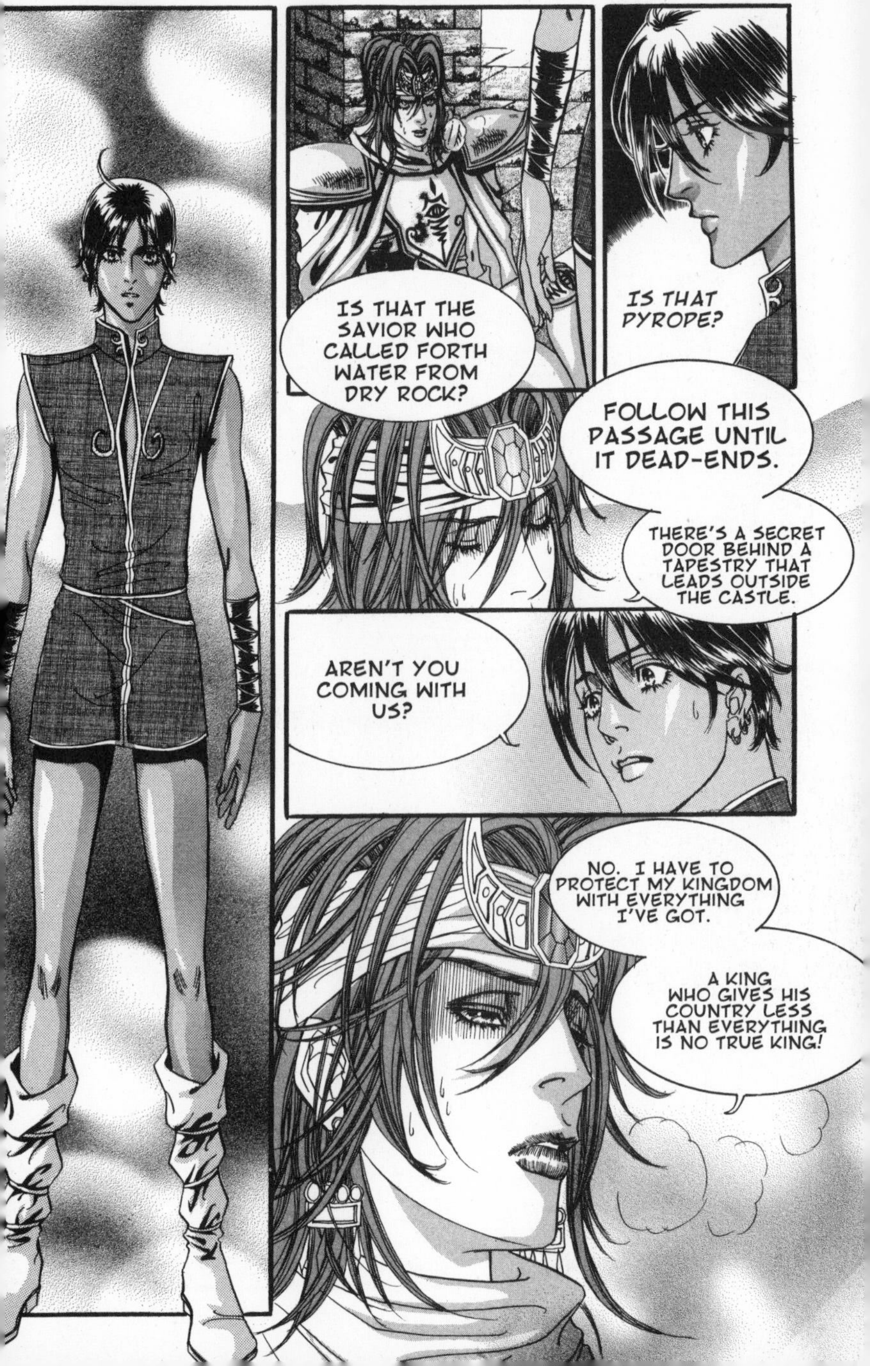
IS THAT THE SAVIOR WHO CALLED FORTH WATER FROM DRY ROCK?
IS THAT PYROPE?
FOLLOW THIS PASSAGE UNTIL IT DEAD-ENDS.
THERE'S A SECRET DOOR BEHIND A TAPESTRY THAT LEADS OUTSIDE THE CASTLE.
AREN'T YOU COMING WITH US?
NO. I HAVE TO PROTECT MY KINGDOM WITH EVERYTHING I'VE GOT.
A KING WHO GIVES HIS COUNTRY LESS THAN EVERYTHING IS NO TRUE KING!

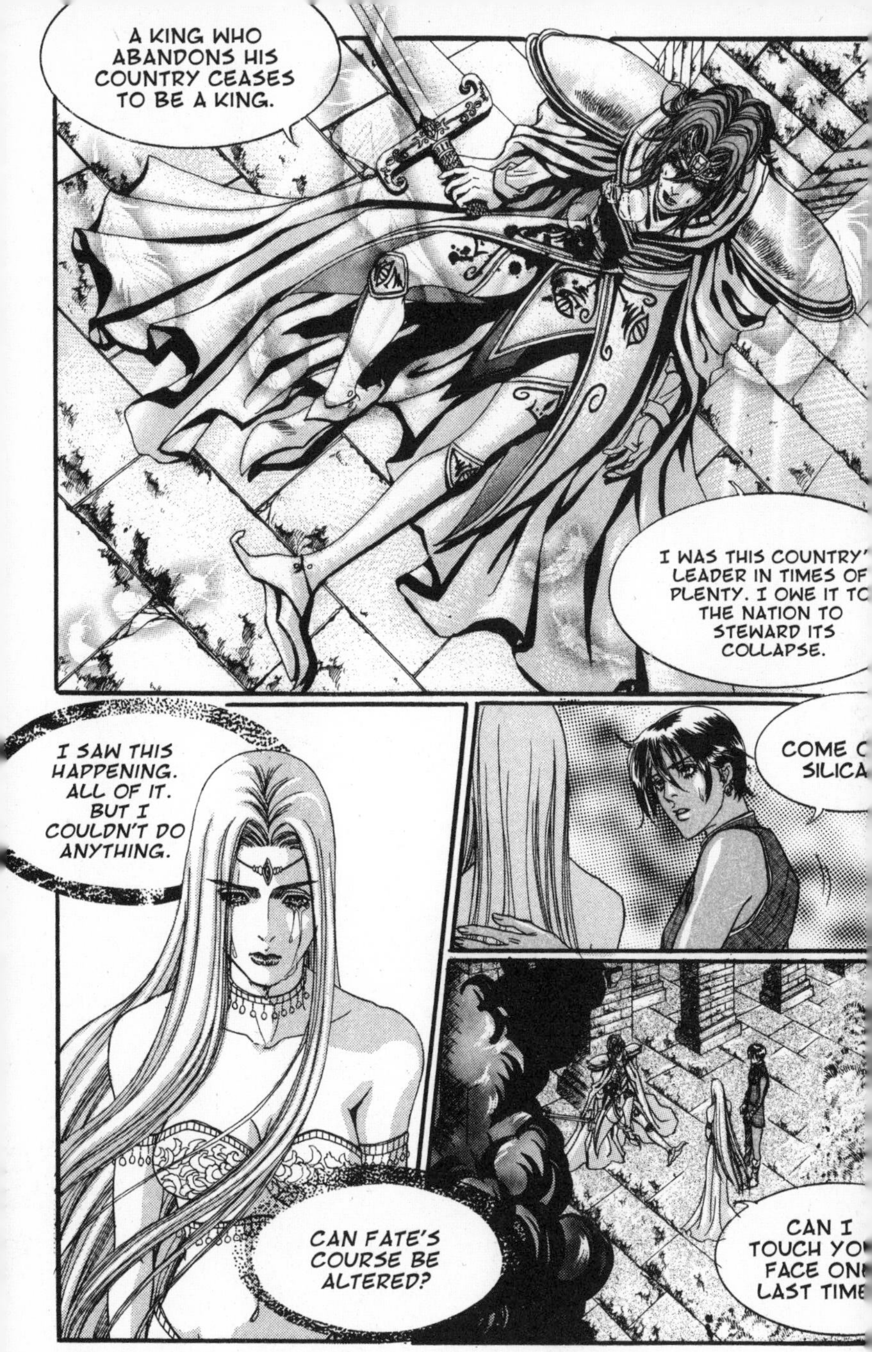
A KING WHO ABANDONS HIS COUNTRY CEASES TO BE A KING.
I WAS THIS COUNTRY' LEADER IN TIMES OF PLENTY. I OWE IT TO THE NATION TO STEWARD ITS COLLAPSE.
I SAW THIS HAPPENING. ALL OF IT. BUT I COULDN'T DO ANYTHING.
CAN FATE'S COURSE BE ALTERED?
COME C SILICA
CAN I TOUCH YO FACE ON LAST TIME

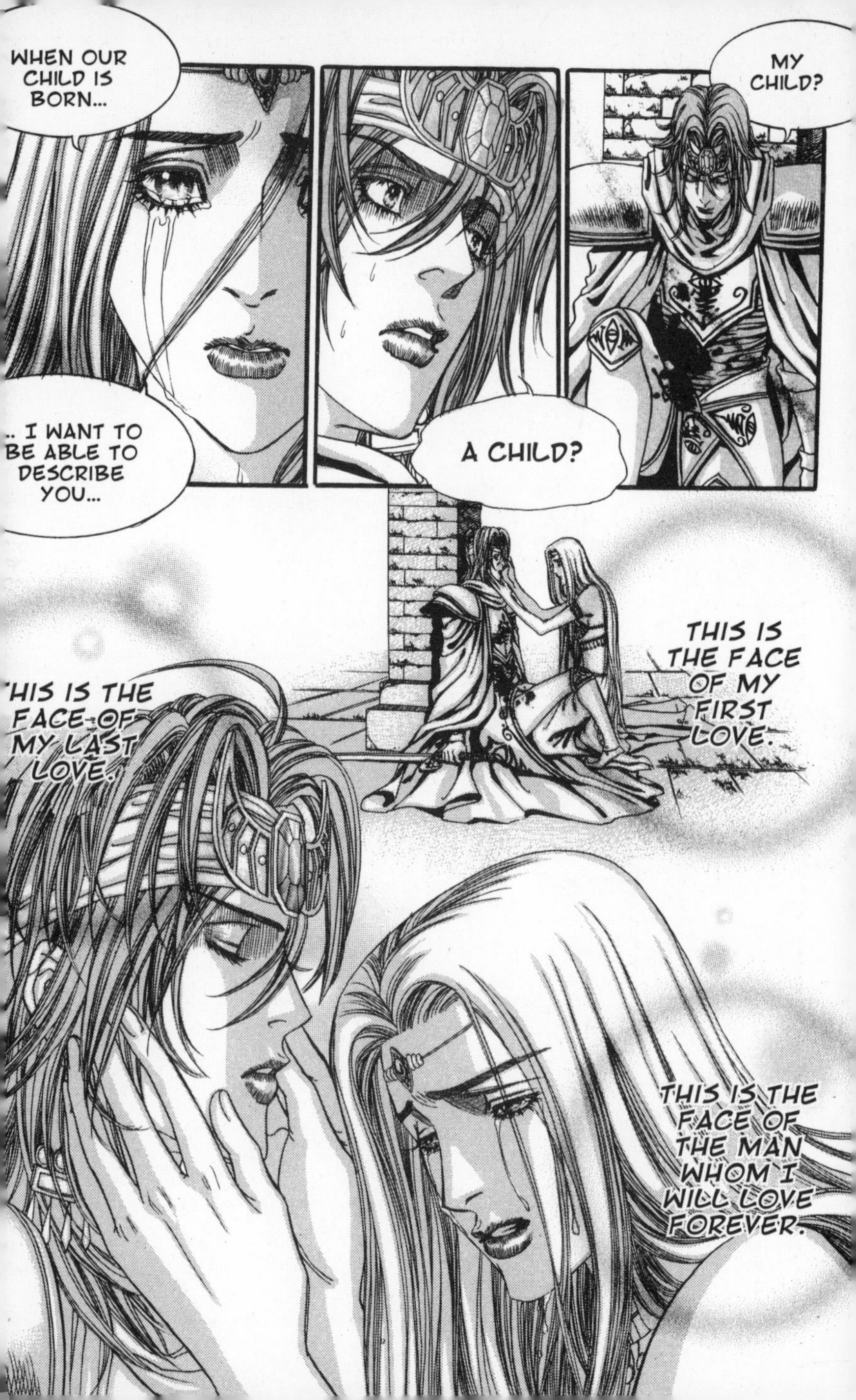
WHEN OUR CHILD IS BORN...
.. I WANT TO BE ABLE TO DESCRIBE YOU...
A CHILD?
MY CHILD?
THIS IS THE FACE OF MY FIRST LOVE.
THIS IS THE FACE OF MY LAST LOVE.
THIS IS THE FACE OF THE MAN WHOM I WILL LOVE FOREVER.

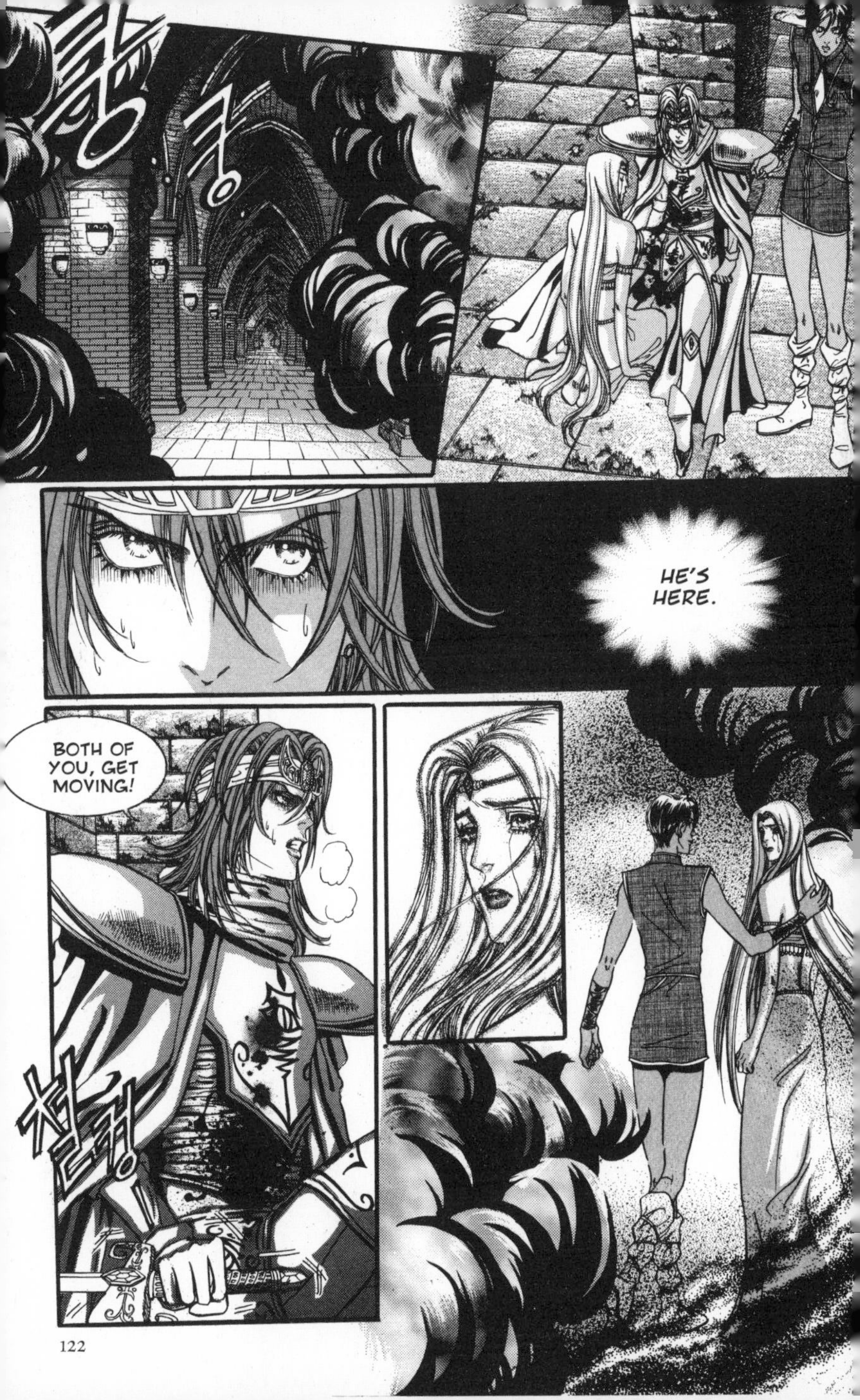
HE'S HERE.
BOTH OF YOU, GET MOVING!

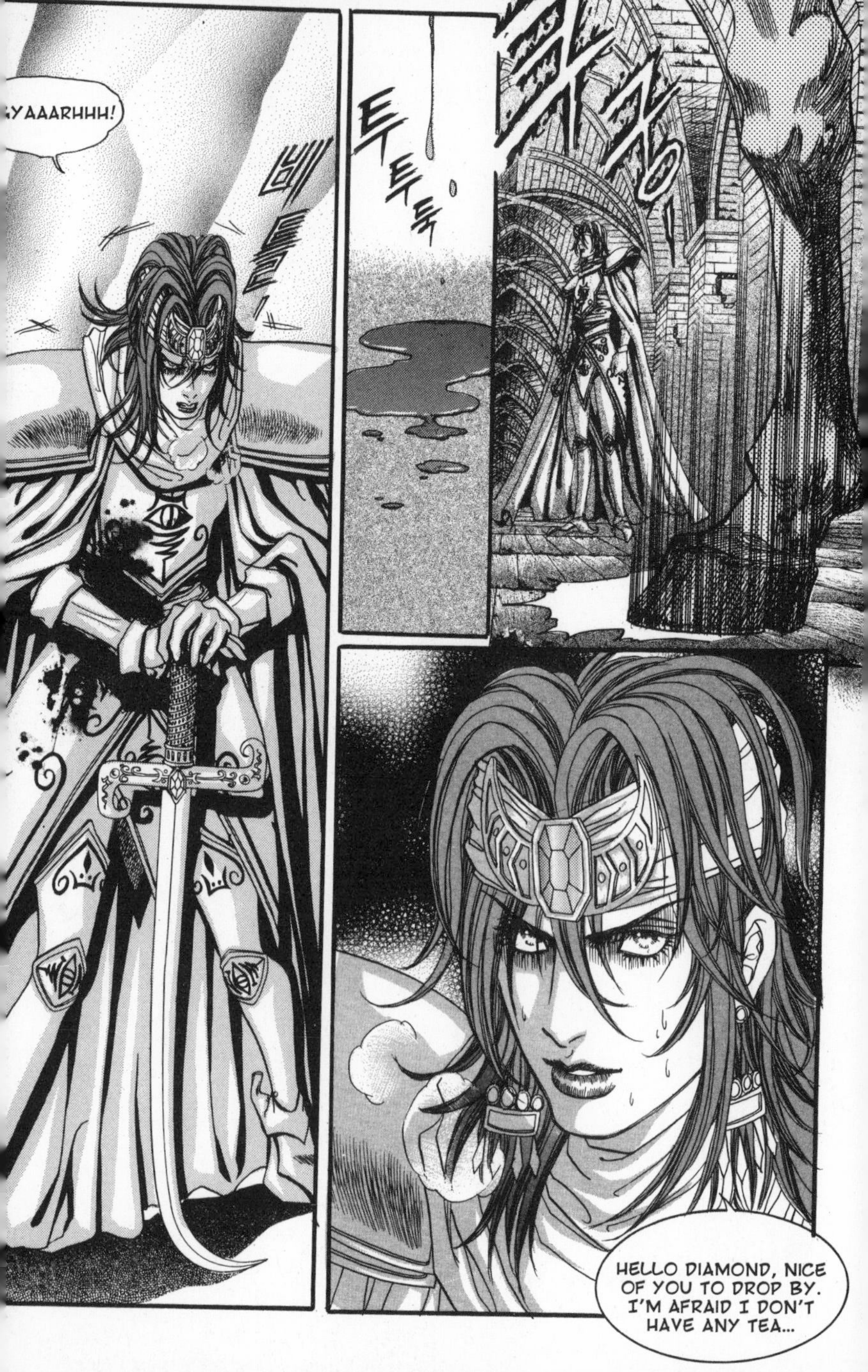
YAAARHHH!
비틀!
투투둑
HELLO DIAMOND, NICE OF YOU TO DROP BY. I'M AFRAID I DON'T HAVE ANY TEA...

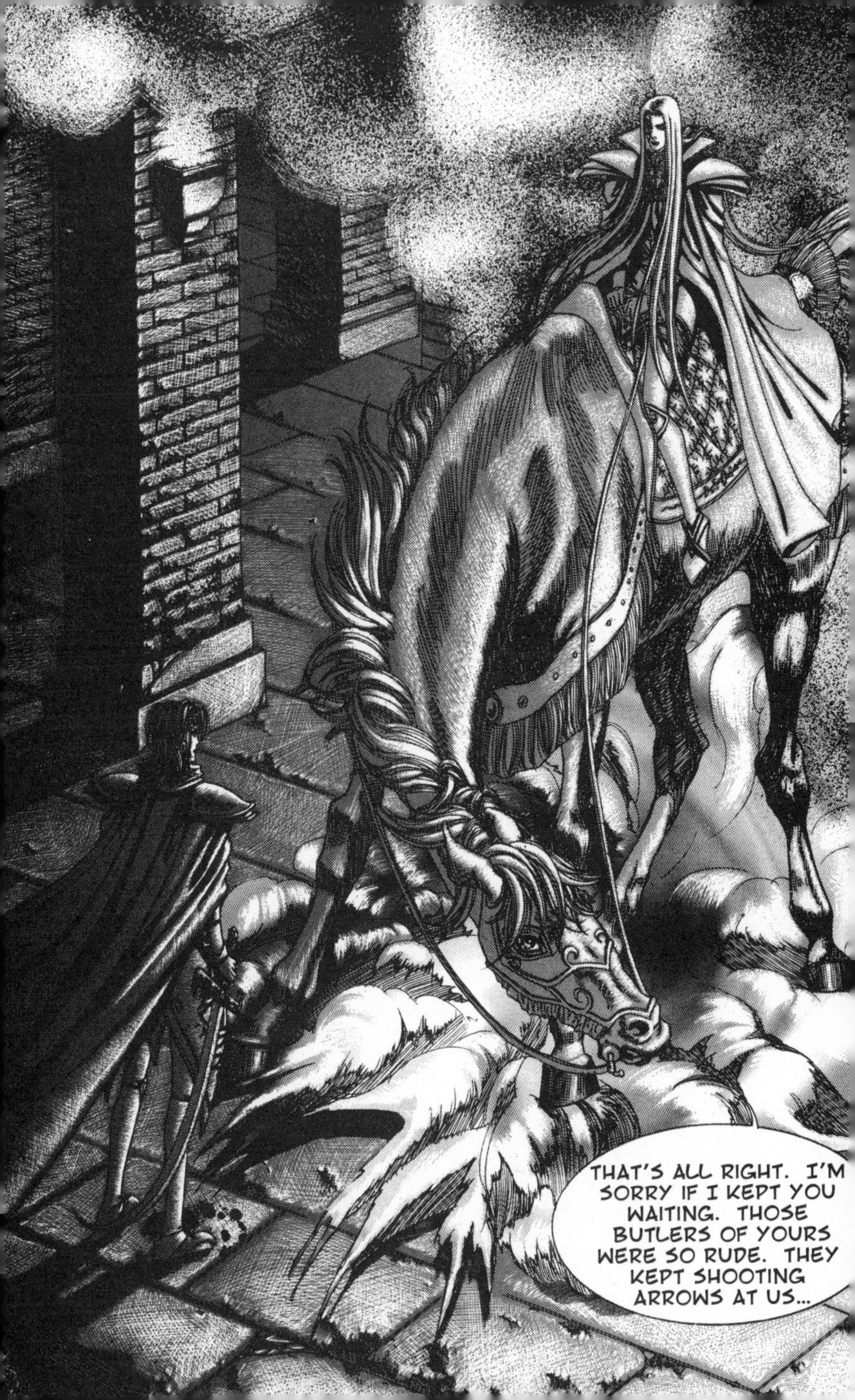
THAT'S ALL RIGHT. I'M SORRY IF I KEPT YOU WAITING. THOSE BUTLERS OF YOURS WERE SO RUDE. THEY KEPT SHOOTING ARROWS AT US...

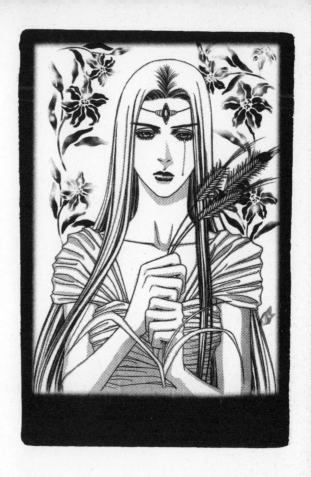

Silica
실리카

Whose heart is pure and clear,
But shatters with a careless touch.
Like glass that was
Born from the dry sands.

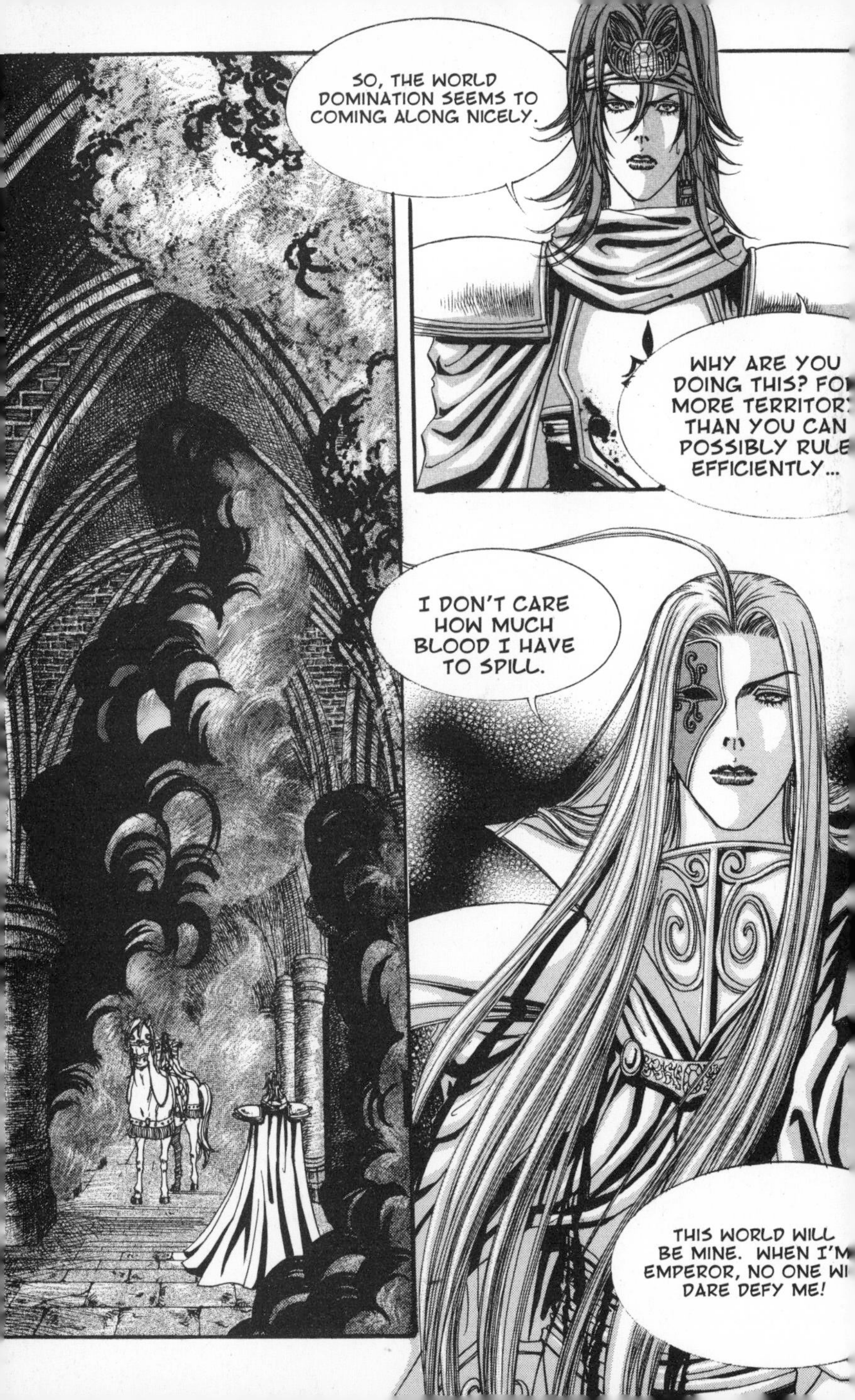
SO, THE WORLD DOMINATION SEEMS TO COMING ALONG NICELY.
WHY ARE YOU DOING THIS? FO MORE TERRITOR THAN YOU CAN POSSIBLY RULE EFFICIENTLY...
I DON'T CARE HOW MUCH BLOOD I HAVE TO SPILL.
THIS WORLD WILL BE MINE. WHEN I'M EMPEROR, NO ONE WI DARE DEFY ME!

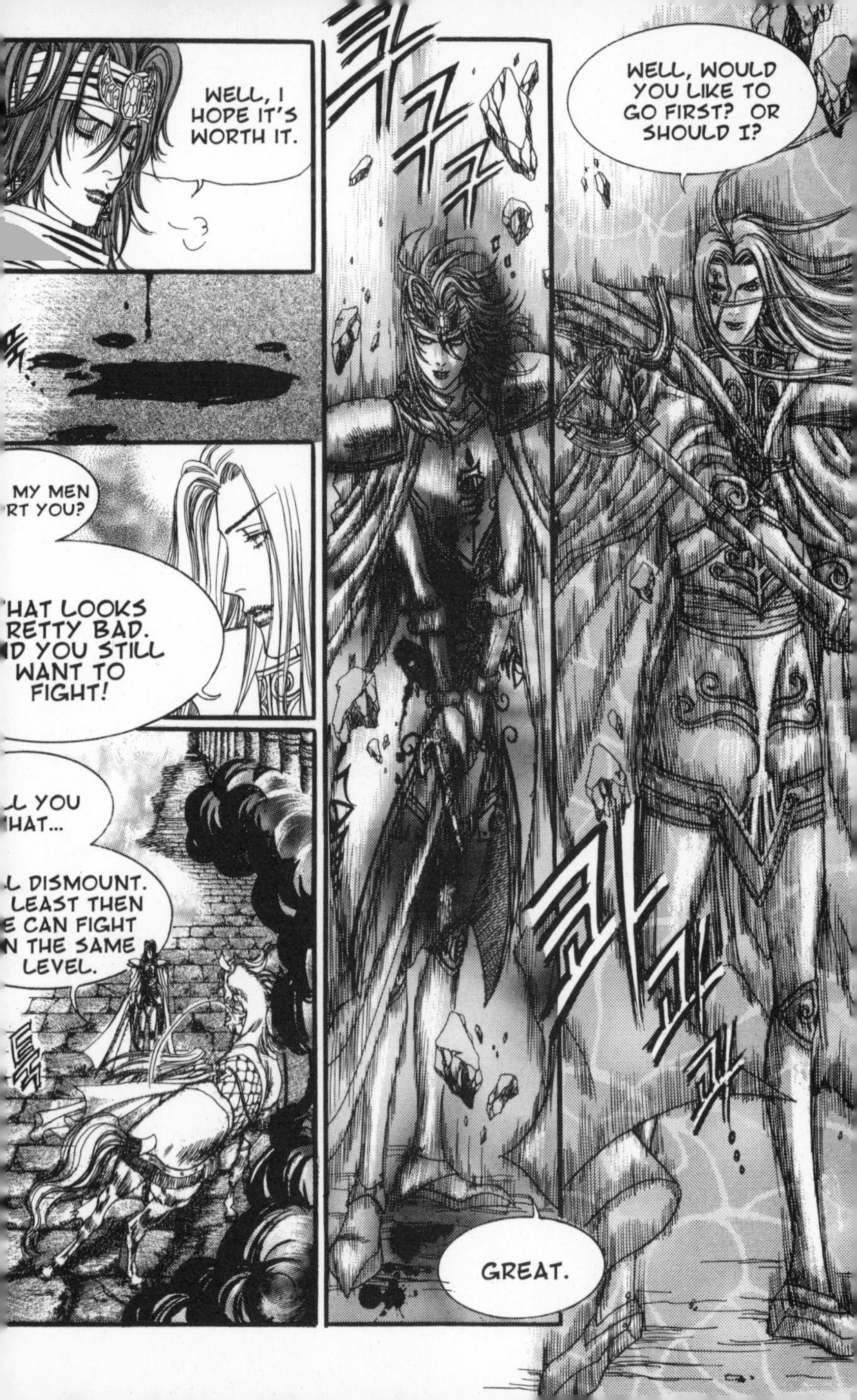
WELL, I HOPE IT'S WORTH IT.
MY MEN
RT YOU?
HAT LOOKS RETTY BAD. D YOU STILL WANT TO FIGHT!
L YOU HAT...
L DISMOUNT. LEAST THEN E CAN FIGHT N THE SAME LEVEL.
GREAT.
WELL, WOULD YOU LIKE TO GO FIRST? OR SHOULD I?

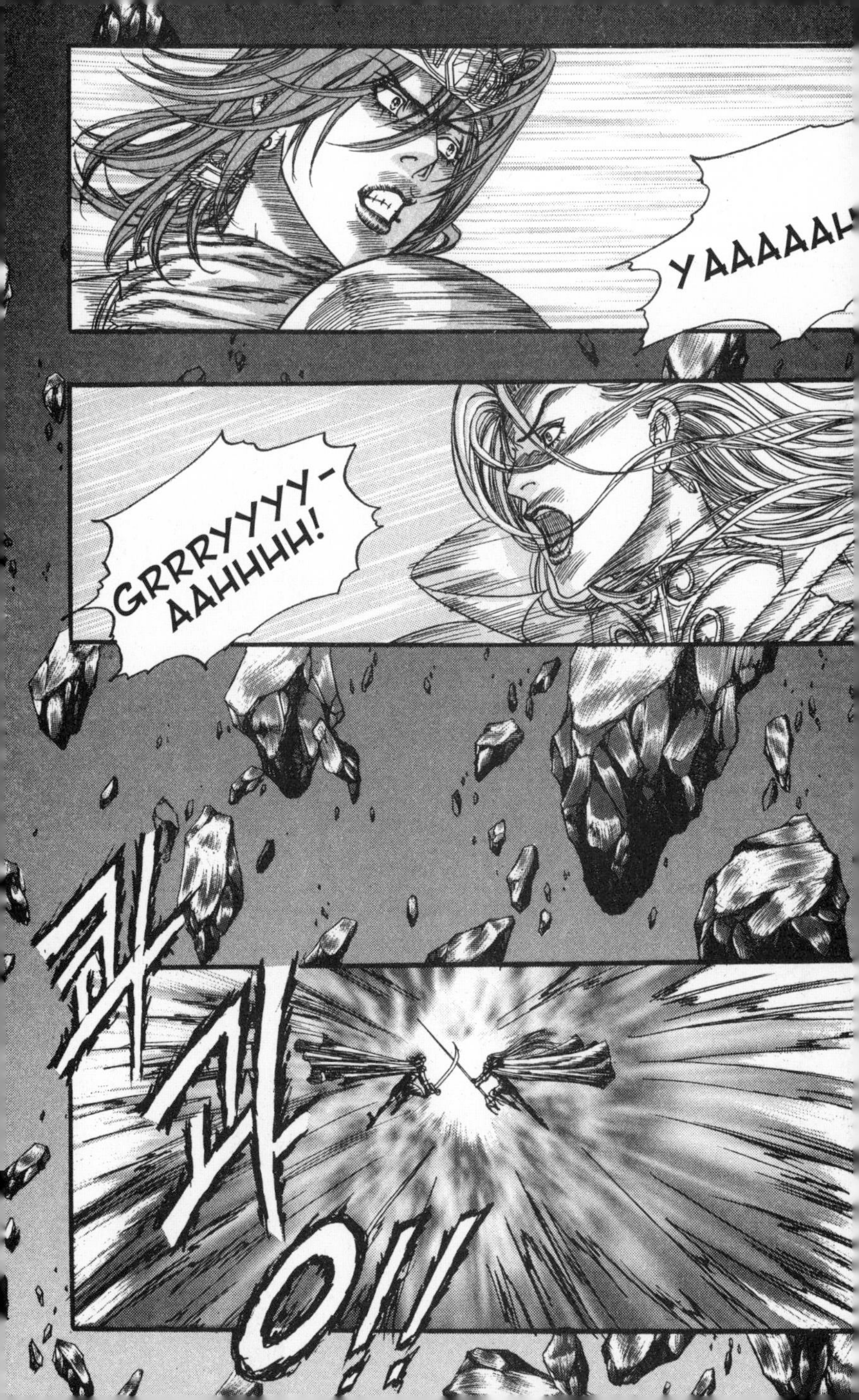
YAAAAAH
GRRRYYYY-AAHHHH!

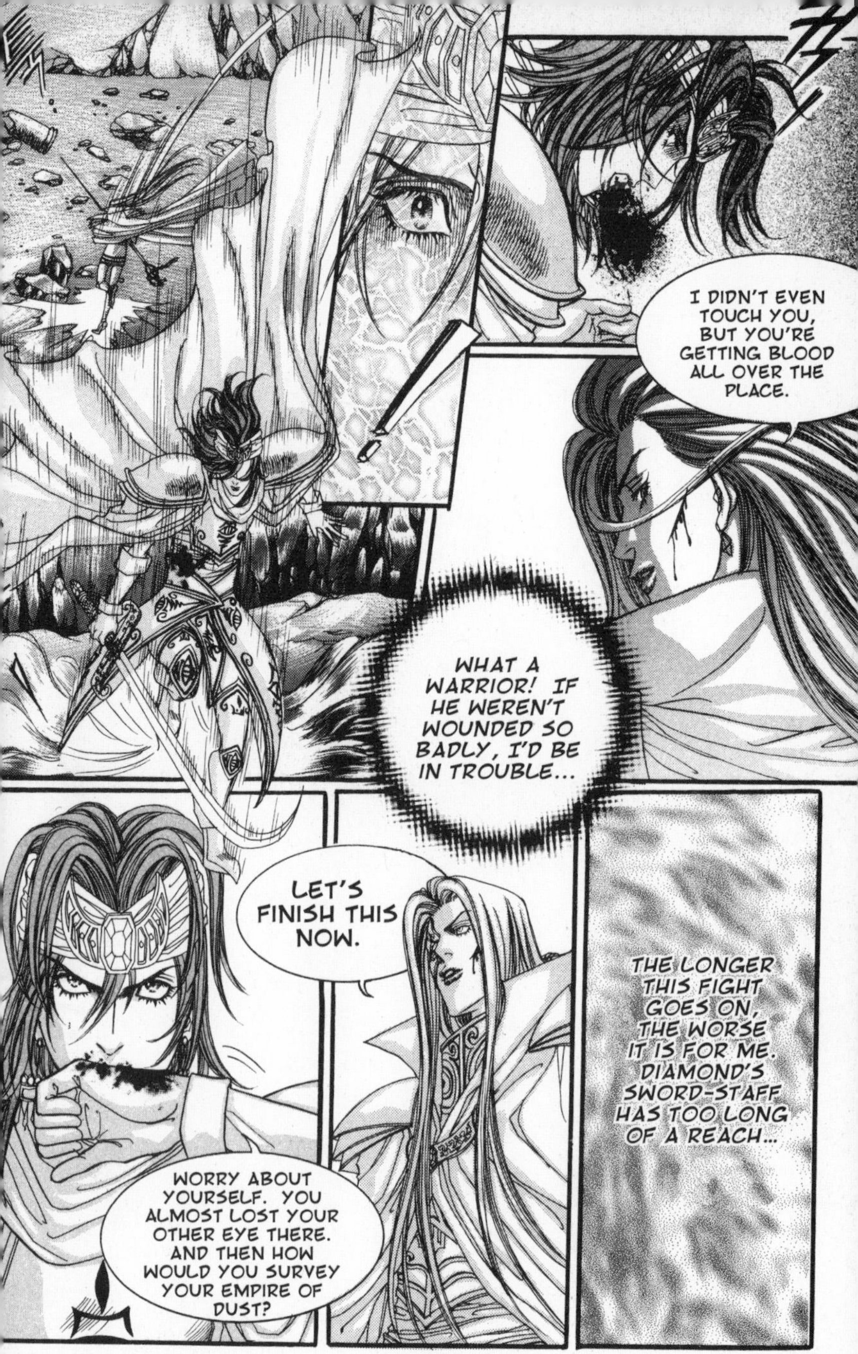
I DIDN'T EVEN TOUCH YOU, BUT YOU'RE GETTING BLOOD ALL OVER THE PLACE.
WHAT A WARRIOR! IF HE WEREN'T WOUNDED SO BADLY, I'D BE IN TROUBLE...
WORRY ABOUT YOURSELF. YOU ALMOST LOST YOUR OTHER EYE THERE. AND THEN HOW WOULD YOU SURVEY YOUR EMPIRE OF DUST?
LET'S FINISH THIS NOW.
THE LONGER THIS FIGHT GOES ON, THE WORSE IT IS FOR ME. DIAMOND'S SWORD-STAFF HAS TOO LONG OF A REACH...

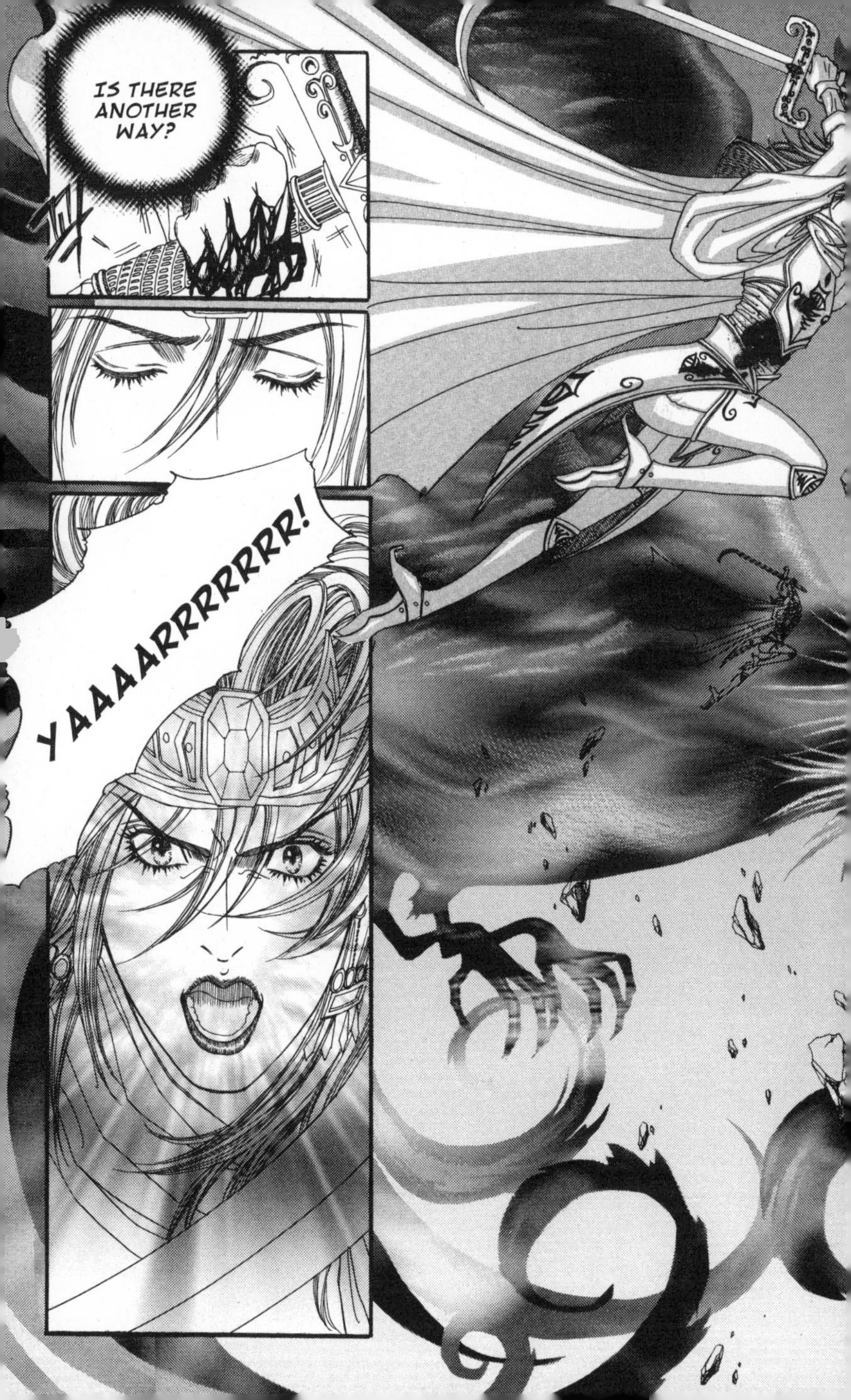
IS THERE ANOTHER WAY?
YAAAARRRRRRR!

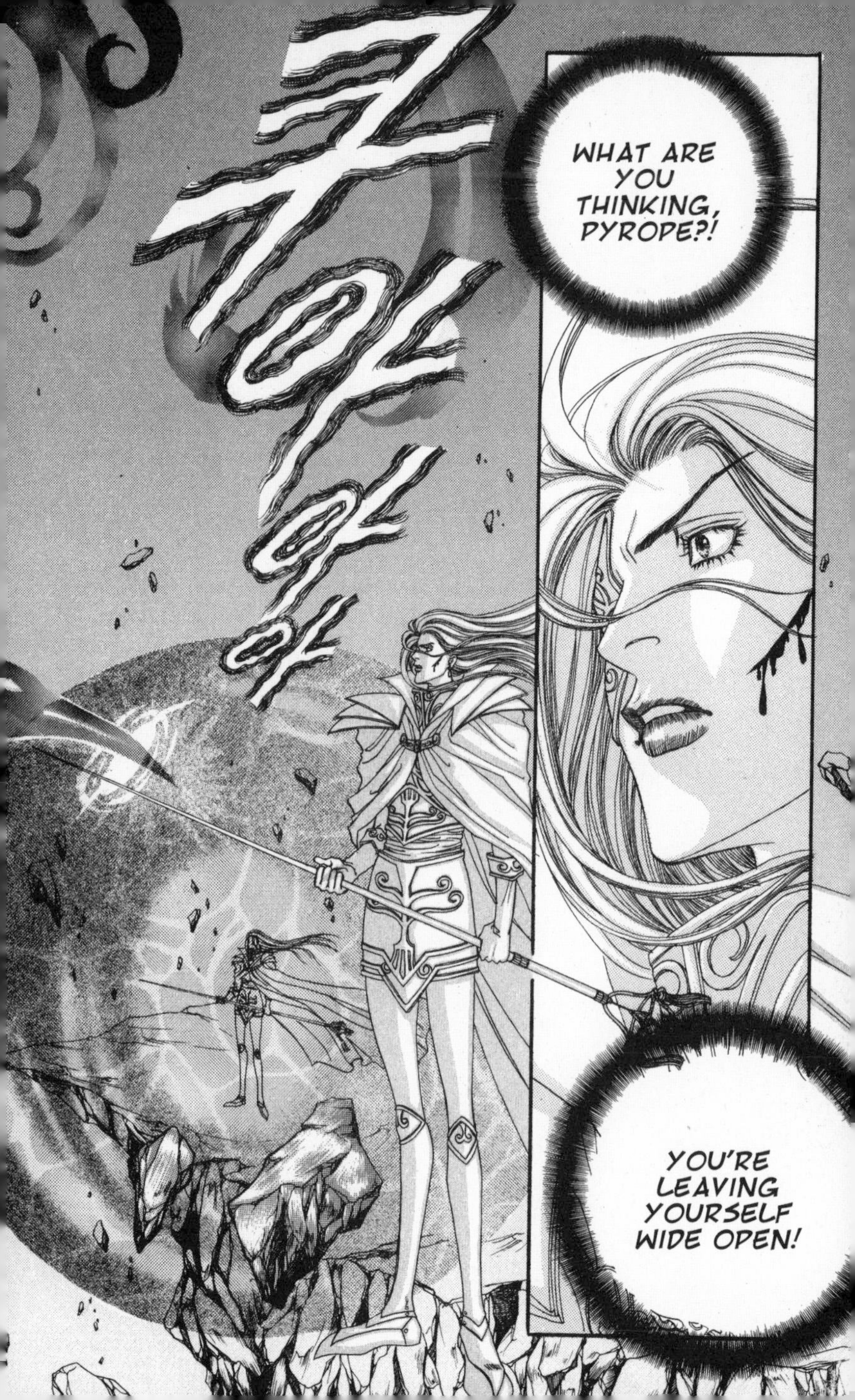
WHAT ARE YOU THINKING, PYROPE?!
YOU'RE LEAVING YOURSELF WIDE OPEN!

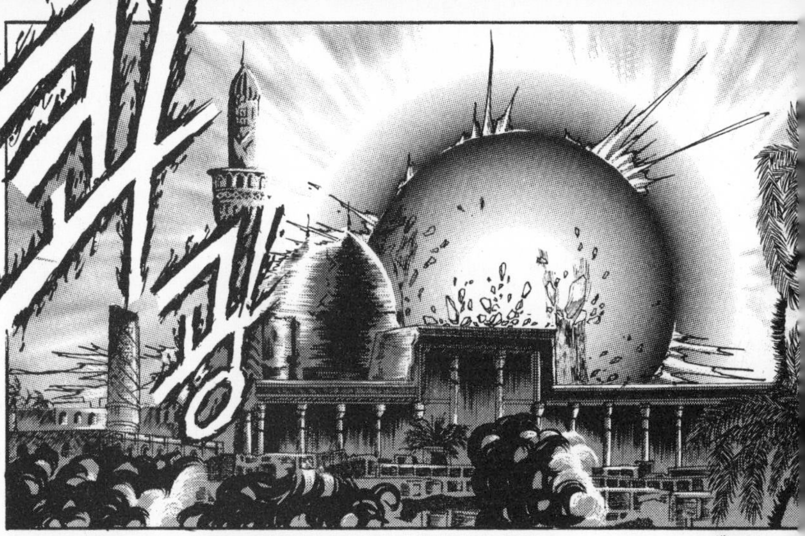
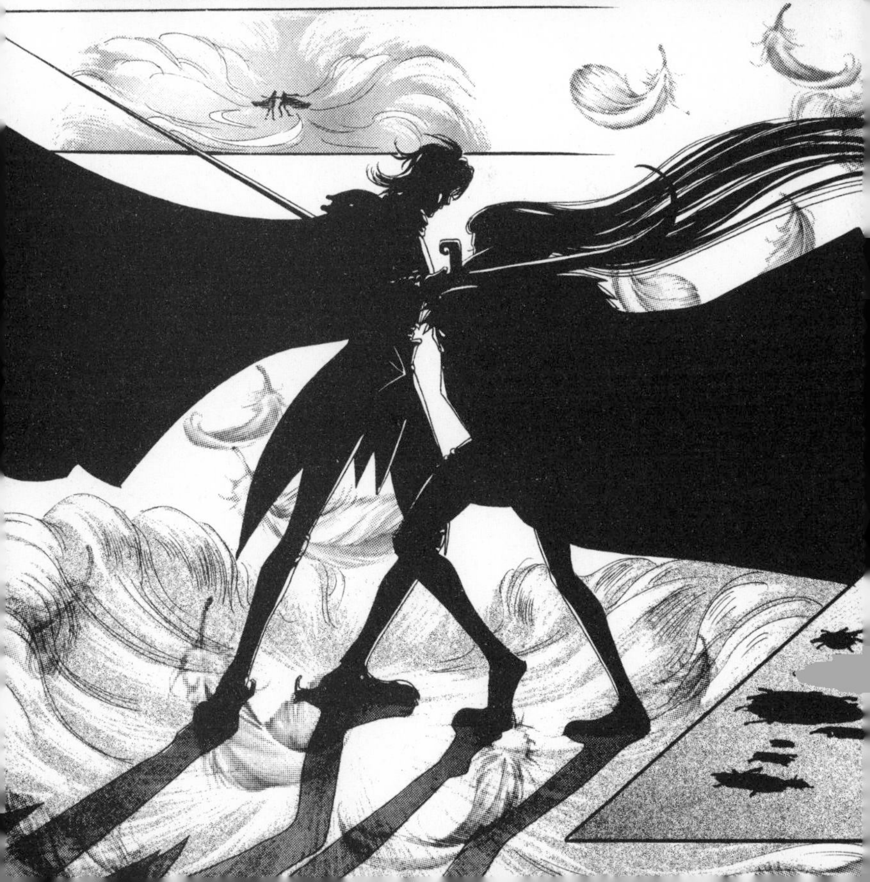

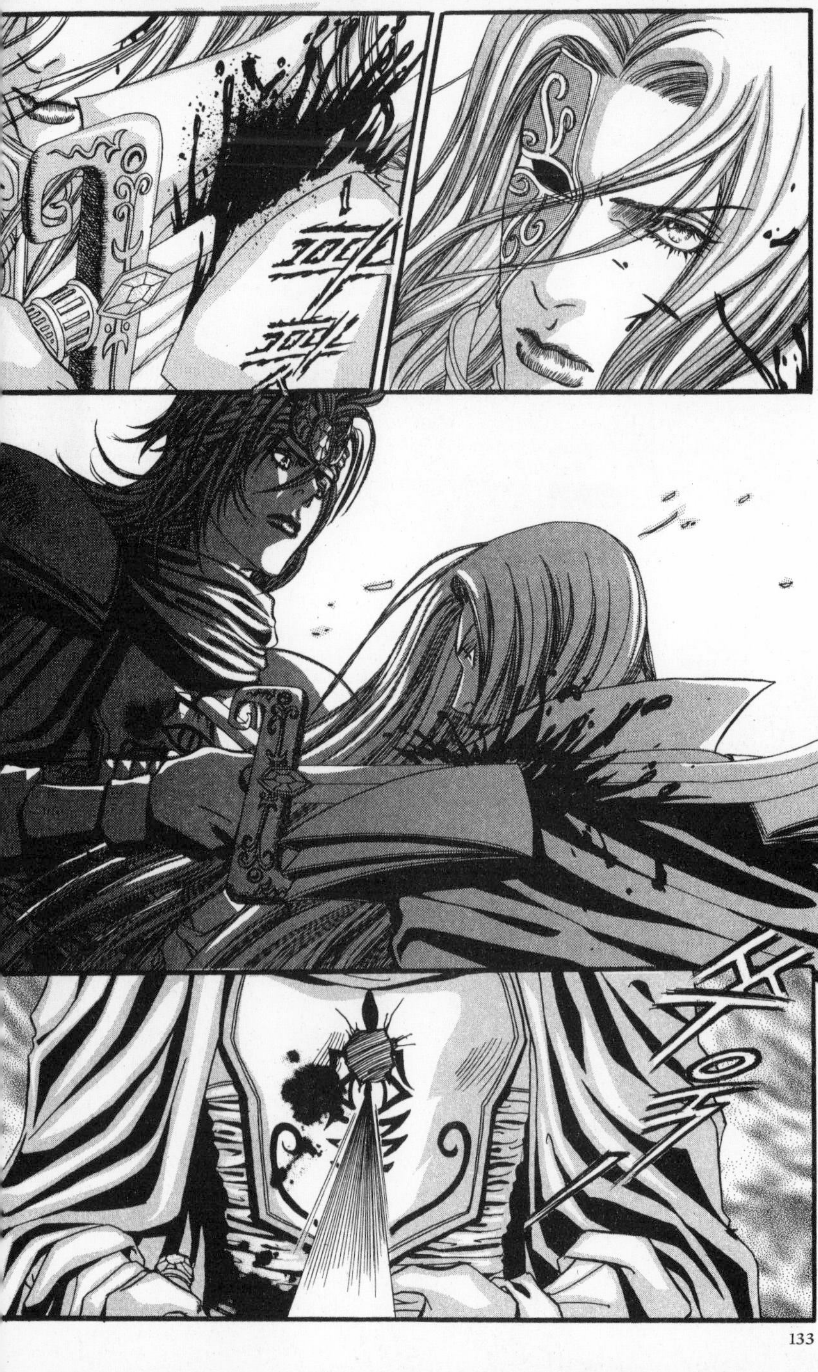

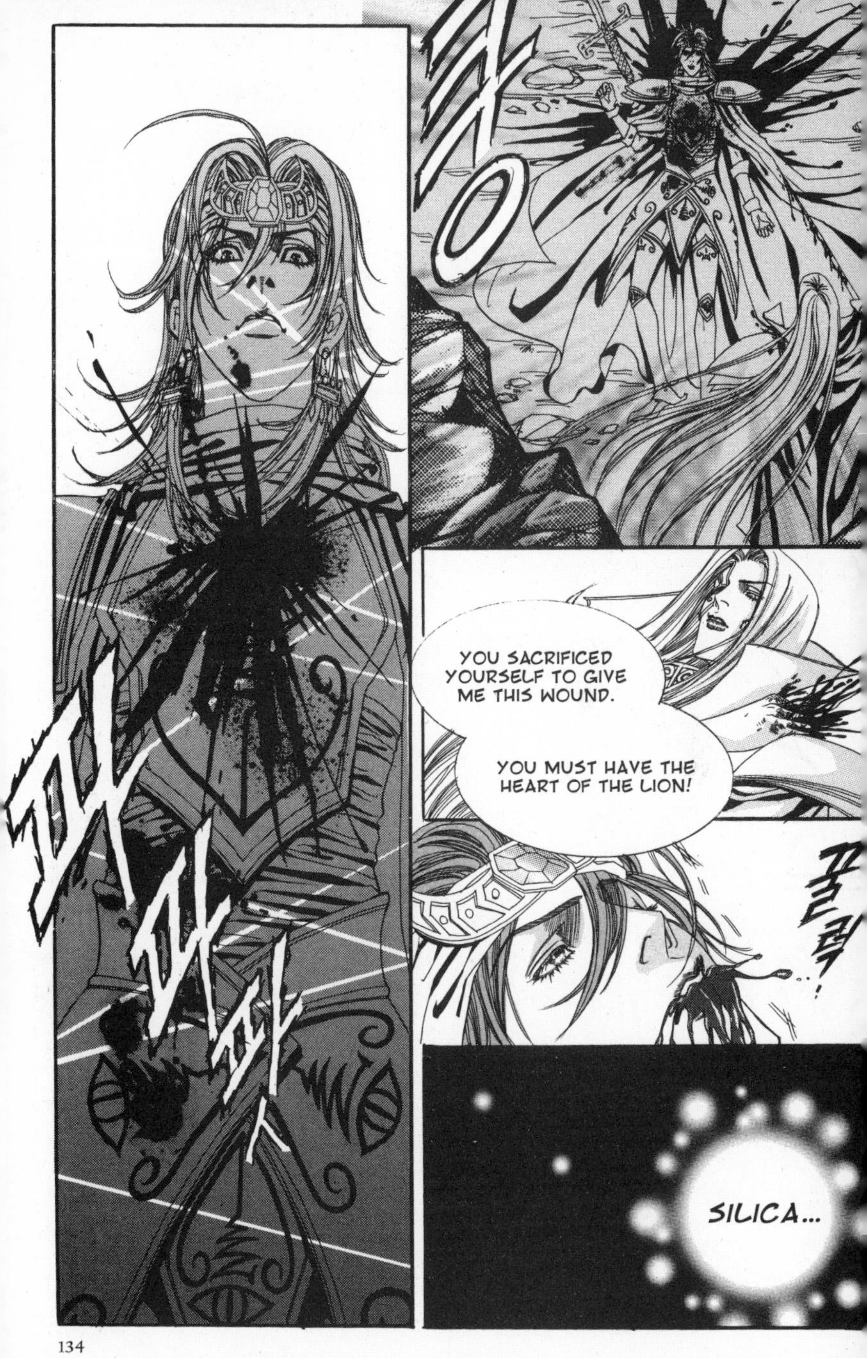
YOU SACRIFICED YOURSELF TO GIVE ME THIS WOUND.
YOU MUST HAVE THE HEART OF THE LION!
SILICA...

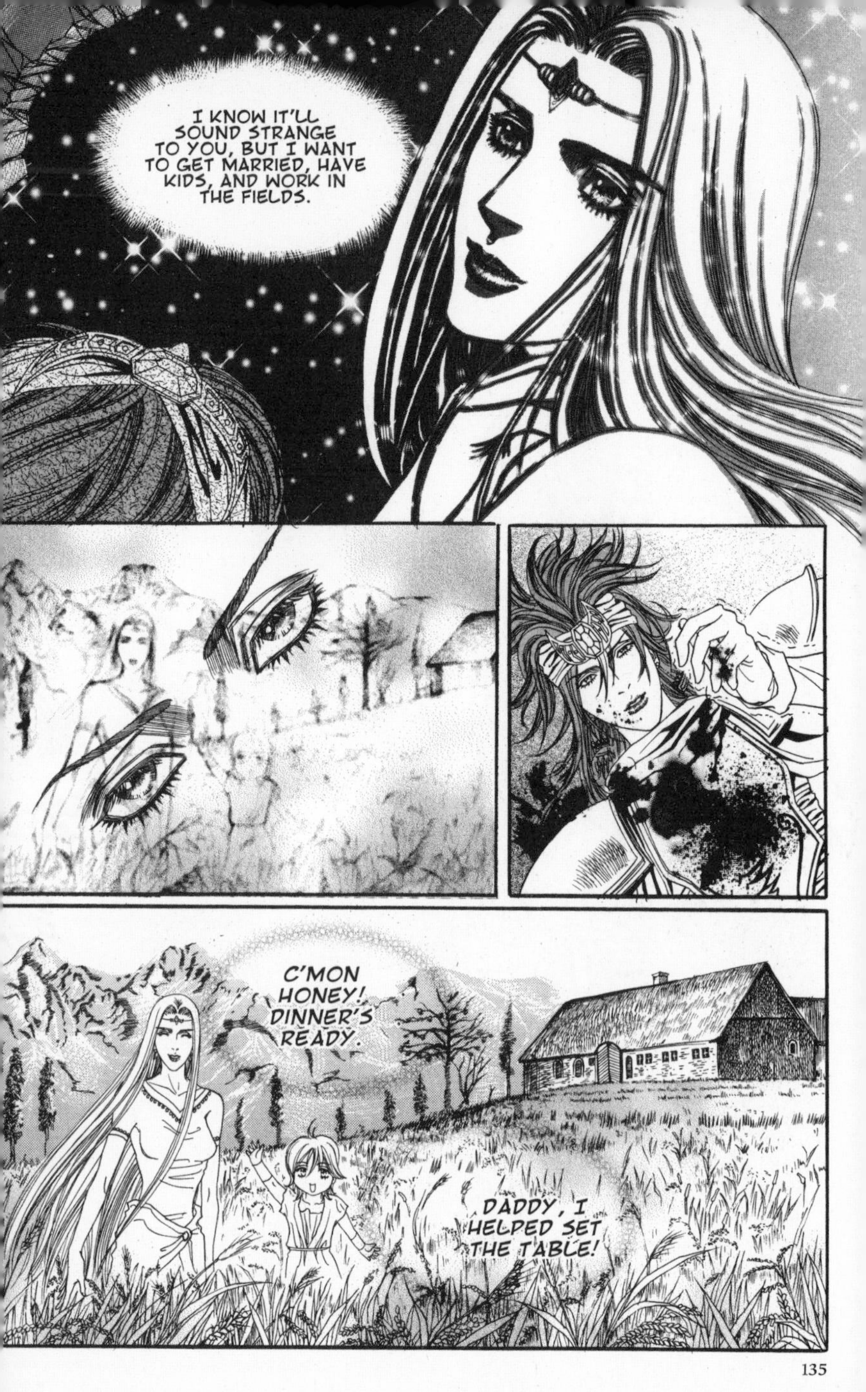
I KNOW IT'LL SOUND STRANGE TO YOU, BUT I WANT TO GET MARRIED, HAVE KIDS, AND WORK IN THE FIELDS.
C'MON HONEY! DINNER'S READY.
DADDY, I HELPED SET THE TABLE!

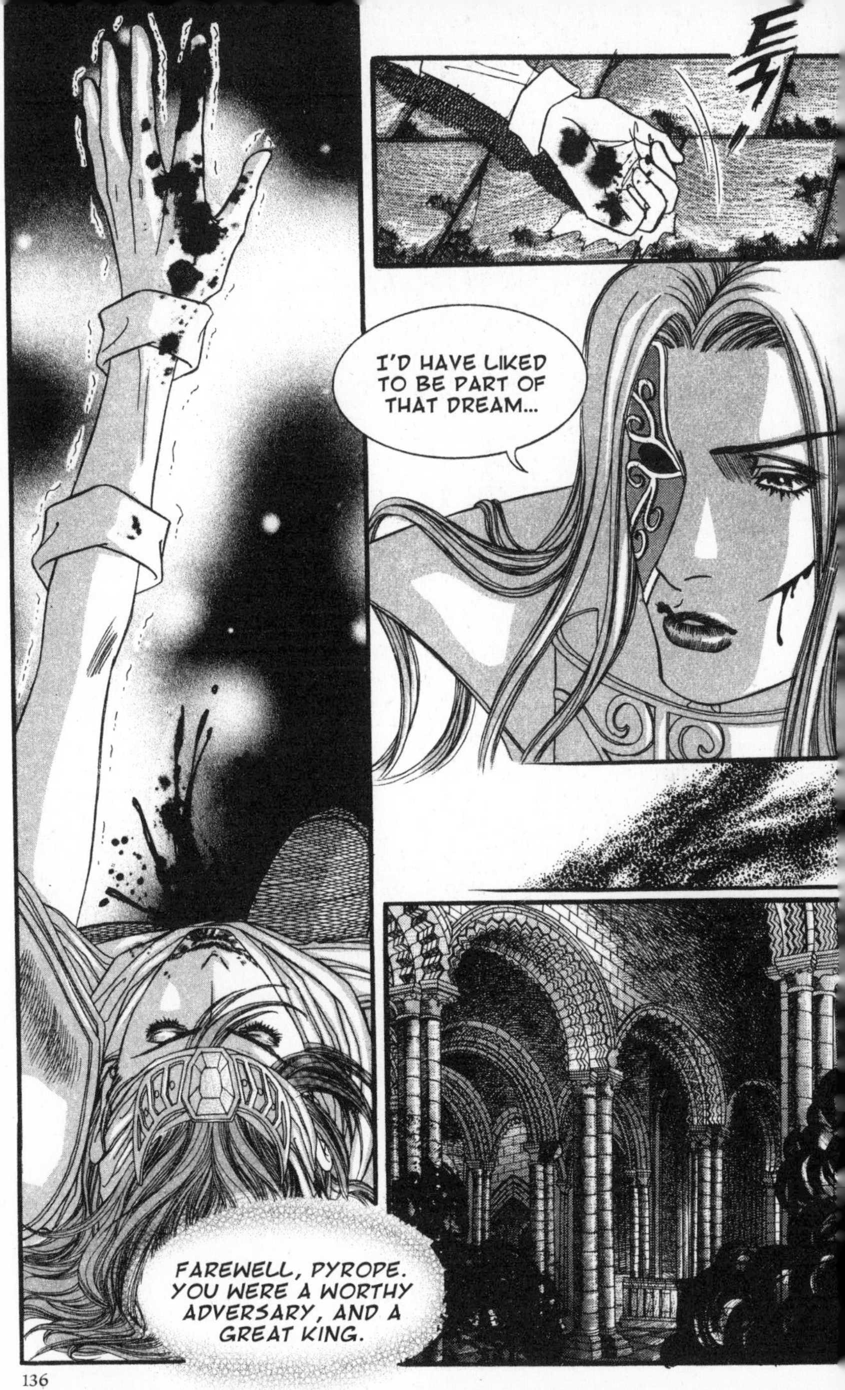
FAREWELL, PYROPE. YOU WERE A WORTHY ADVERSARY, AND A GREAT KING.
I'D HAVE LIKED TO BE PART OF THAT DREAM...

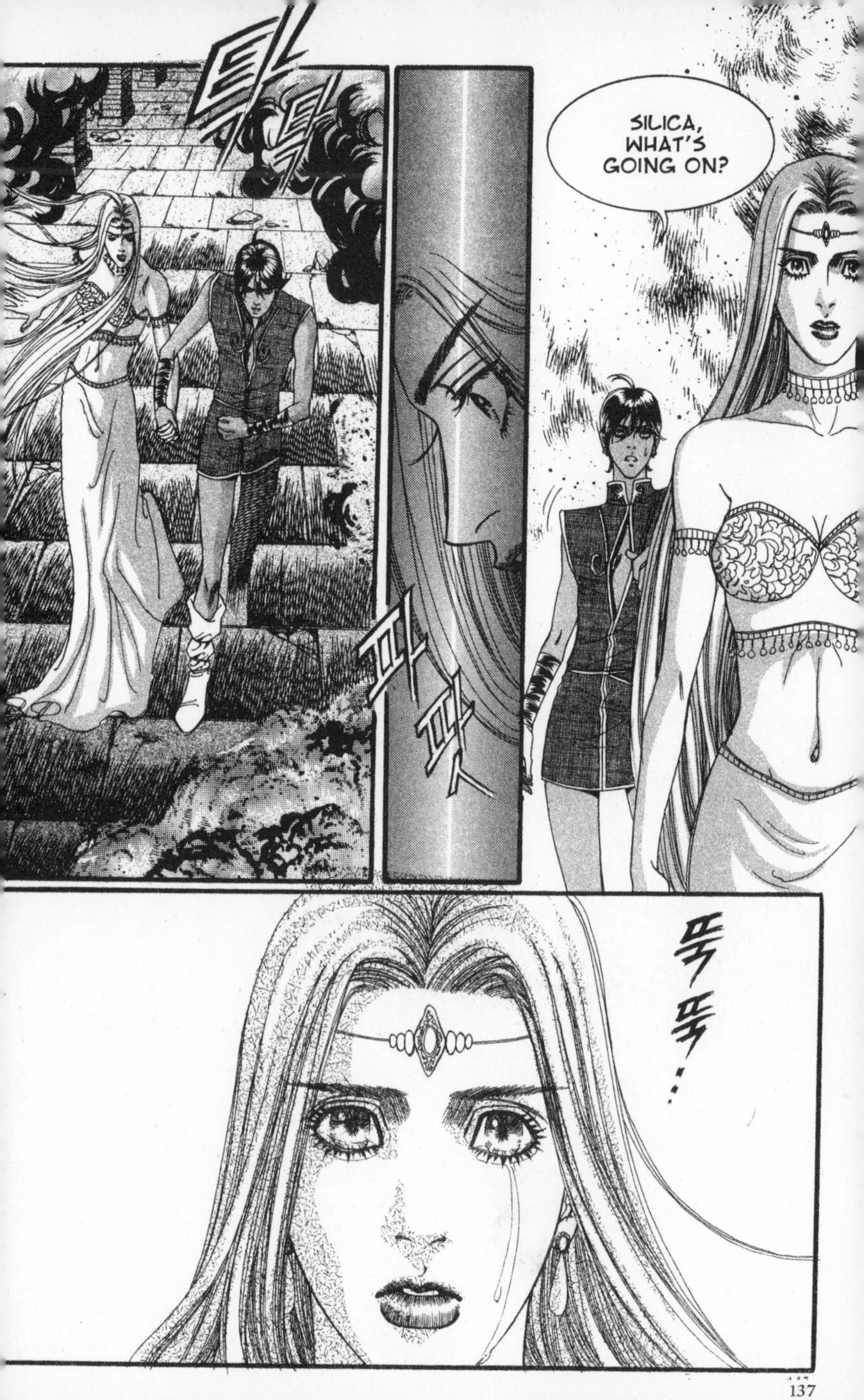
SILICA,
WHAT'S
GOING ON?
뚝 뚝...

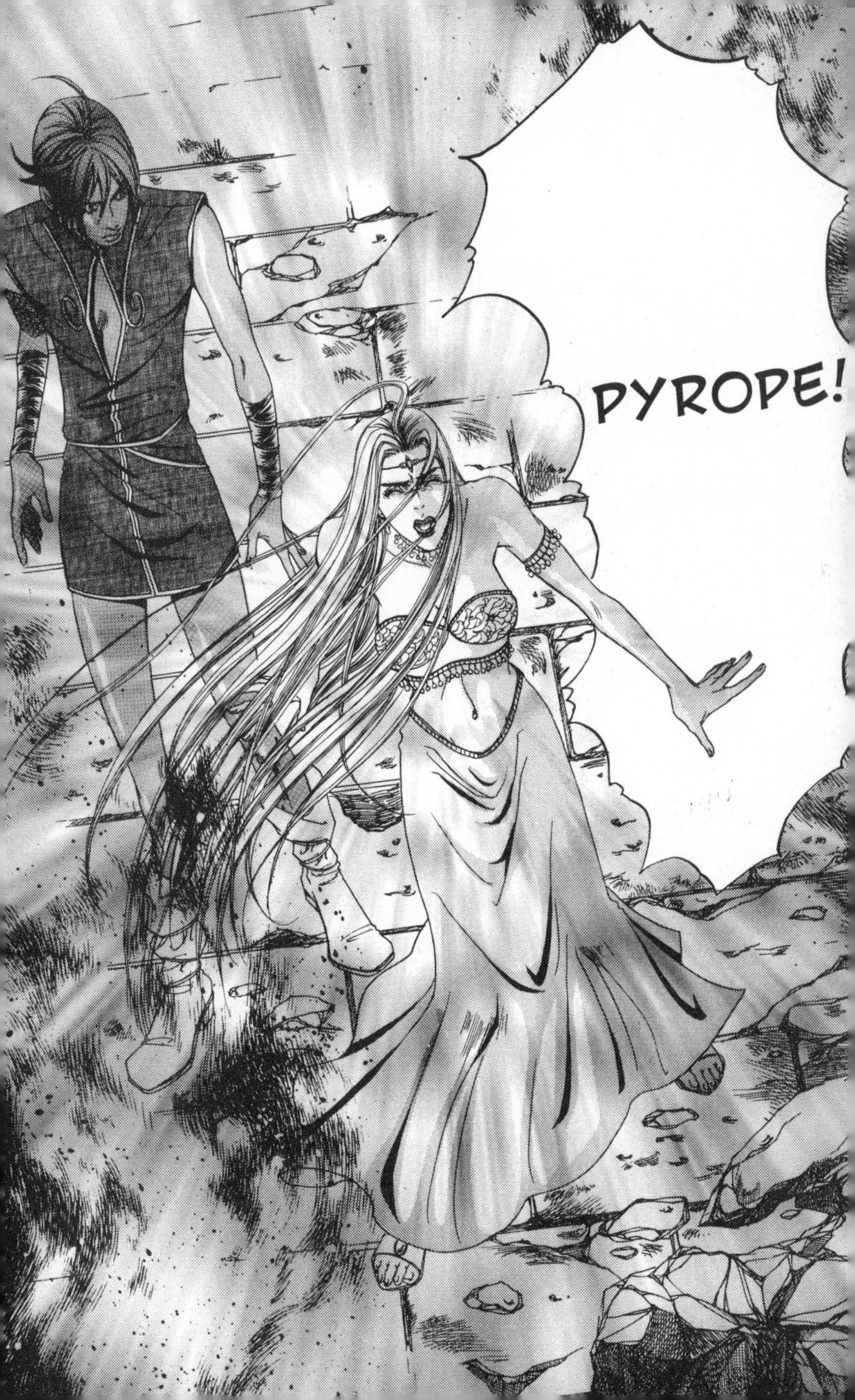
PYROPE!

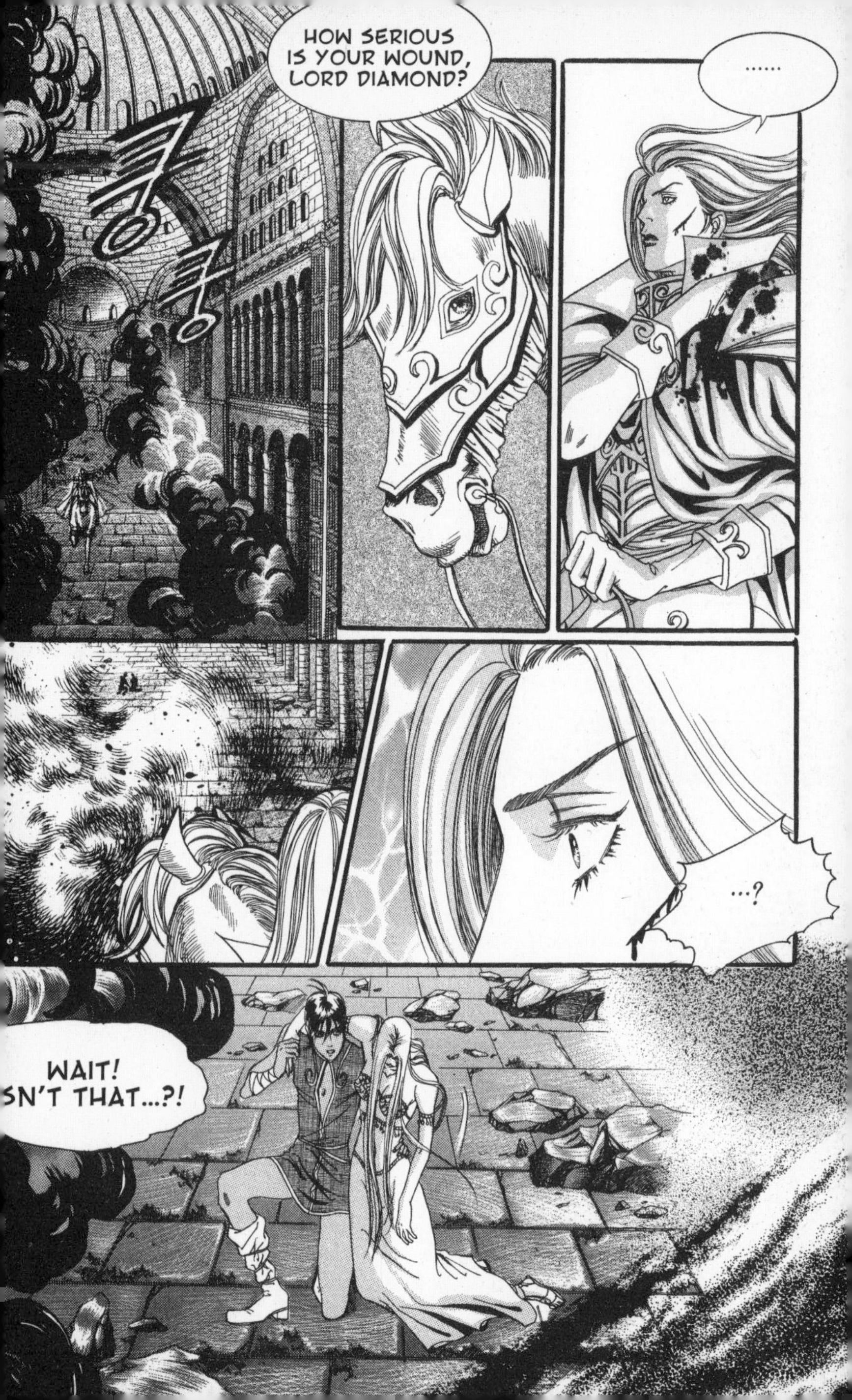
HOW SERIOUS IS YOUR WOUND, LORD DIAMOND?
......
...?
WAIT! SN'T THAT...?!

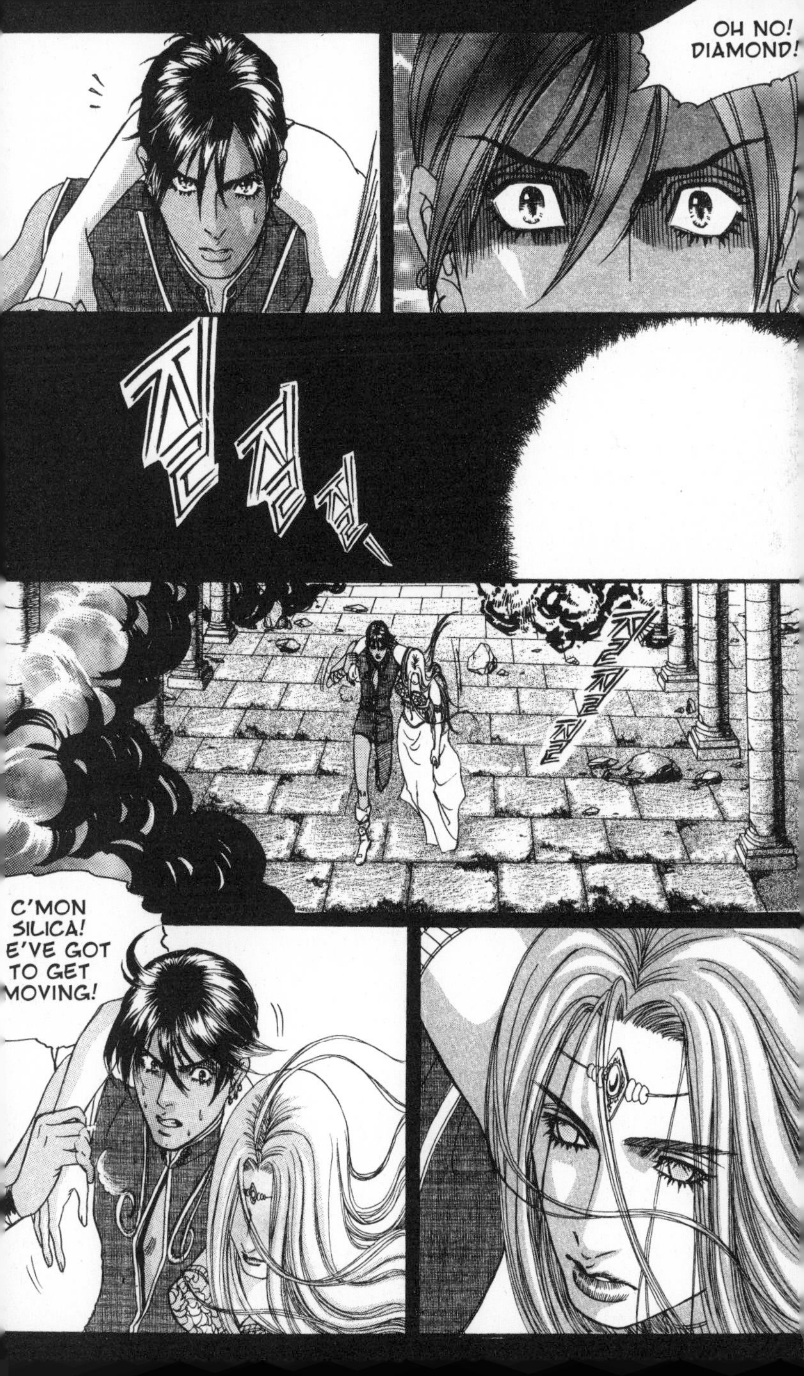
OH NO! DIAMOND!
C'MON SILICA! E'VE GOT TO GET MOVING!

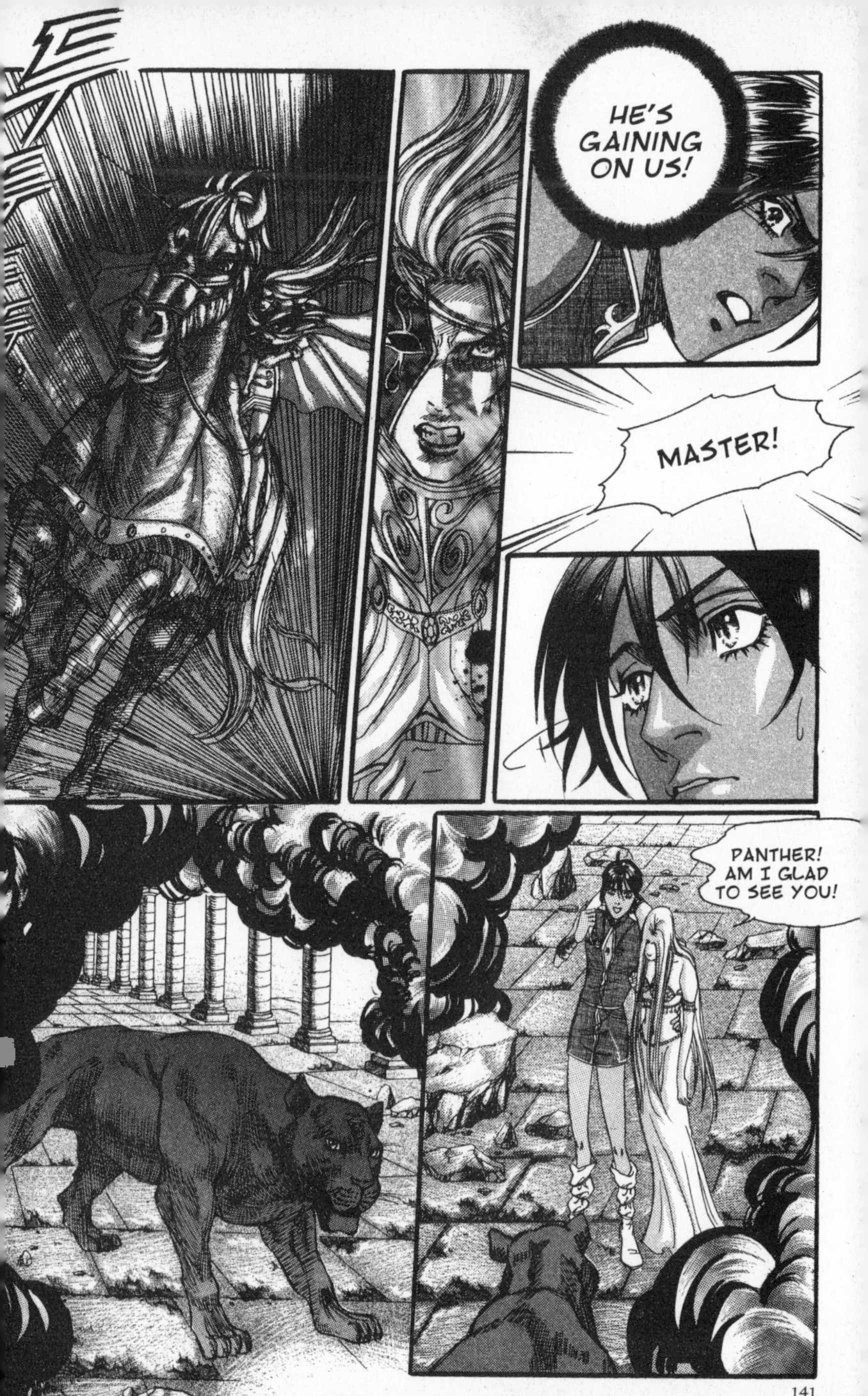
HE'S GAINING ON US!
MASTER!
PANTHER! AM I GLAD TO SEE YOU!

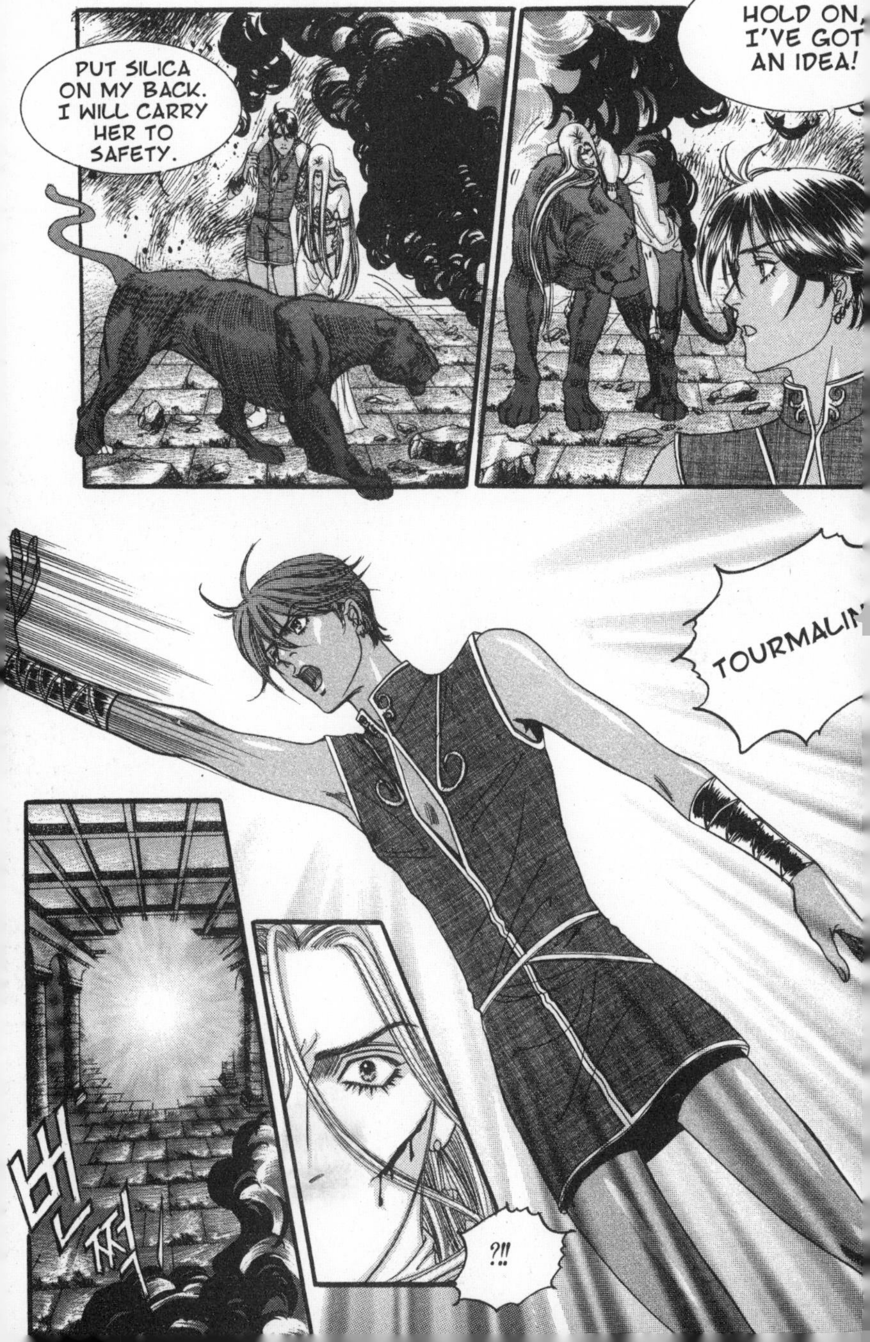
PUT SILICA ON MY BACK. I WILL CARRY HER TO SAFETY.
HOLD ON, I'VE GOT AN IDEA!
TOURMALIN
번쩍
?!!

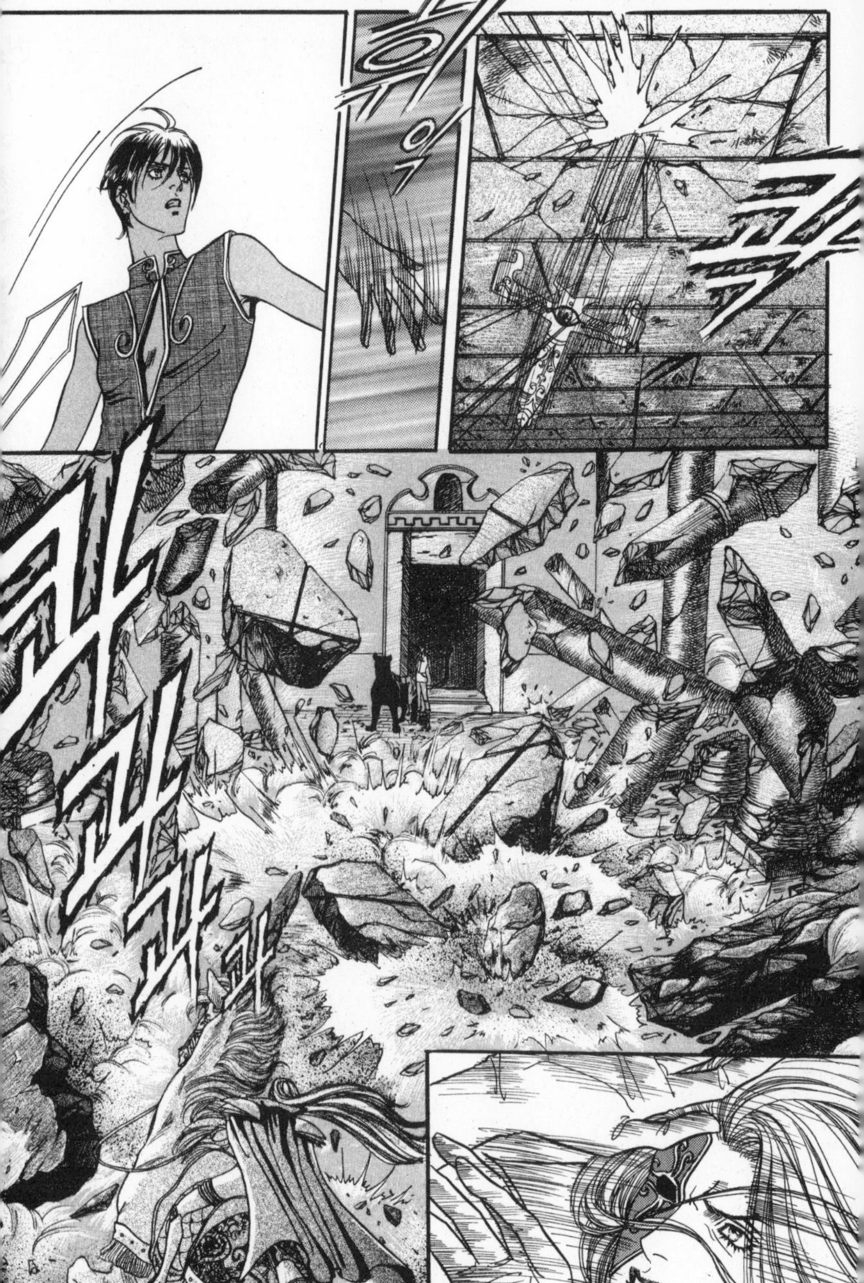

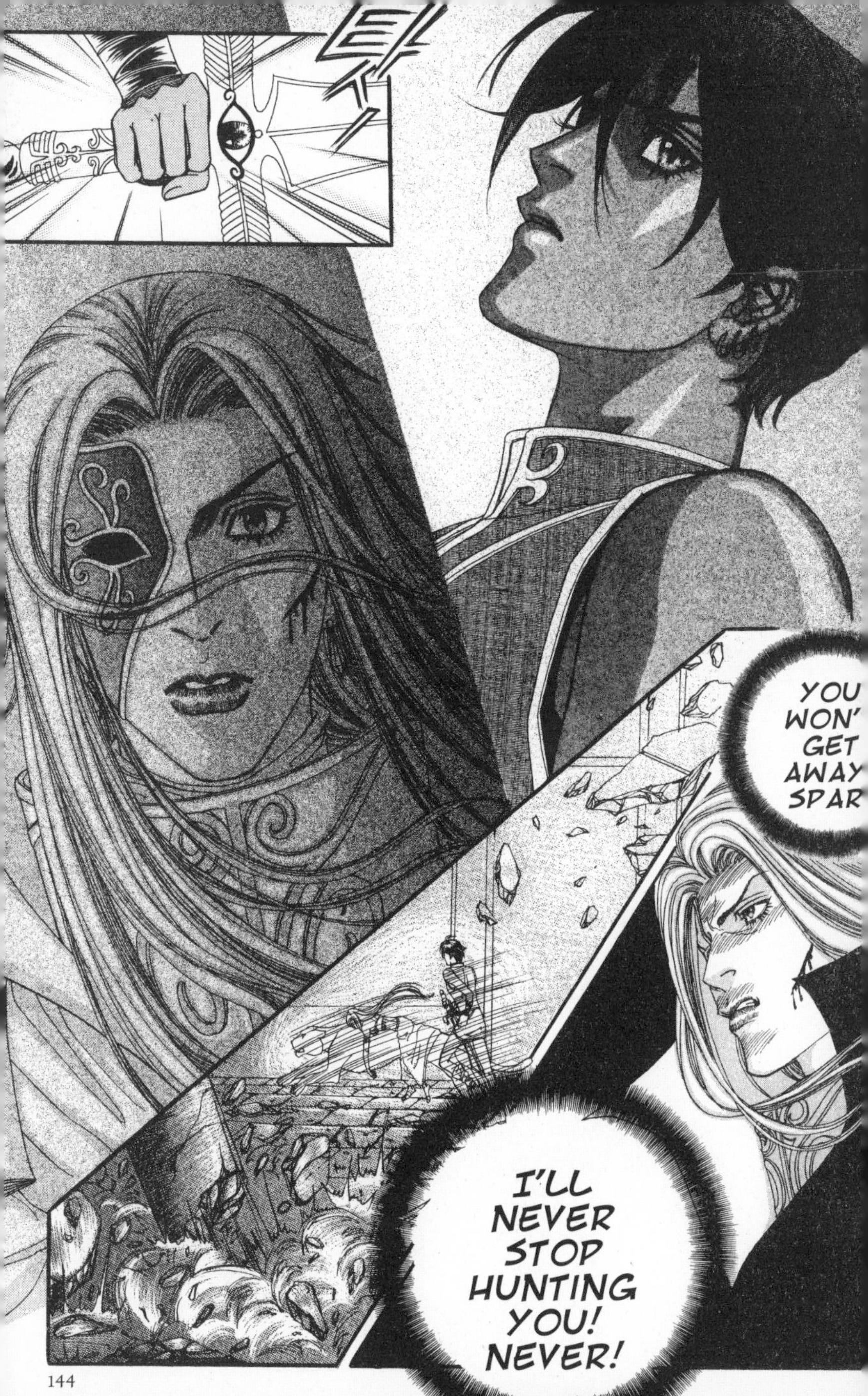
YOU WON' GET AWAY SPAR
I'LL NEVER STOP HUNTING YOU! NEVER!

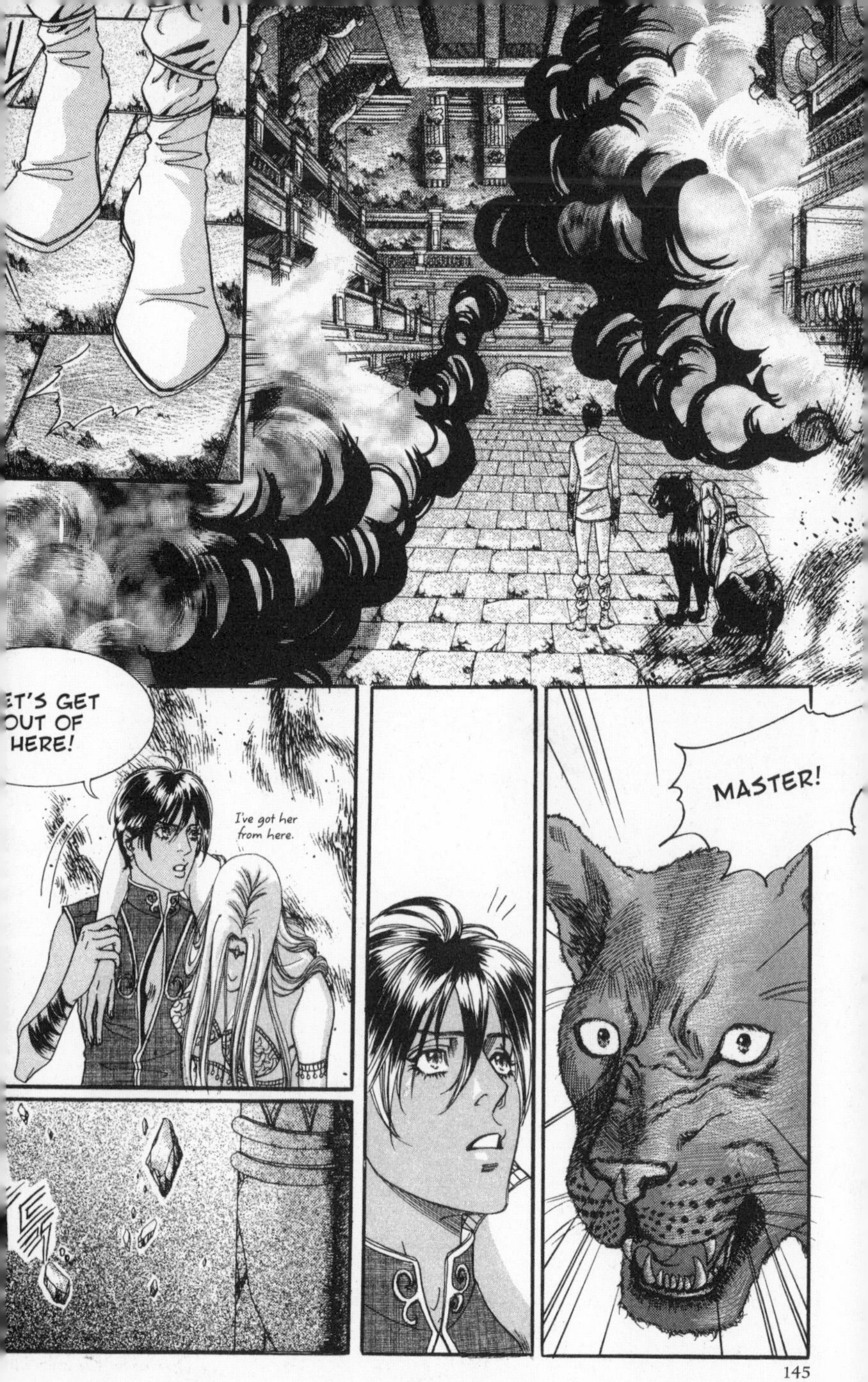
ET'S GET OUT OF HERE!
I've got her from here.
MASTER!

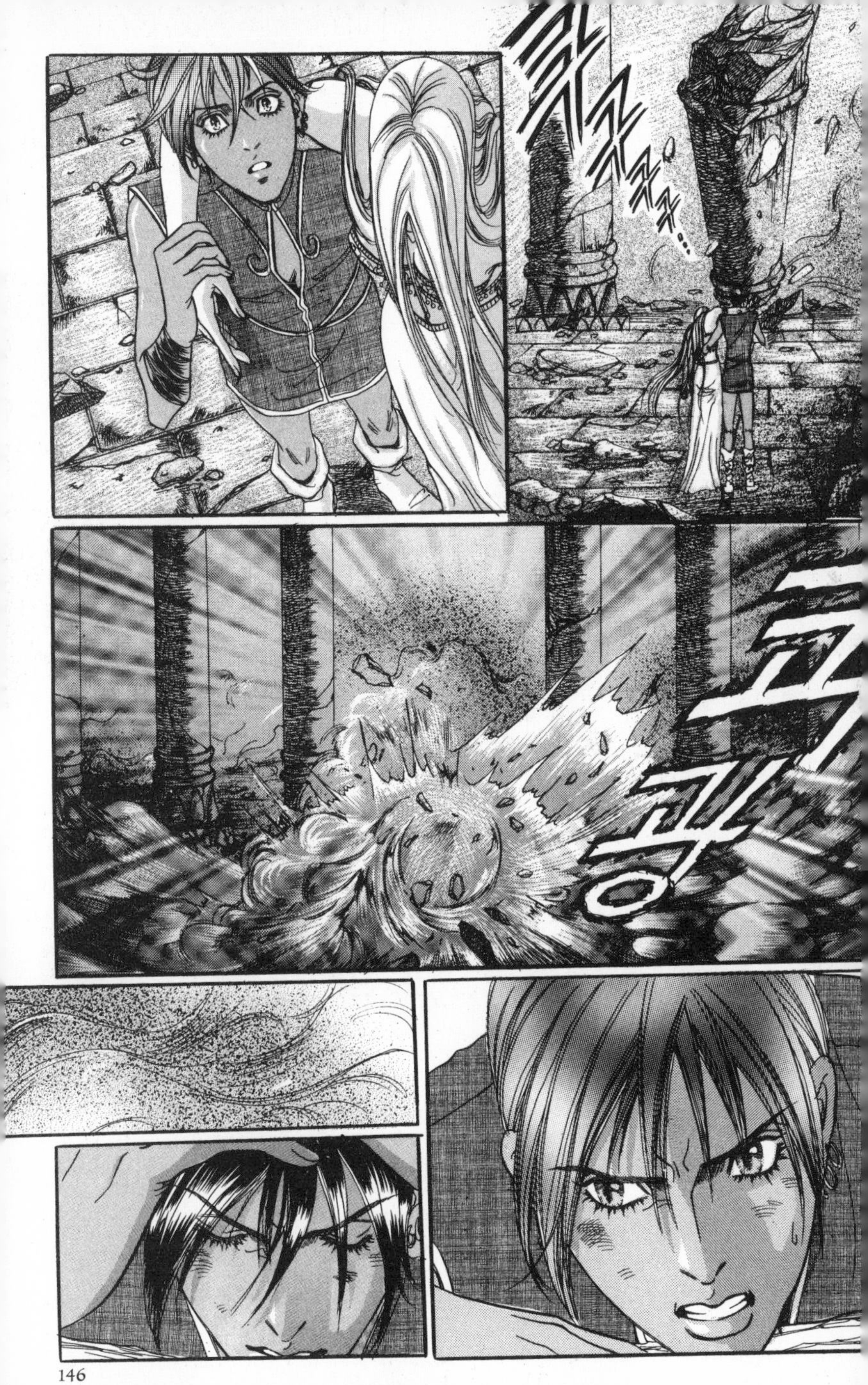

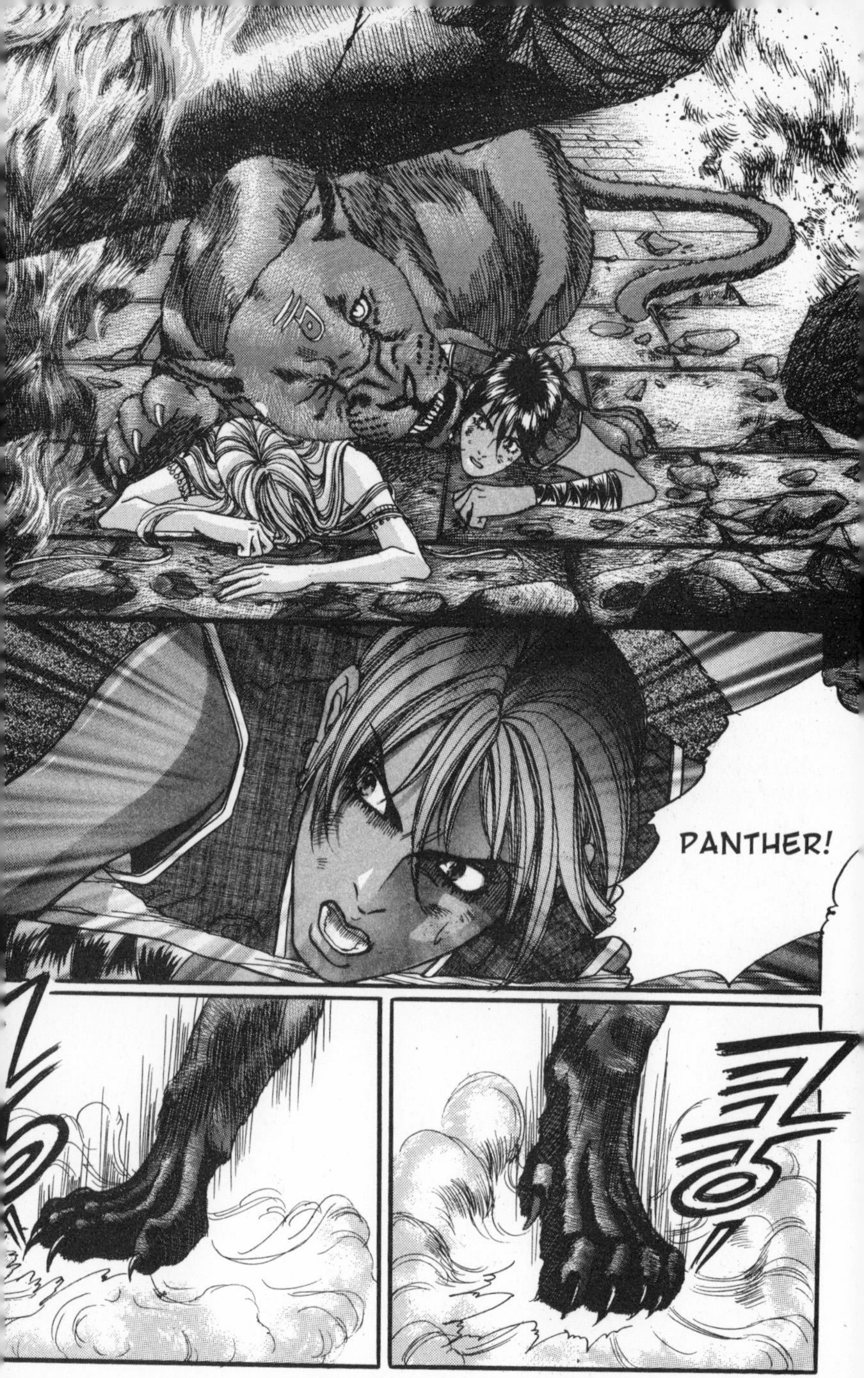
PANTHER!

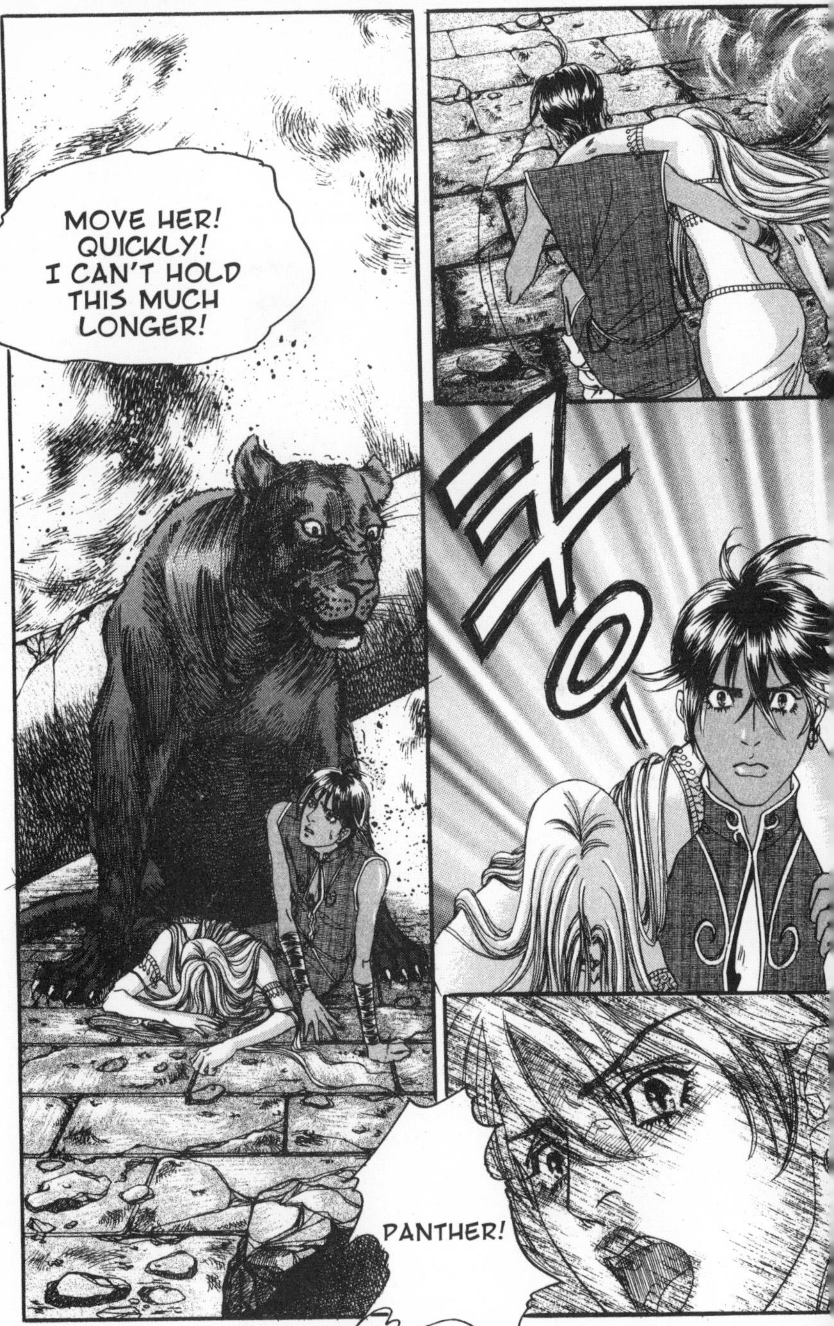
PANTHER!
MOVE HER! QUICKLY! I CAN'T HOLD THIS MUCH LONGER!

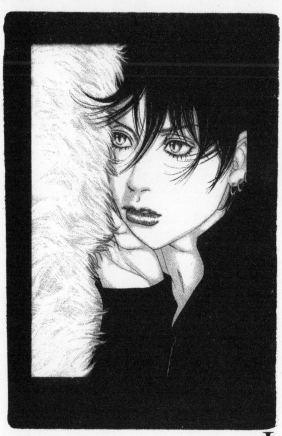

Lapis
라피스

He feels his
weaknesses keenly,
but not even the
strongest can stop
the cruel wheel of
fate.
He is a savior of
divided mind.

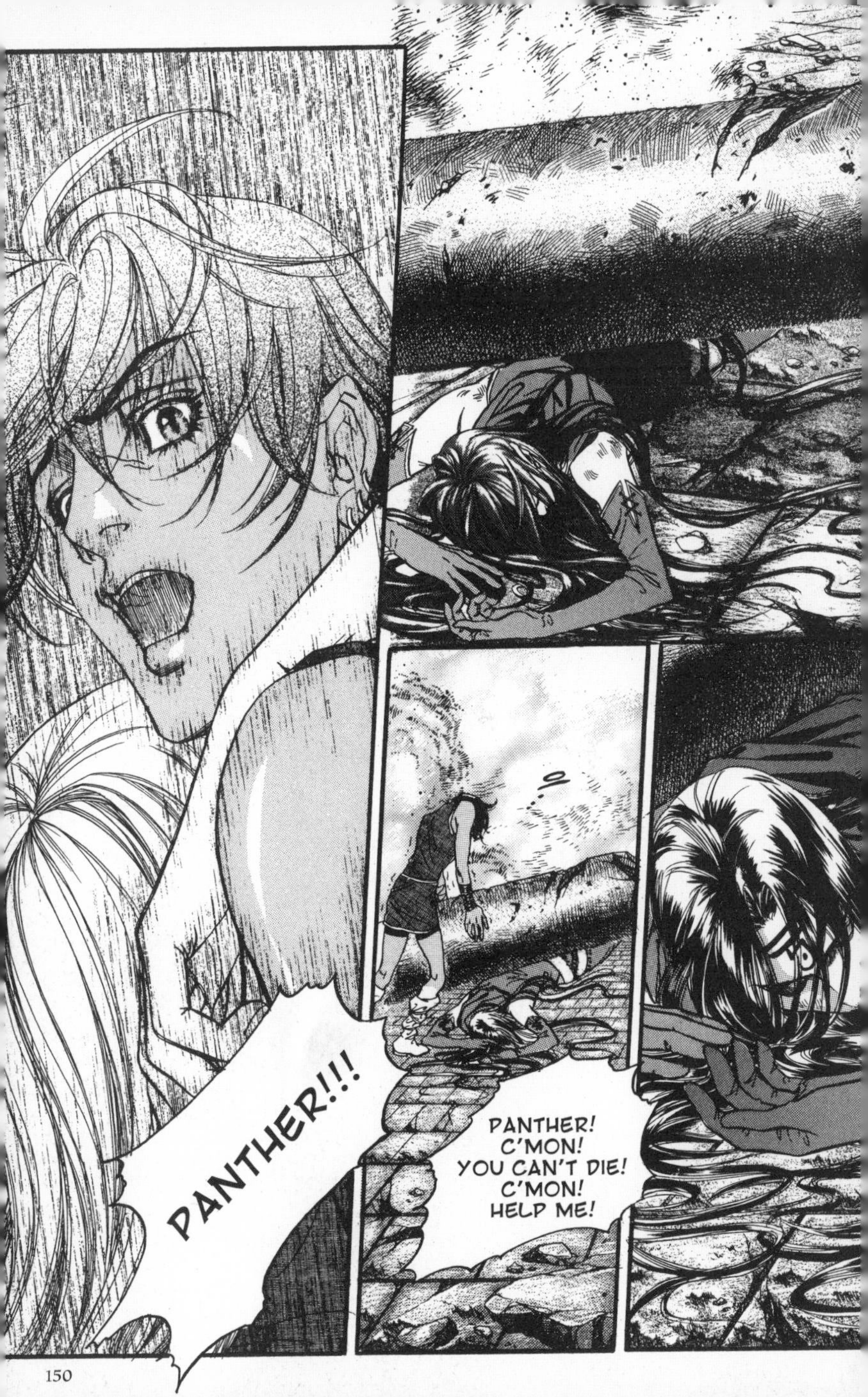
PANTHER!!!
PANTHER! C'MON! YOU CAN'T DIE! C'MON! HELP ME!

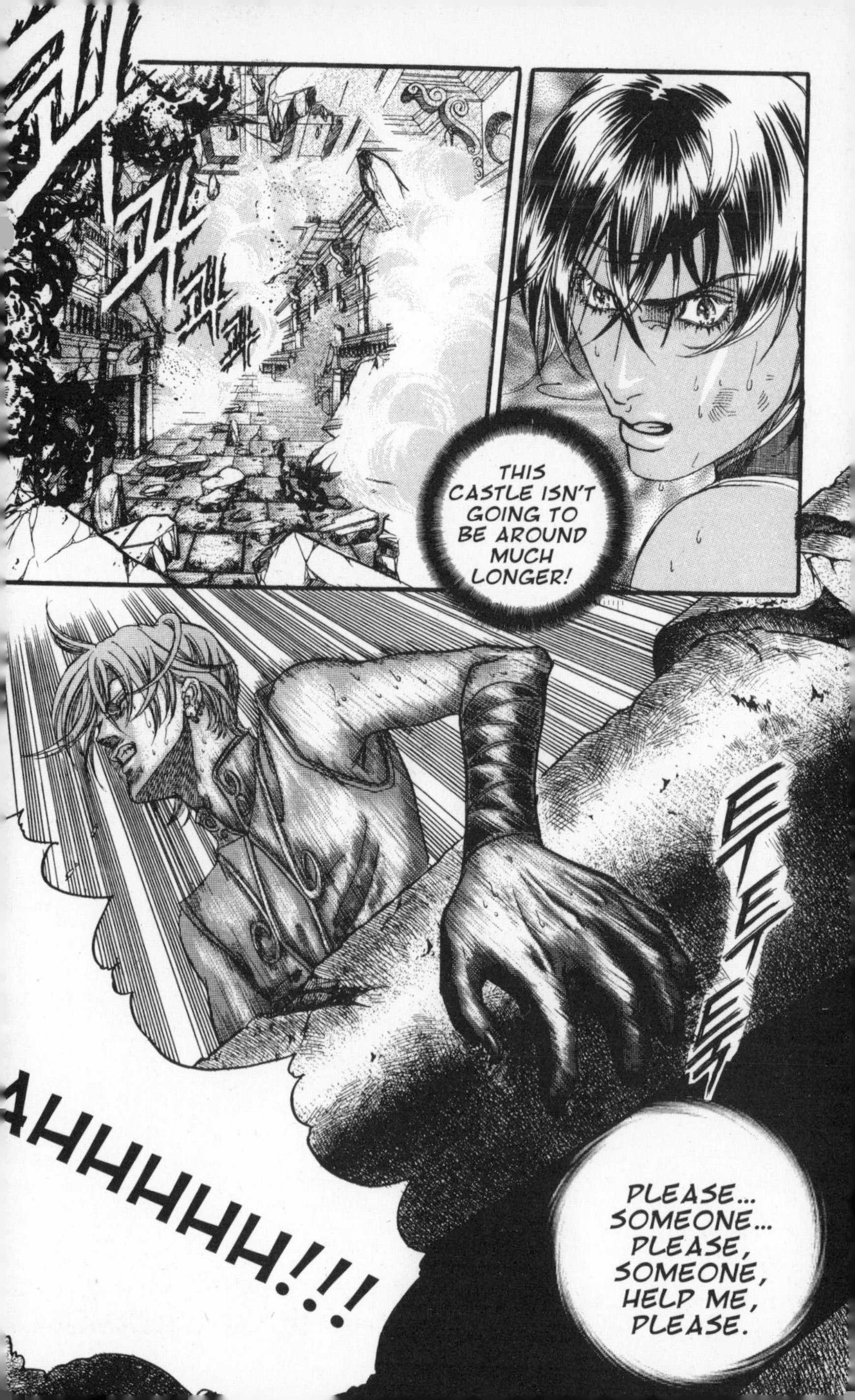
THIS CASTLE ISN'T GOING TO BE AROUND MUCH LONGER!
AHHHHHH!!!
PLEASE... SOMEONE... PLEASE, SOMEONE, HELP ME, PLEASE.

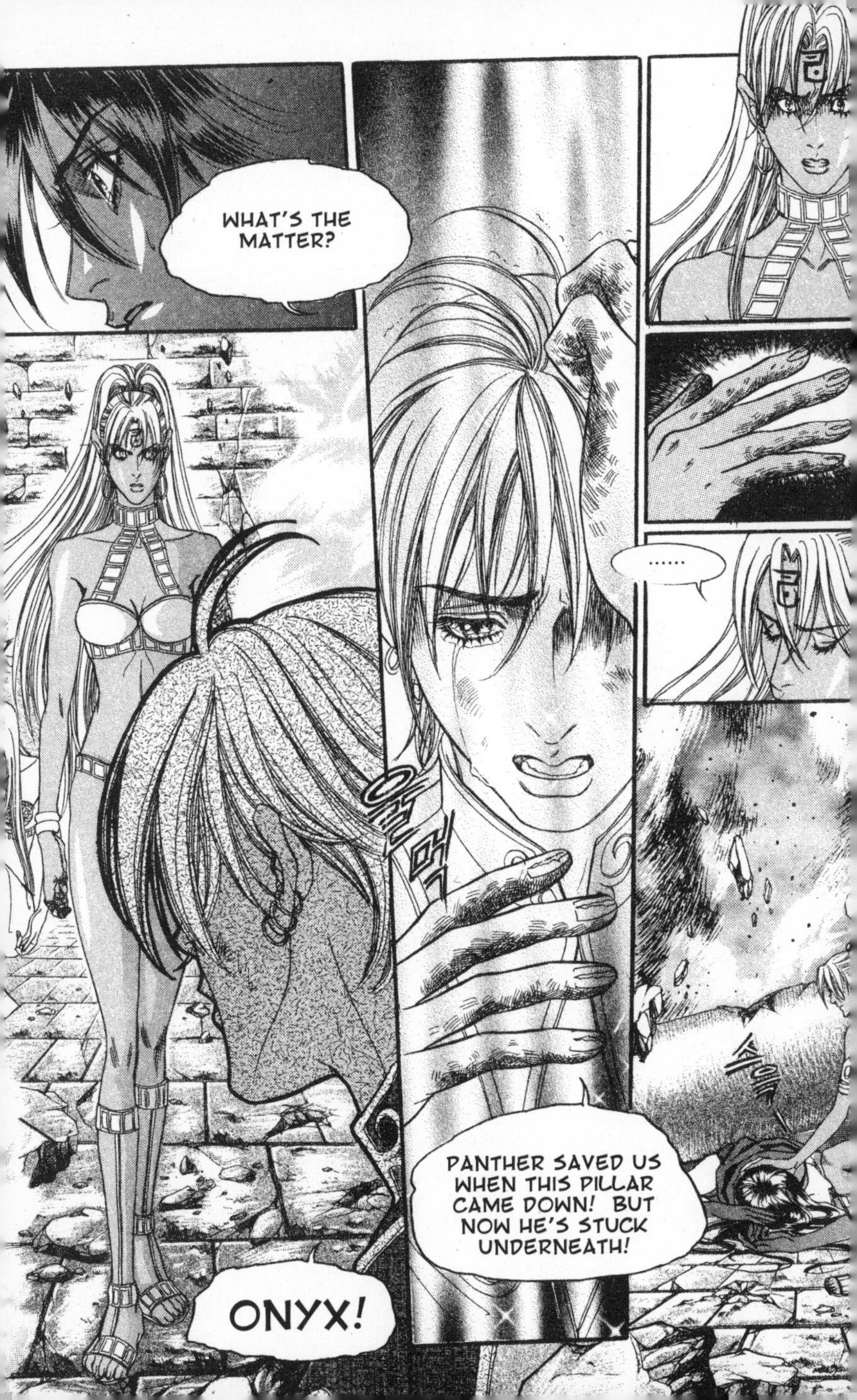
WHAT'S THE MATTER?
......
ONYX!
PANTHER SAVED US WHEN THIS PILLAR CAME DOWN! BUT NOW HE'S STUCK UNDERNEATH!

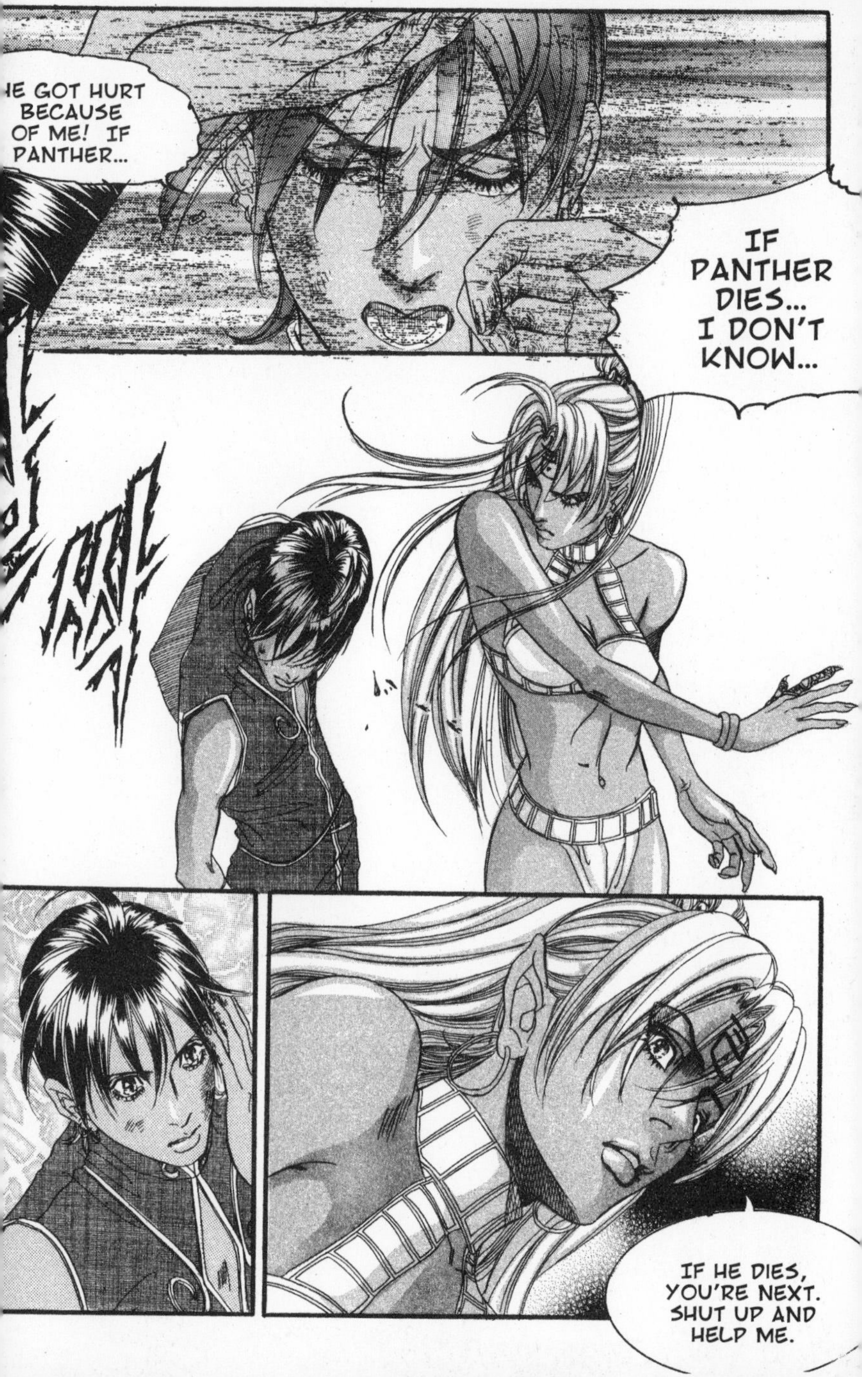
HE GOT HURT BECAUSE OF ME! IF PANTHER...
IF PANTHER DIES... I DON'T KNOW...
IF HE DIES, YOU'RE NEXT. SHUT UP AND HELP ME.

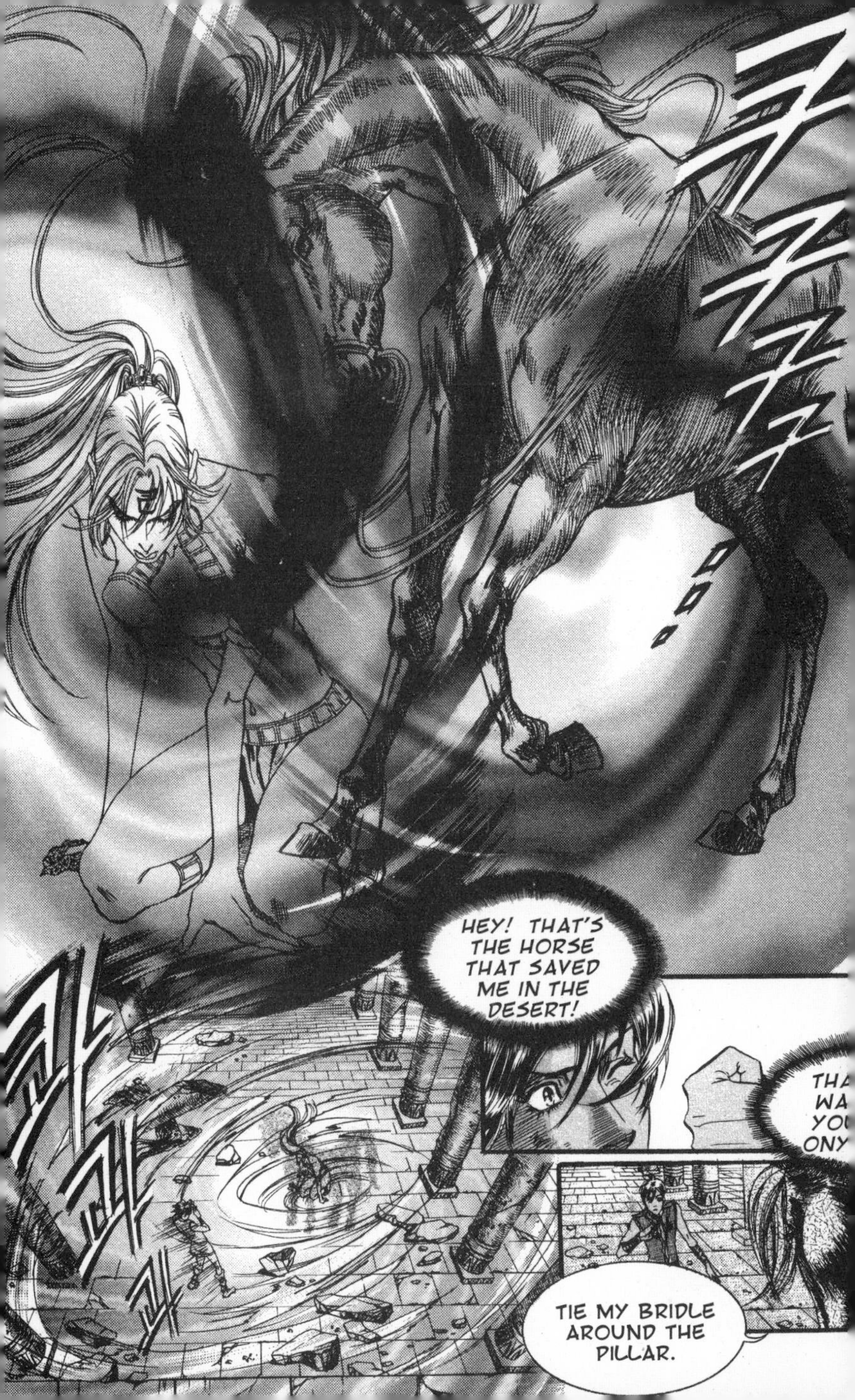
HEY! THAT'S THE HORSE THAT SAVED ME IN THE DESERT!
TIE MY BRIDLE AROUND THE PILLAR.

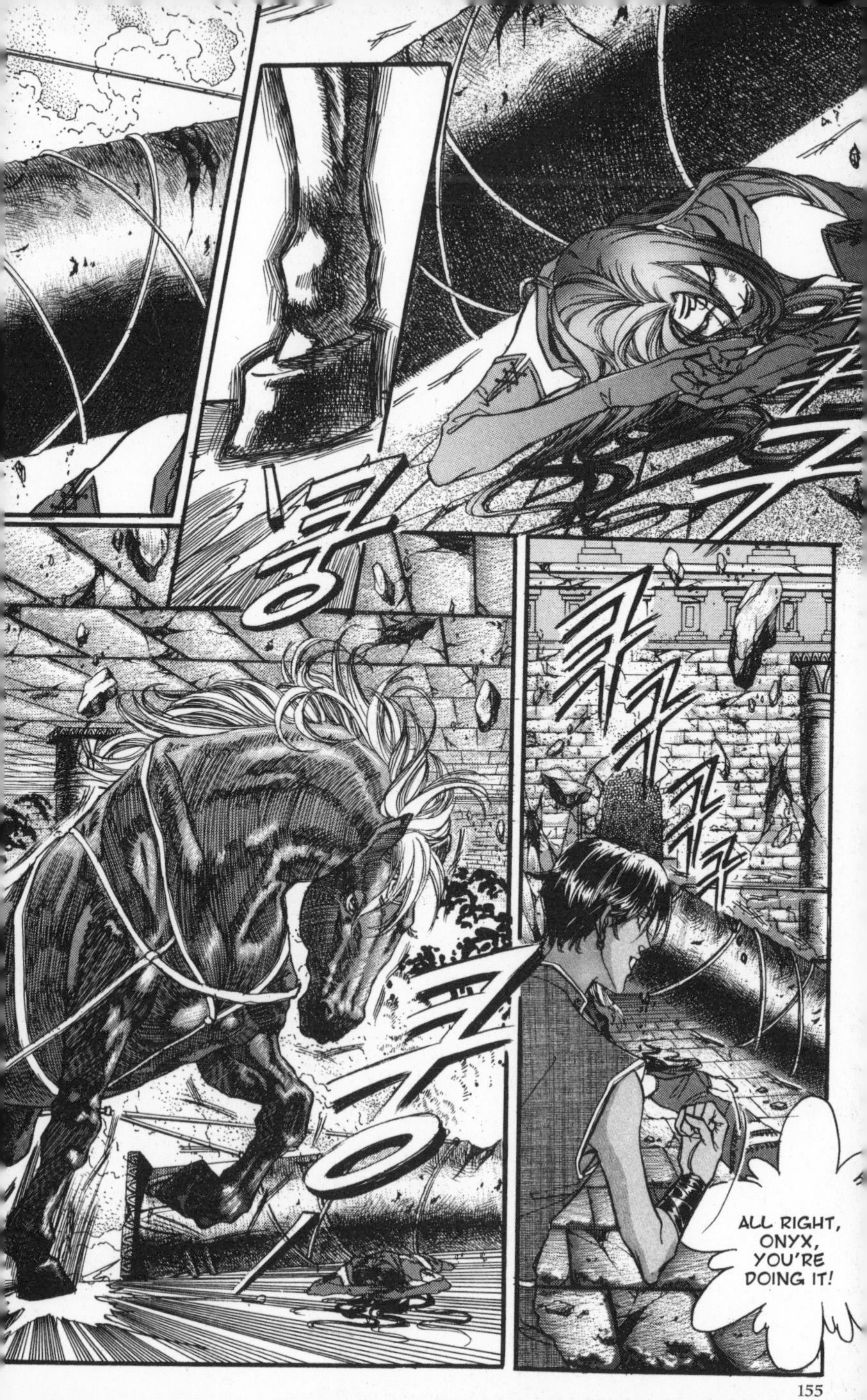
ALL RIGHT, ONYX, YOU'RE DOING IT!

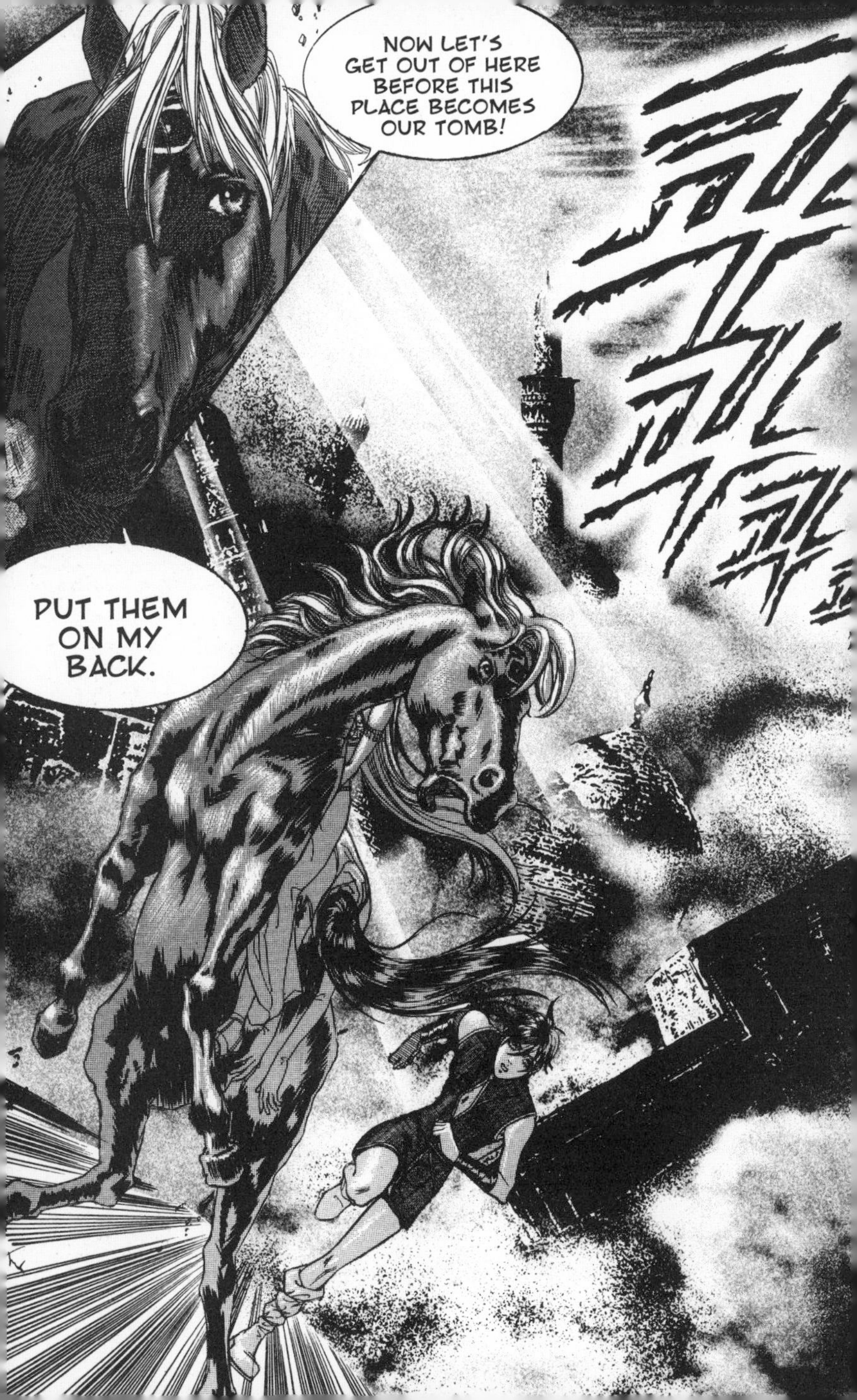
NOW LET'S GET OUT OF HERE BEFORE THIS PLACE BECOMES OUR TOMB!
PUT THEM ON MY BACK.

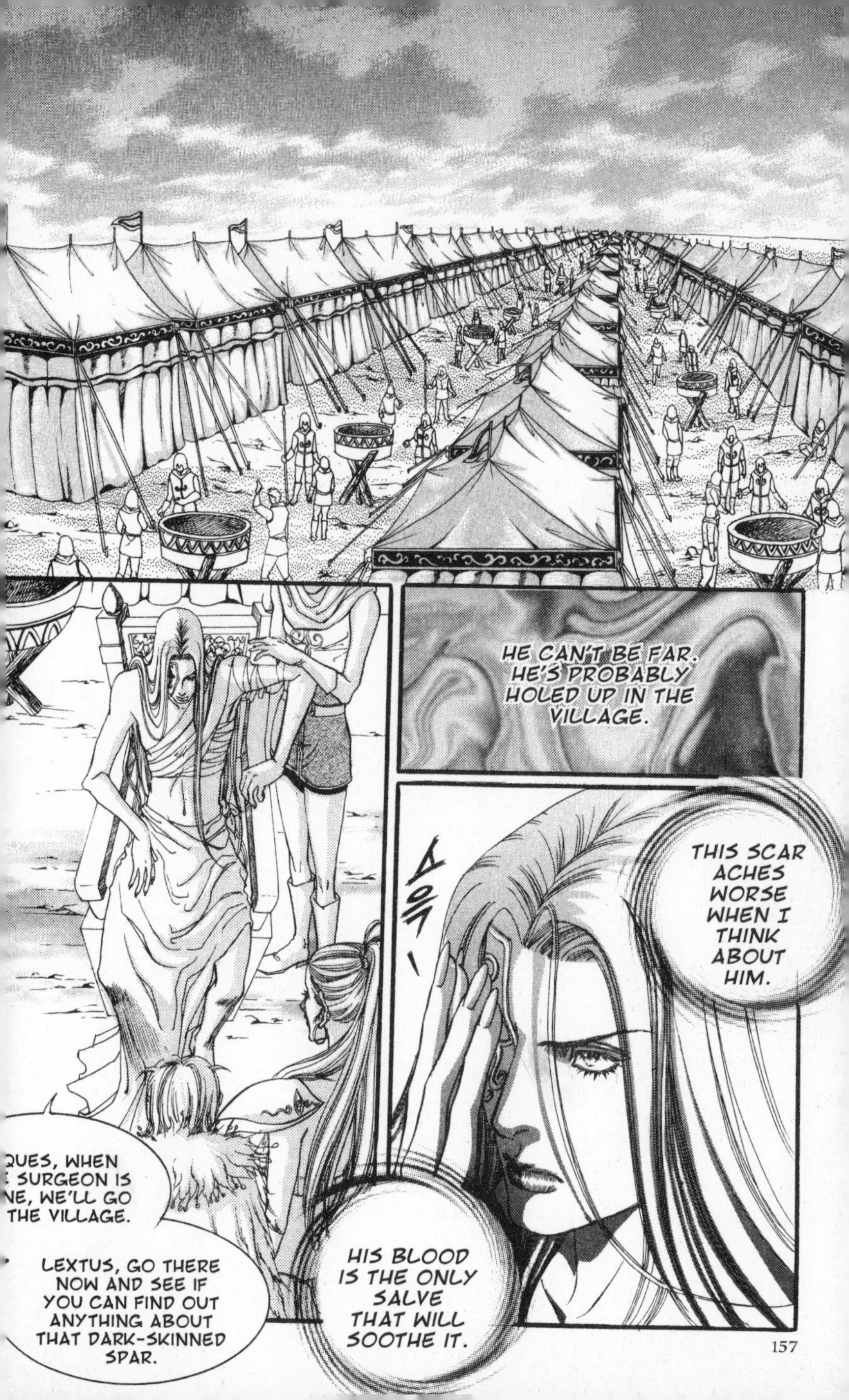
QUES, WHEN E SURGEON IS NE, WE'LL GO THE VILLAGE.
LEXTUS, GO THERE NOW AND SEE IF YOU CAN FIND OUT ANYTHING ABOUT THAT DARK-SKINNED SPAR.
HE CAN'T BE FAR. HE'S PROBABLY HOLED UP IN THE VILLAGE.
THIS SCAR ACHES WORSE WHEN I THINK ABOUT HIM.
HIS BLOOD IS THE ONLY SALVE THAT WILL SOOTHE IT.

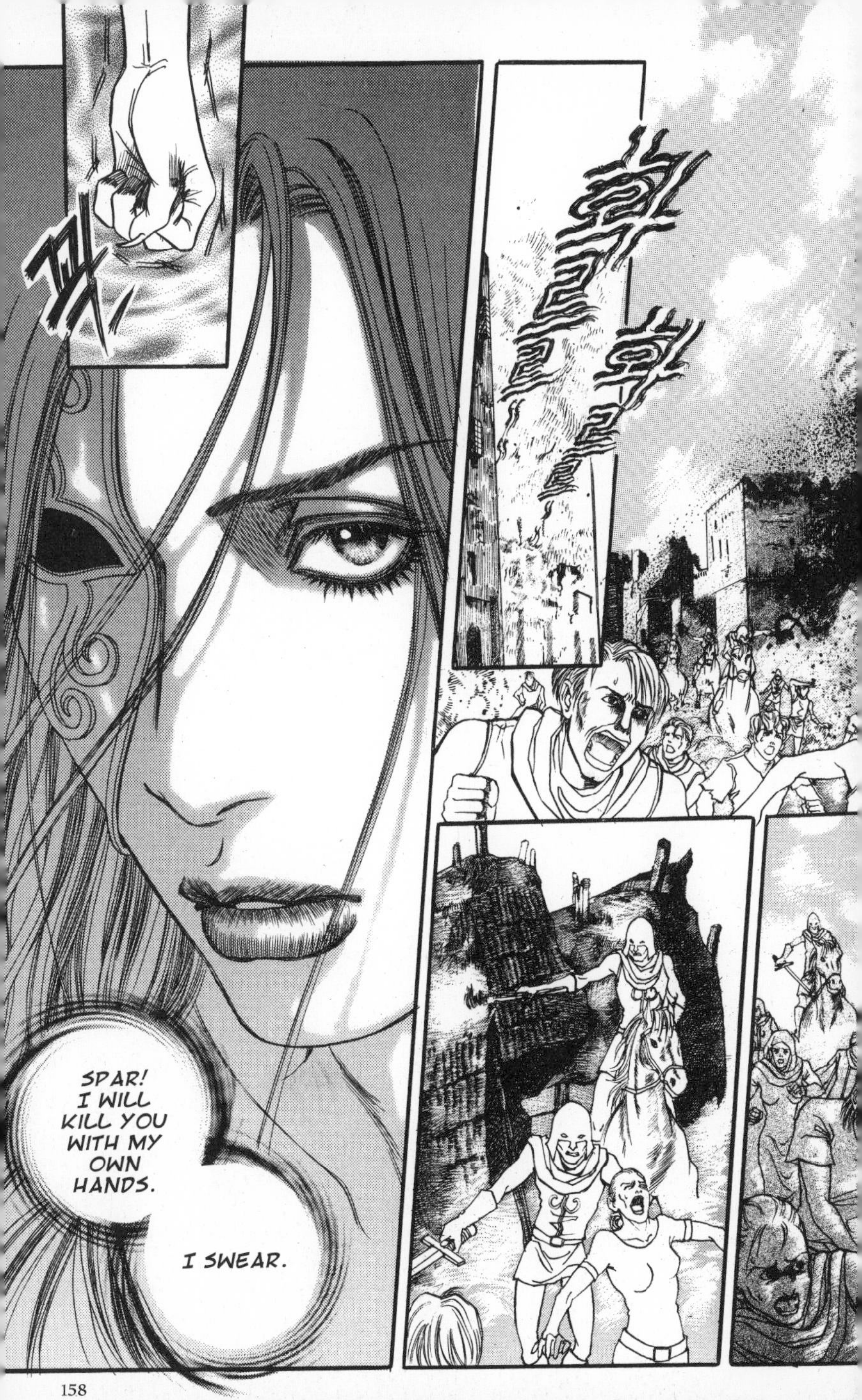
SPAR! I WILL KILL YOU WITH MY OWN HANDS.
I SWEAR.

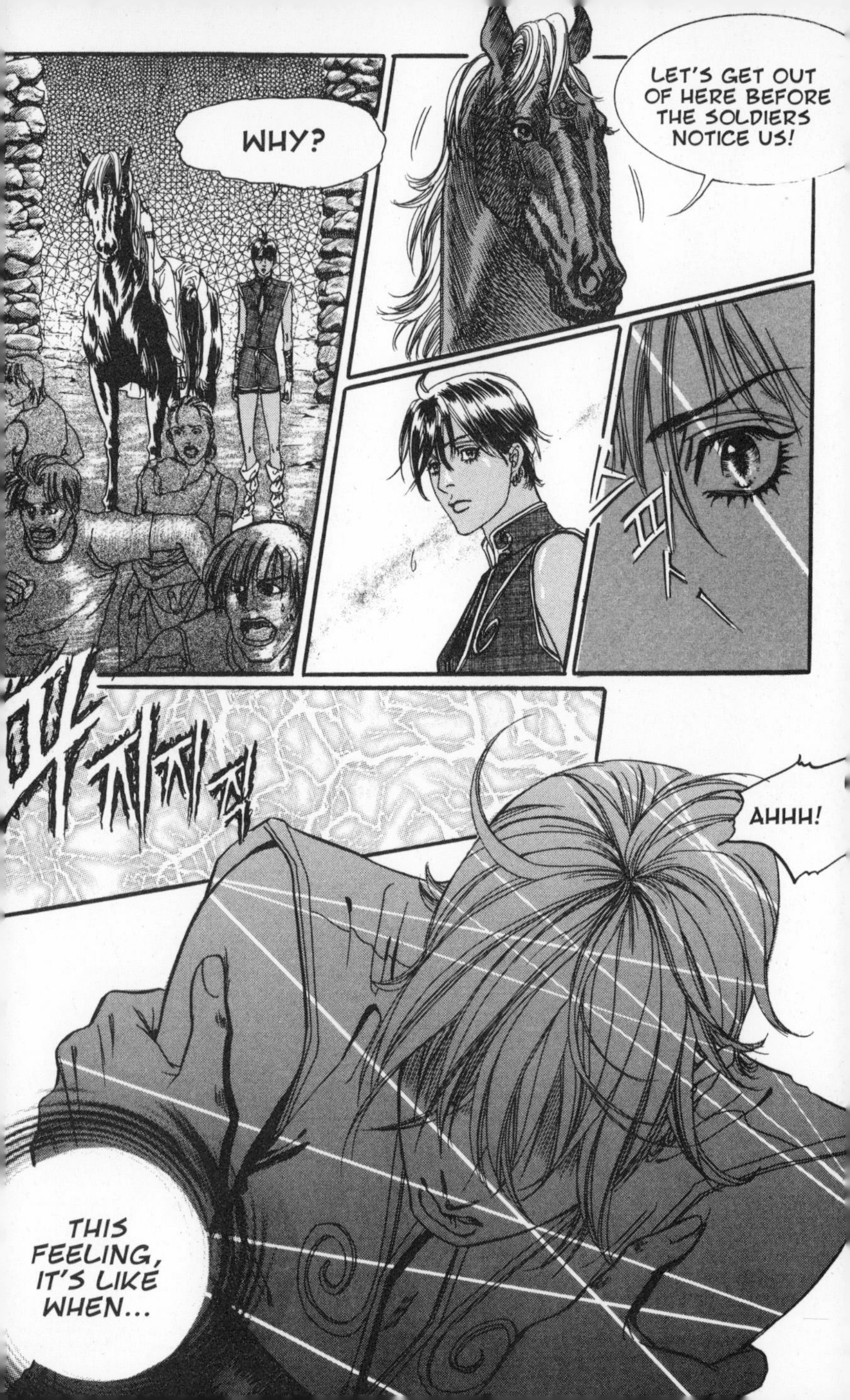
WHY?
LET'S GET OUT OF HERE BEFORE THE SOLDIERS NOTICE US!
AHHH!
THIS FEELING, IT'S LIKE WHEN...

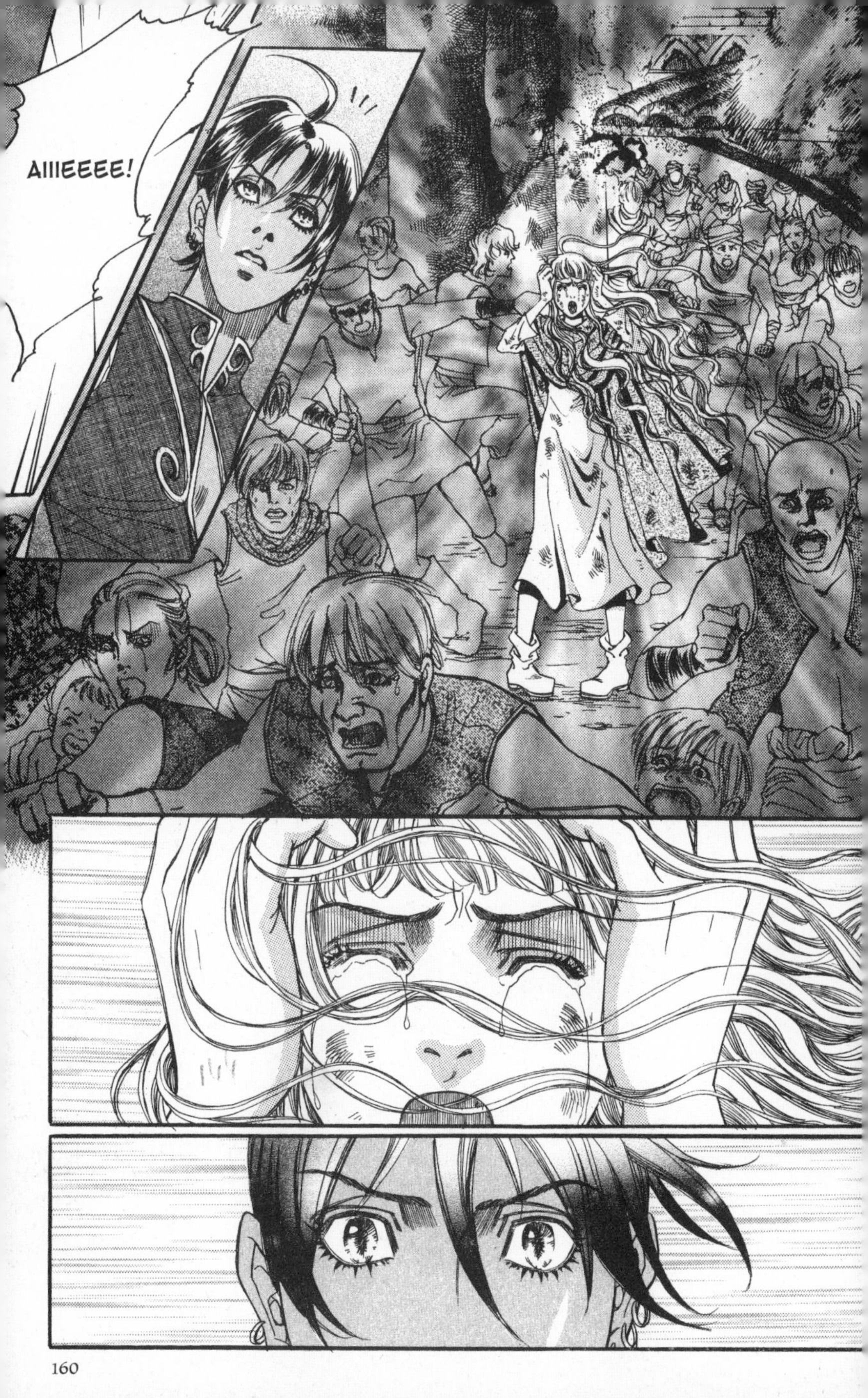
AIIIEEEE!

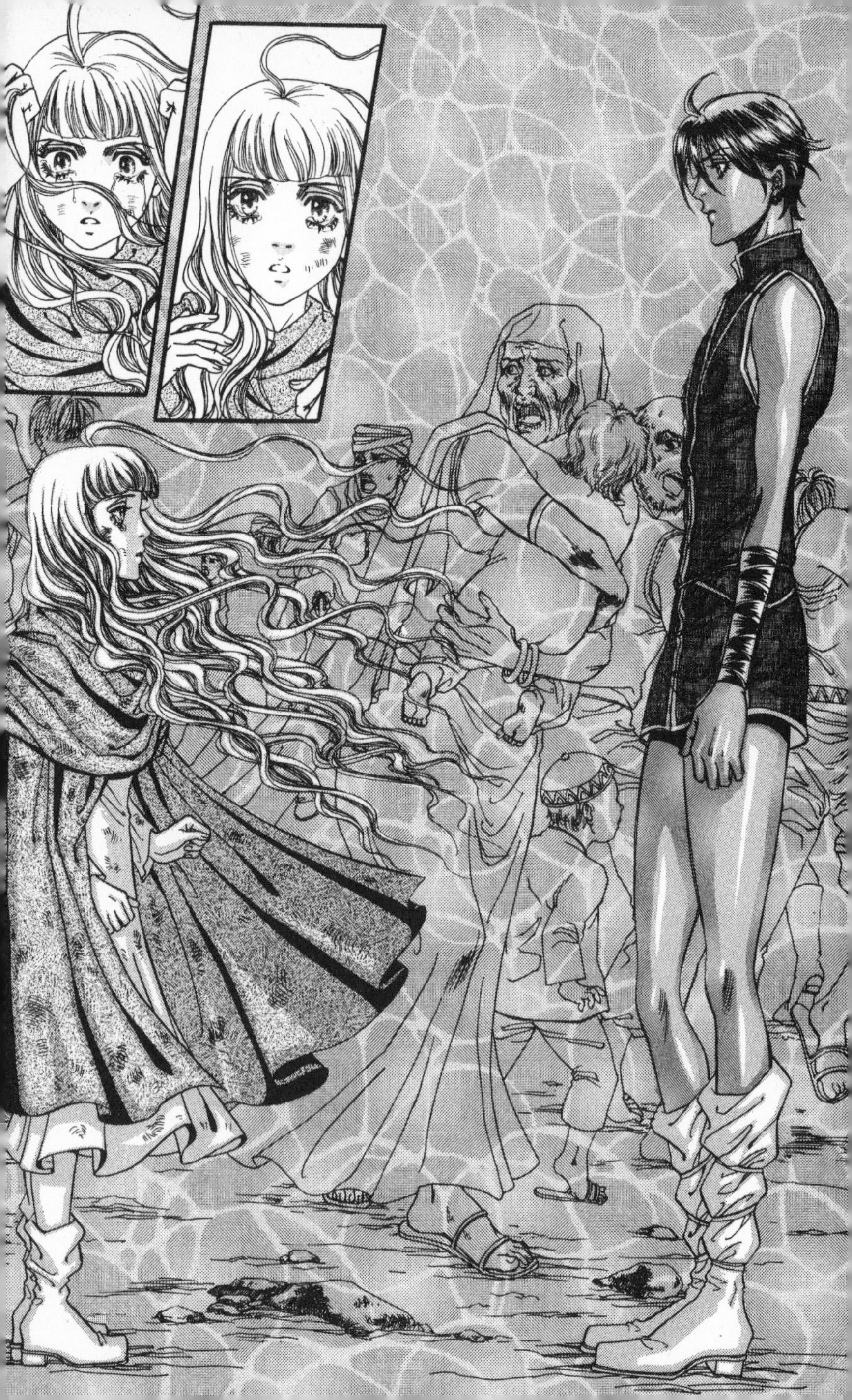

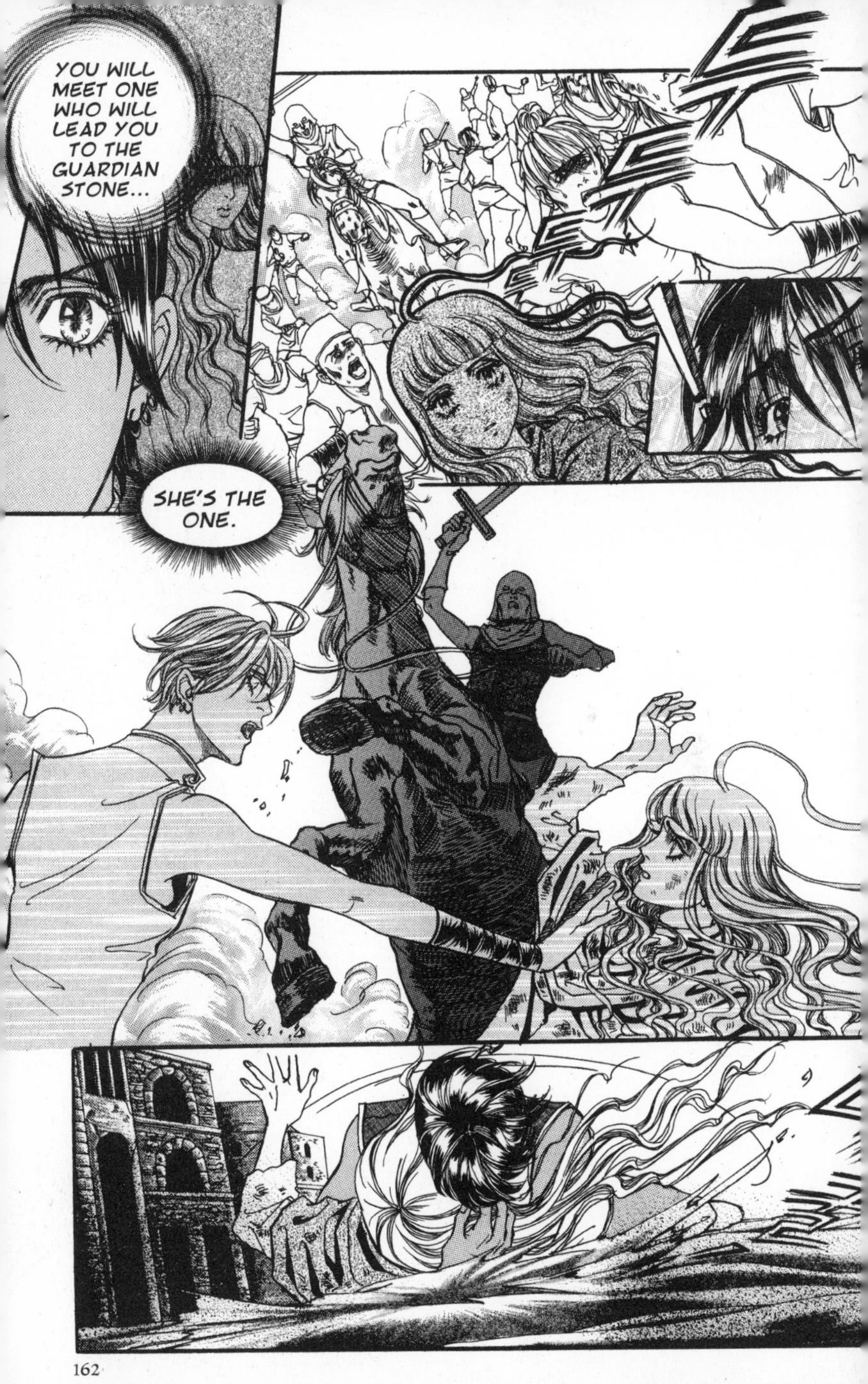
YOU WILL MEET ONE WHO WILL LEAD YOU TO THE GUARDIAN STONE...
SHE'S THE ONE.

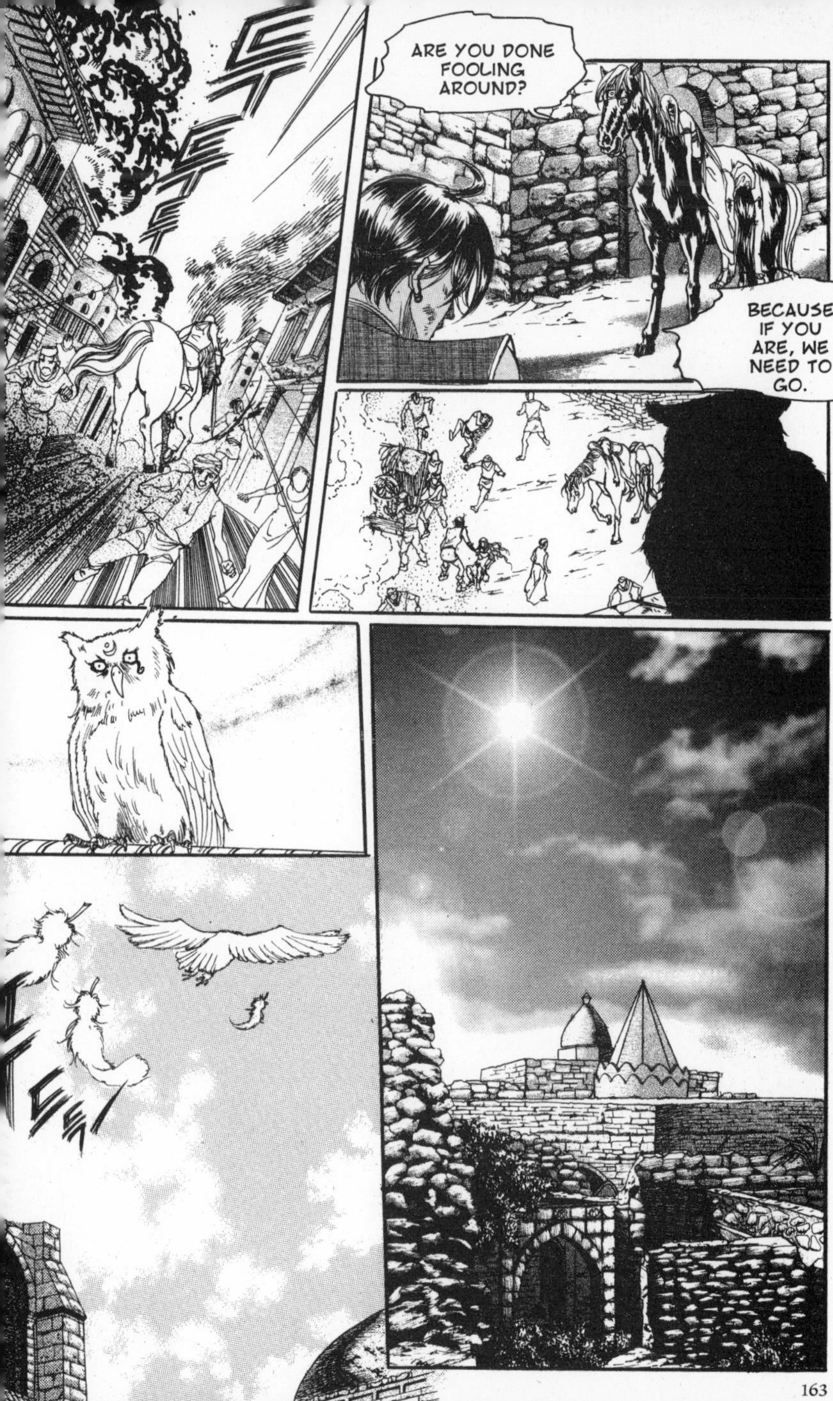
ARE YOU DONE FOOLING AROUND?
BECAUSE IF YOU ARE, WE NEED TO GO.

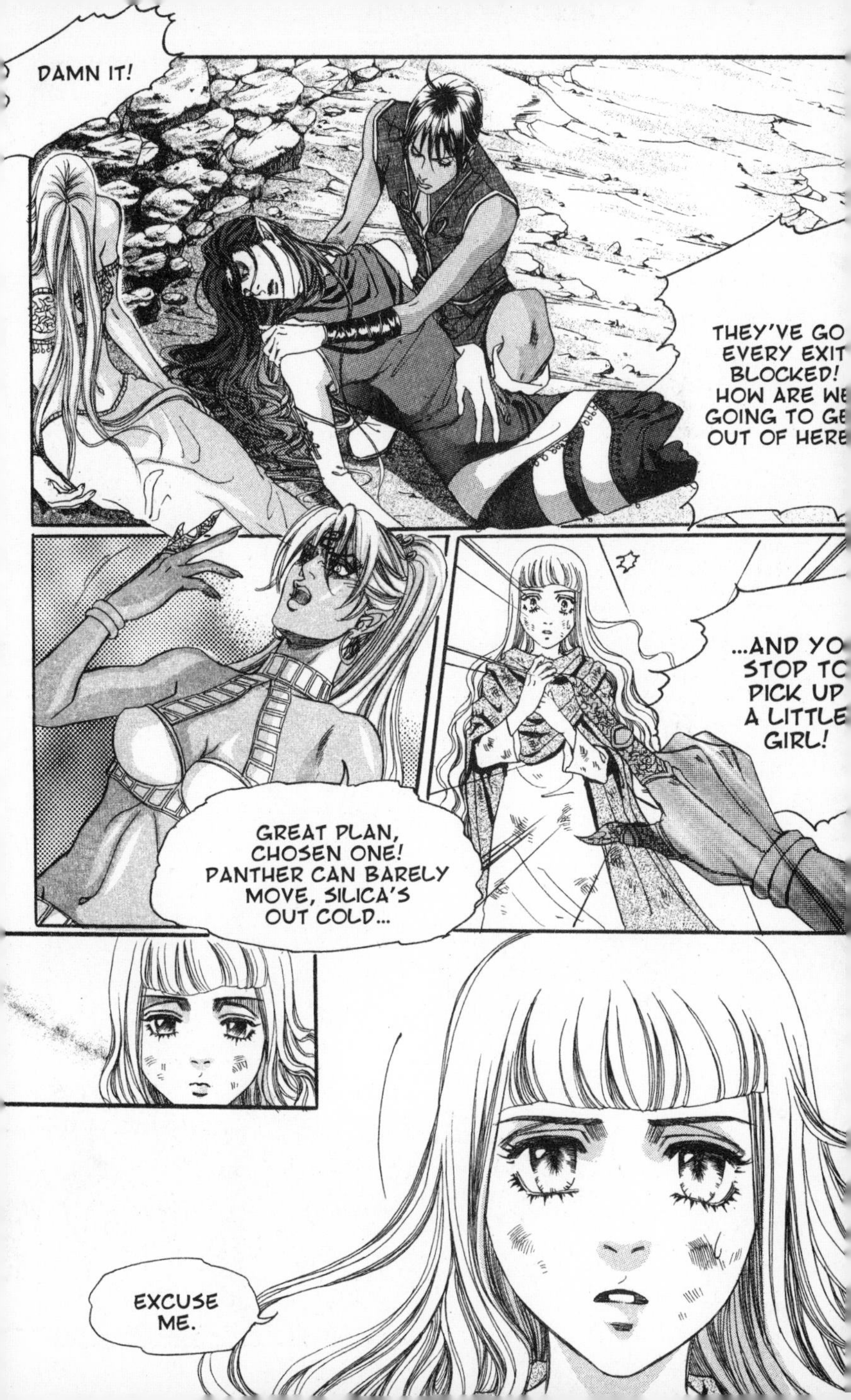
DAMN IT!
THEY'VE GO EVERY EXIT BLOCKED! HOW ARE WE GOING TO GE OUT OF HERE
GREAT PLAN, CHOSEN ONE! PANTHER CAN BARELY MOVE, SILICA'S OUT COLD...
...AND YO STOP TO PICK UP A LITTLE GIRL!
EXCUSE ME.

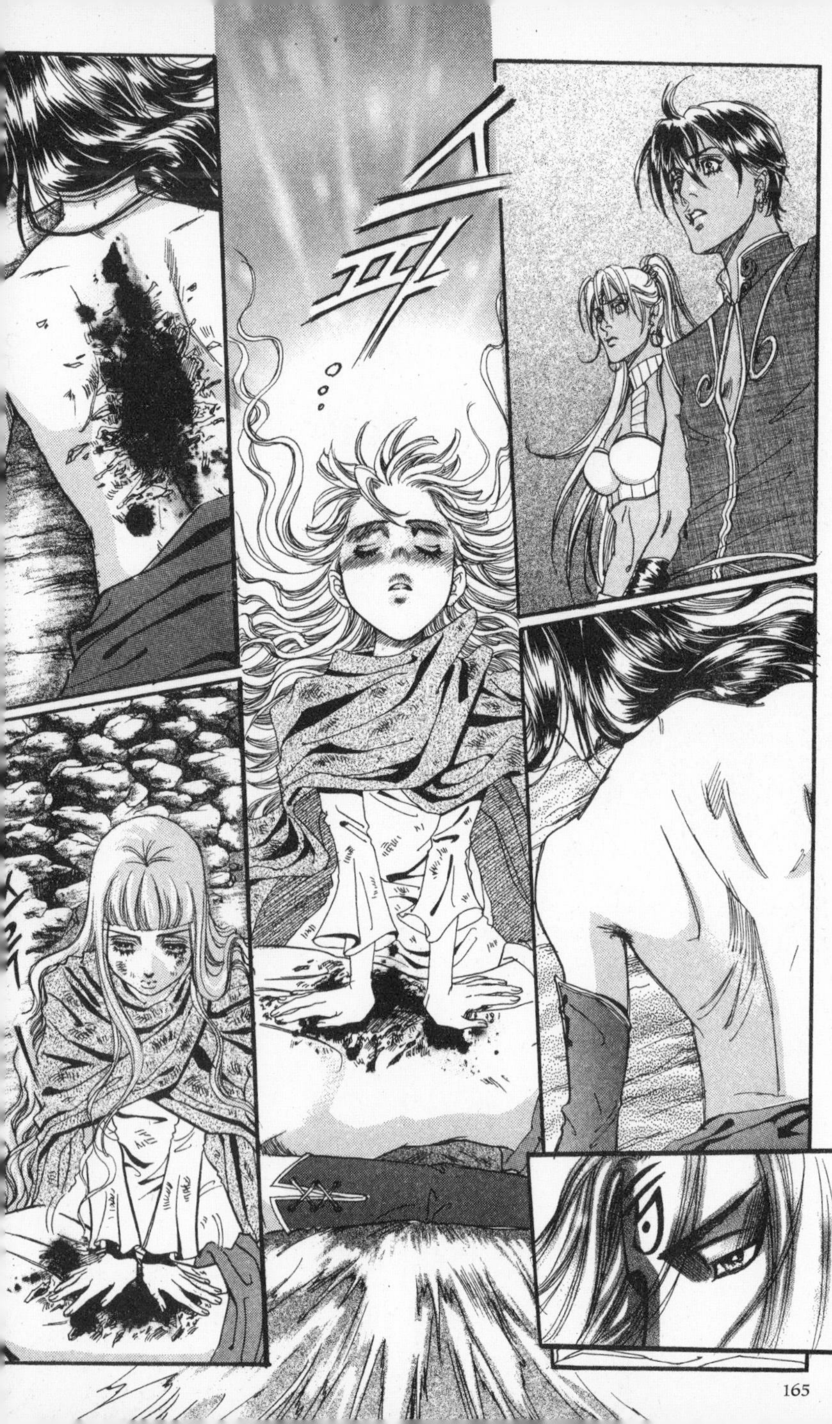

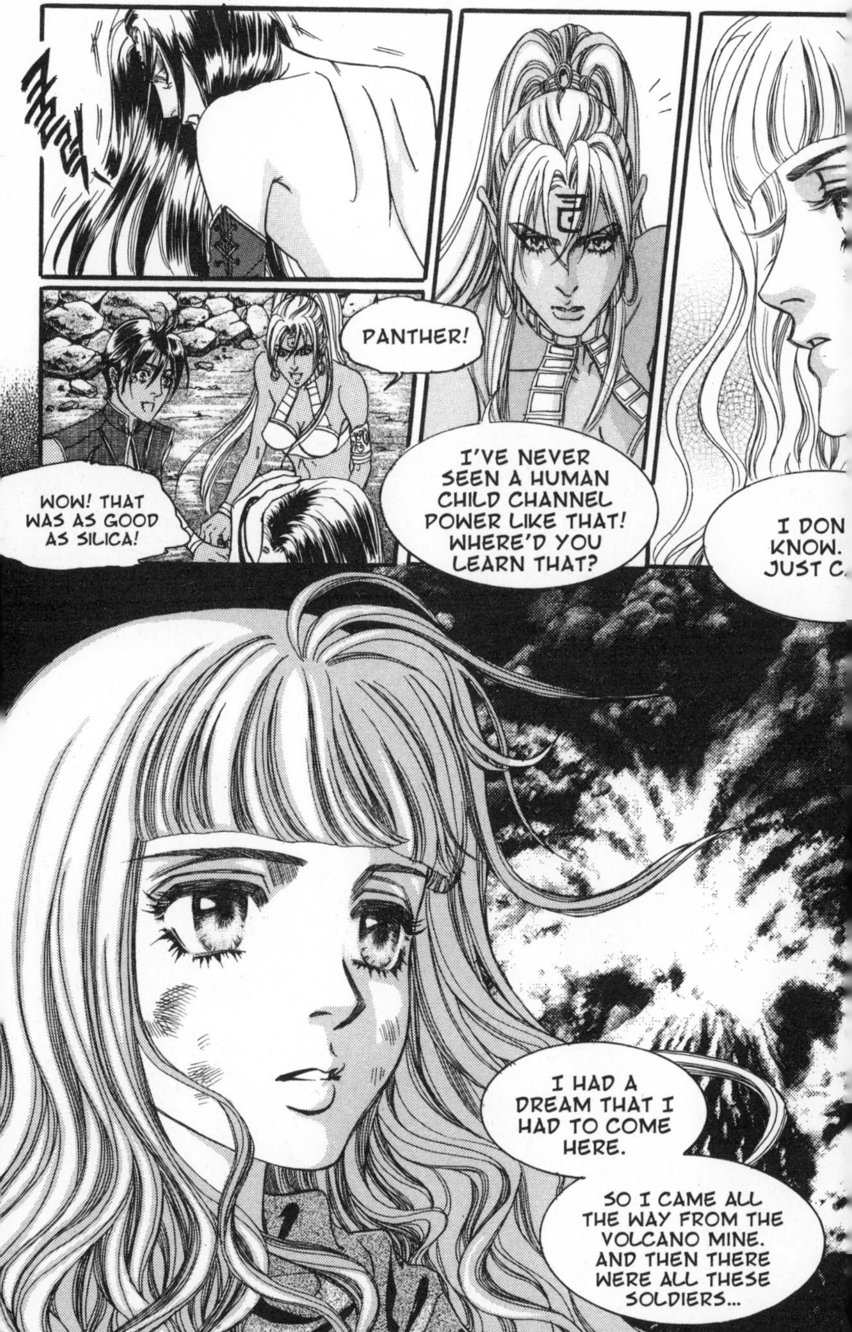
콜럭
PANTHER!
WOW! THAT WAS AS GOOD AS SILICA!
I'VE NEVER SEEN A HUMAN CHILD CHANNEL POWER LIKE THAT! WHERE'D YOU LEARN THAT?
I DON KNOW. JUST C
I HAD A DREAM THAT I HAD TO COME HERE.
SO I CAME ALL THE WAY FROM THE VOLCANO MINE. AND THEN THERE WERE ALL THESE SOLDIERS...

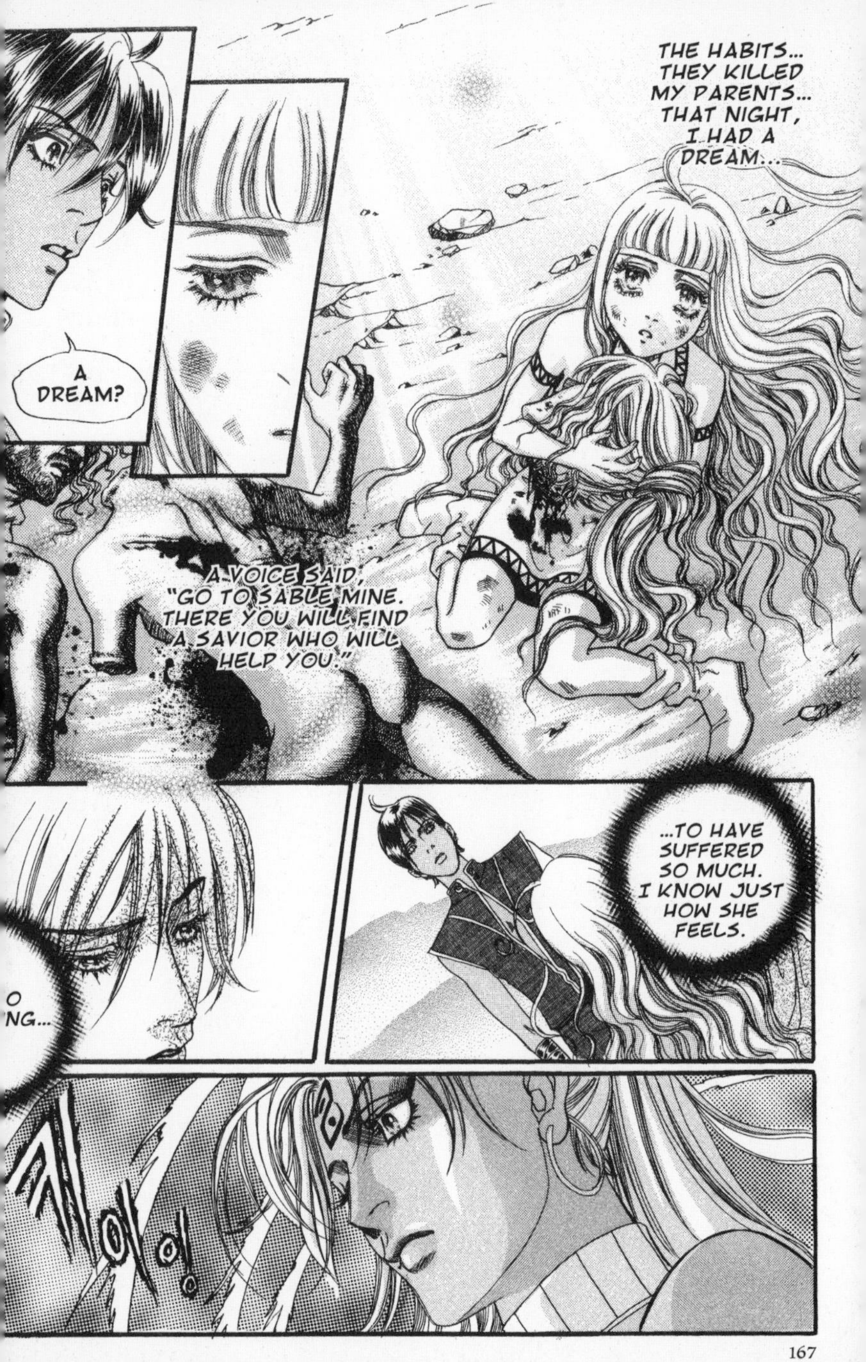
THE HABITS... THEY KILLED MY PARENTS... THAT NIGHT, I HAD A DREAM...
A DREAM?
A VOICE SAID, "GO TO SABLE MINE. THERE YOU WILL FIND A SAVIOR WHO WILL HELP YOU."
O NG...
...TO HAVE SUFFERED SO MUCH. I KNOW JUST HOW SHE FEELS.

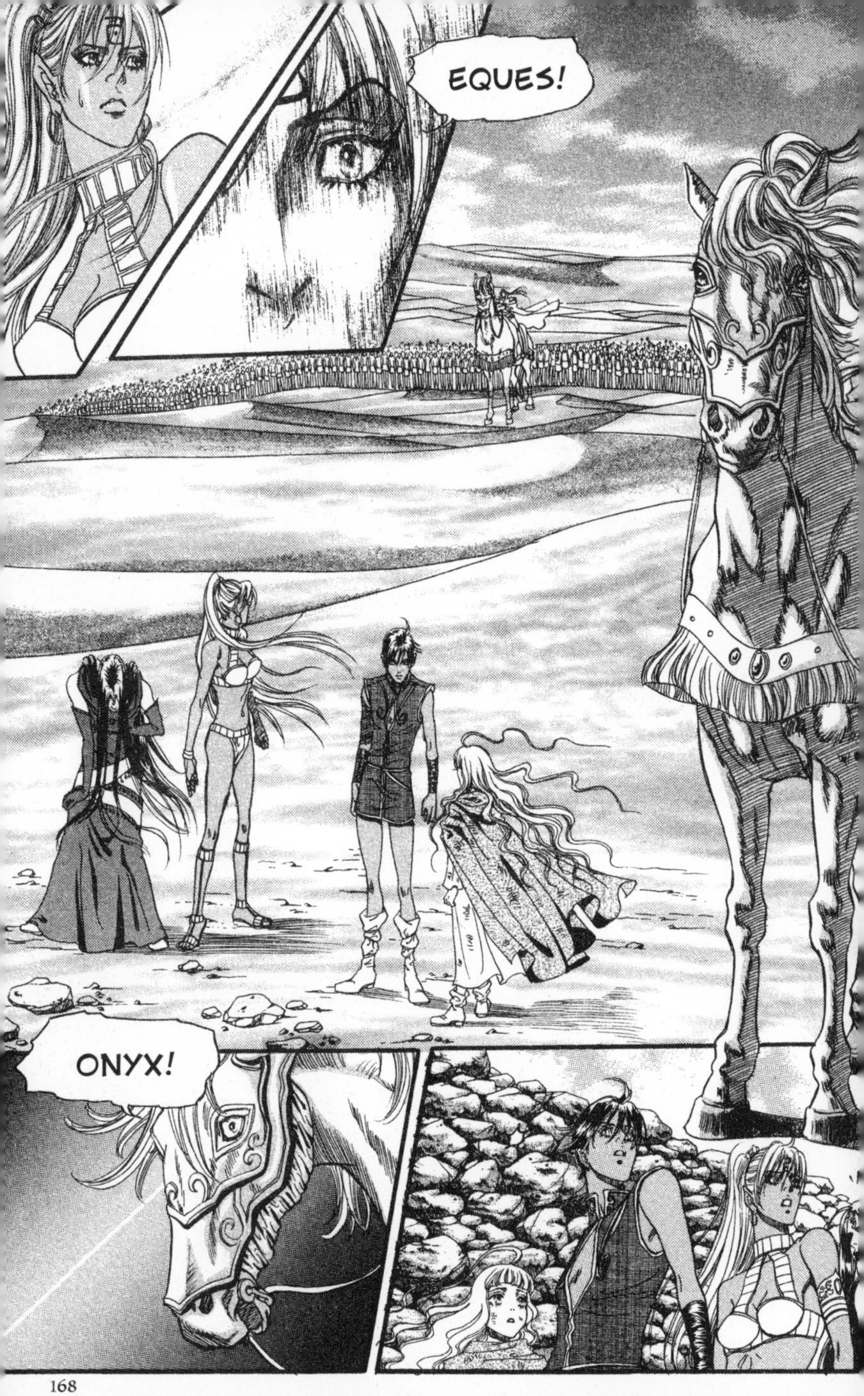
EQUES!
ONYX!

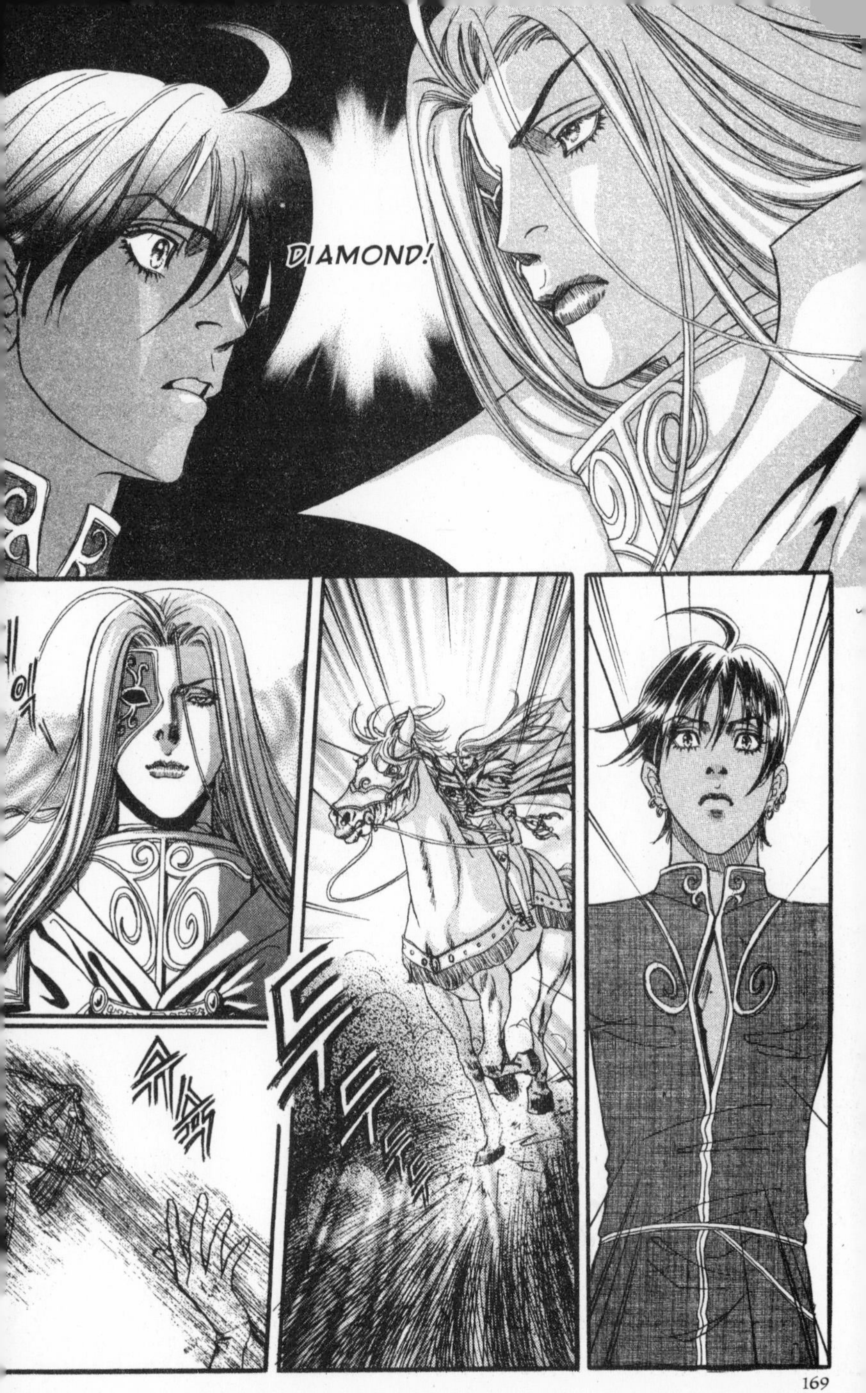
DIAMOND!

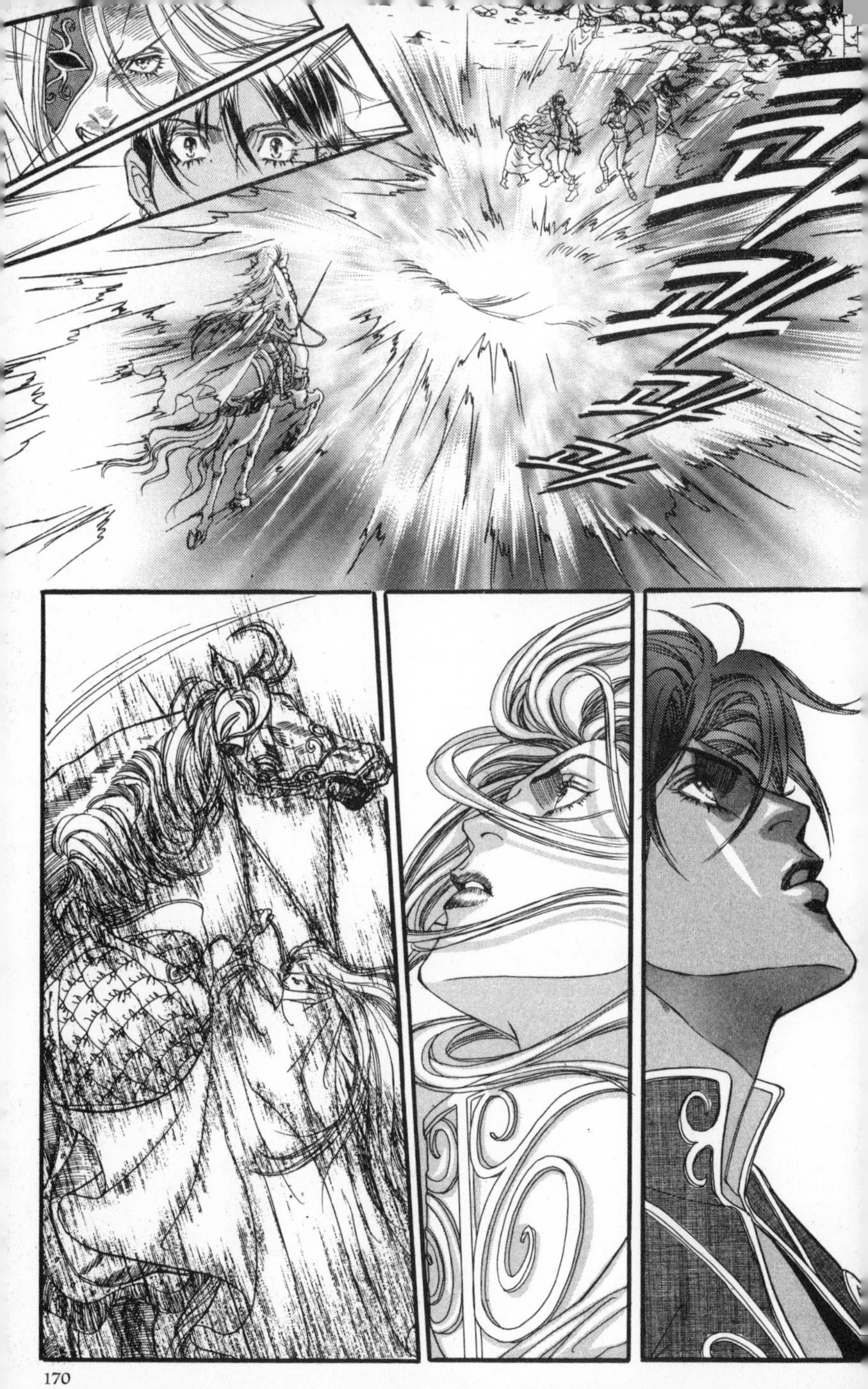

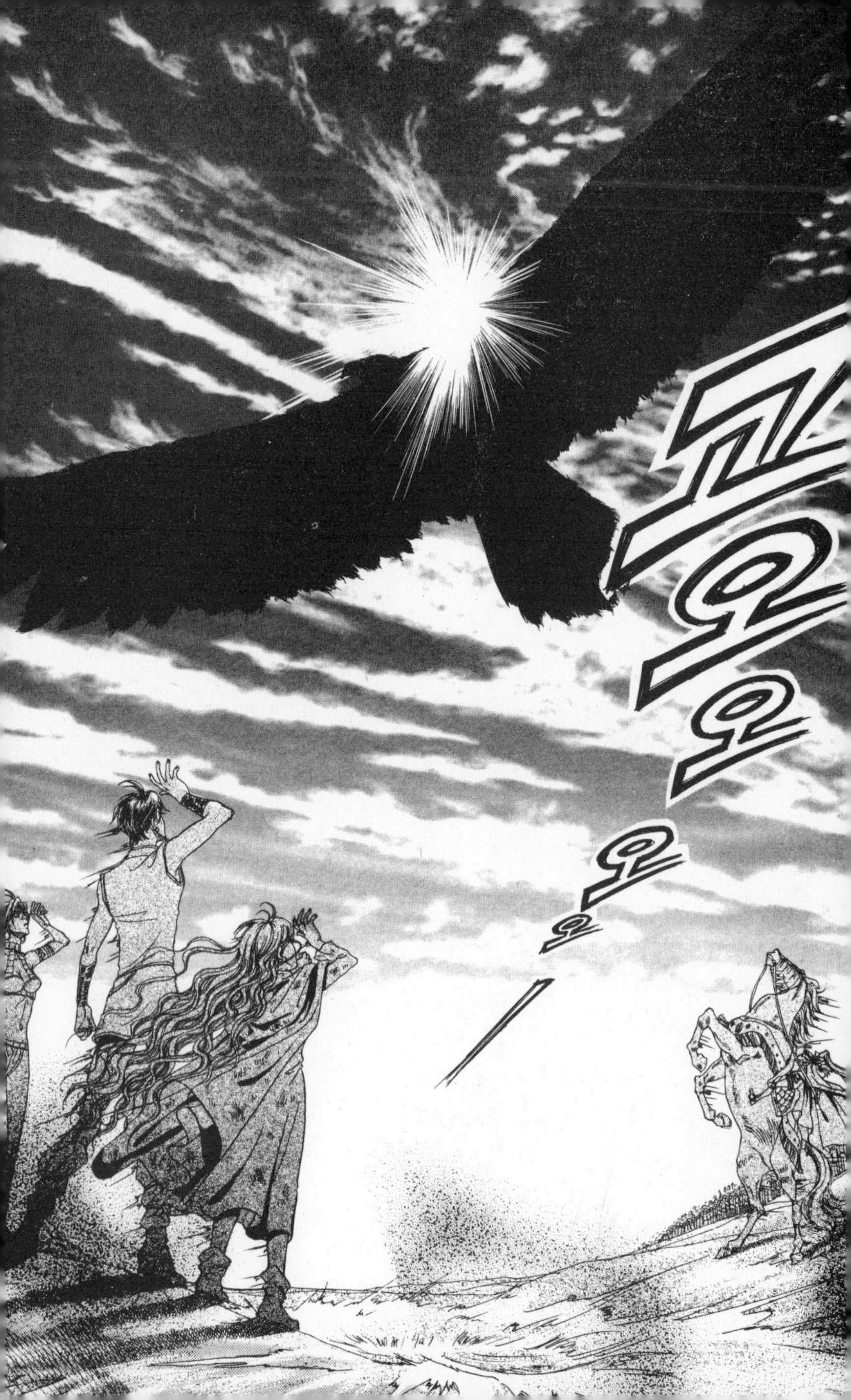

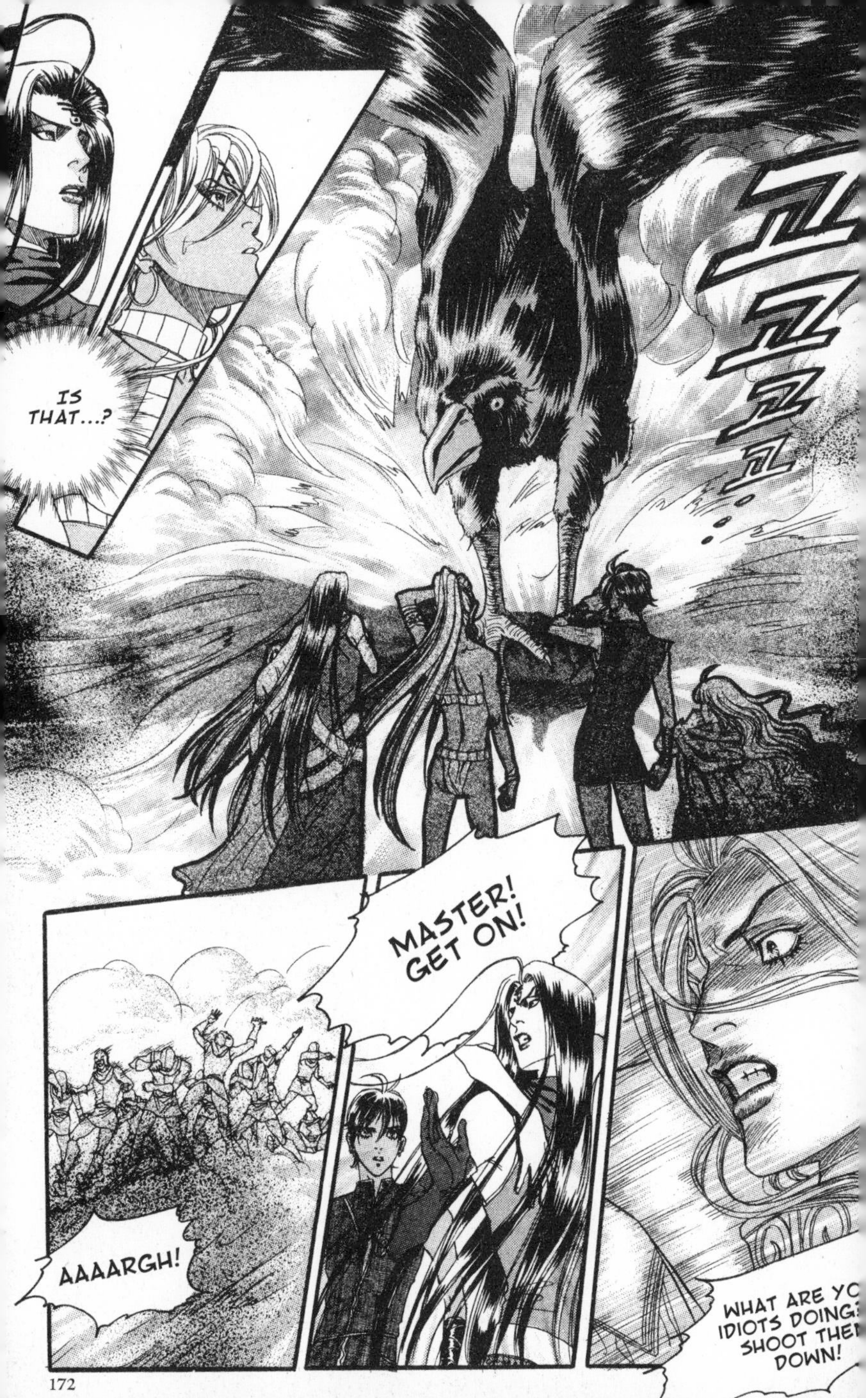
IS THAT...?
FZZZZZ...
MASTER! GET ON!
AAAARGH!
WHAT ARE YO
IDIOTS DOING
SHOOT THE
DOWN!

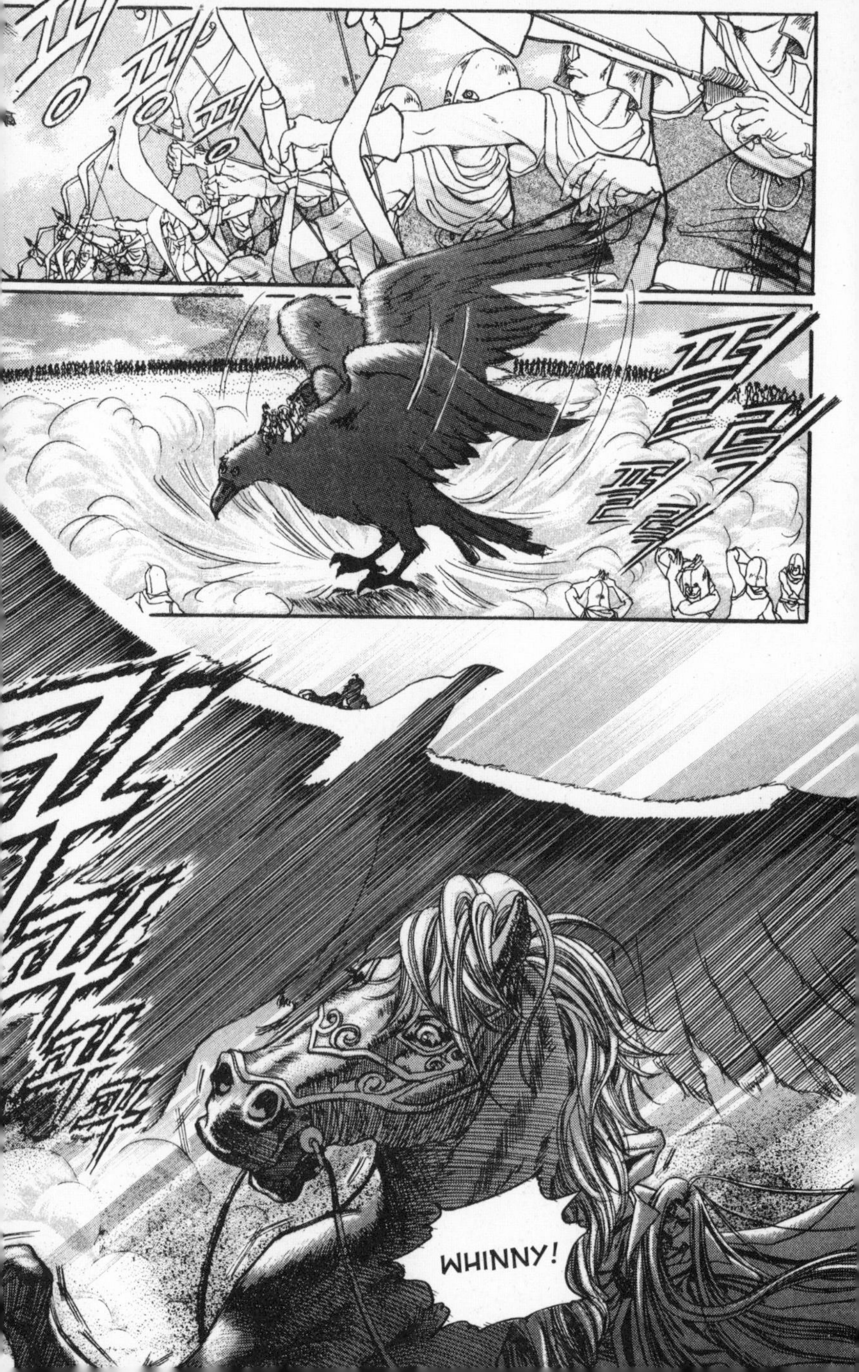
WHINNY!

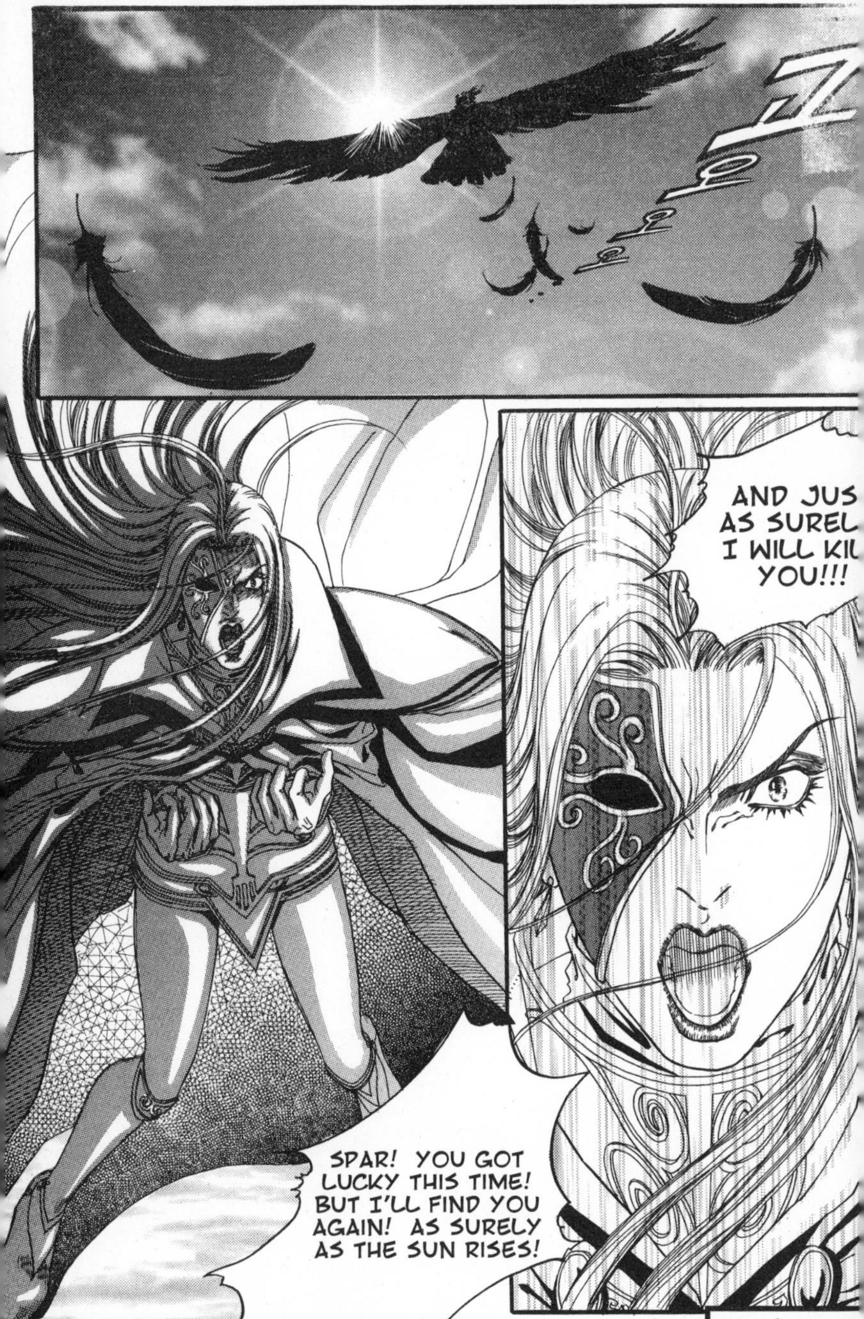
SPAR! YOU GOT LUCKY THIS TIME! BUT I'LL FIND YOU AGAIN! AS SURELY AS THE SUN RISES!
AND JUS AS SUREL I WILL KIL YOU!!!

End of Les Bijoux

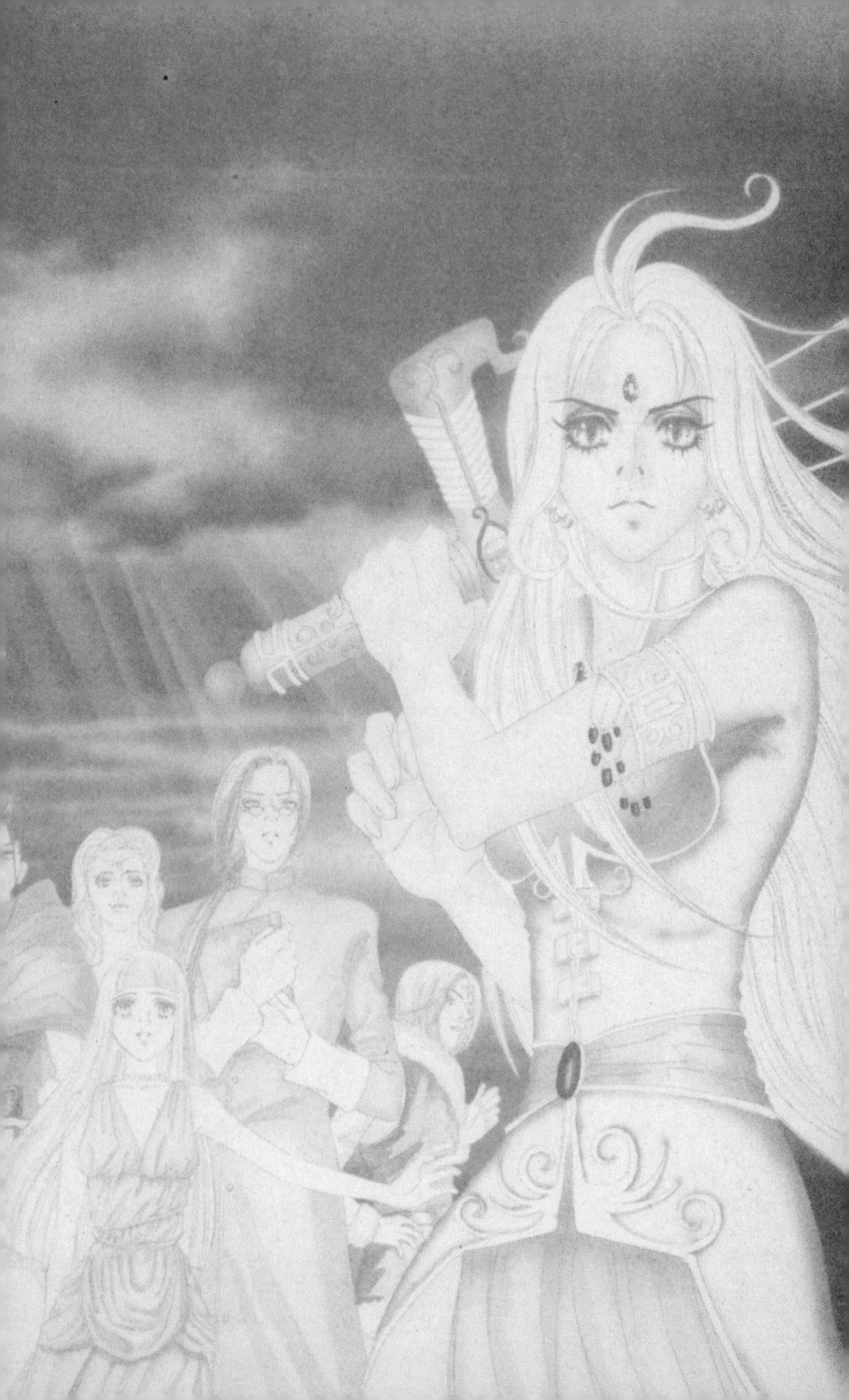

IN THE NEXT VOLUME OF

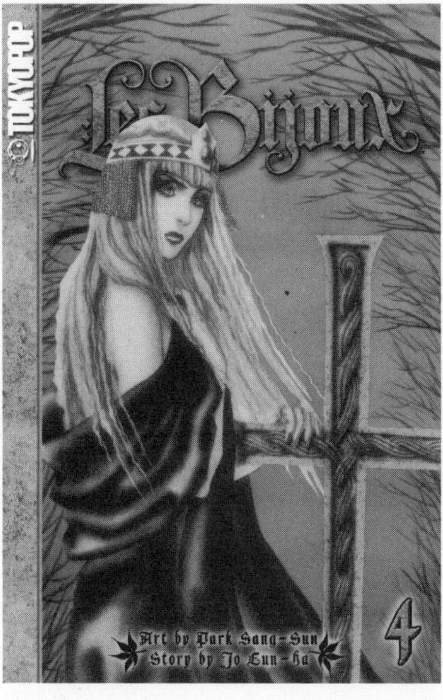
TOKYOPOP
Le Bijoux
4
Art by Park Sang-Sun
Story by Jo Eun-Ha

Lazuli in the Sky with Diamond

As power-hungry Diamond's plans for conquest begin to come to fruition, the one thing he covets most still eludes him--the mysterious Lazuli. In order to get on Diamond's good side, Emerald sets out to capture Lazuli. Meanwhile, although Lapis has vowed to kill Diamond, his female form is beginning to see a softer side of the Neige Mine's lord. Will Diamond become this girl's best friend?

Snow Drop™

Like love, a fragile flower
often blooms in unlikely places.

TOKYOPOP®

ALSO AVAILABLE FROM 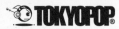 TOKYOPOP®

MANGA

.HACK//LEGEND OF THE TWILIGHT
@LARGE
ABENOBASHI: MAGICAL SHOPPING ARCADE
A.I. LOVE YOU
AI YORI AOSHI
ANGELIC LAYER
ARM OF KANNON
BABY BIRTH
BATTLE ROYALE
BATTLE VIXENS
BRAIN POWERED
BRIGADOON
B'TX
CANDIDATE FOR GODDESS, THE
CARDCAPTOR SAKURA
CARDCAPTOR SAKURA - MASTER OF THE CLOW
CHOBITS
CHRONICLES OF THE CURSED SWORD
CLAMP SCHOOL DETECTIVES
CLOVER
COMIC PARTY
CONFIDENTIAL CONFESSIONS
CORRECTOR YUI
COWBOY BEBOP
COWBOY BEBOP: SHOOTING STAR
CRAZY LOVE STORY
CRESCENT MOON
CROSS
CULDCEPT
CYBORG 009
D•N•ANGEL
DEMON DIARY
DEMON ORORON, THE
DEUS VITAE
DIABOLO
DIGIMON
DIGIMON TAMERS
DIGIMON ZERO TWO
DOLL
DRAGON HUNTER
DRAGON KNIGHTS
DRAGON VOICE
DREAM SAGA
DUKLYON: CLAMP SCHOOL DEFENDERS
EERIE QUEERIE!
END, THE
ERICA SAKURAZAWA: COLLECTED WORKS
ET CETERA
ETERNITY
EVIL'S RETURN
FAERIES' LANDING
FAKE
FLCL
FLOWER OF THE DEEP SLEEP, THE
FORBIDDEN DANCE
FRUITS BASKET
G GUNDAM
GATEKEEPERS

GETBACKERS
GIRL GOT GAME
GIRL'S EDUCATIONAL CHARTER
GRAVITATION
GTO
GUNDAM BLUE DESTINY
GUNDAM SEED ASTRAY
GUNDAM WING
GUNDAM WING: BATTLEFIELD OF PACIFISTS
GUNDAM WING: ENDLESS WALTZ
GUNDAM WING: THE LAST OUTPOST (G-UNIT)
GUYS' GUIDE TO GIRLS
HANDS OFF!
HAPPY MANIA
HARLEM BEAT
HONEY MUSTARD
HYPER * RUN
I.N.V.U.
IMMORTAL RAIN
INITIAL D
INSTANT TEEN: JUST ADD NUTS
ISLAND
JING: KING OF BANDITS
JING: KING OF BANDITS - TWILIGHT TALES
JULINE
KARE KANO
KILL ME, KISS ME
KINDAICHI CASE FILES, THE
KING OF HELL
KODOCHA: SANA'S STAGE
LAMENT OF THE LAMB
LEGAL DRUG
LEGEND OF CHUN HYANG, THE
LES BIJOUX
LOVE HINA
LUPIN III
LUPIN III: WORLD'S MOST WANTED
MAGIC KNIGHT RAYEARTH I
MAGIC KNIGHT RAYEARTH II
MAHOROMATIC: AUTOMATIC MAIDEN
MAN OF MANY FACES
MARMALADE BOY
MARS
MARS: HORSE WITH NO NAME
METROID
MINK
MIRACLE GIRLS
MIYUKI-CHAN IN WONDERLAND
MODEL
MOU RYO-KIDEN
MY LOVE
NECK AND NECK
ONE
ONE I LOVE, THE
PARADISE KISS
PARASYTE
PASSION FRUIT
PEACH GIRL
PEACH GIRL: CHANGE OF HEART
PET SHOP OF HORRORS

03.22.04T

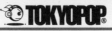
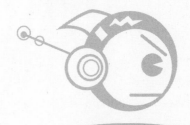

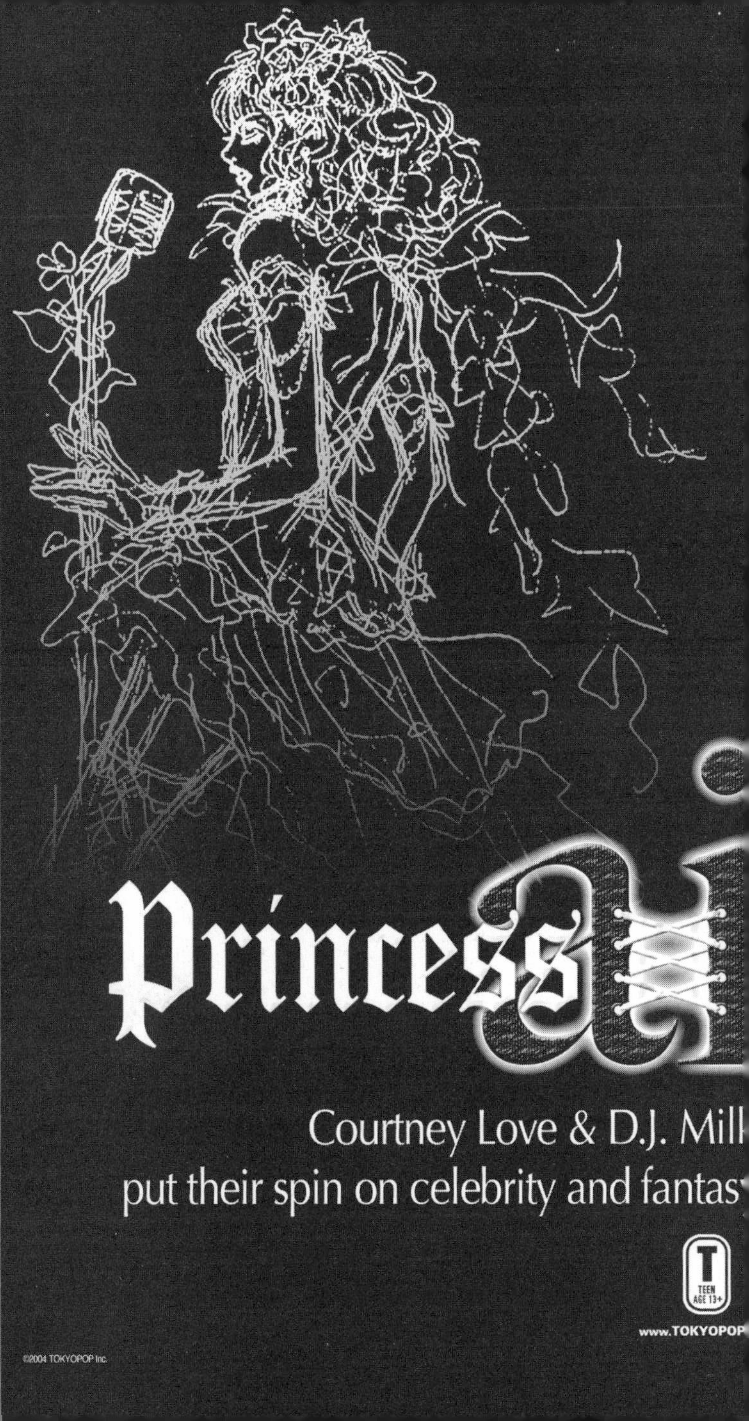
Princess
Courtney Love & D.J. Mill
put their spin on celebrity and fantas
T
TEEN AGE 13+
www.TOKYOPOP
©2004 TOKYOPOP Inc.

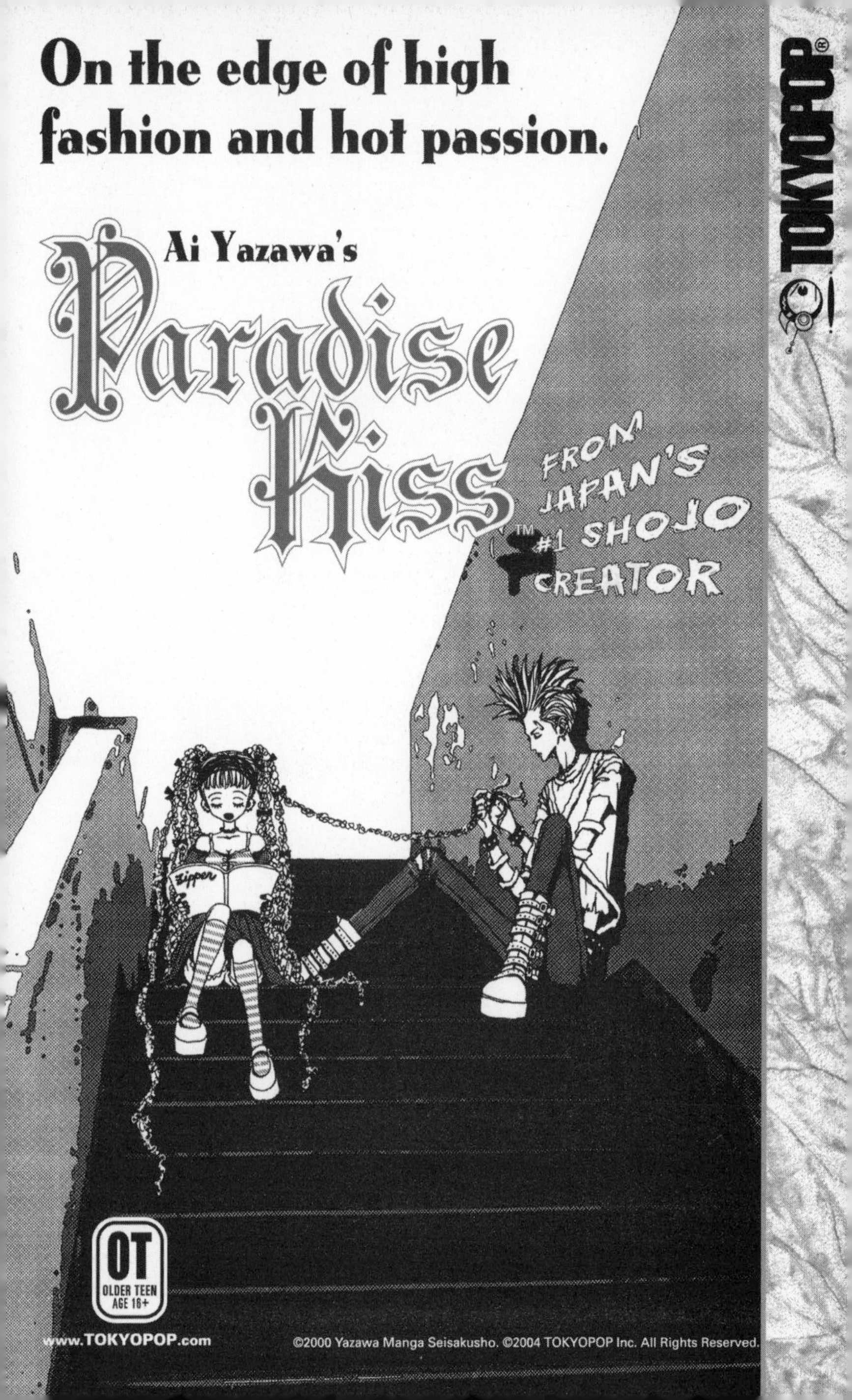
On the edge of high fashion and hot passion.
Ai Yazawa's
Paradise Kiss™
FROM JAPAN'S #1 SHOJO CREATOR
Zipper
TOKYOPOP®
OT OLDER TEEN AGE 16+
www.TOKYOPOP.com
©2000 Yazawa Manga Seisakusho. ©2004 TOKYOPOP Inc. All Rights Reserved.

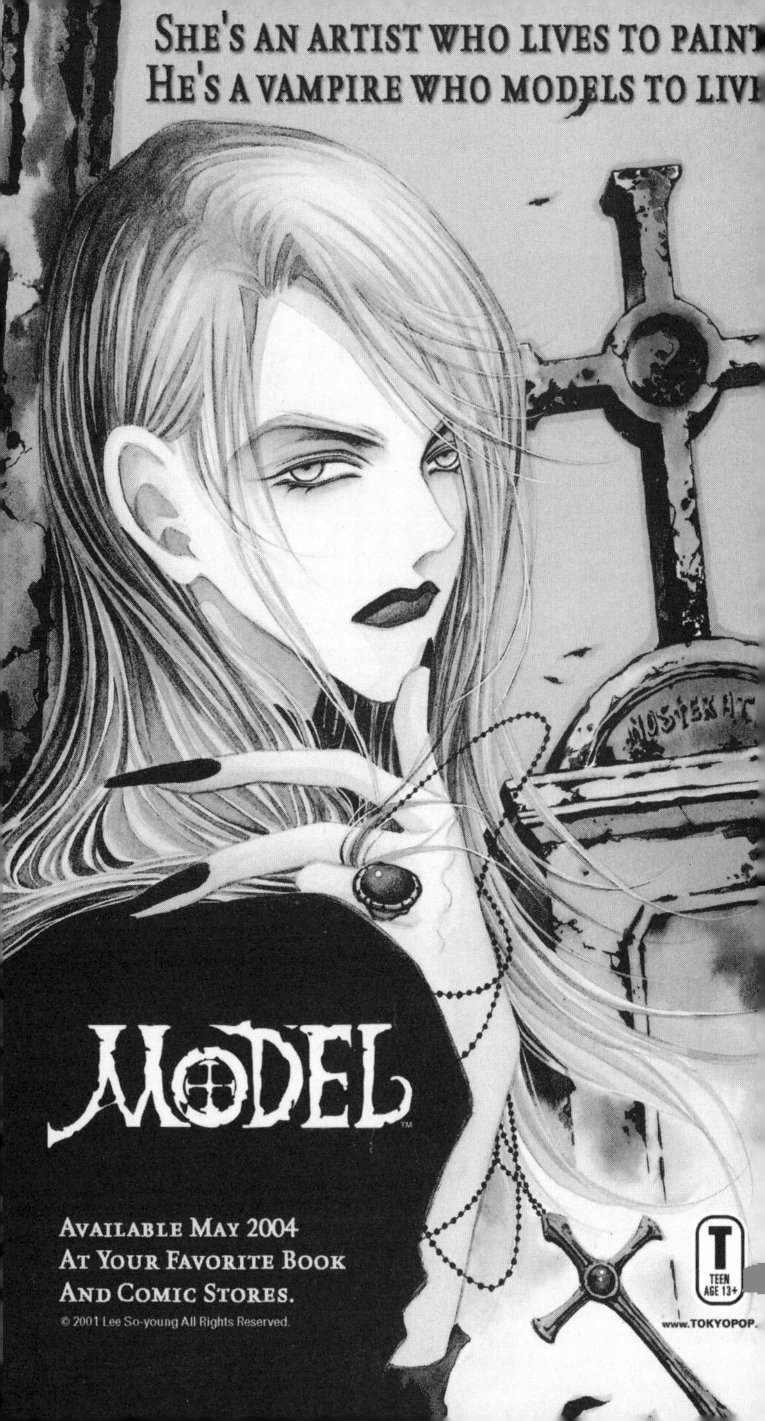
SHE'S AN ARTIST WHO LIVES TO PAIN
HE'S A VAMPIRE WHO MODELS TO LIV
MODEL™
AVAILABLE MAY 2004
AT YOUR FAVORITE BOOK
AND COMIC STORES.
© 2001 Lee So-young All Rights Reserved.
T
TEEN AGE 13+
www.TOKYOPOP.

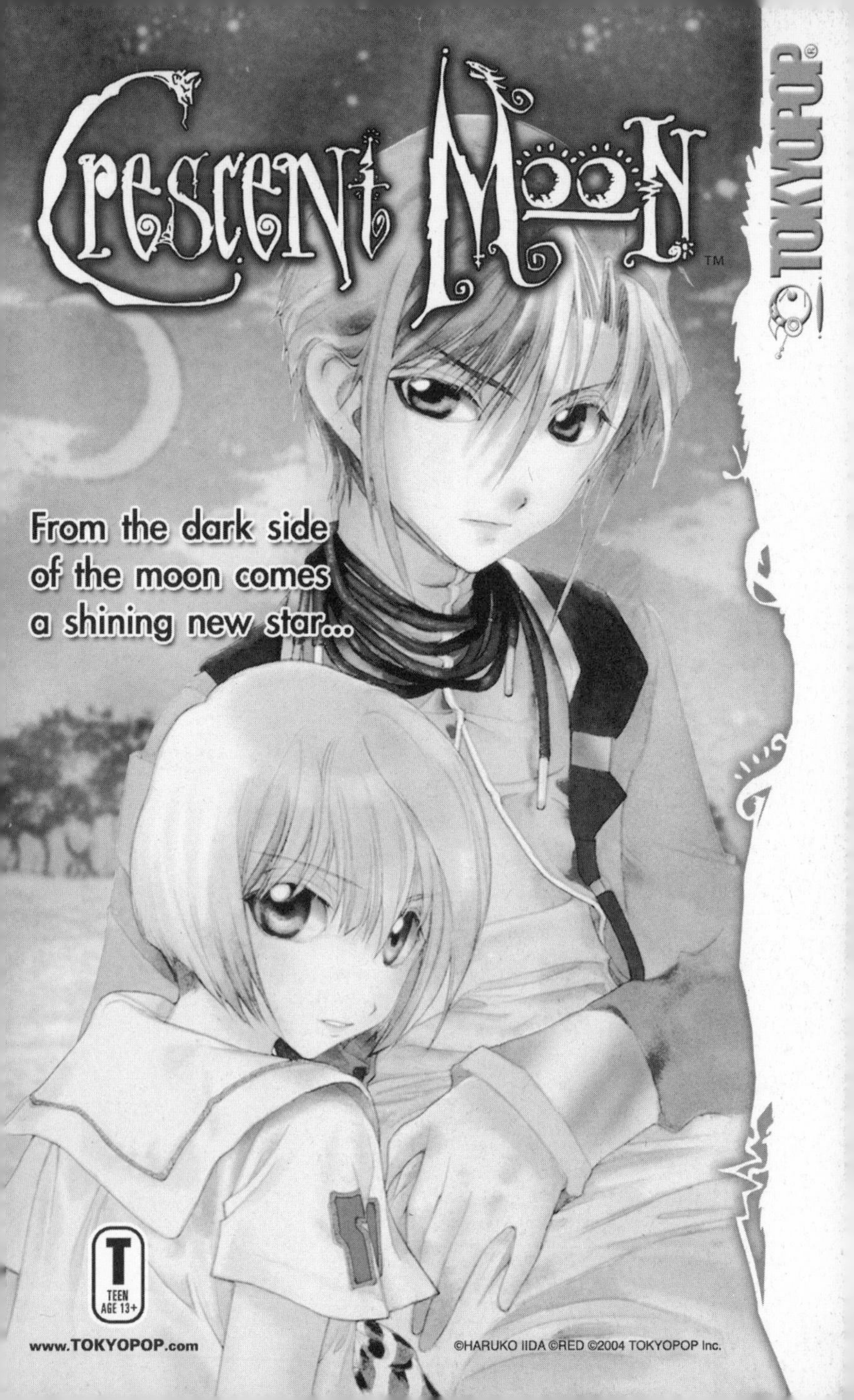
Crescent Moon™
TOKYOPOP®
From the dark side of the moon comes a shining new star...
T TEEN AGE 13+
www.TOKYOPOP.com
©HARUKO IIDA ©RED ©2004 TOKYOPOP Inc.

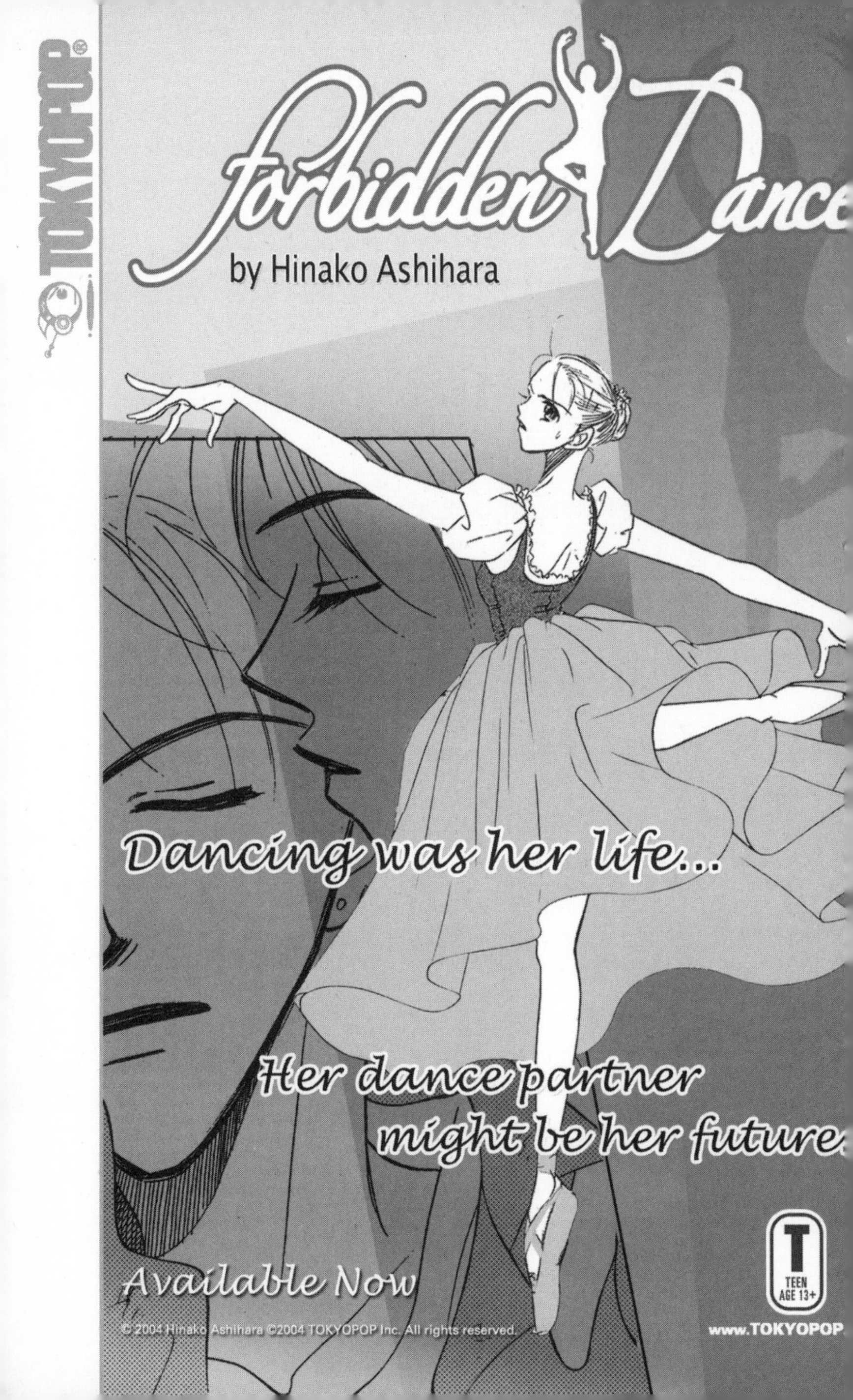
TOKYOPOP
forbidden Dance
by Hinako Ashihara
Dancing was her life...
Her dance partner
might be her future.
T
TEEN
AGE 13+
Available Now
© 2004 Hinako Ashihara ©2004 TOKYOPOP Inc. All rights reserved.
www.TOKYOPOP.

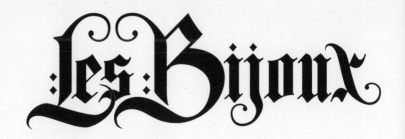

Les Bijoux

Story by
Jo Eun-Ha

Art by
Park Sang-Sun

Volume 3

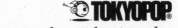

Los Angeles • Tokyo • London • Hamburg

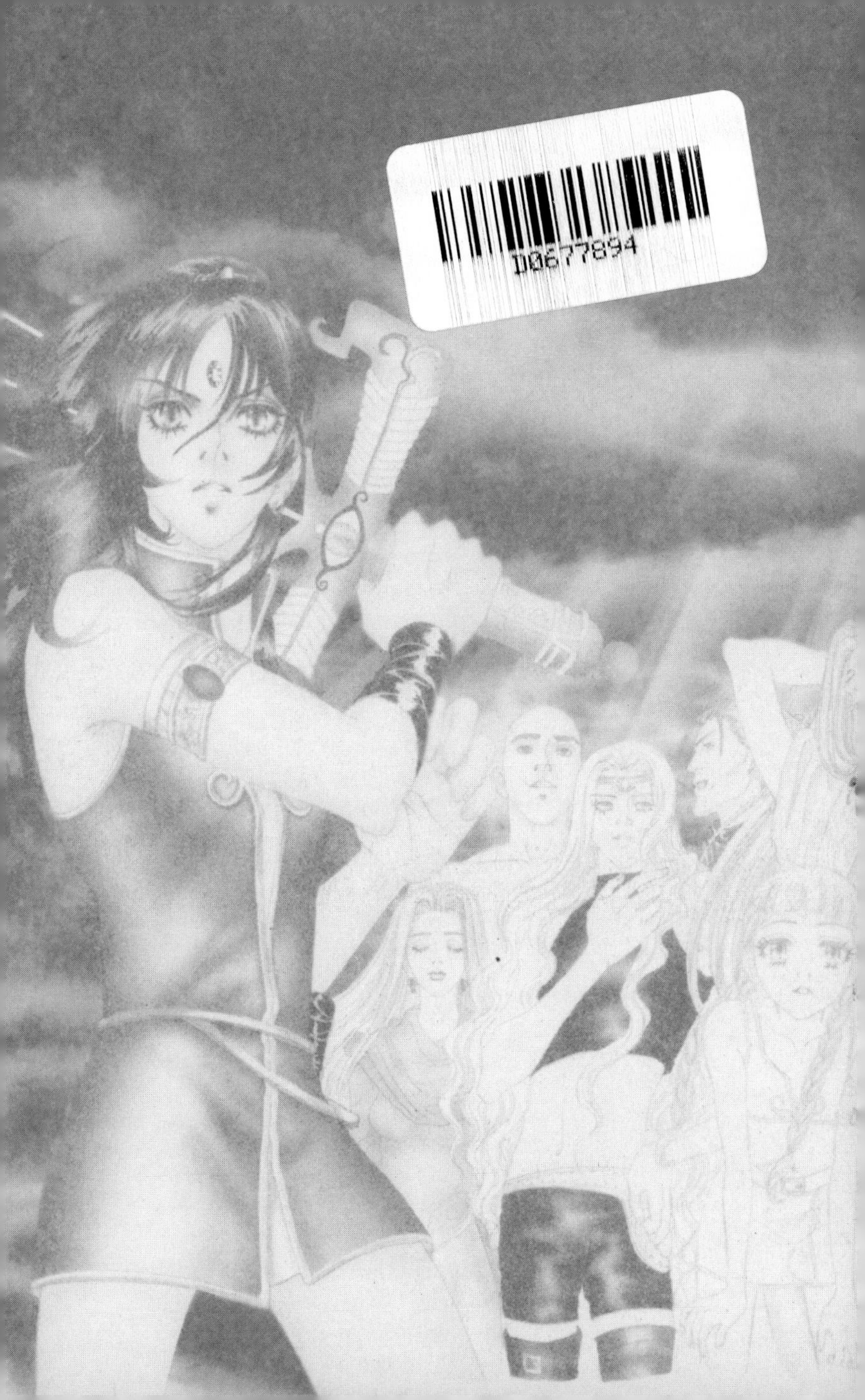